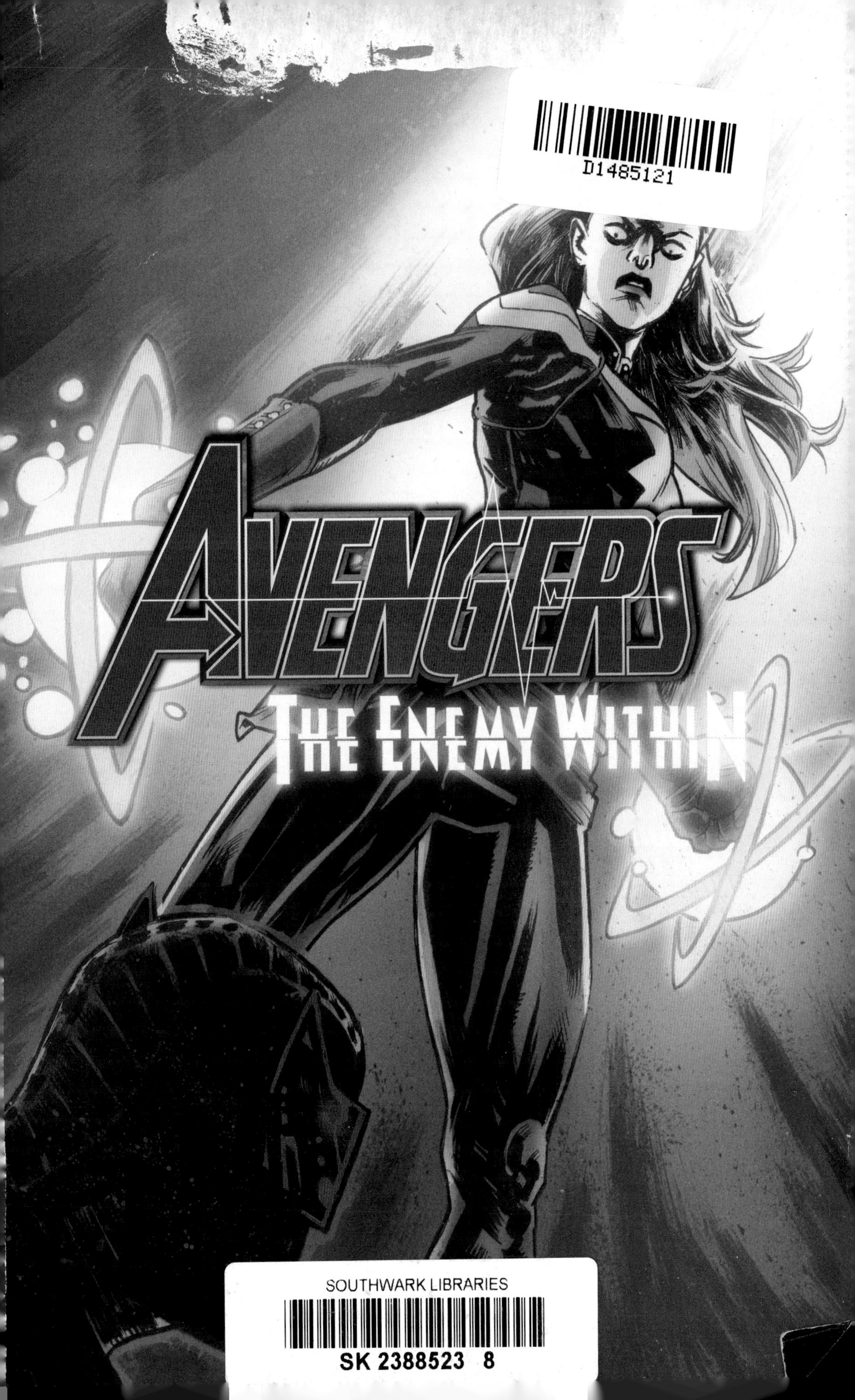
AVENGERS
THE ENEMY WITHIN

AVENGERS
THE ENEMY WITHIN

WRITER
KELLY SUE DeCONNICK

AVENGERS: THE ENEMY WITHIN #1
ARTIST
SCOTT HEPBURN

COLOR ARTIST
JORDIE BELLAIRE

LETTERER
VC'S JOE CARAMAGNA

AVENGERS ASSEMBLE #16-17
ARTIST
MATTEO BUFFAGNI
WITH **PEPE LARRAZ** (#17)

COLOR ARTIST
JORDIE BELLAIRE
WITH **MATTHEW WILSON** (#16)
& **NOLAN WOODARD** (#17)

LETTERER
VC'S CLAYTON COWLES

CAPTAIN MARVEL #13-14
ARTIST
SCOTT HEPBURN
WITH **GERARDO SANDOVAL**

COLOR ARTISTS
JORDIE BELLAIRE
& **ANDY TROY**

LETTERER
VC'S JOE CARAMAGNA

CAPTAIN MARVEL #17
ARTIST
FILIPE ANDRADE

COLOR ARTIST
JORDIE BELLAIRE

LETTERER
VC'S JOE CARAMAGNA

COVER ARTIST
JOE QUINONES

ASSISTANT EDITORS
JAKE THOMAS & DEVIN LEWIS

ASSOCIATE EDITOR
TOM BRENNAN

EDITORS
SANA AMANAT & LAUREN SANKOVITCH

SENIOR EDITOR
STEPHEN WACKER

EXECUTIVE EDITOR
TOM BREVOORT

Collection Editor: Cory Levine • Assistant Editors: Alex Starbuck & Nelson Ribeiro
Editors, Special Projects: Jennifer Grünwald & Mark D. Beazley • Senior Editor, Special Projects: Jeff Youngquist
SVP of Print & Digital Publishing Sales: David Gabriel • Book Design: Jeff Powell

Editor in Chief: Axel Alonso • Chief Creative Officer: Joe Quesada
Publisher: Dan Buckley • Executive Producer: Alan Fine

AVENGERS: THE ENEMY WITHIN. Contains material originally published in magazine form as AVENGERS: THE ENEMY WITHIN #1, CAPTAIN MARVEL #13-14 and #17, and AVENGERS ASSEMBLE #16-17. First printing 2013. ISBN# 978-0-7851-8403-4. Published by MARVEL WORLDWIDE, INC., a subsidiary of MARVEL ENTERTAINMENT, LLC. OFFICE OF PUBLICATION: 135 West 50th Street, New York, NY 10020. Copyright © 2013 Marvel Characters, Inc. All rights reserved. All characters featured in this issue and the distinctive names and likenesses thereof, and all related indicia are trademarks of Marvel Characters, Inc. No similarity between any of the names, characters, persons, and/or institutions in this magazine with those of any living or dead person or institution is intended, and any such similarity which may exist is purely coincidental. **Printed in the U.S.A.** ALAN FINE, EVP - Office of the President, Marvel Worldwide, Inc. and EVP & CMO Marvel Characters B.V.; DAN BUCKLEY, Publisher & President - Print, Animation & Digital Divisions; JOE QUESADA, Chief Creative Officer; TOM BREVOORT, SVP of Publishing; DAVID BOGART, SVP of Operations & Procurement, Publishing; C.B. CEBULSKI, SVP of Creator & Content Development; DAVID GABRIEL, SVP of Print & Digital Publishing Sales; JIM O'KEEFE, VP of Operations & Logistics; DAN CARR, Executive Director of Publishing Technology; SUSAN CRESPI, Editorial Operations Manager; ALEX MORALES, Publishing Operations Manager; STAN LEE, Chairman Emeritus. For information regarding advertising in Marvel Comics or on Marvel.com, please contact Niza Disla, Director of Marvel Partnerships, at ndisla@marvel.com. For Marvel subscription inquiries, please call 800-217-9158. **Manufactured between 10/11/2013 and 11/18/2013 by QUAD/GRAPHICS, VERSAILLES, KY, USA.**

10 9 8 7 6 5 4 3 2 1

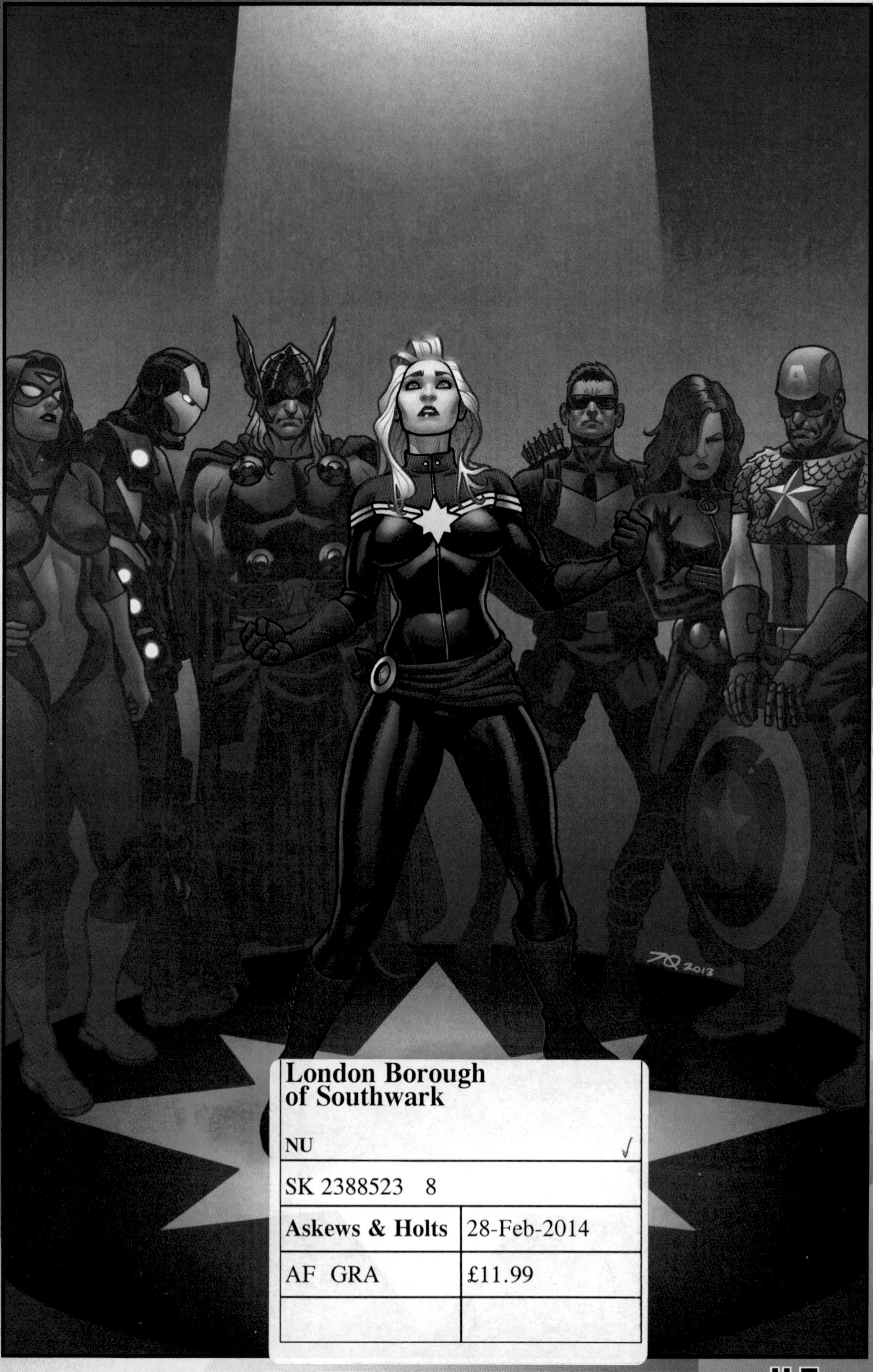

AVENGERS: THE ENEMY WITHIN #1

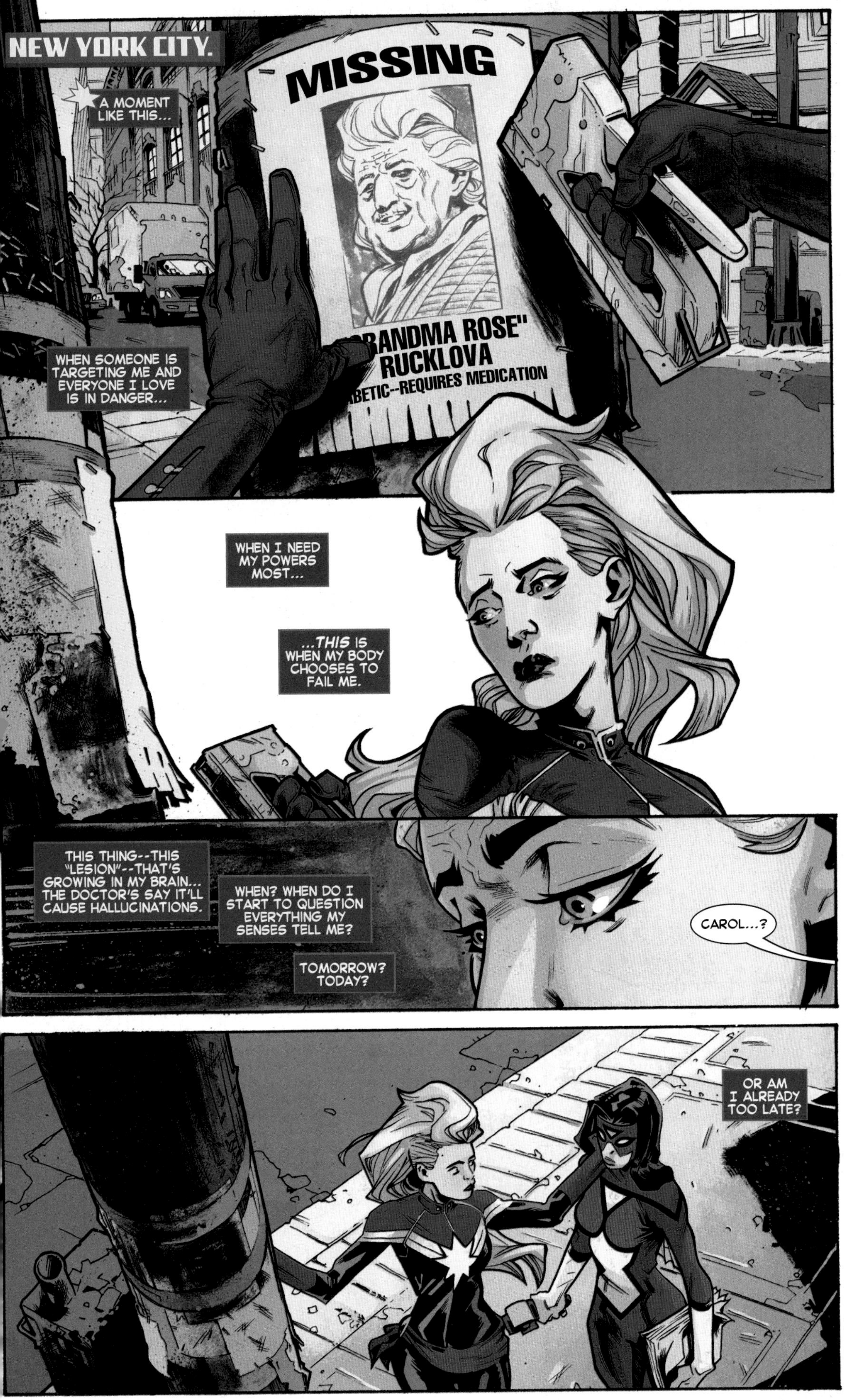

NEW YORK CITY.
A MOMENT LIKE THIS...
MISSING
"GRANDMA ROSE" RUCKLOVA
ABETIC--REQUIRES MEDICATION
WHEN SOMEONE IS TARGETING ME AND EVERYONE I LOVE IS IN DANGER...
WHEN I NEED MY POWERS MOST...
...THIS IS WHEN MY BODY CHOOSES TO FAIL ME.
THIS THING--THIS "LESION"--THAT'S GROWING IN MY BRAIN... THE DOCTOR'S SAY IT'LL CAUSE HALLUCINATIONS.
WHEN? WHEN DO I START TO QUESTION EVERYTHING MY SENSES TELL ME?
TOMORROW? TODAY?
CAROL...?
OR AM I ALREADY TOO LATE?

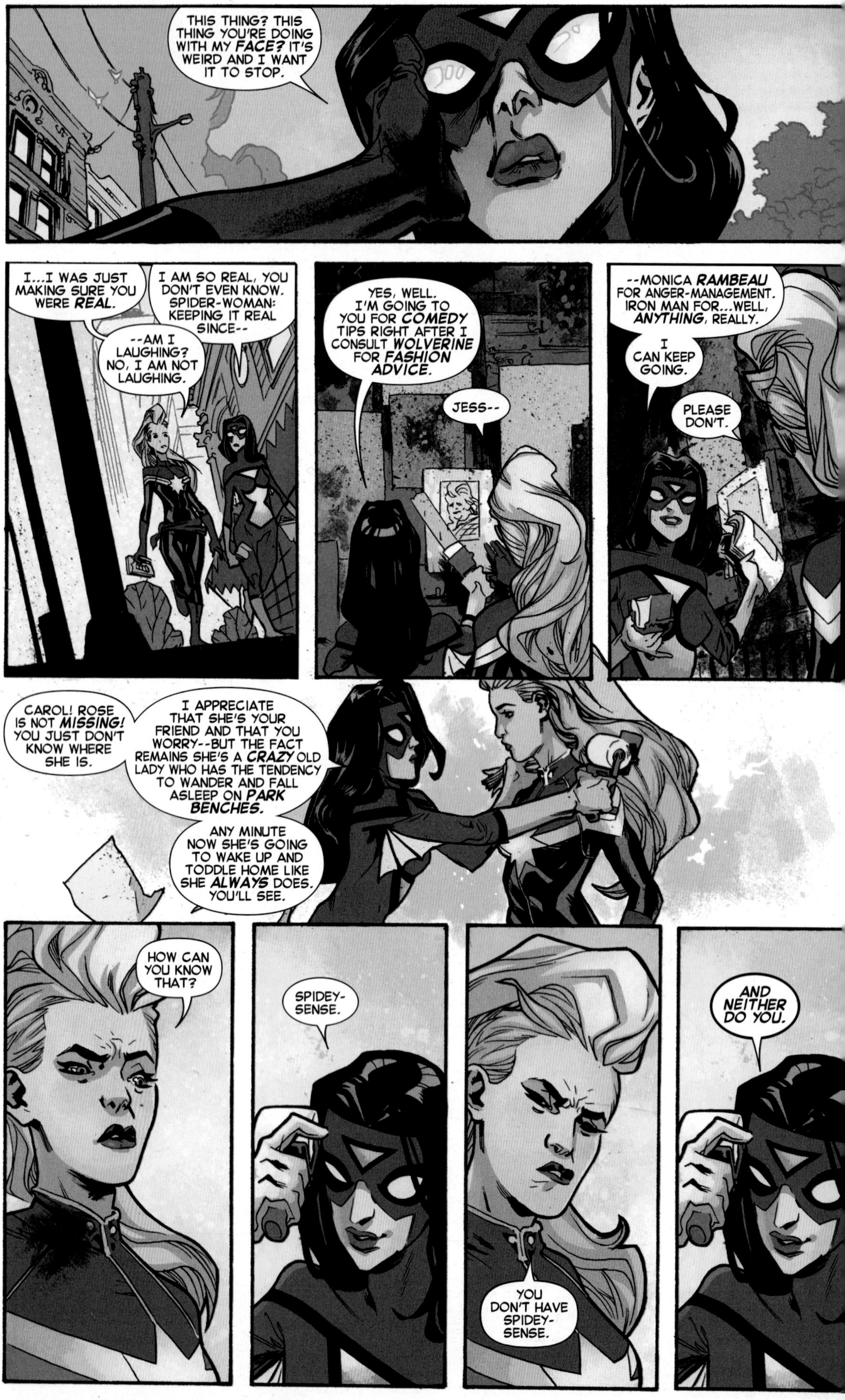

THIS THING? THIS THING YOU'RE DOING WITH MY FACE? IT'S WEIRD AND I WANT IT TO STOP.
I...I WAS JUST MAKING SURE YOU WERE REAL.
I AM SO REAL, YOU DON'T EVEN KNOW. SPIDER-WOMAN: KEEPING IT REAL SINCE--
--AM I LAUGHING? NO, I AM NOT LAUGHING.
YES, WELL. I'M GOING TO YOU FOR COMEDY TIPS RIGHT AFTER I CONSULT WOLVERINE FOR FASHION ADVICE.
JESS--
--MONICA RAMBEAU FOR ANGER-MANAGEMENT. IRON MAN FOR...WELL, ANYTHING, REALLY.
I CAN KEEP GOING.
PLEASE DON'T.
CAROL! ROSE IS NOT MISSING! YOU JUST DON'T KNOW WHERE SHE IS.
I APPRECIATE THAT SHE'S YOUR FRIEND AND THAT YOU WORRY--BUT THE FACT REMAINS SHE'S A CRAZY OLD LADY WHO HAS THE TENDENCY TO WANDER AND FALL ASLEEP ON PARK BENCHES.
ANY MINUTE NOW SHE'S GOING TO WAKE UP AND TODDLE HOME LIKE SHE ALWAYS DOES. YOU'LL SEE.
HOW CAN YOU KNOW THAT?
SPIDEY-SENSE.
YOU DON'T HAVE SPIDEY-SENSE.
AND NEITHER DO YOU.

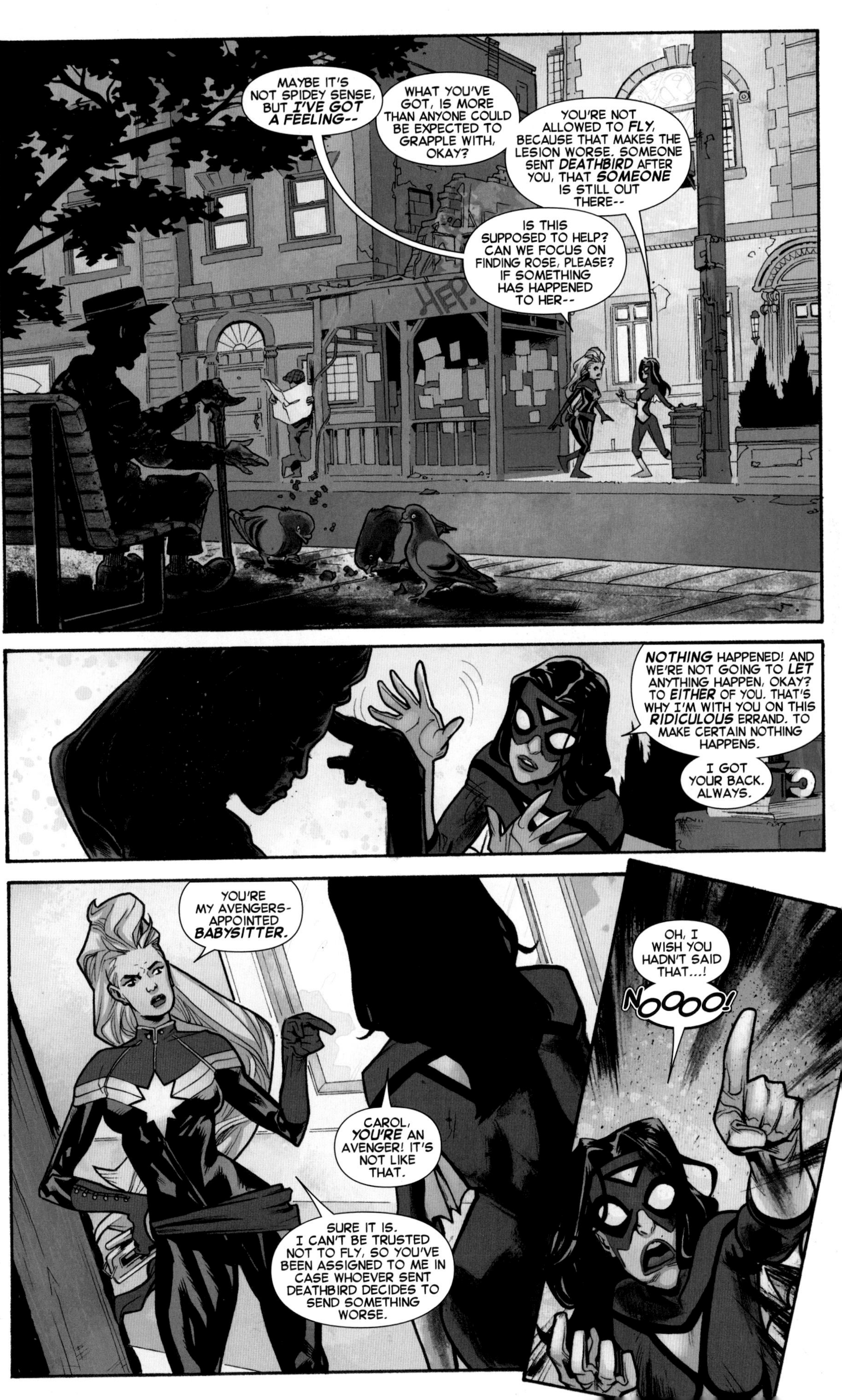
MAYBE IT'S NOT SPIDEY SENSE, BUT I'VE GOT A FEELING--
WHAT YOU'VE GOT, IS MORE THAN ANYONE COULD BE EXPECTED TO GRAPPLE WITH, OKAY?
YOU'RE NOT ALLOWED TO FLY, BECAUSE THAT MAKES THE LESION WORSE. SOMEONE SENT DEATHBIRD AFTER YOU, THAT SOMEONE IS STILL OUT THERE--
IS THIS SUPPOSED TO HELP? CAN WE FOCUS ON FINDING ROSE, PLEASE? IF SOMETHING HAS HAPPENED TO HER--
HEP.
NOTHING HAPPENED! AND WE'RE NOT GOING TO LET ANYTHING HAPPEN, OKAY? TO EITHER OF YOU. THAT'S WHY I'M WITH YOU ON THIS RIDICULOUS ERRAND. TO MAKE CERTAIN NOTHING HAPPENS.
I GOT YOUR BACK. ALWAYS.
YOU'RE MY AVENGERS-APPOINTED BABYSITTER.
CAROL, YOU'RE AN AVENGER! IT'S NOT LIKE THAT.
SURE IT IS. I CAN'T BE TRUSTED NOT TO FLY, SO YOU'VE BEEN ASSIGNED TO ME IN CASE WHOEVER SENT DEATHBIRD DECIDES TO SEND SOMETHING WORSE.
OH, I WISH YOU HADN'T SAID THAT...!
NOOOO!

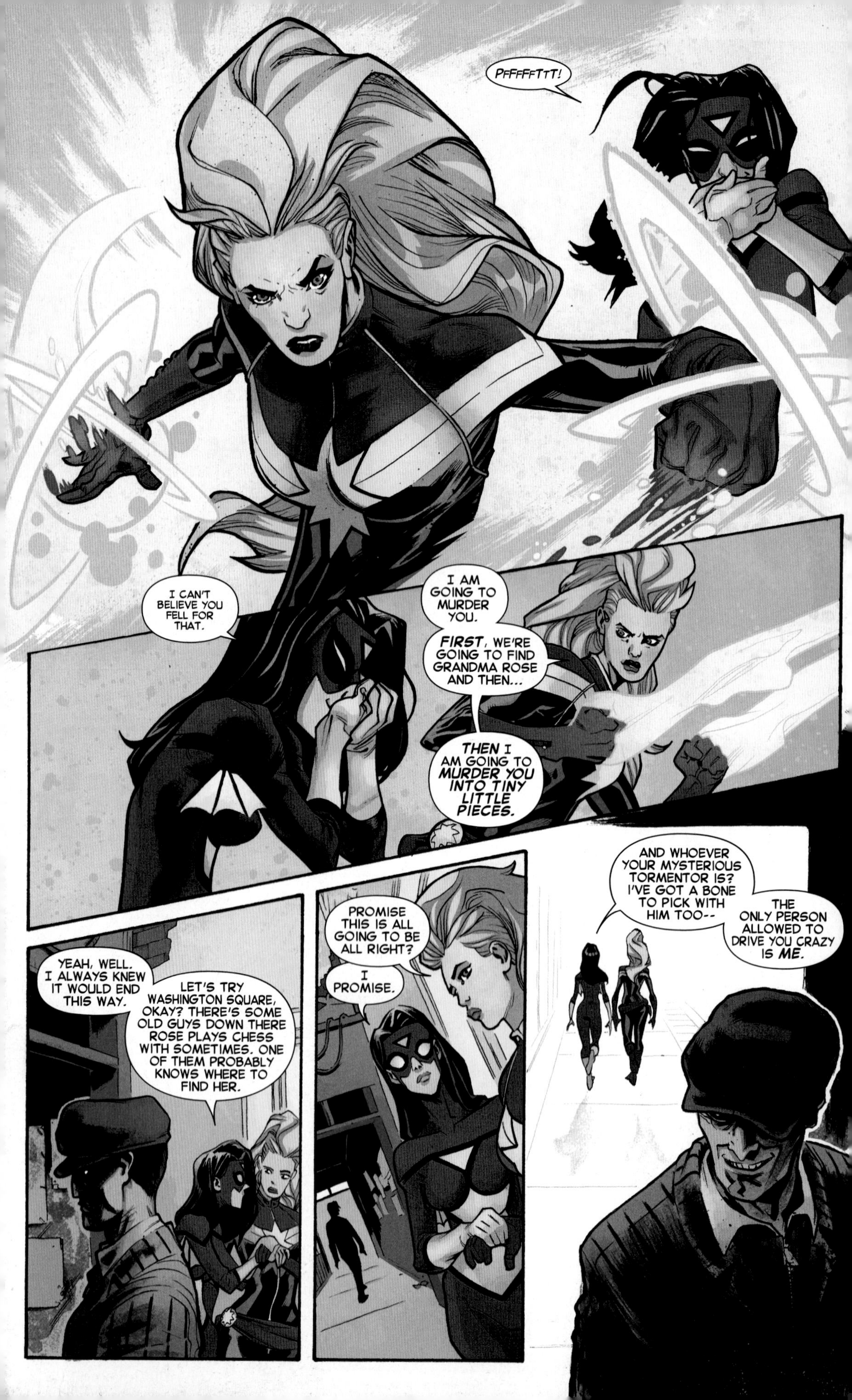
PFFFFFTTT!
I CAN'T BELIEVE YOU FELL FOR THAT.
I AM GOING TO MURDER YOU.
FIRST, WE'RE GOING TO FIND GRANDMA ROSE AND THEN...
THEN I AM GOING TO MURDER YOU INTO TINY LITTLE PIECES.
YEAH, WELL. I ALWAYS KNEW IT WOULD END THIS WAY.
LET'S TRY WASHINGTON SQUARE, OKAY? THERE'S SOME OLD GUYS DOWN THERE ROSE PLAYS CHESS WITH SOMETIMES. ONE OF THEM PROBABLY KNOWS WHERE TO FIND HER.
PROMISE THIS IS ALL GOING TO BE ALL RIGHT?
I PROMISE.
AND WHOEVER YOUR MYSTERIOUS TORMENTOR IS? I'VE GOT A BONE TO PICK WITH HIM TOO--
THE ONLY PERSON ALLOWED TO DRIVE YOU CRAZY IS ME.

When former U.S. Air Force pilot, Carol Danvers was caught in the explosion of an alien device called the Psyche-Magnitron, she was transformed into one of the world's most powerful super beings. She now uses her abilities to protect her planet and fight for justice as an Avenger. She is Earth's Mightiest Hero...she is...

CAPTAIN MARVEL

And there came a day, a day unlike any other, when Earth's mightiest heroes found themselves united against a common threat! On that day, the Avengers were born, to fight the foes no single super hero could withstand!

AVENGERS ASSEMBLE

THE HARDEST FOE TO BEAT...

IS THE ONE INSIDE HER HEAD.

THE ENEMY WITHIN

WHEN I WAS A CHILD, FAR AWAY FROM HERE, WE PLAYED A *GAME*, CAPTAIN MARVEL.

SOMETHING SIMILAR TO ONE YOU HAVE HERE. A *COMPETITIVE* VERSION OF...

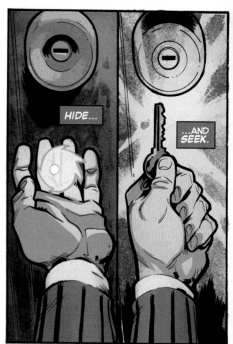

HIDE...

...AND *SEEK*.

WE EACH HID SOMETHING FOR THE OTHER TO FIND.

EACH PLAYER HAD *UNTIL THE BELL TOWER CHIMED* TO FIND OUR PRIZE AND RETURN TO BASE...

WHERE HAVE YOU HIDDEN *MY PRIZE*, CAPTAIN?

WHERE HAVE YOU HIDDEN THE KEY TO ALL THAT IS OWED ME?

READY, SET...

HSSSSS

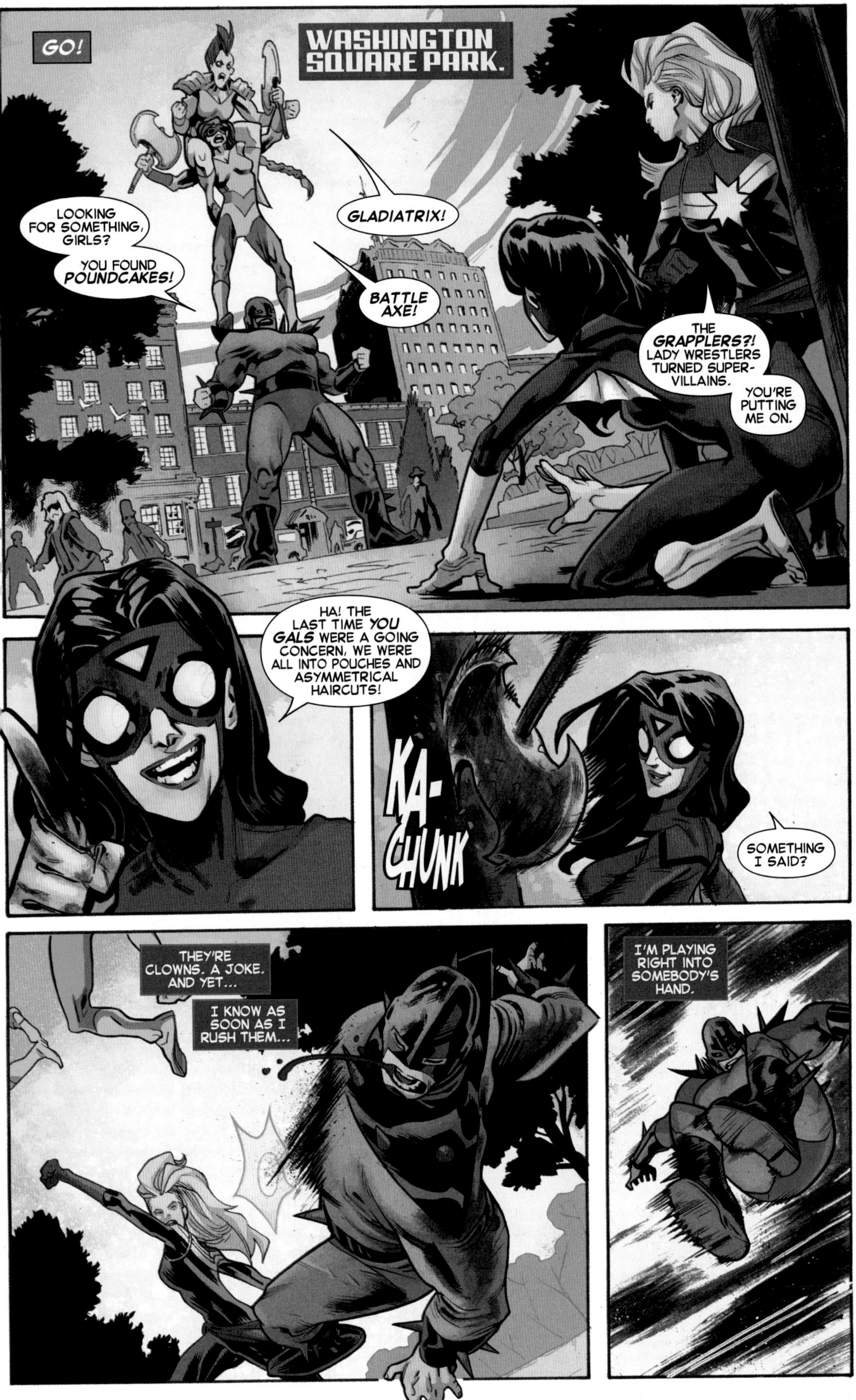
GO!
WASHINGTON SQUARE PARK.
LOOKING FOR SOMETHING, GIRLS?
YOU FOUND POUNDCAKES!
GLADIATRIX!
BATTLE AXE!
THE GRAPPLERS?! LADY WRESTLERS TURNED SUPER-VILLAINS.
YOU'RE PUTTING ME ON.
HA! THE LAST TIME YOU GALS WERE A GOING CONCERN, WE WERE ALL INTO POUCHES AND ASYMMETRICAL HAIRCUTS!
KA-CHUNK
SOMETHING I SAID?
THEY'RE CLOWNS. A JOKE. AND YET...
I KNOW AS SOON AS I RUSH THEM...
I'M PLAYING RIGHT INTO SOMEBODY'S HAND.

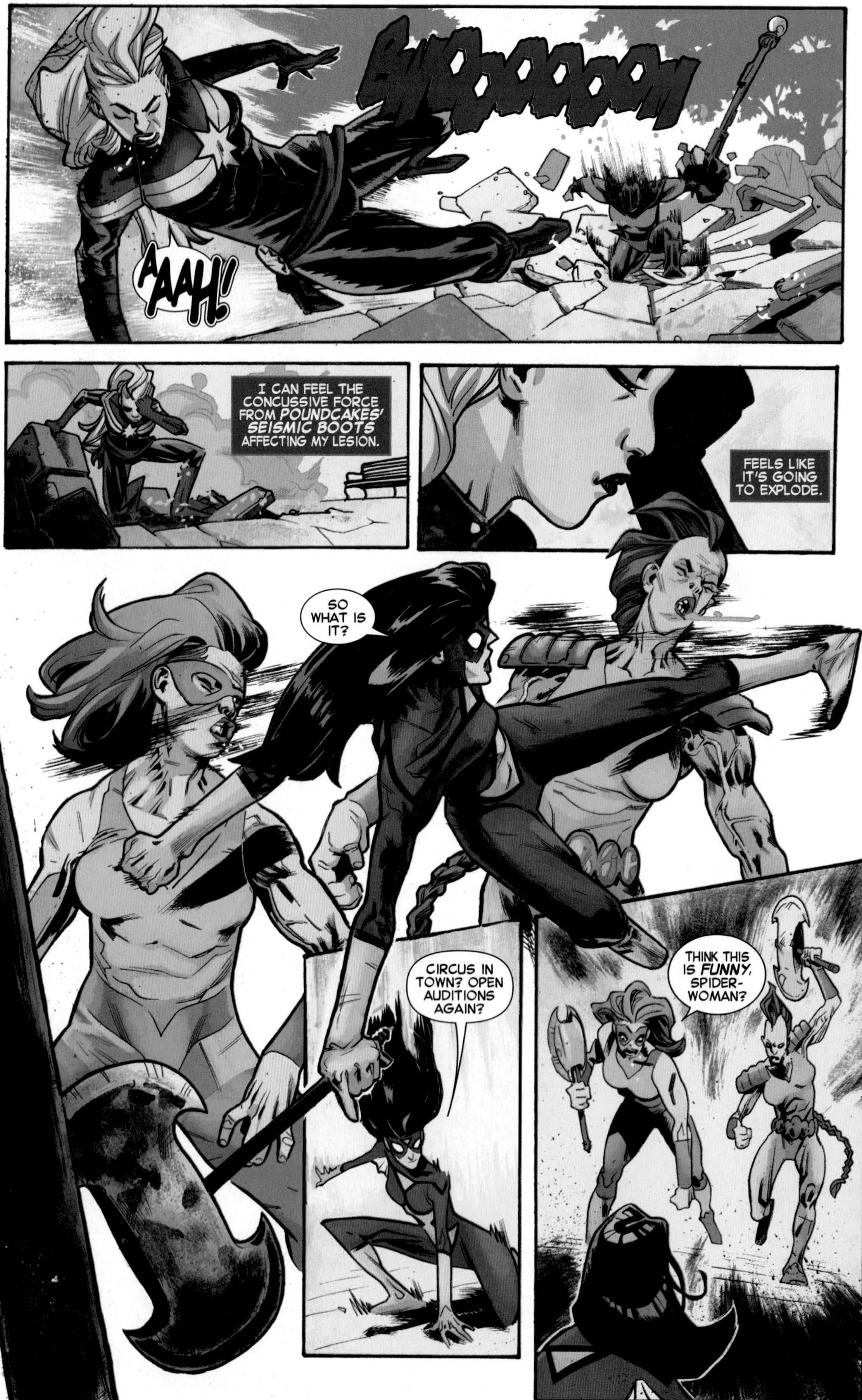
BHOOOOOOM
AAAH!
I CAN FEEL THE CONCUSSIVE FORCE FROM POUNDCAKES' SEISMIC BOOTS AFFECTING MY LESION.
FEELS LIKE IT'S GOING TO EXPLODE.
SO WHAT IS IT?
CIRCUS IN TOWN? OPEN AUDITIONS AGAIN?
THINK THIS IS FUNNY, SPIDER-WOMAN?

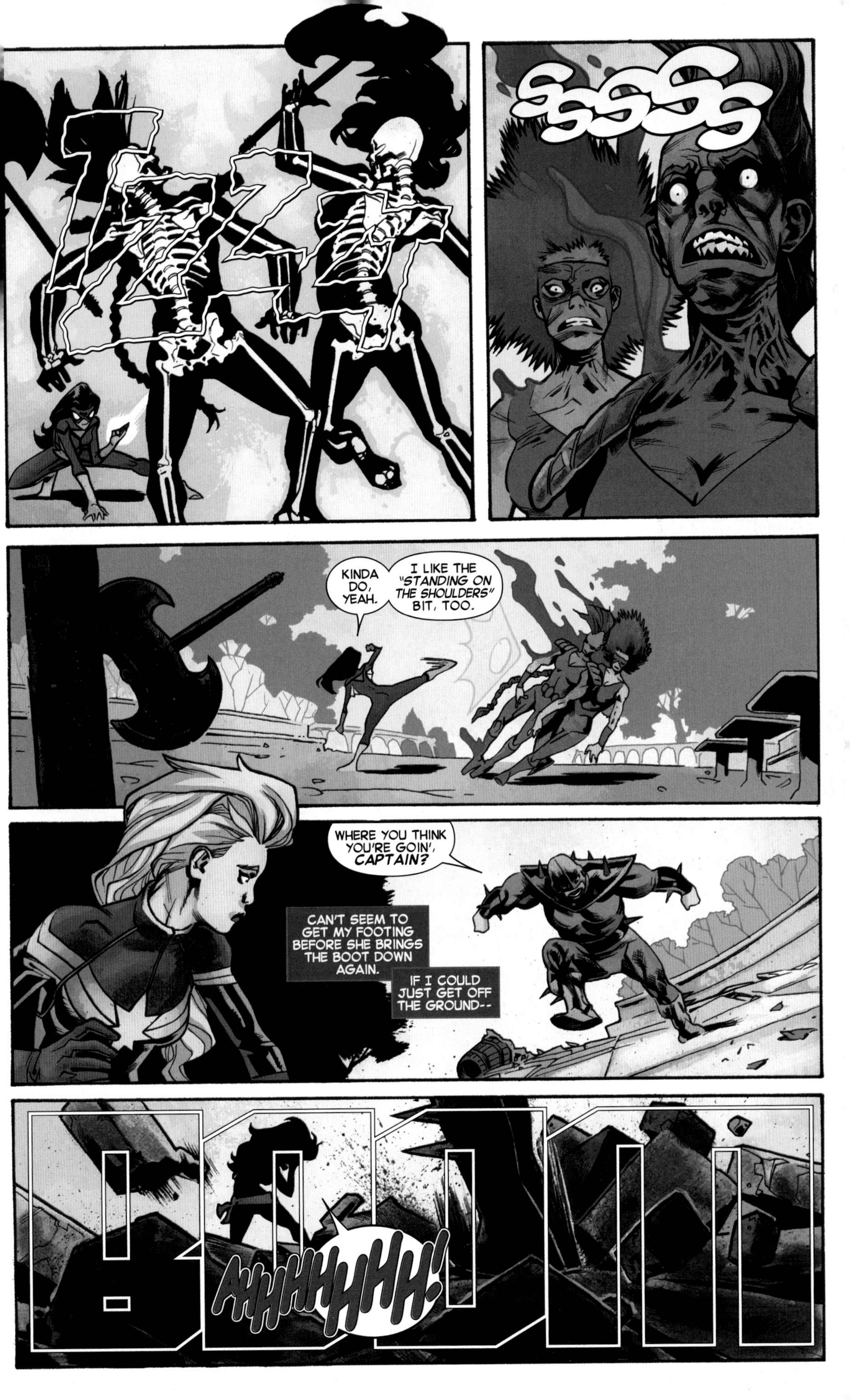
KINDA DO, YEAH.
I LIKE THE "STANDING ON THE SHOULDERS" BIT, TOO.
WHERE YOU THINK YOU'RE GOIN', CAPTAIN?
CAN'T SEEM TO GET MY FOOTING BEFORE SHE BRINGS THE BOOT DOWN AGAIN.
IF I COULD JUST GET OFF THE GROUND--

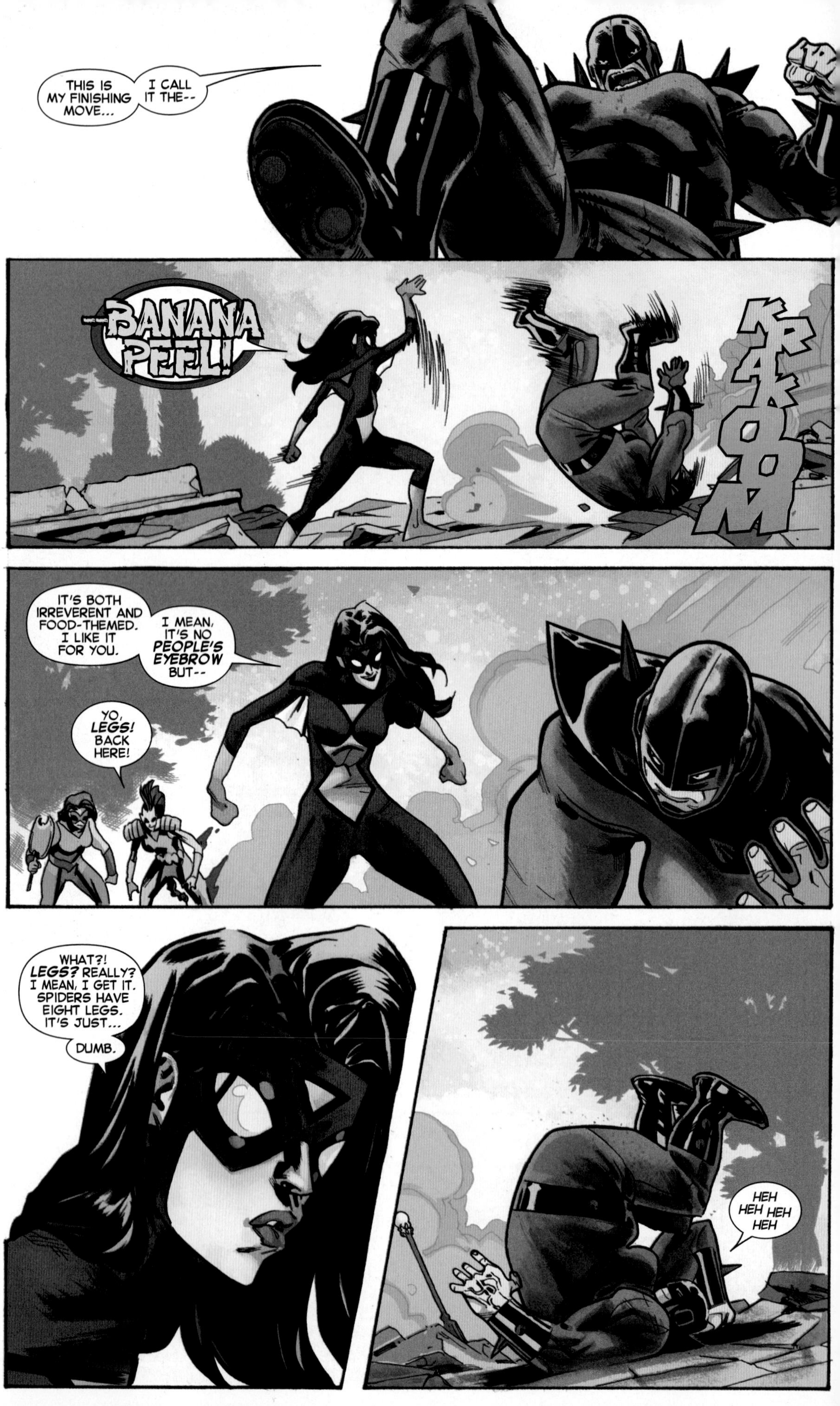
THIS IS MY FINISHING MOVE...
I CALL IT THE--
BANANA PEEL!
KRAKOOM
IT'S BOTH IRREVERENT AND FOOD-THEMED. I LIKE IT FOR YOU.
I MEAN, IT'S NO *PEOPLE'S EYEBROW* BUT--
YO, *LEGS!* BACK HERE!
WHAT?! *LEGS?* REALLY? I MEAN, I GET IT. SPIDERS HAVE EIGHT LEGS. IT'S JUST...
DUMB.
HEH HEH HEH HEH

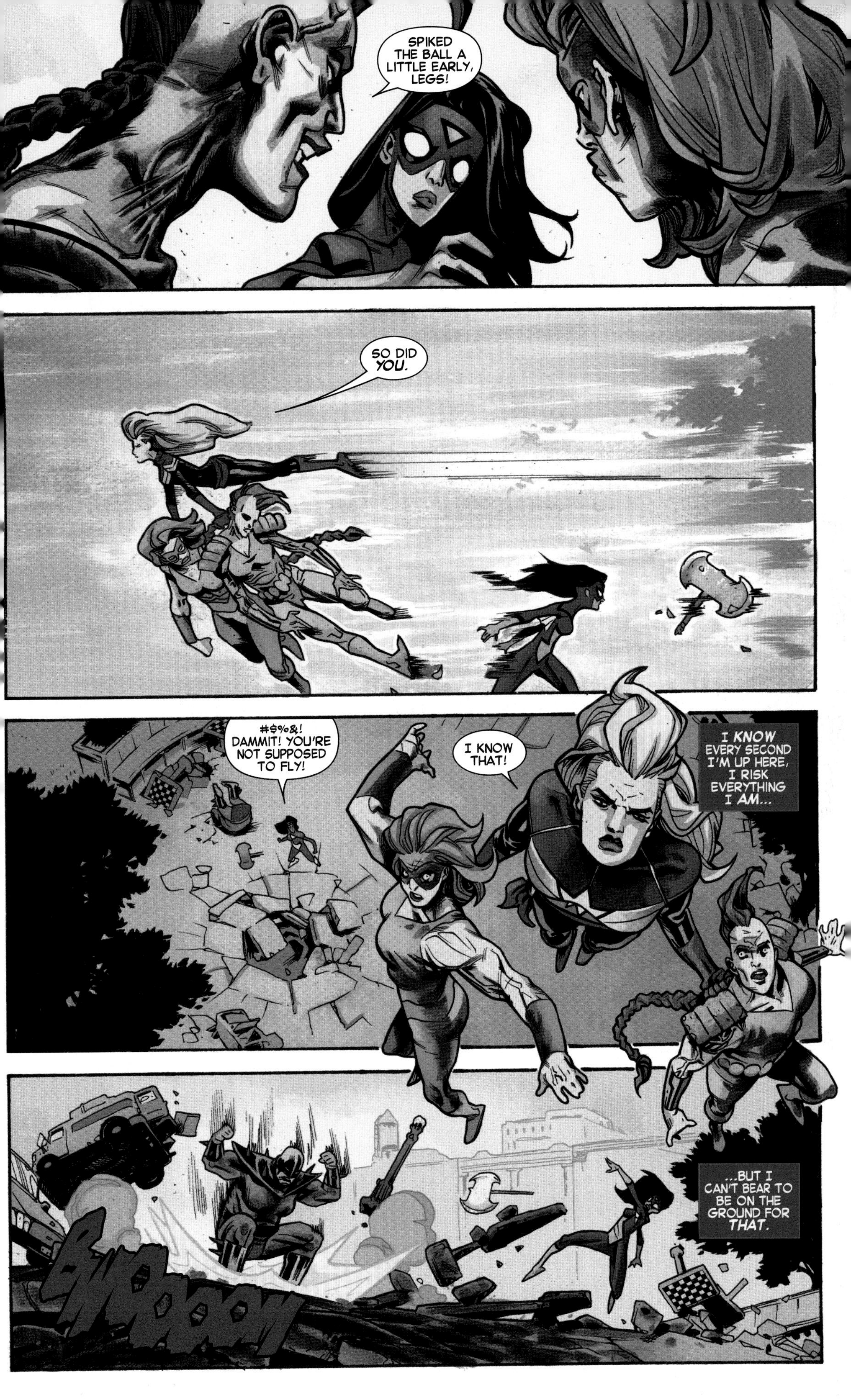

SPIKED THE BALL A LITTLE EARLY, LEGS!
SO DID YOU.
#$%&! DAMMIT! YOU'RE NOT SUPPOSED TO FLY!
I KNOW THAT!
I KNOW EVERY SECOND I'M UP HERE, I RISK EVERYTHING I AM...
...BUT I CAN'T BEAR TO BE ON THE GROUND FOR THAT.

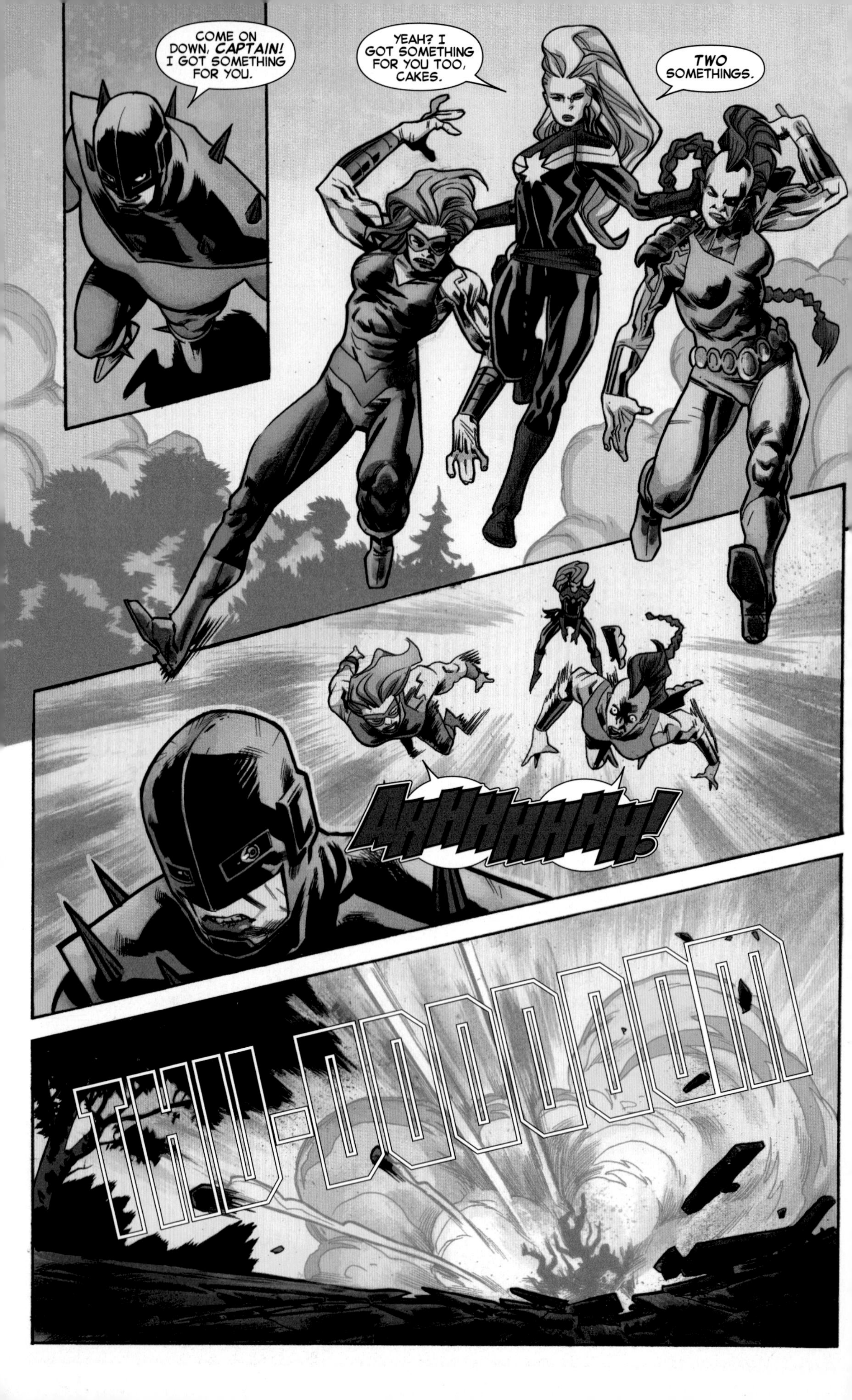
COME ON DOWN, CAPTAIN! I GOT SOMETHING FOR YOU.
YEAH? I GOT SOMETHING FOR YOU TOO, CAKES.
TWO SOMETHINGS.
AHHHHHHH!
THU-DOOOOOM

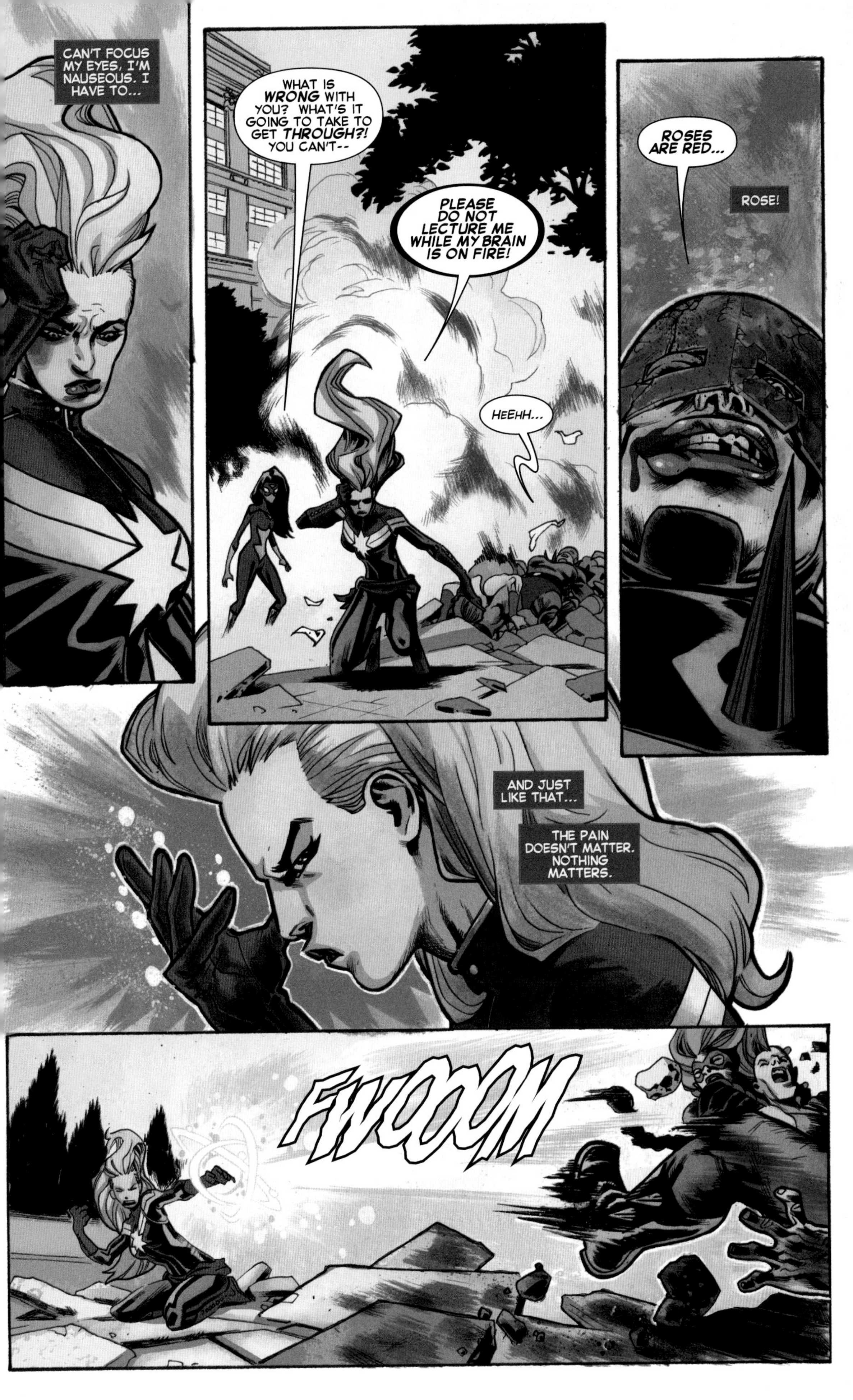
CAN'T FOCUS MY EYES, I'M NAUSEOUS. I HAVE TO...
WHAT IS WRONG WITH YOU? WHAT'S IT GOING TO TAKE TO GET THROUGH?! YOU CAN'T--
PLEASE DO NOT LECTURE ME WHILE MY BRAIN IS ON FIRE!
HEEHH...
ROSES ARE RED...
ROSE!
AND JUST LIKE THAT...
THE PAIN DOESN'T MATTER. NOTHING MATTERS.
FWOOOM

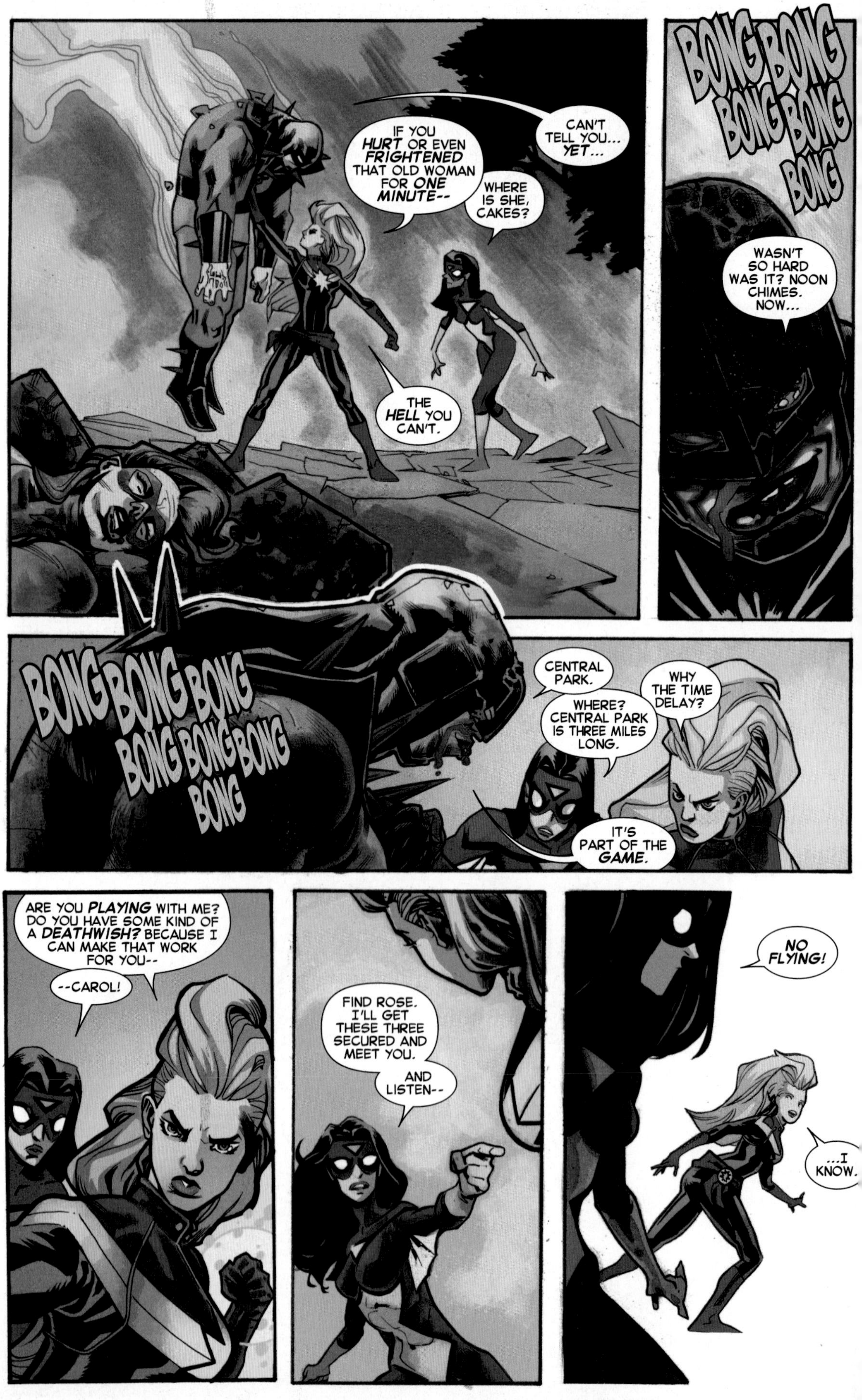
IF YOU HURT OR EVEN FRIGHTENED THAT OLD WOMAN FOR ONE MINUTE--
CAN'T TELL YOU... YET...
WHERE IS SHE, CAKES?
THE HELL YOU CAN'T.
BONG BONG BONG BONG BONG
WASN'T SO HARD WAS IT? NOON CHIMES. NOW...
BONG BONG BONG BONG BONG BONG BONG
CENTRAL PARK.
WHERE? CENTRAL PARK IS THREE MILES LONG.
WHY THE TIME DELAY?
IT'S PART OF THE GAME.
ARE YOU PLAYING WITH ME? DO YOU HAVE SOME KIND OF A DEATHWISH? BECAUSE I CAN MAKE THAT WORK FOR YOU--
--CAROL!
FIND ROSE. I'LL GET THESE THREE SECURED AND MEET YOU.
AND LISTEN--
NO FLYING!
...I KNOW.

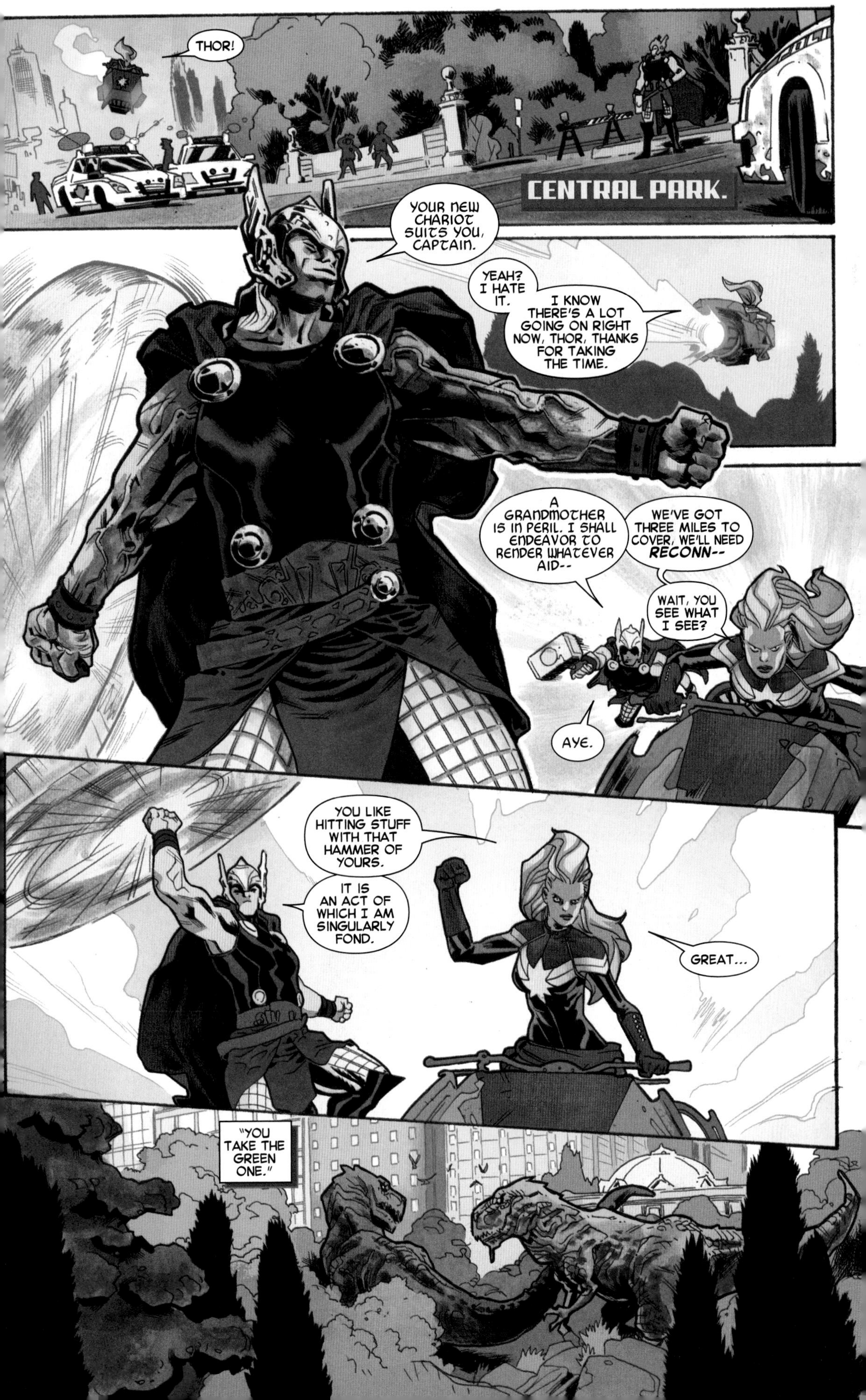
THOR!
CENTRAL PARK.
YOUR NEW CHARIOT SUITS YOU, CAPTAIN.
YEAH? I HATE IT.
I KNOW THERE'S A LOT GOING ON RIGHT NOW, THOR, THANKS FOR TAKING THE TIME.
A GRANDMOTHER IS IN PERIL. I SHALL ENDEAVOR TO RENDER WHATEVER AID--
WE'VE GOT THREE MILES TO COVER, WE'LL NEED RECONN--
WAIT, YOU SEE WHAT I SEE?
AYE.
YOU LIKE HITTING STUFF WITH THAT HAMMER OF YOURS.
IT IS AN ACT OF WHICH I AM SINGULARLY FOND.
GREAT...
"YOU TAKE THE GREEN ONE."

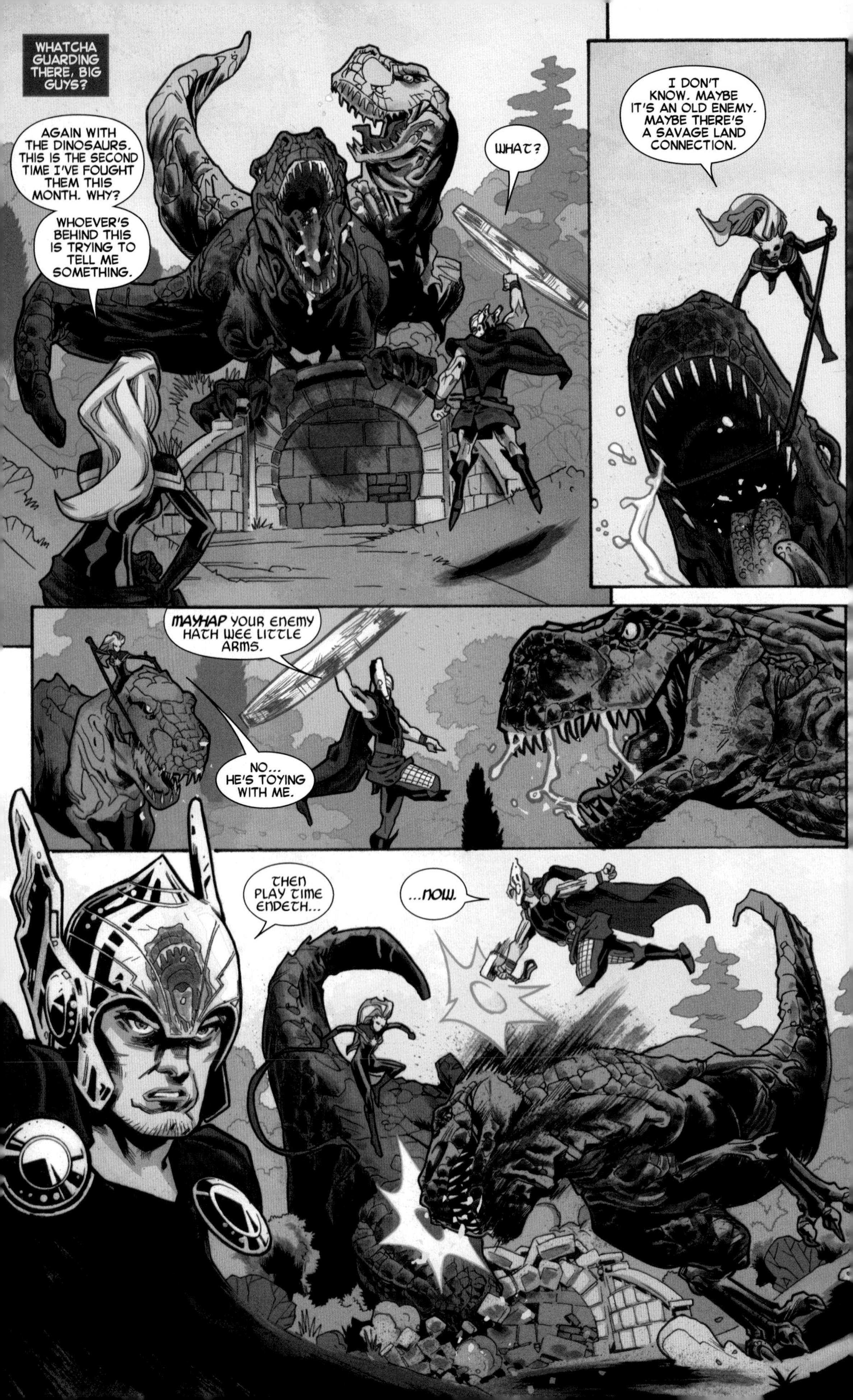
WHATCHA GUARDING THERE, BIG GUYS?
AGAIN WITH THE DINOSAURS. THIS IS THE SECOND TIME I'VE FOUGHT THEM THIS MONTH. WHY?
WHOEVER'S BEHIND THIS IS TRYING TO TELL ME SOMETHING.
WHAT?
I DON'T KNOW. MAYBE IT'S AN OLD ENEMY. MAYBE THERE'S A SAVAGE LAND CONNECTION.
MAYHAP YOUR ENEMY HATH WEE LITTLE ARMS.
NO... HE'S TOYING WITH ME.
THEN PLAY TIME ENDETH...
...NOW.

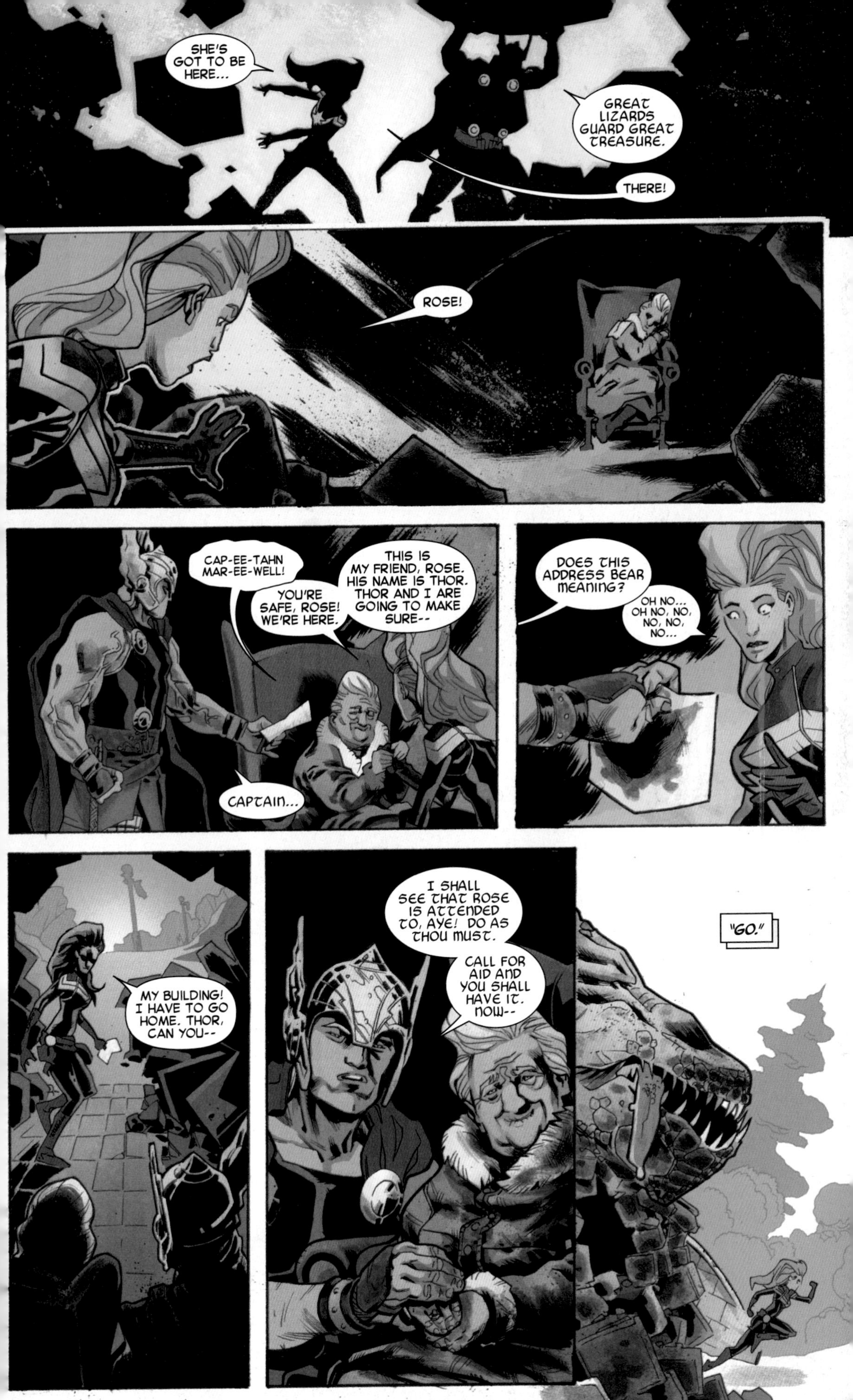
SHE'S GOT TO BE HERE...
GREAT LIZARDS GUARD GREAT TREASURE.
THERE!
ROSE!
CAP-EE-TAHN MAR-EE-WELL!
YOU'RE SAFE, ROSE! WE'RE HERE.
THIS IS MY FRIEND, ROSE. HIS NAME IS THOR. THOR AND I ARE GOING TO MAKE SURE--
CAPTAIN...
DOES THIS ADDRESS BEAR MEANING?
OH NO... OH NO, NO, NO, NO, NO...
MY BUILDING! I HAVE TO GO HOME. THOR, CAN YOU--
I SHALL SEE THAT ROSE IS ATTENDED TO, AYE! DO AS THOU MUST.
CALL FOR AID AND YOU SHALL HAVE IT. NOW--
"GO."

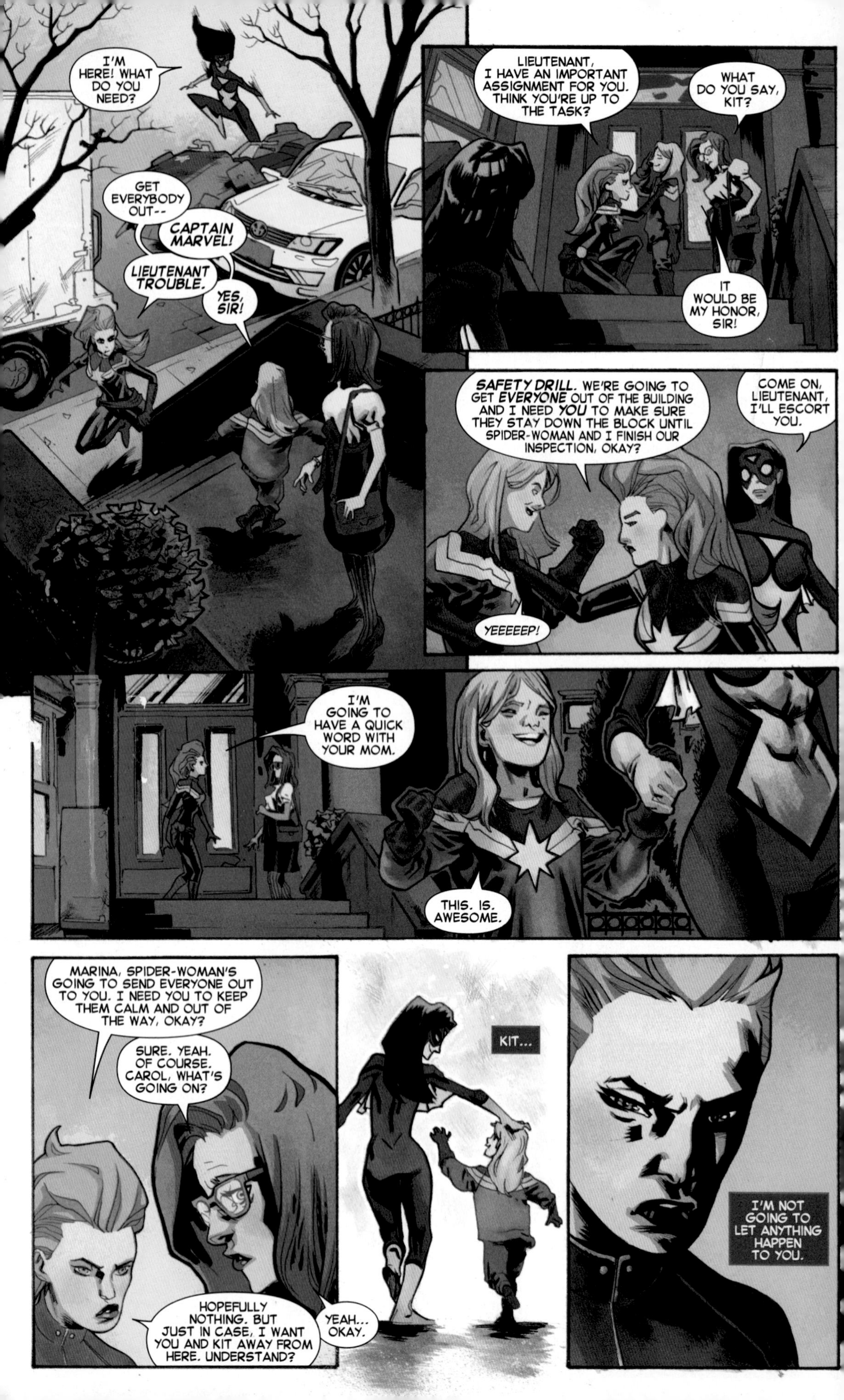
I'M HERE! WHAT DO YOU NEED?
GET EVERYBODY OUT--
CAPTAIN MARVEL!
LIEUTENANT TROUBLE.
YES, SIR!
LIEUTENANT, I HAVE AN IMPORTANT ASSIGNMENT FOR YOU. THINK YOU'RE UP TO THE TASK?
WHAT DO YOU SAY, KIT?
IT WOULD BE MY HONOR, SIR!
SAFETY DRILL. WE'RE GOING TO GET EVERYONE OUT OF THE BUILDING AND I NEED YOU TO MAKE SURE THEY STAY DOWN THE BLOCK UNTIL SPIDER-WOMAN AND I FINISH OUR INSPECTION, OKAY?
COME ON, LIEUTENANT, I'LL ESCORT YOU.
YEEEEEP!
I'M GOING TO HAVE A QUICK WORD WITH YOUR MOM.
THIS. IS. AWESOME.
MARINA, SPIDER-WOMAN'S GOING TO SEND EVERYONE OUT TO YOU. I NEED YOU TO KEEP THEM CALM AND OUT OF THE WAY, OKAY?
SURE. YEAH. OF COURSE. CAROL, WHAT'S GOING ON?
HOPEFULLY NOTHING. BUT JUST IN CASE, I WANT YOU AND KIT AWAY FROM HERE. UNDERSTAND?
YEAH... OKAY.
KIT...
I'M NOT GOING TO LET ANYTHING HAPPEN TO YOU.

COME OUT, COME OUT...
...WHOEVER YOU ARE.
HAAAAAAAA!
HISSSSSS!
...!
CHEWIE! OH, BABY GIRL, I DIDN'T MEAN TO SCARE YOU! IT'S OKAY. IT'S GOING TO BE OKAY.
CAROL... LOOK.

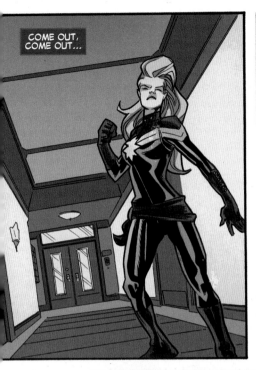

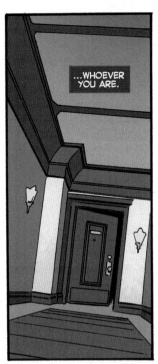

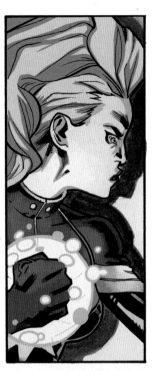

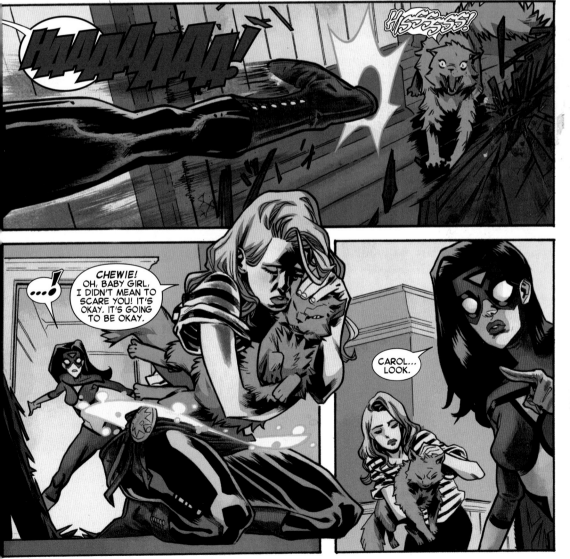

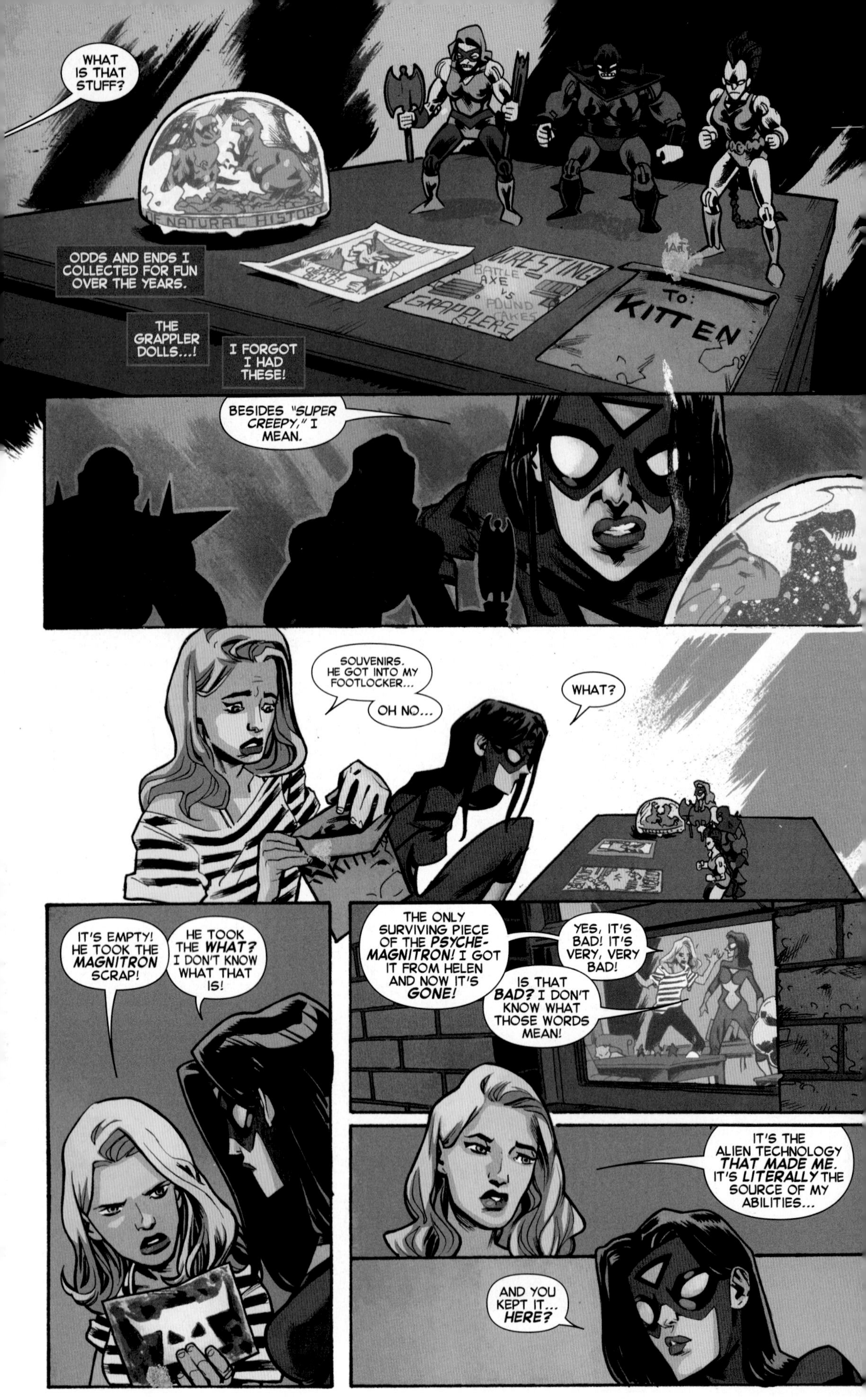
WHAT IS THAT STUFF?
ODDS AND ENDS I COLLECTED FOR FUN OVER THE YEARS.
THE GRAPPLER DOLLS...!
I FORGOT I HAD THESE!
OF NATURAL HISTORY
WRESTLING
BATTLE AXE VS POUND CAKES
GRAPPLERS
TO: KITTEN
BESIDES "SUPER CREEPY," I MEAN.
SOUVENIRS. HE GOT INTO MY FOOTLOCKER...
OH NO...
WHAT?
IT'S EMPTY! HE TOOK THE MAGNITRON SCRAP!
HE TOOK THE WHAT? I DON'T KNOW WHAT THAT IS!
THE ONLY SURVIVING PIECE OF THE PSYCHE-MAGNITRON! I GOT IT FROM HELEN AND NOW IT'S GONE!
IS THAT BAD? I DON'T KNOW WHAT THOSE WORDS MEAN!
YES, IT'S BAD! IT'S VERY, VERY BAD!
IT'S THE ALIEN TECHNOLOGY THAT MADE ME. IT'S LITERALLY THE SOURCE OF MY ABILITIES...
AND YOU KEPT IT... HERE?

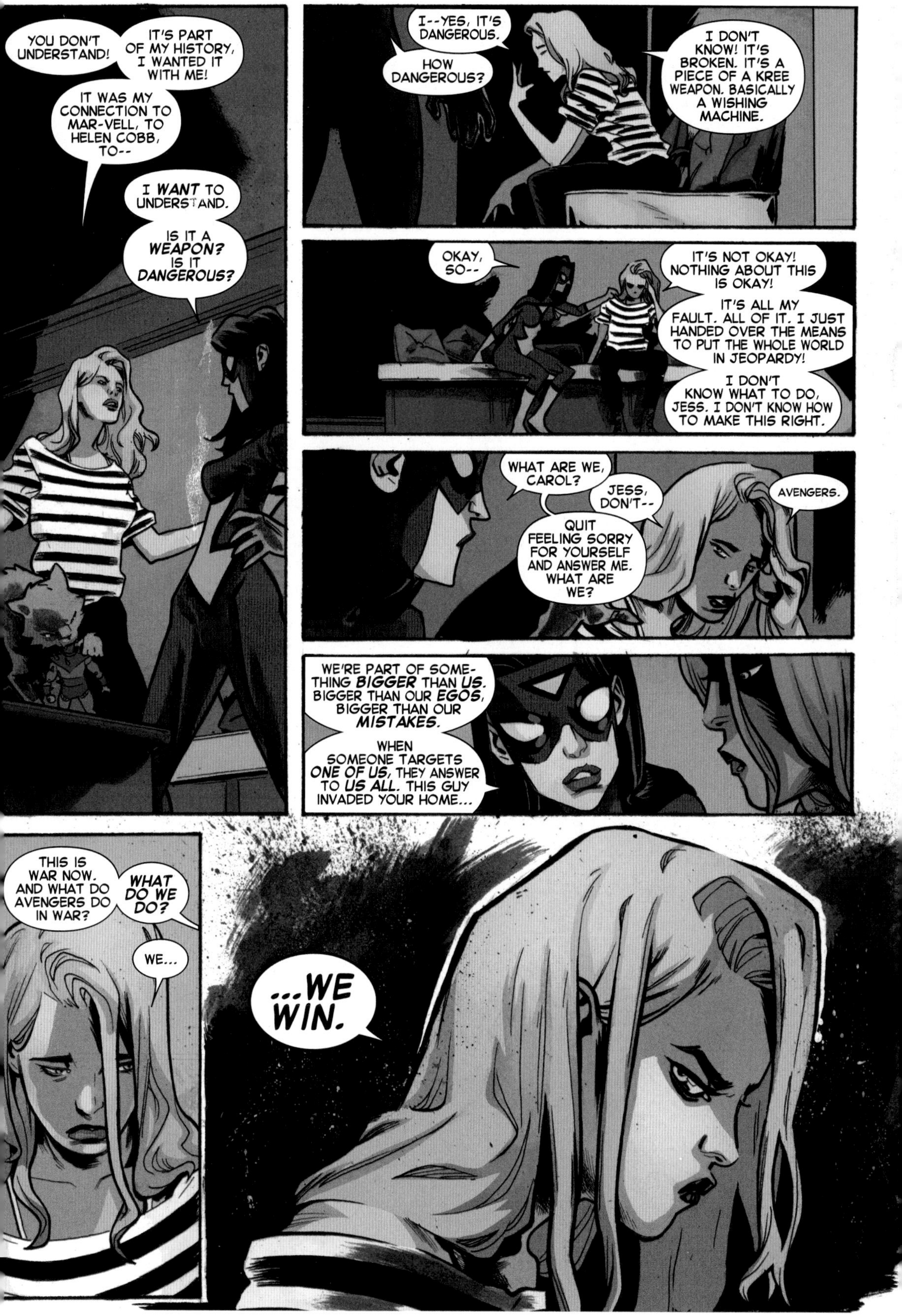

YOU DON'T UNDERSTAND!
IT'S PART OF MY HISTORY, I WANTED IT WITH ME!
IT WAS MY CONNECTION TO MAR-VELL, TO HELEN COBB, TO--
I WANT TO UNDERSTAND.
IS IT A WEAPON? IS IT DANGEROUS?
I--YES, IT'S DANGEROUS.
HOW DANGEROUS?
I DON'T KNOW! IT'S BROKEN. IT'S A PIECE OF A KREE WEAPON. BASICALLY A WISHING MACHINE.
OKAY, SO--
IT'S NOT OKAY! NOTHING ABOUT THIS IS OKAY!
IT'S ALL MY FAULT. ALL OF IT. I JUST HANDED OVER THE MEANS TO PUT THE WHOLE WORLD IN JEOPARDY!
I DON'T KNOW WHAT TO DO, JESS. I DON'T KNOW HOW TO MAKE THIS RIGHT.
WHAT ARE WE, CAROL?
JESS, DON'T--
QUIT FEELING SORRY FOR YOURSELF AND ANSWER ME. WHAT ARE WE?
AVENGERS.
WE'RE PART OF SOMETHING BIGGER THAN US. BIGGER THAN OUR EGOS, BIGGER THAN OUR MISTAKES.
WHEN SOMEONE TARGETS ONE OF US, THEY ANSWER TO US ALL. THIS GUY INVADED YOUR HOME...
THIS IS WAR NOW. AND WHAT DO AVENGERS DO IN WAR?
WHAT DO WE DO?
WE...
...WE WIN.

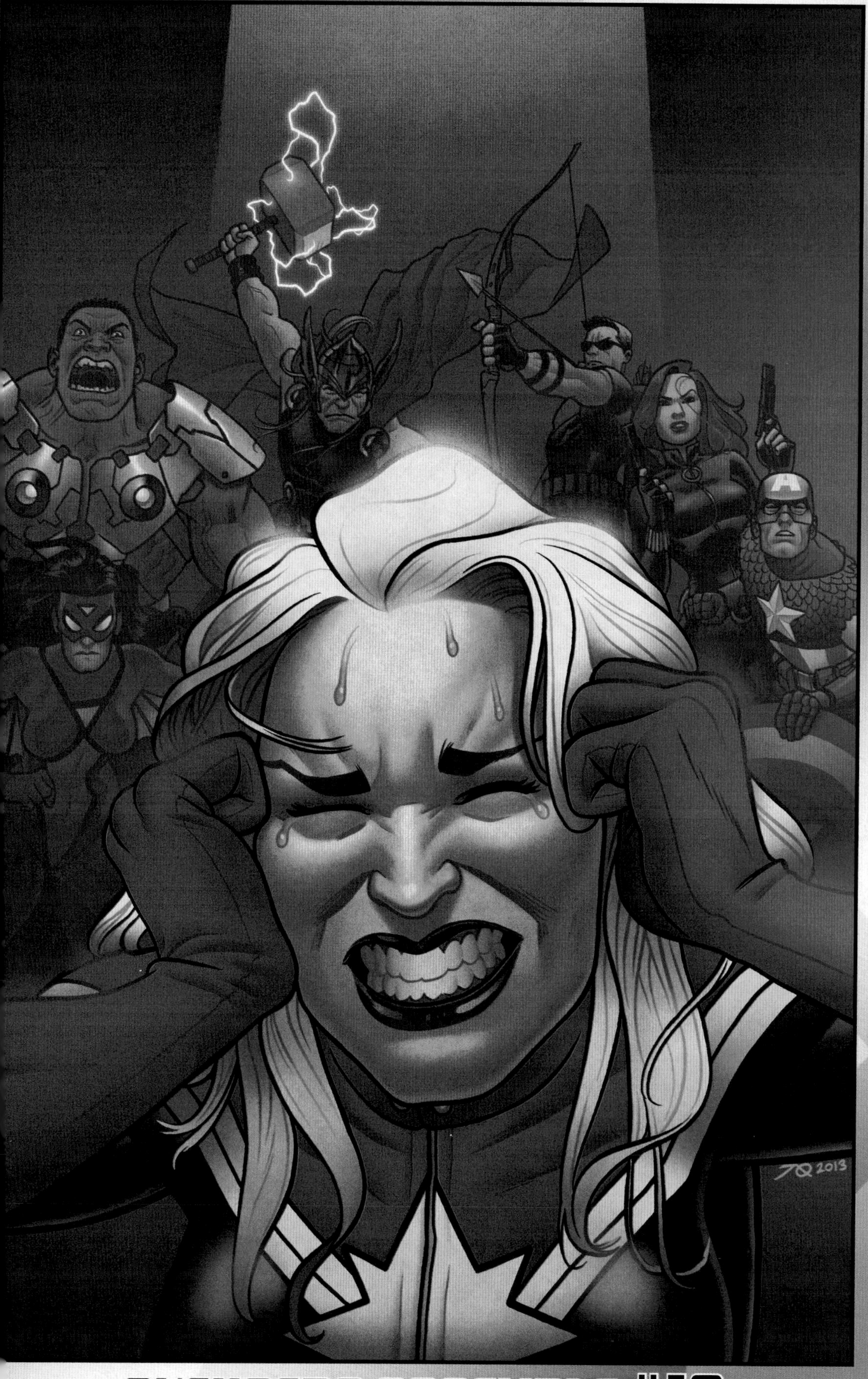
JQ 2013

AVENGERS ASSEMBLE #16

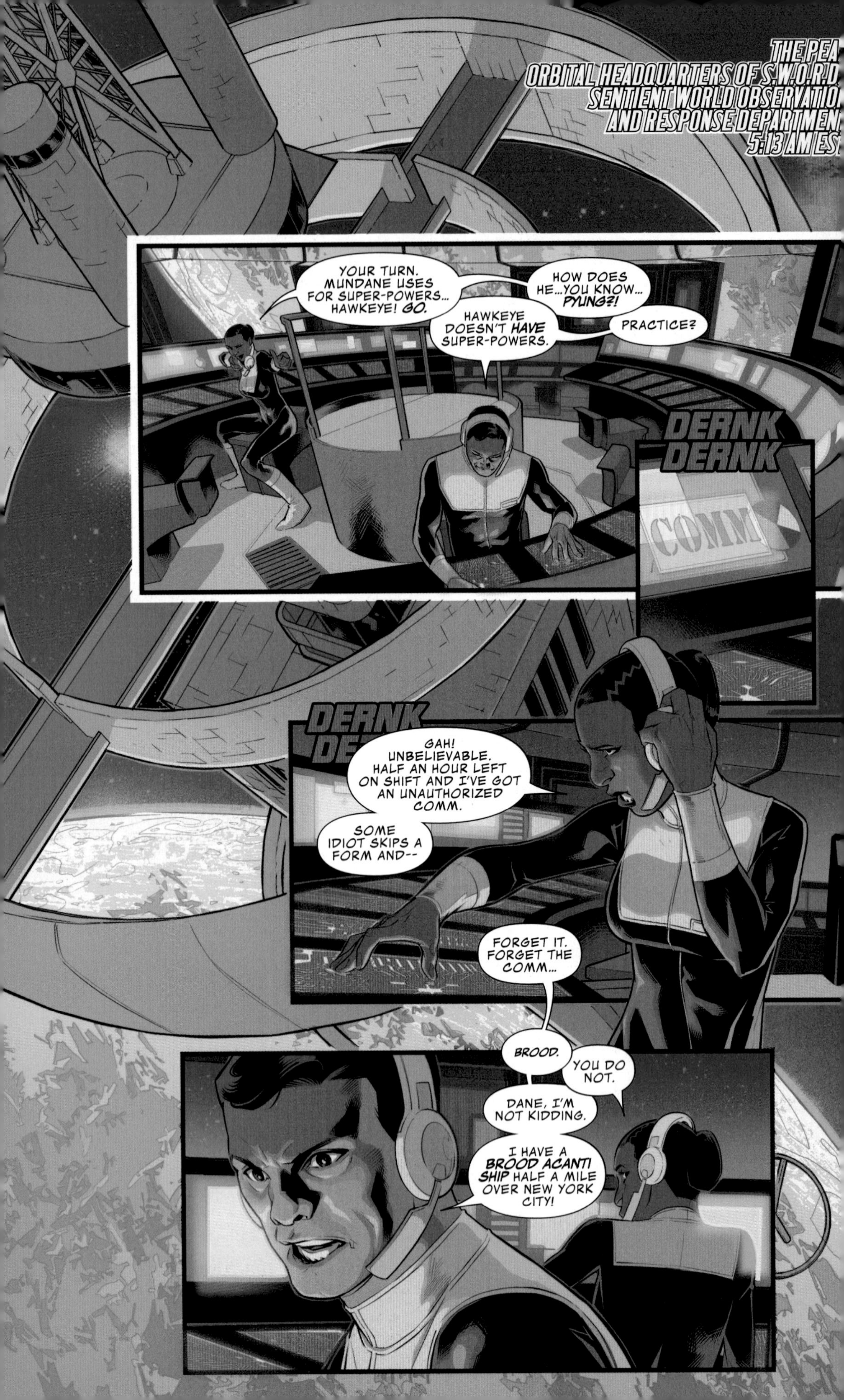
THE PEA
ORBITAL HEADQUARTERS OF S.W.O.R.D.
SENTIENT WORLD OBSERVATIO
AND RESPONSE DEPARTMEN
5:13 AM ES
YOUR TURN. MUNDANE USES FOR SUPER-POWERS... HAWKEYE! GO.
HOW DOES HE...YOU KNOW... PYUNG?!
HAWKEYE DOESN'T HAVE SUPER-POWERS.
PRACTICE?
DERNK DERNK
COMM
DERNK
GAH! UNBELIEVABLE. HALF AN HOUR LEFT ON SHIFT AND I'VE GOT AN UNAUTHORIZED COMM.
SOME IDIOT SKIPS A FORM AND--
FORGET IT. FORGET THE COMM...
BROOD.
YOU DO NOT.
DANE, I'M NOT KIDDING.
I HAVE A BROOD ACANTI SHIP HALF A MILE OVER NEW YORK CITY!

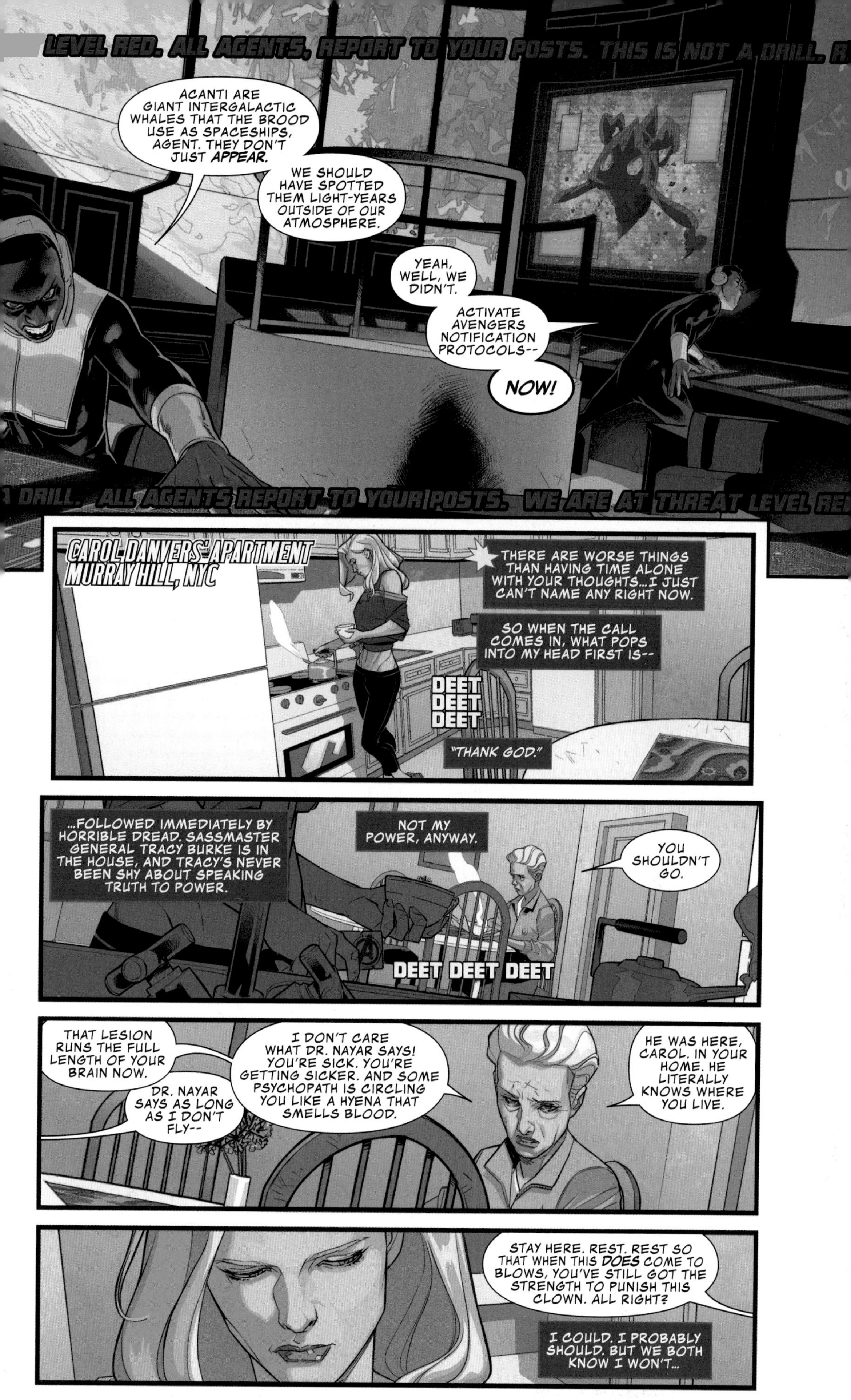

LEVEL RED. ALL AGENTS, REPORT TO YOUR POSTS. THIS IS NOT A DRILL.
ACANTI ARE GIANT INTERGALACTIC WHALES THAT THE BROOD USE AS SPACESHIPS, AGENT. THEY DON'T JUST APPEAR.
WE SHOULD HAVE SPOTTED THEM LIGHT-YEARS OUTSIDE OF OUR ATMOSPHERE.
YEAH, WELL, WE DIDN'T.
ACTIVATE AVENGERS NOTIFICATION PROTOCOLS--
NOW!
DRILL. ALL AGENTS REPORT TO YOUR POSTS. WE ARE AT THREAT LEVEL
CAROL DANVERS' APARTMENT MURRAY HILL, NYC
THERE ARE WORSE THINGS THAN HAVING TIME ALONE WITH YOUR THOUGHTS...I JUST CAN'T NAME ANY RIGHT NOW.
SO WHEN THE CALL COMES IN, WHAT POPS INTO MY HEAD FIRST IS--
DEET DEET DEET
"THANK GOD."
...FOLLOWED IMMEDIATELY BY HORRIBLE DREAD. SASSMASTER GENERAL TRACY BURKE IS IN THE HOUSE, AND TRACY'S NEVER BEEN SHY ABOUT SPEAKING TRUTH TO POWER.
NOT MY POWER, ANYWAY.
YOU SHOULDN'T GO.
DEET DEET DEET
THAT LESION RUNS THE FULL LENGTH OF YOUR BRAIN NOW.
DR. NAYAR SAYS AS LONG AS I DON'T FLY--
I DON'T CARE WHAT DR. NAYAR SAYS! YOU'RE SICK. YOU'RE GETTING SICKER. AND SOME PSYCHOPATH IS CIRCLING YOU LIKE A HYENA THAT SMELLS BLOOD.
HE WAS HERE, CAROL. IN YOUR HOME. HE LITERALLY KNOWS WHERE YOU LIVE.
STAY HERE. REST. REST SO THAT WHEN THIS DOES COME TO BLOWS, YOU'VE STILL GOT THE STRENGTH TO PUNISH THIS CLOWN. ALL RIGHT?
I COULD. I PROBABLY SHOULD. BUT WE BOTH KNOW I WON'T...

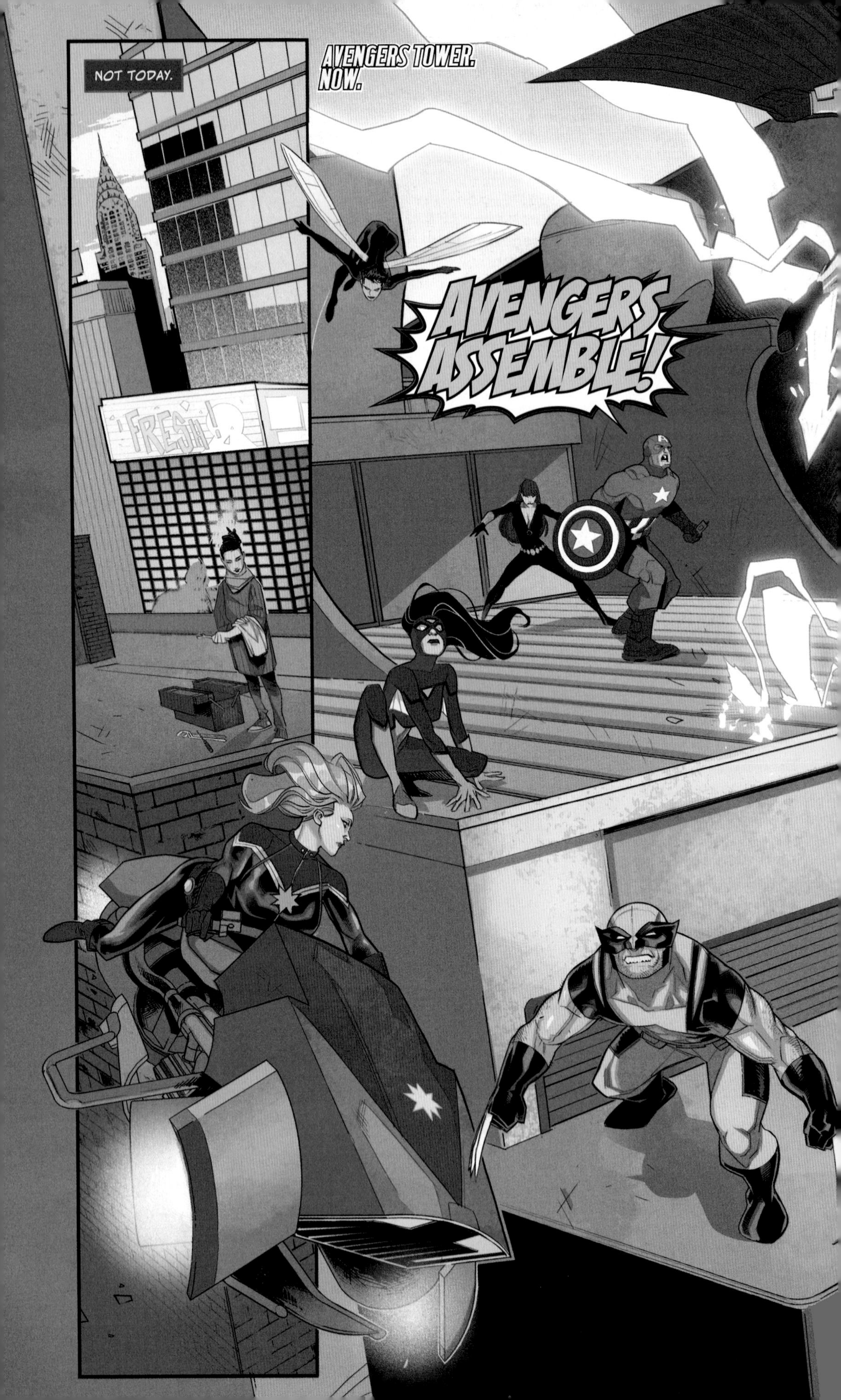

NOT TODAY.
FRESH!
AVENGERS TOWER.
NOW.
AVENGERS ASSEMBLE!

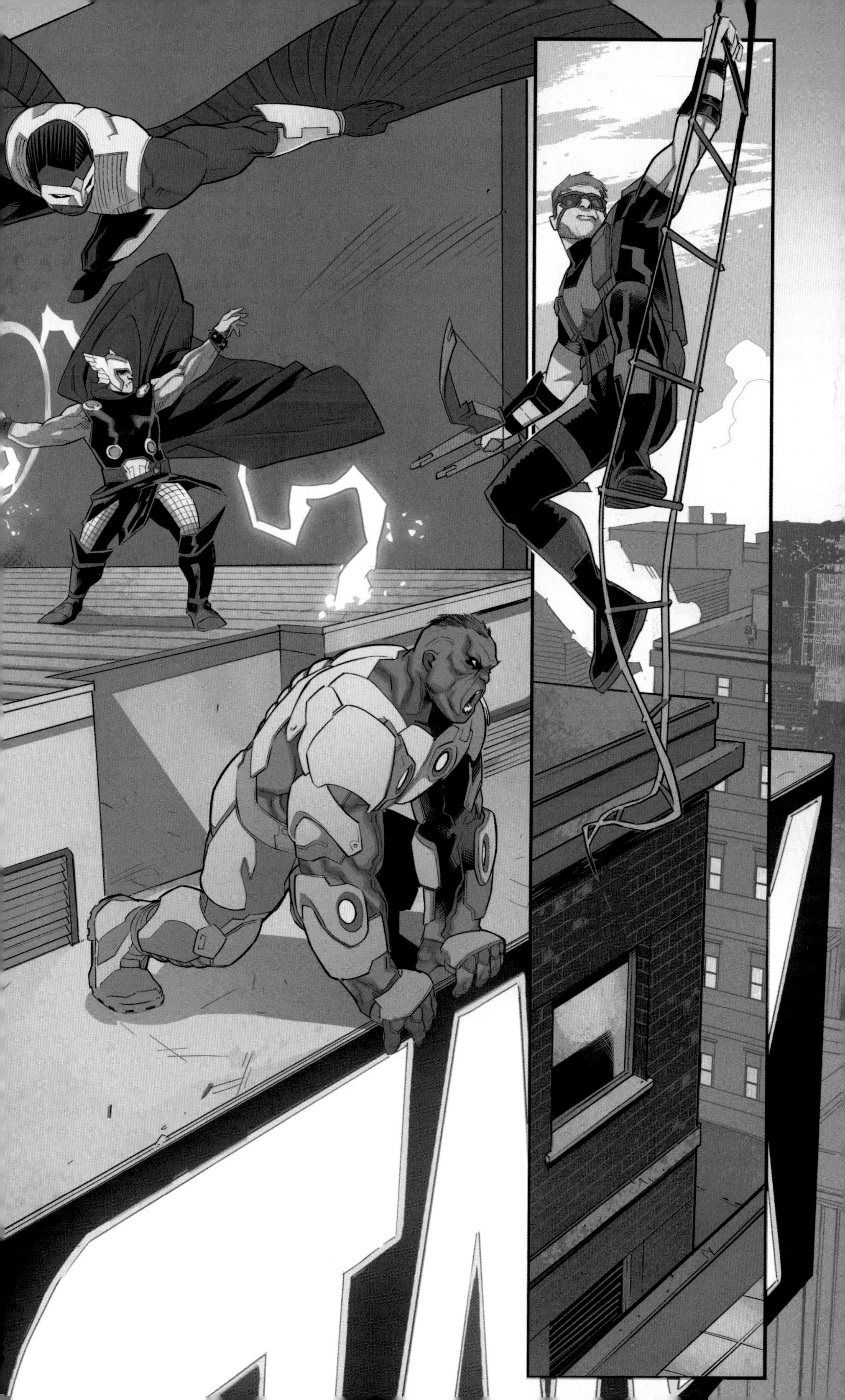

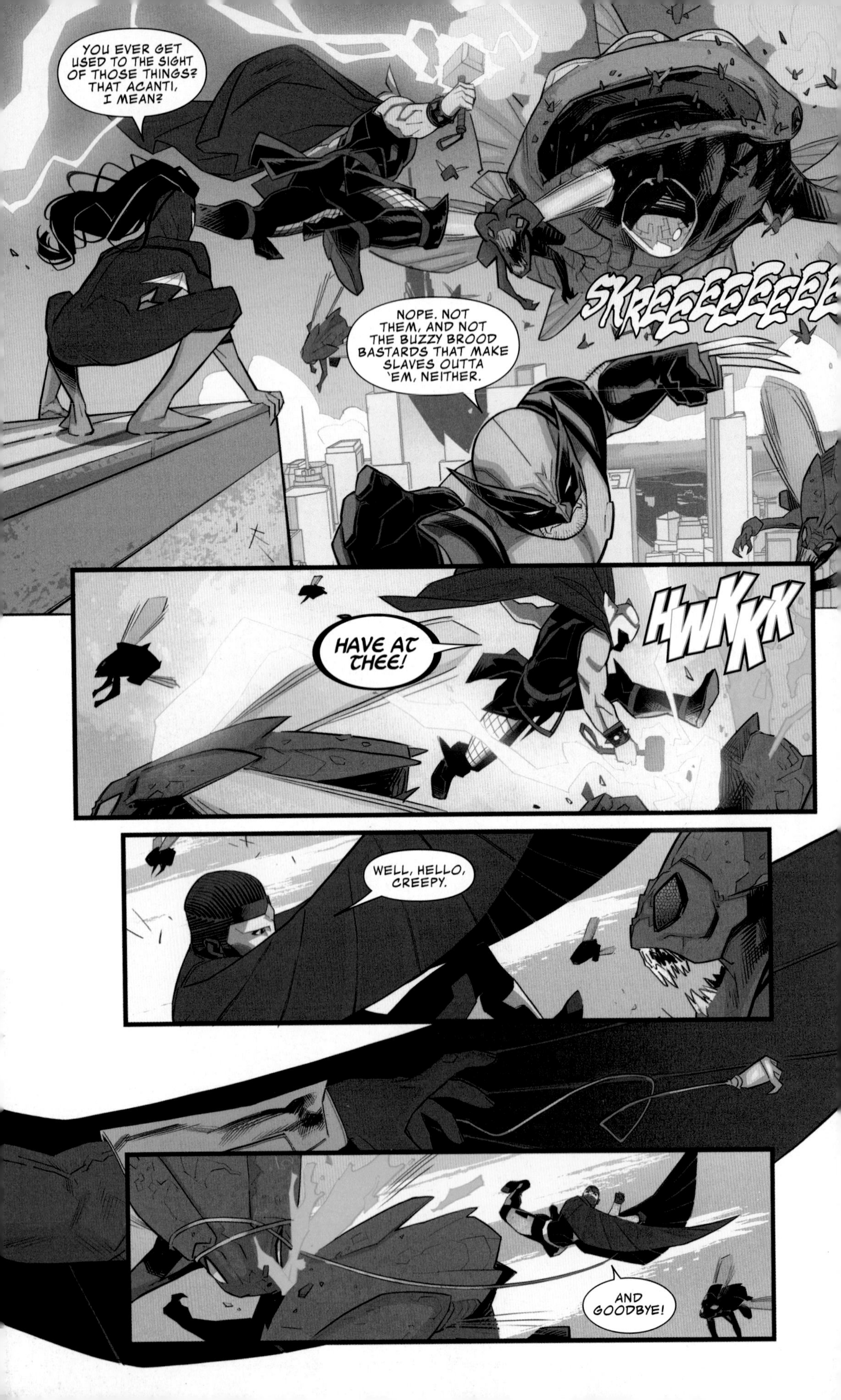

YOU EVER GET USED TO THE SIGHT OF THOSE THINGS? THAT ACANTI, I MEAN?
SKREEEEEEEEE
NOPE. NOT THEM, AND NOT THE BUZZY BROOD BASTARDS THAT MAKE SLAVES OUTTA 'EM, NEITHER.
HAVE AT THEE!
HWKKK
WELL, HELLO, CREEPY.
AND GOODBYE!

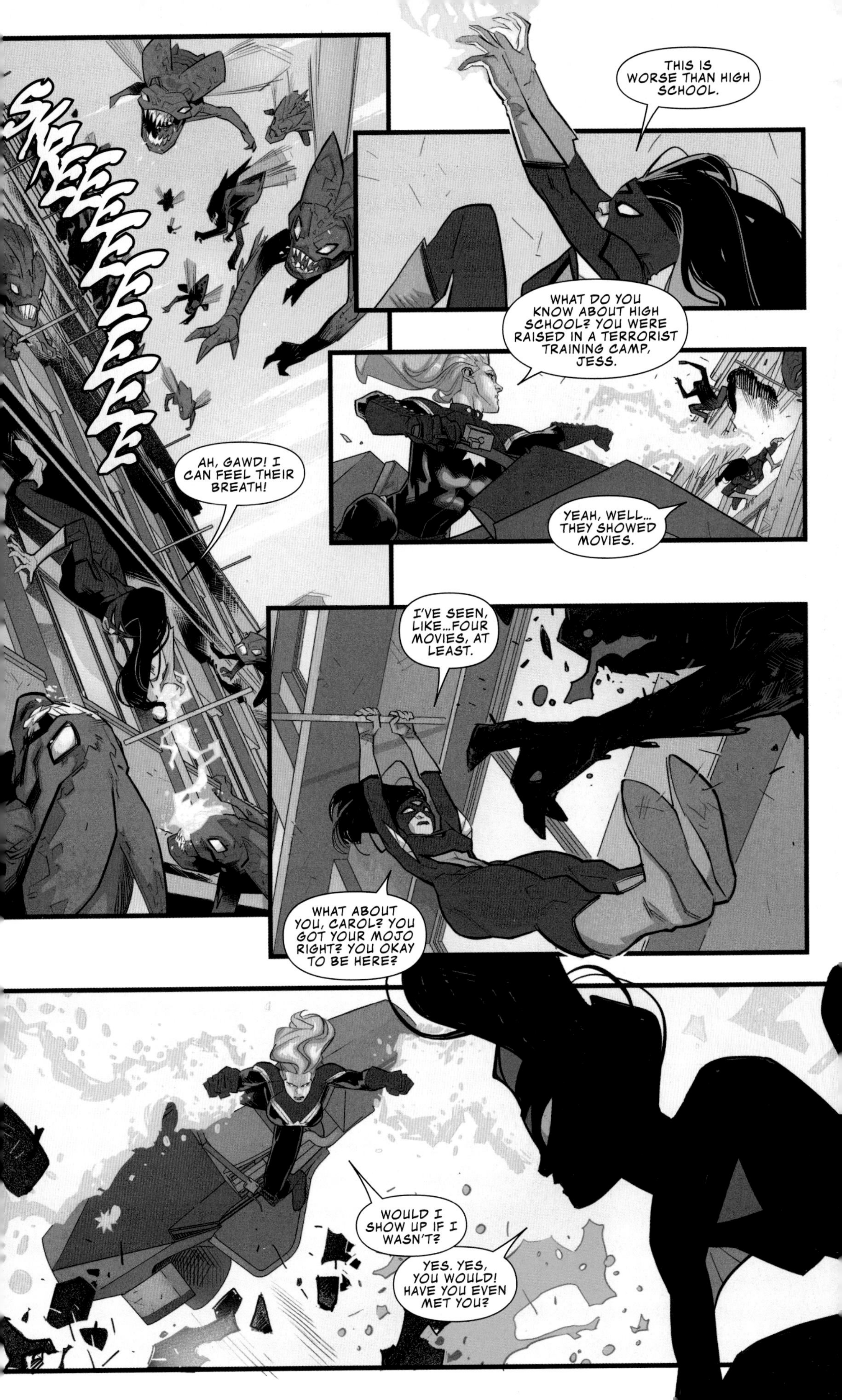
SKREEEEEEEEE
THIS IS WORSE THAN HIGH SCHOOL.
WHAT DO YOU KNOW ABOUT HIGH SCHOOL? YOU WERE RAISED IN A TERRORIST TRAINING CAMP, JESS.
AH, GAWD! I CAN FEEL THEIR BREATH!
YEAH, WELL... THEY SHOWED MOVIES.
I'VE SEEN, LIKE...FOUR MOVIES, AT LEAST.
WHAT ABOUT YOU, CAROL? YOU GOT YOUR MOJO RIGHT? YOU OKAY TO BE HERE?
WOULD I SHOW UP IF I WASN'T?
YES. YES, YOU WOULD! HAVE YOU EVEN MET YOU?

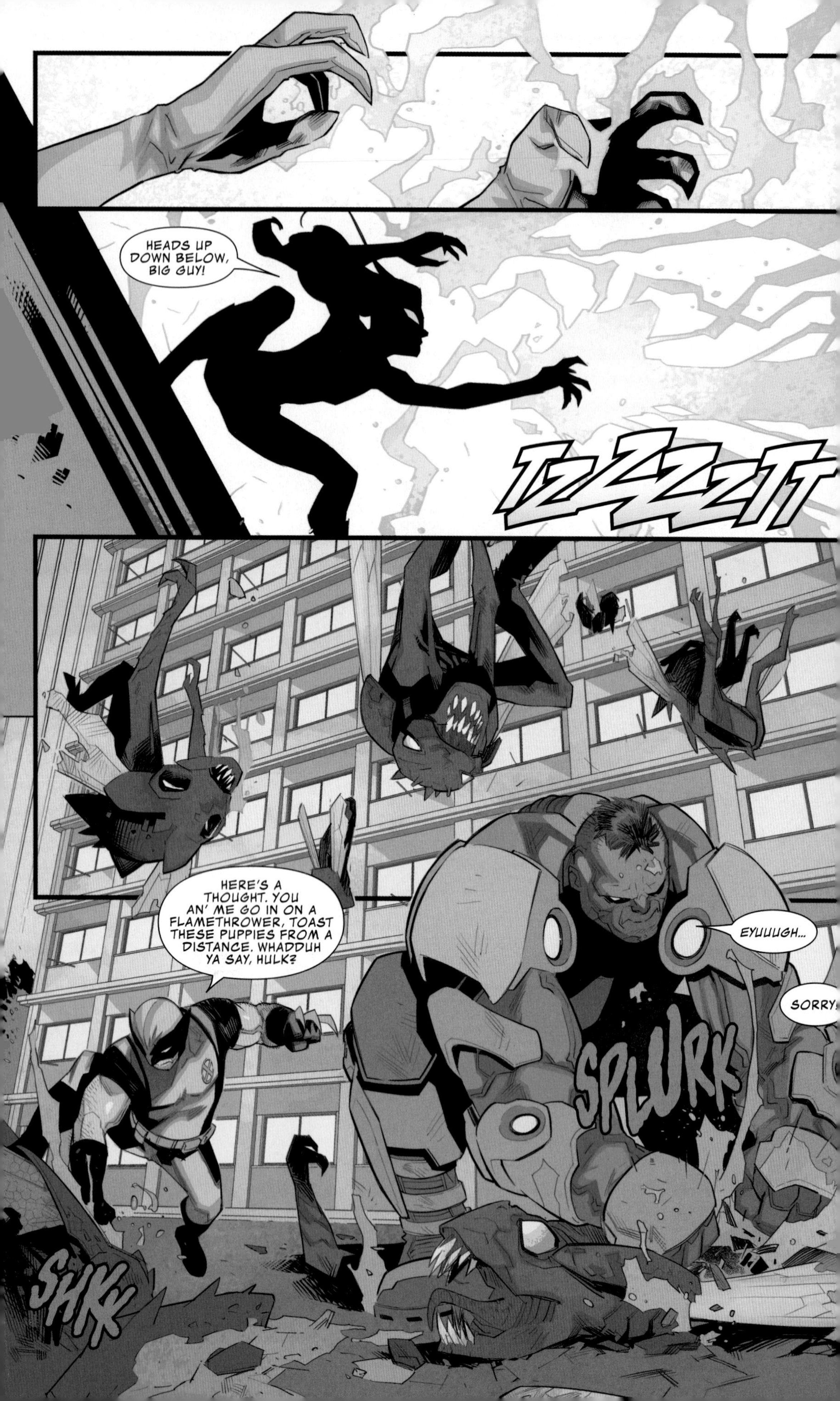

HEADS UP DOWN BELOW, BIG GUY!
TZZZZZTT
HERE'S A THOUGHT. YOU AN' ME GO IN ON A FLAMETHROWER, TOAST THESE PUPPIES FROM A DISTANCE. WHADDUH YA SAY, HULK?
EYUUUGH...
SORRY.
SPLURK
SHKK

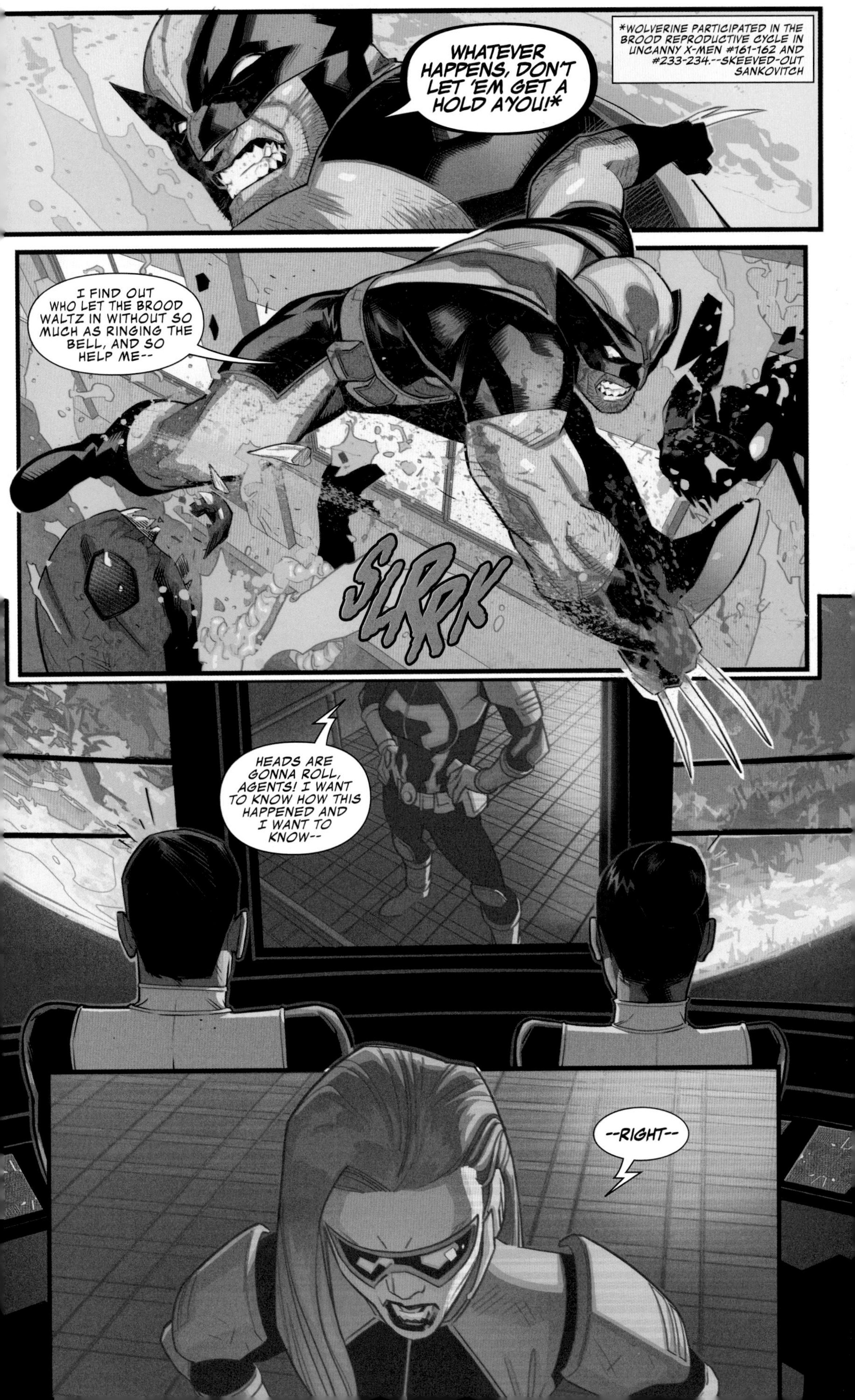
*WOLVERINE PARTICIPATED IN THE BROOD REPRODUCTIVE CYCLE IN UNCANNY X-MEN #161-162 AND #233-234.--SKEEVED-OUT SANKOVITCH
WHATEVER HAPPENS, DON'T LET 'EM GET A HOLD A'YOU!*
I FIND OUT WHO LET THE BROOD WALTZ IN WITHOUT SO MUCH AS RINGING THE BELL, AND SO HELP ME--
SLRRK
HEADS ARE GONNA ROLL, AGENTS! I WANT TO KNOW HOW THIS HAPPENED AND I WANT TO KNOW--
--RIGHT--

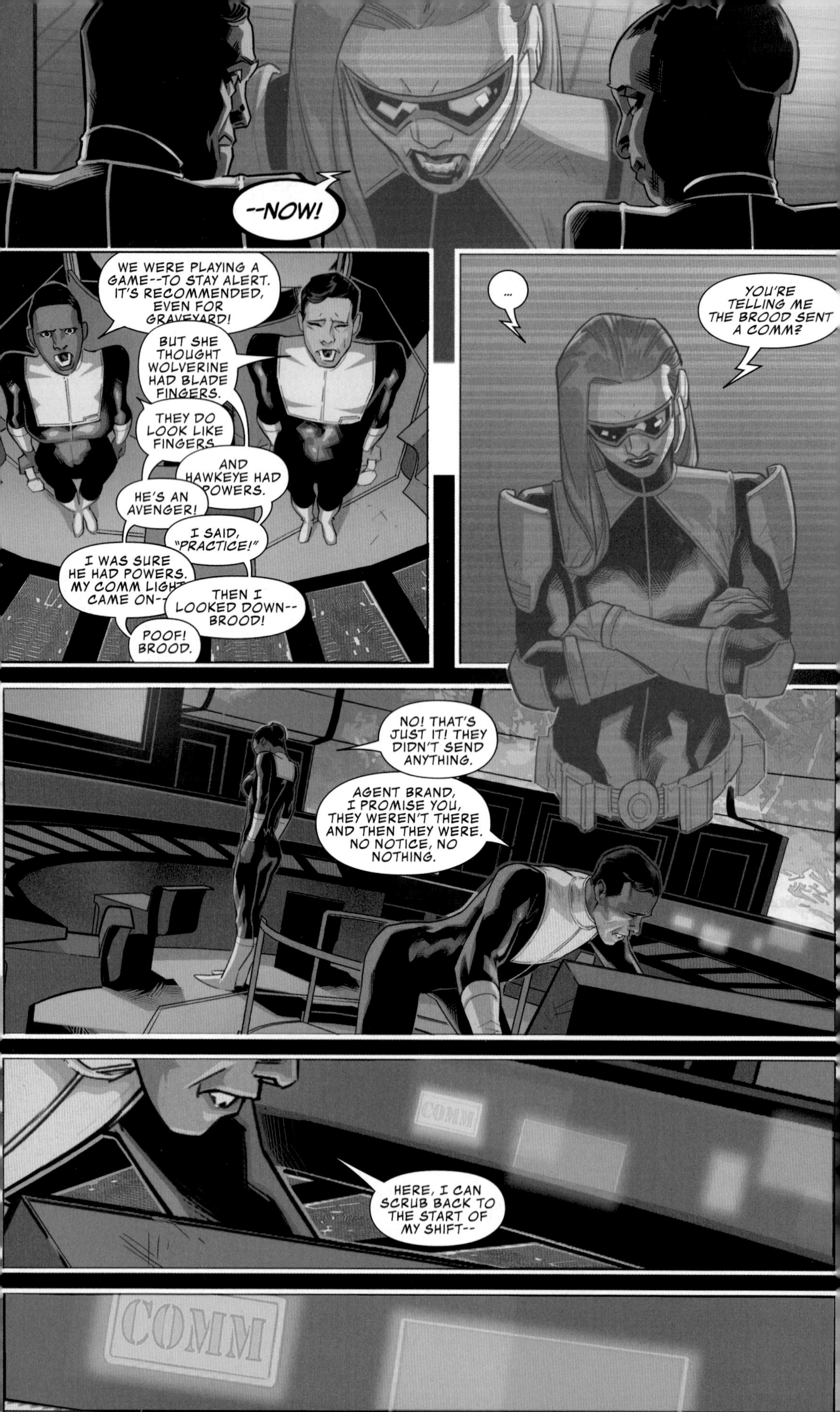
--NOW!
WE WERE PLAYING A GAME--TO STAY ALERT. IT'S RECOMMENDED, EVEN FOR GRAVEYARD!
BUT SHE THOUGHT WOLVERINE HAD BLADE FINGERS.
THEY DO LOOK LIKE FINGERS.
AND HAWKEYE HAD POWERS.
HE'S AN AVENGER!
I SAID, "PRACTICE!"
I WAS SURE HE HAD POWERS. MY COMM LIGHT CAME ON--
THEN I LOOKED DOWN--BROOD!
POOF! BROOD.
...
YOU'RE TELLING ME THE BROOD SENT A COMM?
NO! THAT'S JUST IT! THEY DIDN'T SEND ANYTHING.
AGENT BRAND, I PROMISE YOU, THEY WEREN'T THERE AND THEN THEY WERE. NO NOTICE, NO NOTHING.
COMM
HERE, I CAN SCRUB BACK TO THE START OF MY SHIFT--
COMM

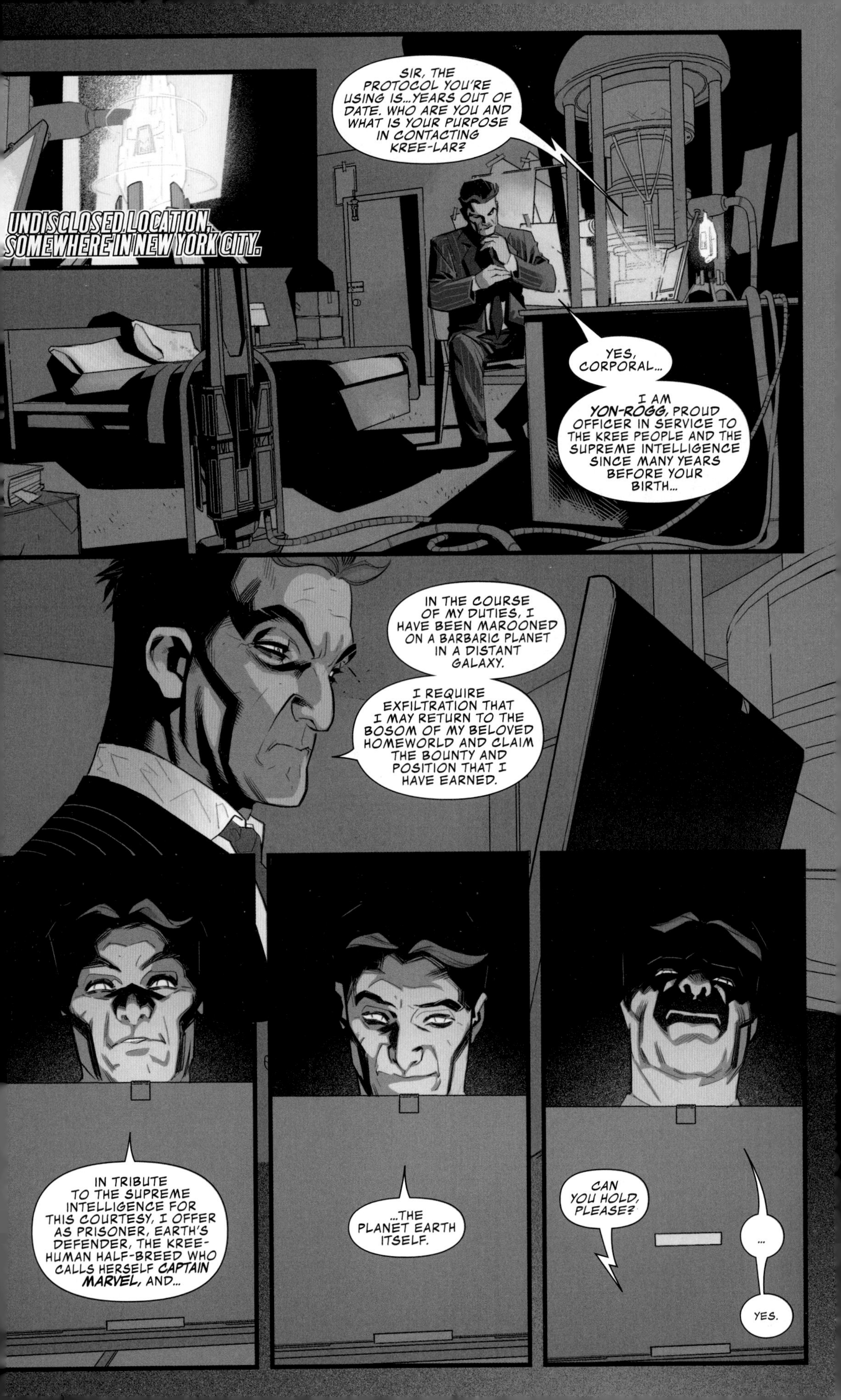
UNDISCLOSED LOCATION, SOMEWHERE IN NEW YORK CITY.
SIR, THE PROTOCOL YOU'RE USING IS...YEARS OUT OF DATE. WHO ARE YOU AND WHAT IS YOUR PURPOSE IN CONTACTING KREE-LAR?
YES, CORPORAL...
I AM YON-ROGG, PROUD OFFICER IN SERVICE TO THE KREE PEOPLE AND THE SUPREME INTELLIGENCE SINCE MANY YEARS BEFORE YOUR BIRTH...
IN THE COURSE OF MY DUTIES, I HAVE BEEN MAROONED ON A BARBARIC PLANET IN A DISTANT GALAXY.
I REQUIRE EXFILTRATION THAT I MAY RETURN TO THE BOSOM OF MY BELOVED HOMEWORLD AND CLAIM THE BOUNTY AND POSITION THAT I HAVE EARNED.
IN TRIBUTE TO THE SUPREME INTELLIGENCE FOR THIS COURTESY, I OFFER AS PRISONER, EARTH'S DEFENDER, THE KREE-HUMAN HALF-BREED WHO CALLS HERSELF CAPTAIN MARVEL, AND...
...THE PLANET EARTH ITSELF.
CAN YOU HOLD, PLEASE?
...
YES.

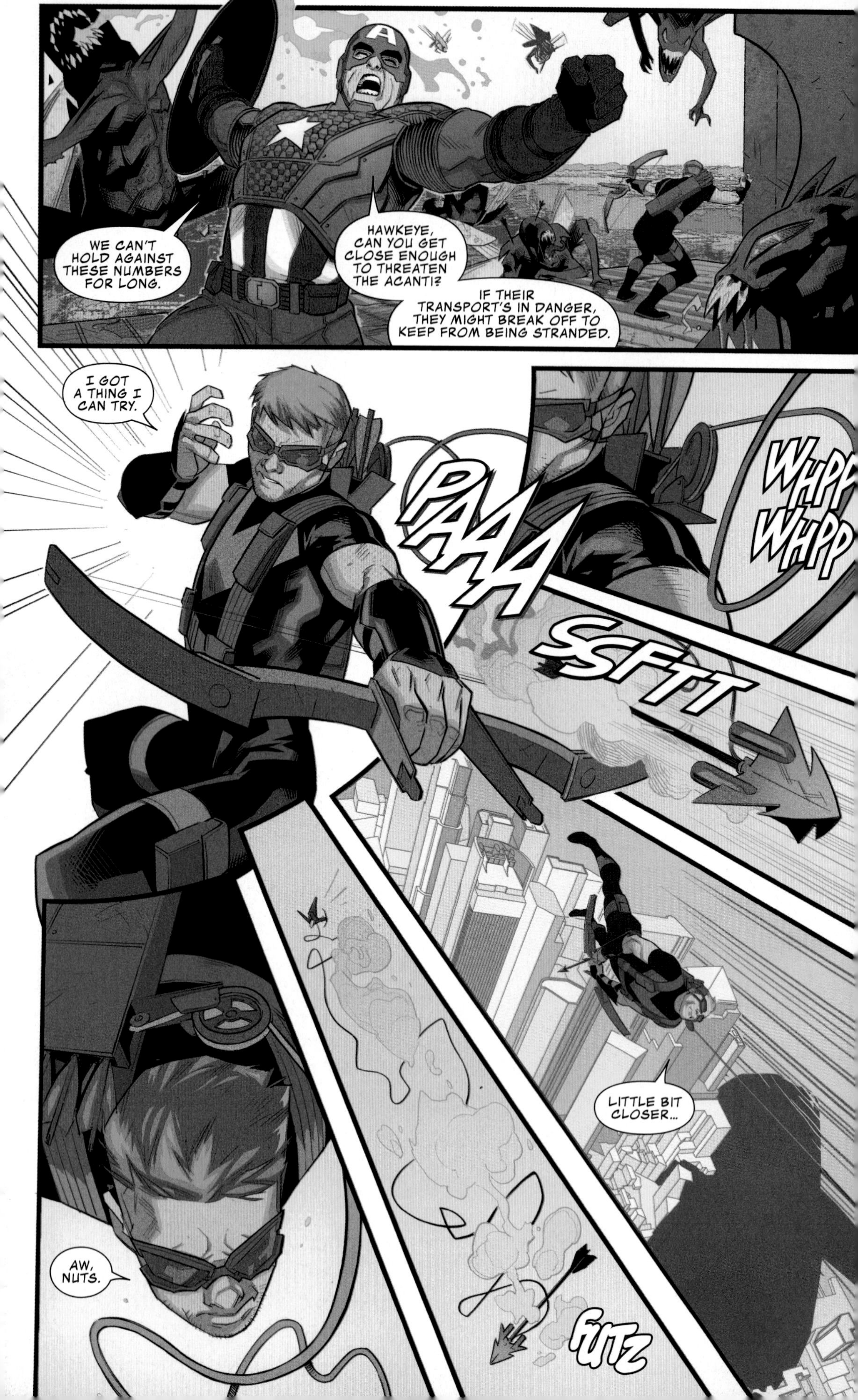
WE CAN'T HOLD AGAINST THESE NUMBERS FOR LONG.
HAWKEYE, CAN YOU GET CLOSE ENOUGH TO THREATEN THE ACANTI?
IF THEIR TRANSPORT'S IN DANGER, THEY MIGHT BREAK OFF TO KEEP FROM BEING STRANDED.
I GOT A THING I CAN TRY.
PAAA
WHPP WHPP
SSFTT
LITTLE BIT CLOSER...
AW, NUTS.
FUTZ

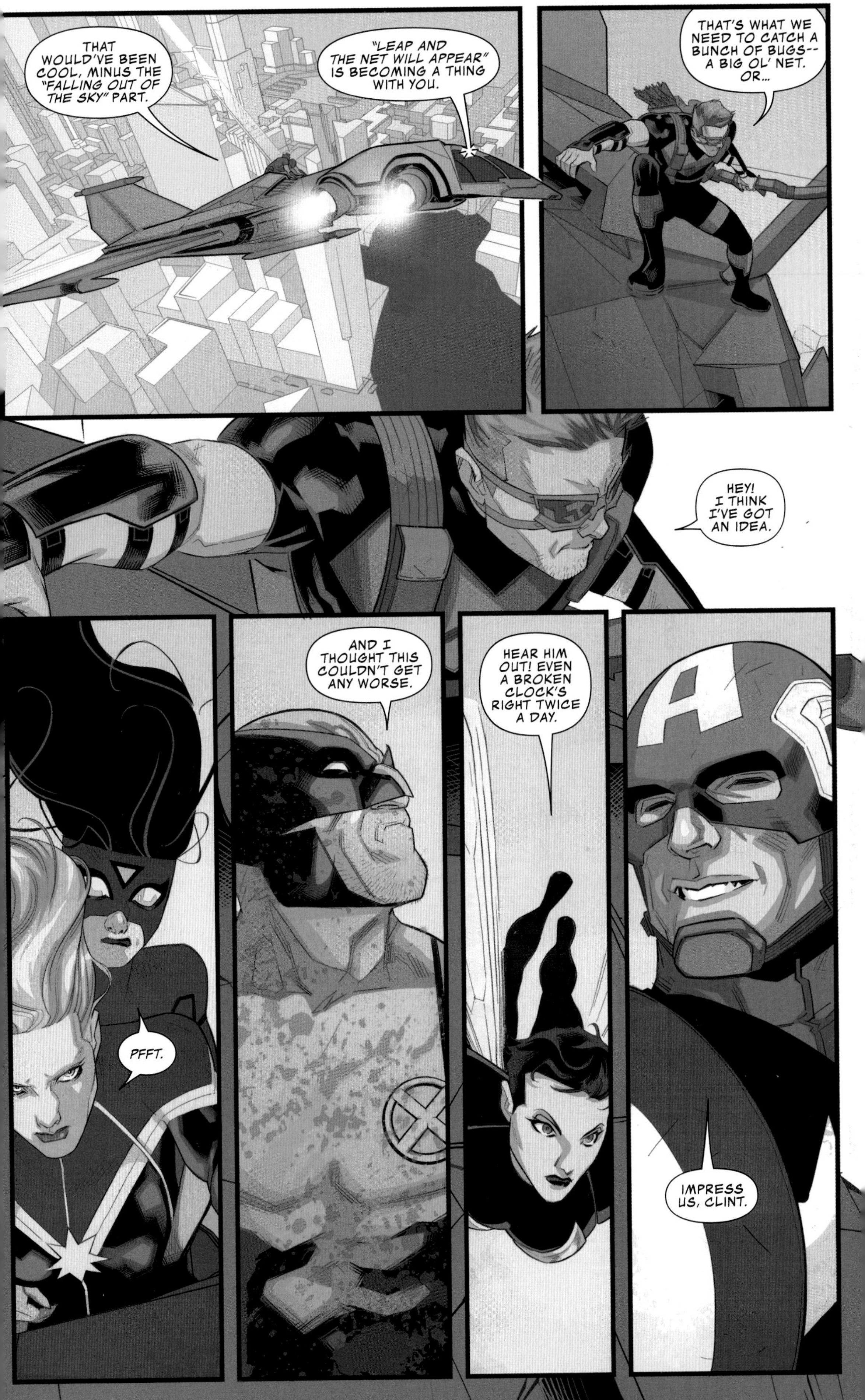
THAT WOULD'VE BEEN COOL, MINUS THE "FALLING OUT OF THE SKY" PART.
"LEAP AND THE NET WILL APPEAR" IS BECOMING A THING WITH YOU.
THAT'S WHAT WE NEED TO CATCH A BUNCH OF BUGS-- A BIG OL' NET. OR...
HEY! I THINK I'VE GOT AN IDEA.
PFFT.
AND I THOUGHT THIS COULDN'T GET ANY WORSE.
HEAR HIM OUT! EVEN A BROKEN CLOCK'S RIGHT TWICE A DAY.
IMPRESS US, CLINT.

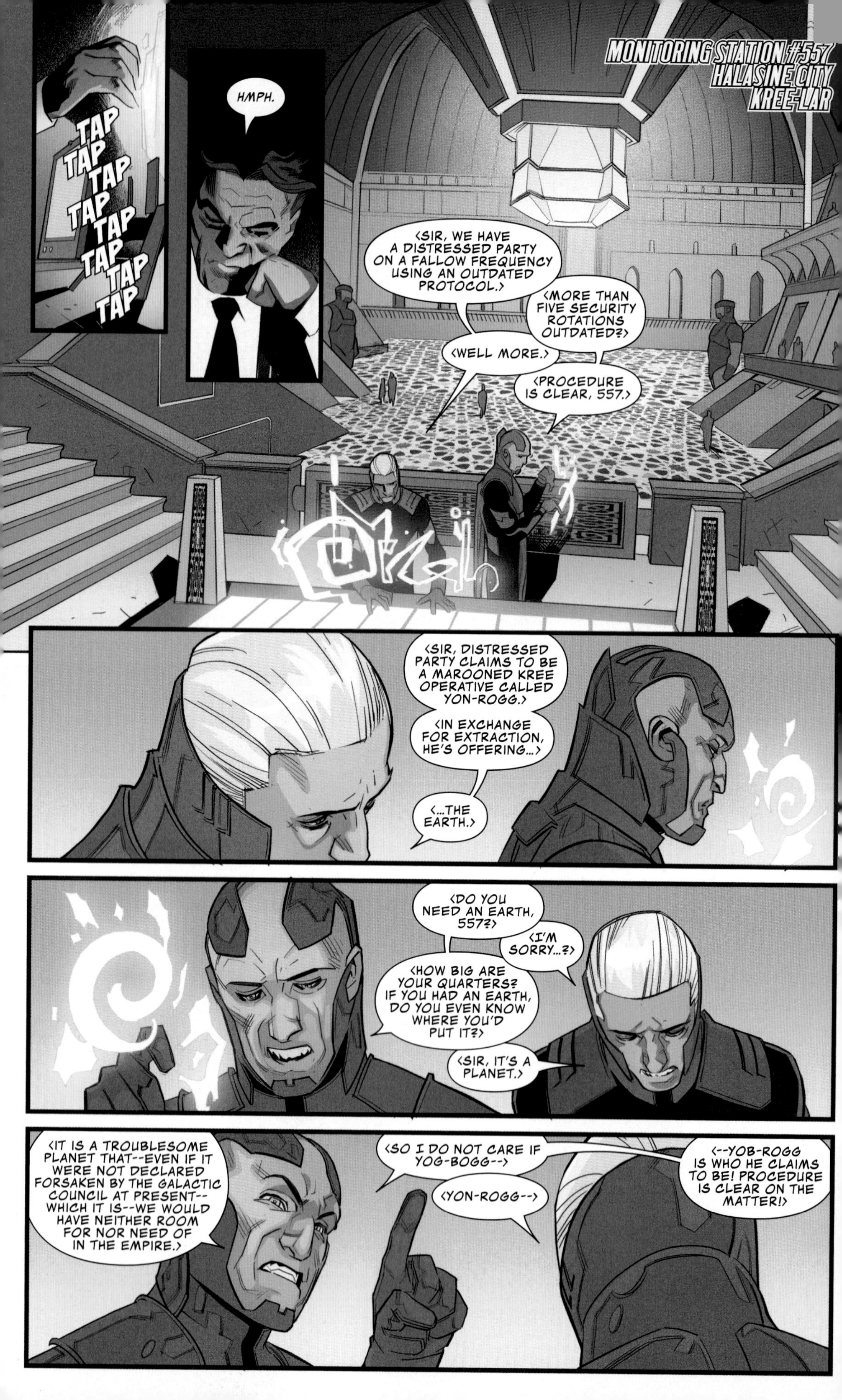
MONITORING STATION #557
HALASINE CITY
KREE-LAR
TAP TAP TAP TAP TAP TAP TAP TAP
HMPH.
<SIR, WE HAVE A DISTRESSED PARTY ON A FALLOW FREQUENCY USING AN OUTDATED PROTOCOL.>
<MORE THAN FIVE SECURITY ROTATIONS OUTDATED?>
<WELL MORE.>
<PROCEDURE IS CLEAR, 557.>
<SIR, DISTRESSED PARTY CLAIMS TO BE A MAROONED KREE OPERATIVE CALLED YON-ROGG.>
<IN EXCHANGE FOR EXTRACTION, HE'S OFFERING...>
<...THE EARTH.>
<DO YOU NEED AN EARTH, 557?>
<I'M SORRY...?>
<HOW BIG ARE YOUR QUARTERS? IF YOU HAD AN EARTH, DO YOU EVEN KNOW WHERE YOU'D PUT IT?>
<SIR, IT'S A PLANET.>
<IT IS A TROUBLESOME PLANET THAT--EVEN IF IT WERE NOT DECLARED FORSAKEN BY THE GALACTIC COUNCIL AT PRESENT--WHICH IT IS--WE WOULD HAVE NEITHER ROOM FOR NOR NEED OF IN THE EMPIRE.>
<SO I DO NOT CARE IF YOG-BOGG-->
<YON-ROGG-->
<--YOB-ROGG IS WHO HE CLAIMS TO BE! PROCEDURE IS CLEAR ON THE MATTER!>

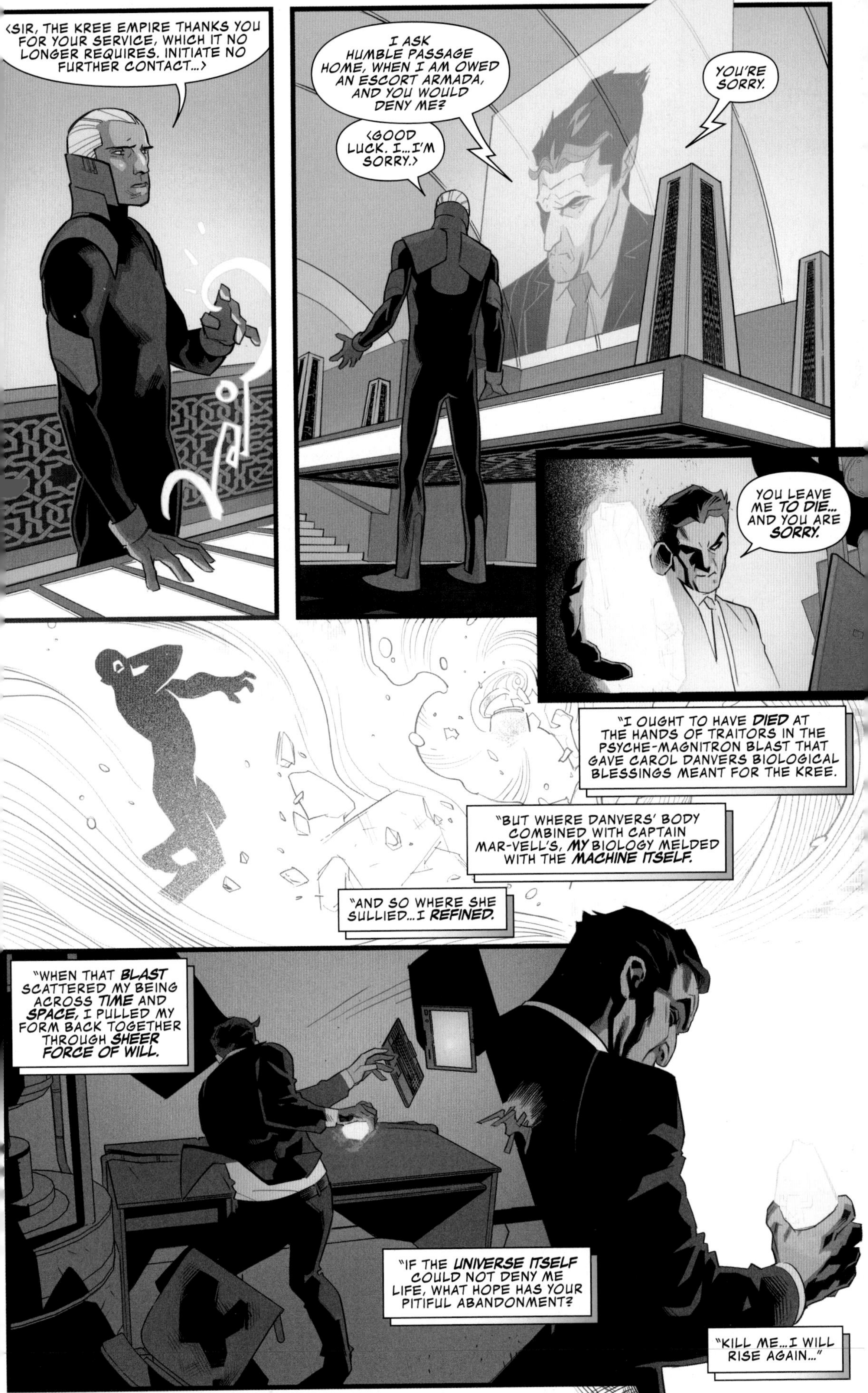
‹SIR, THE KREE EMPIRE THANKS YOU FOR YOUR SERVICE, WHICH IT NO LONGER REQUIRES. INITIATE NO FURTHER CONTACT...›
I ASK HUMBLE PASSAGE HOME, WHEN I AM OWED AN ESCORT ARMADA, AND YOU WOULD DENY ME?
‹GOOD LUCK. I...I'M SORRY.›
YOU'RE SORRY.
YOU LEAVE ME TO DIE... AND YOU ARE SORRY.
"I OUGHT TO HAVE DIED AT THE HANDS OF TRAITORS IN THE PSYCHE-MAGNITRON BLAST THAT GAVE CAROL DANVERS BIOLOGICAL BLESSINGS MEANT FOR THE KREE.
"BUT WHERE DANVERS' BODY COMBINED WITH CAPTAIN MAR-VELL'S, MY BIOLOGY MELDED WITH THE MACHINE ITSELF.
"AND SO WHERE SHE SULLIED...I REFINED.
"WHEN THAT BLAST SCATTERED MY BEING ACROSS TIME AND SPACE, I PULLED MY FORM BACK TOGETHER THROUGH SHEER FORCE OF WILL.
"IF THE UNIVERSE ITSELF COULD NOT DENY ME LIFE, WHAT HOPE HAS YOUR PITIFUL ABANDONMENT?
"KILL ME...I WILL RISE AGAIN..."

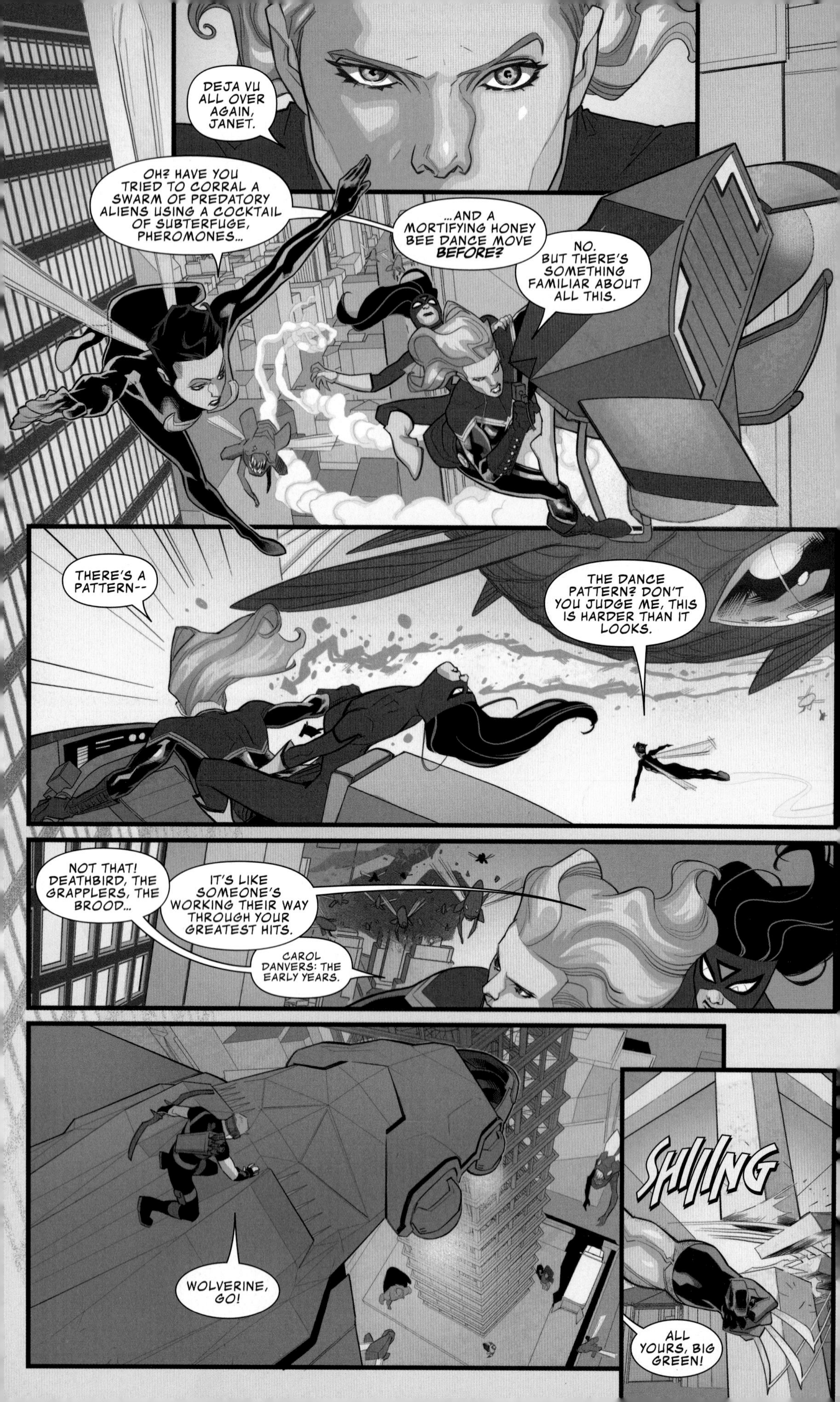
DEJA VU ALL OVER AGAIN, JANET.
OH? HAVE YOU TRIED TO CORRAL A SWARM OF PREDATORY ALIENS USING A COCKTAIL OF SUBTERFUGE, PHEROMONES...
...AND A MORTIFYING HONEY BEE DANCE MOVE BEFORE?
NO. BUT THERE'S SOMETHING FAMILIAR ABOUT ALL THIS.
THERE'S A PATTERN--
THE DANCE PATTERN? DON'T YOU JUDGE ME, THIS IS HARDER THAN IT LOOKS.
NOT THAT! DEATHBIRD, THE GRAPPLERS, THE BROOD...
IT'S LIKE SOMEONE'S WORKING THEIR WAY THROUGH YOUR GREATEST HITS.
CAROL DANVERS: THE EARLY YEARS.
WOLVERINE, GO!
SHIIING
ALL YOURS, BIG GREEN!

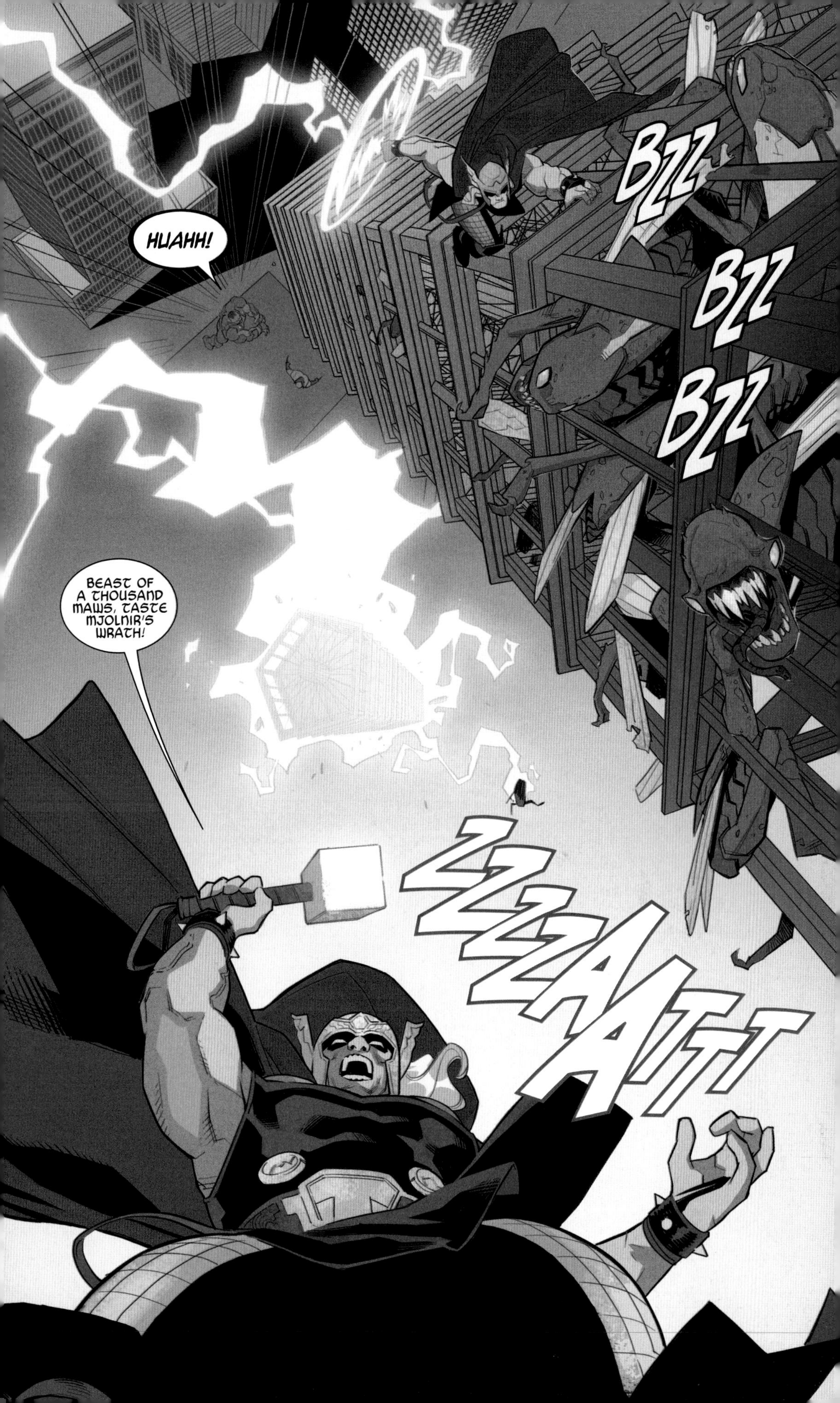
HUAHH!
BZZ
BZZ
BZZ
BEAST OF A THOUSAND MAWS, TASTE MJOLNIR'S WRATH!
ZZZZAAATTT

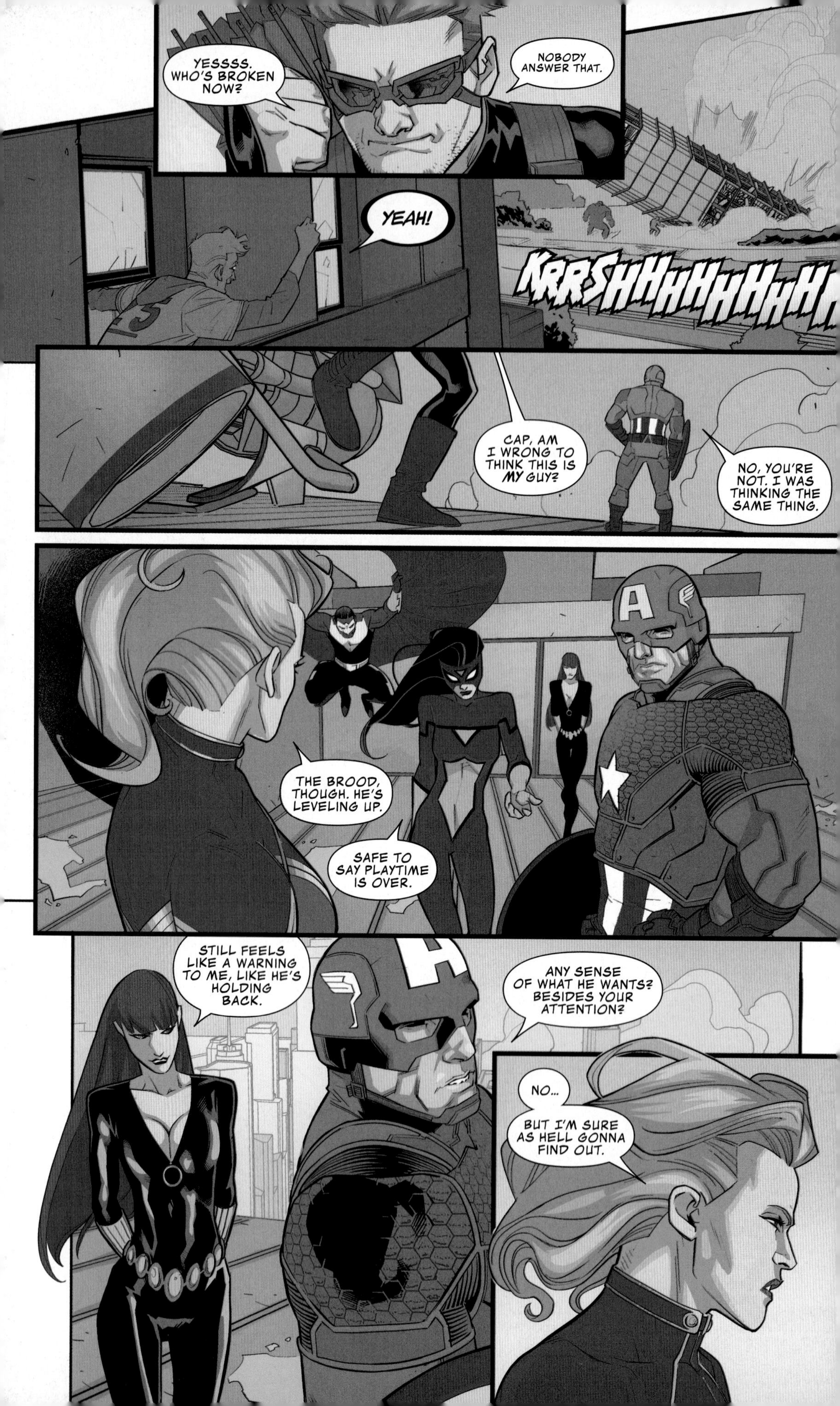

YESSSS. WHO'S BROKEN NOW?
NOBODY ANSWER THAT.
YEAH!
KRRSHHHHHHHHH
CAP, AM I WRONG TO THINK THIS IS MY GUY?
NO, YOU'RE NOT. I WAS THINKING THE SAME THING.
THE BROOD, THOUGH. HE'S LEVELING UP.
SAFE TO SAY PLAYTIME IS OVER.
STILL FEELS LIKE A WARNING TO ME, LIKE HE'S HOLDING BACK.
ANY SENSE OF WHAT HE WANTS? BESIDES YOUR ATTENTION?
NO...
BUT I'M SURE AS HELL GONNA FIND OUT.

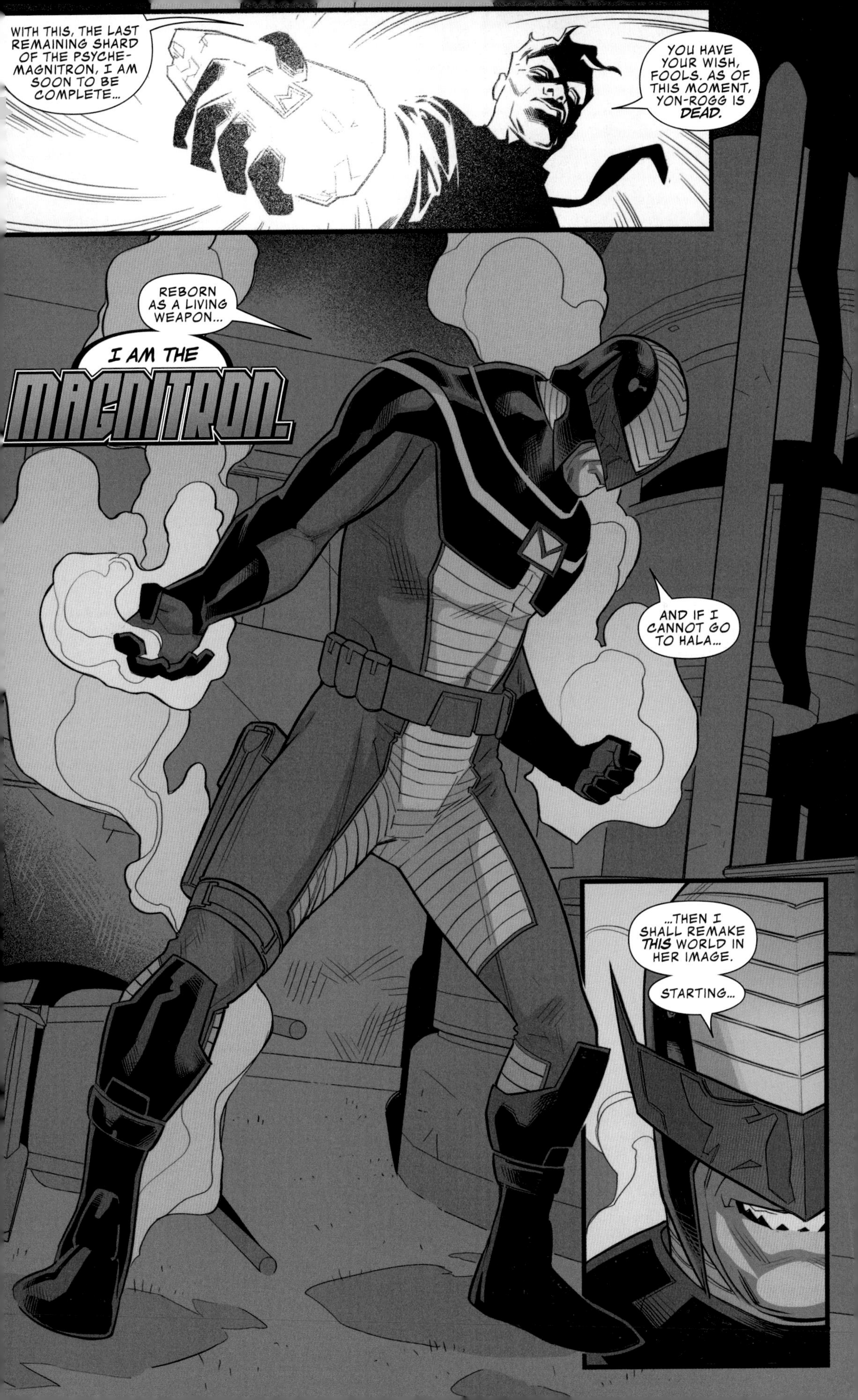
WITH THIS, THE LAST REMAINING SHARD OF THE PSYCHE-MAGNITRON, I AM SOON TO BE COMPLETE...
YOU HAVE YOUR WISH, FOOLS. AS OF THIS MOMENT, YON-ROGG IS DEAD.
REBORN AS A LIVING WEAPON...
I AM THE
MAGNITRON.
AND IF I CANNOT GO TO HALA...
...THEN I SHALL REMAKE THIS WORLD IN HER IMAGE.
STARTING...

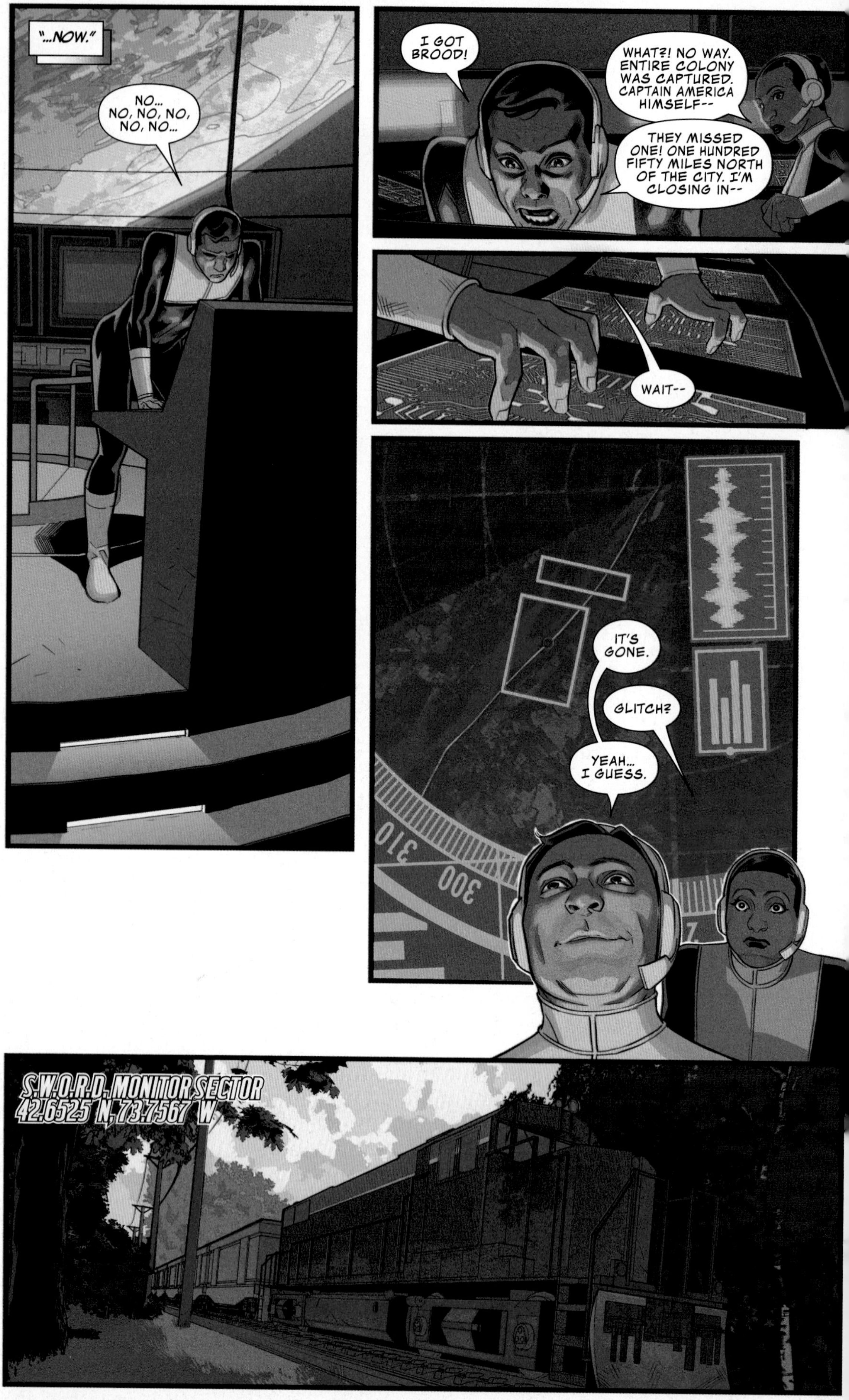

"...NOW."
NO... NO, NO, NO, NO, NO...
I GOT BROOD!
WHAT?! NO WAY. ENTIRE COLONY WAS CAPTURED. CAPTAIN AMERICA HIMSELF--
THEY MISSED ONE! ONE HUNDRED FIFTY MILES NORTH OF THE CITY. I'M CLOSING IN--
WAIT--
IT'S GONE.
GLITCH?
YEAH... I GUESS.
S.W.O.R.D. MONITOR SECTOR 42.6525 N, 73.7567 W.

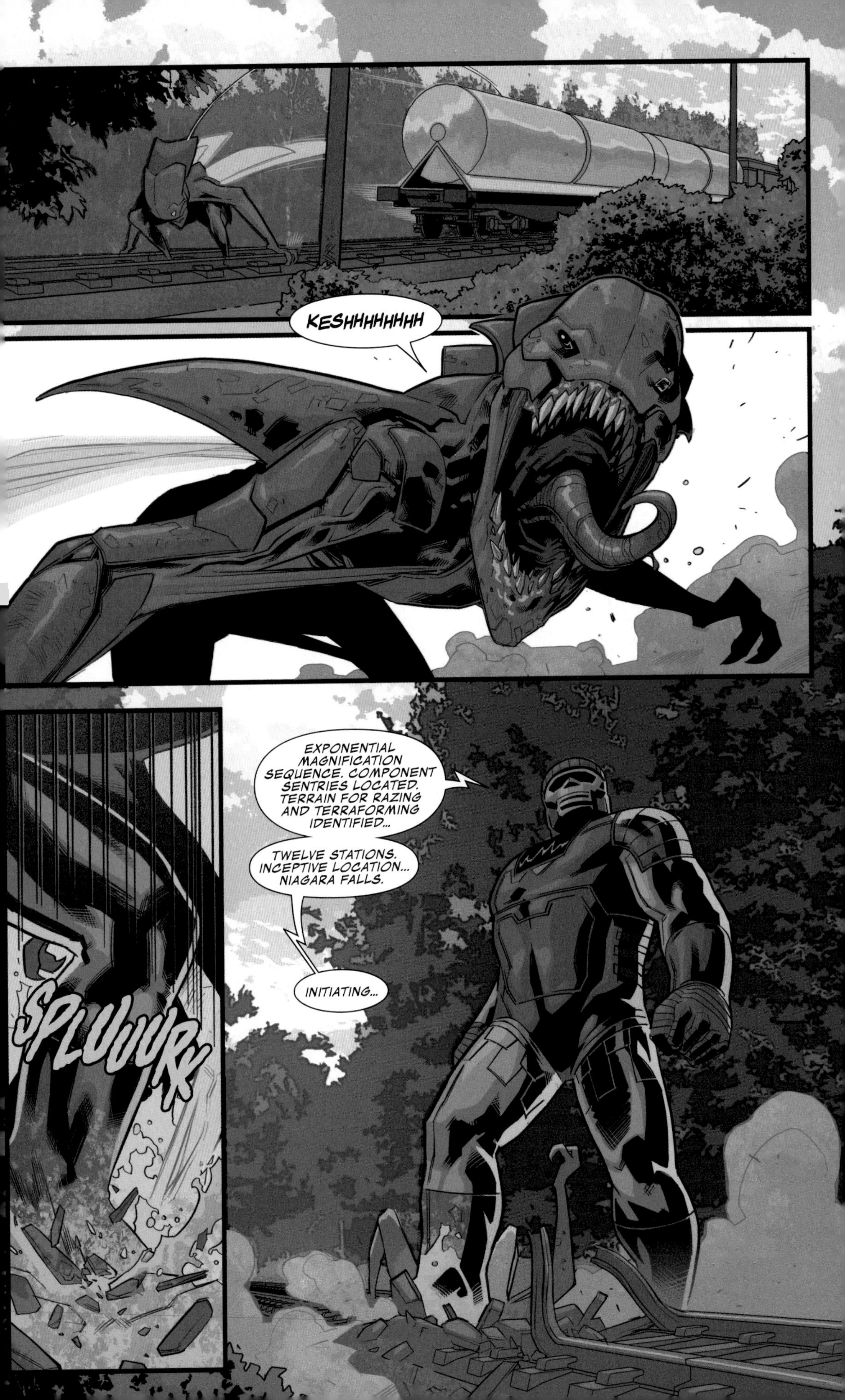
KESHHHHHHHH
EXPONENTIAL MAGNIFICATION SEQUENCE. COMPONENT SENTRIES LOCATED. TERRAIN FOR RAZING AND TERRAFORMING IDENTIFIED...
TWELVE STATIONS. INCEPTIVE LOCATION... NIAGARA FALLS.
INITIATING...
SPLUUURK

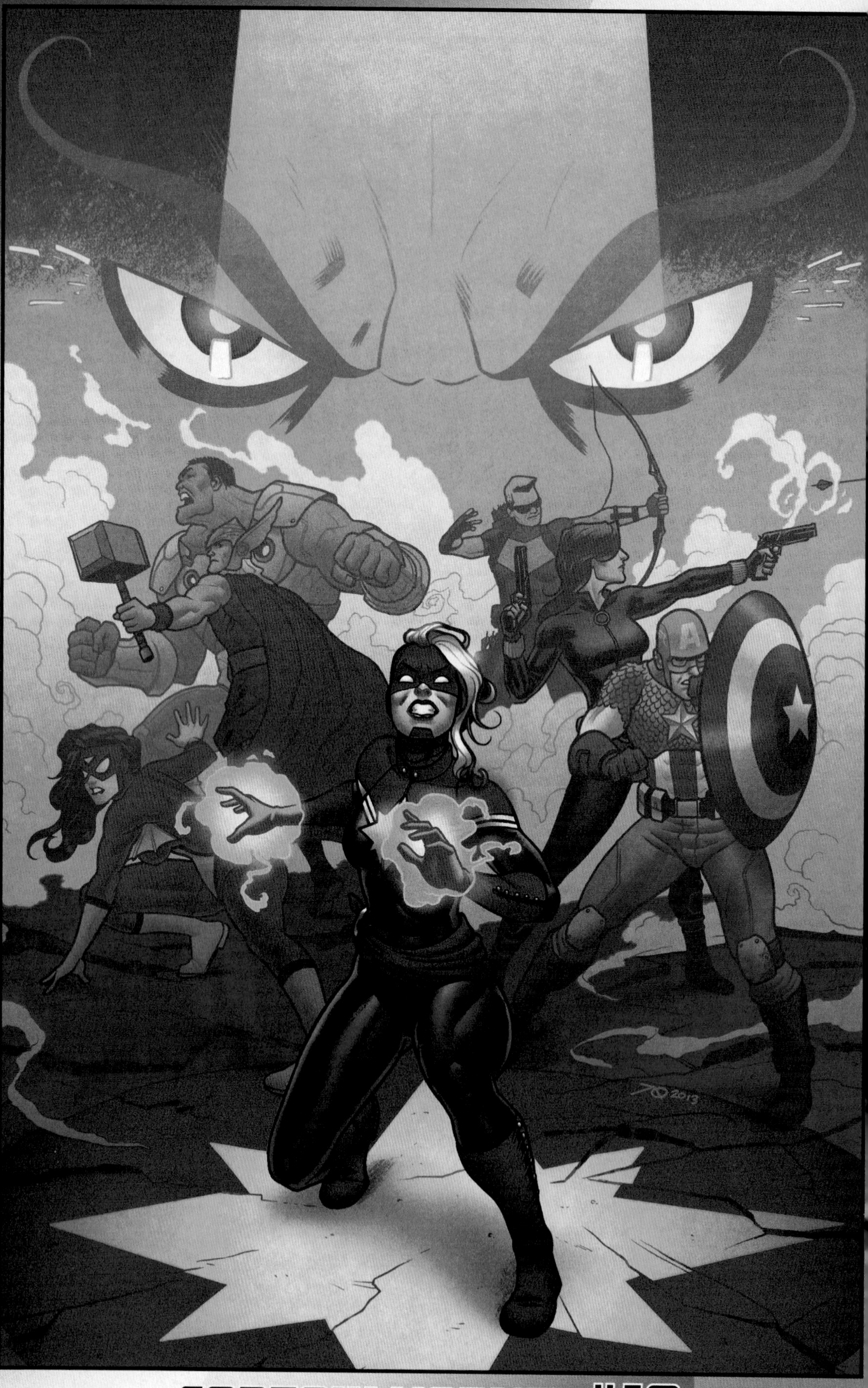

CAPTAIN MARVEL #13

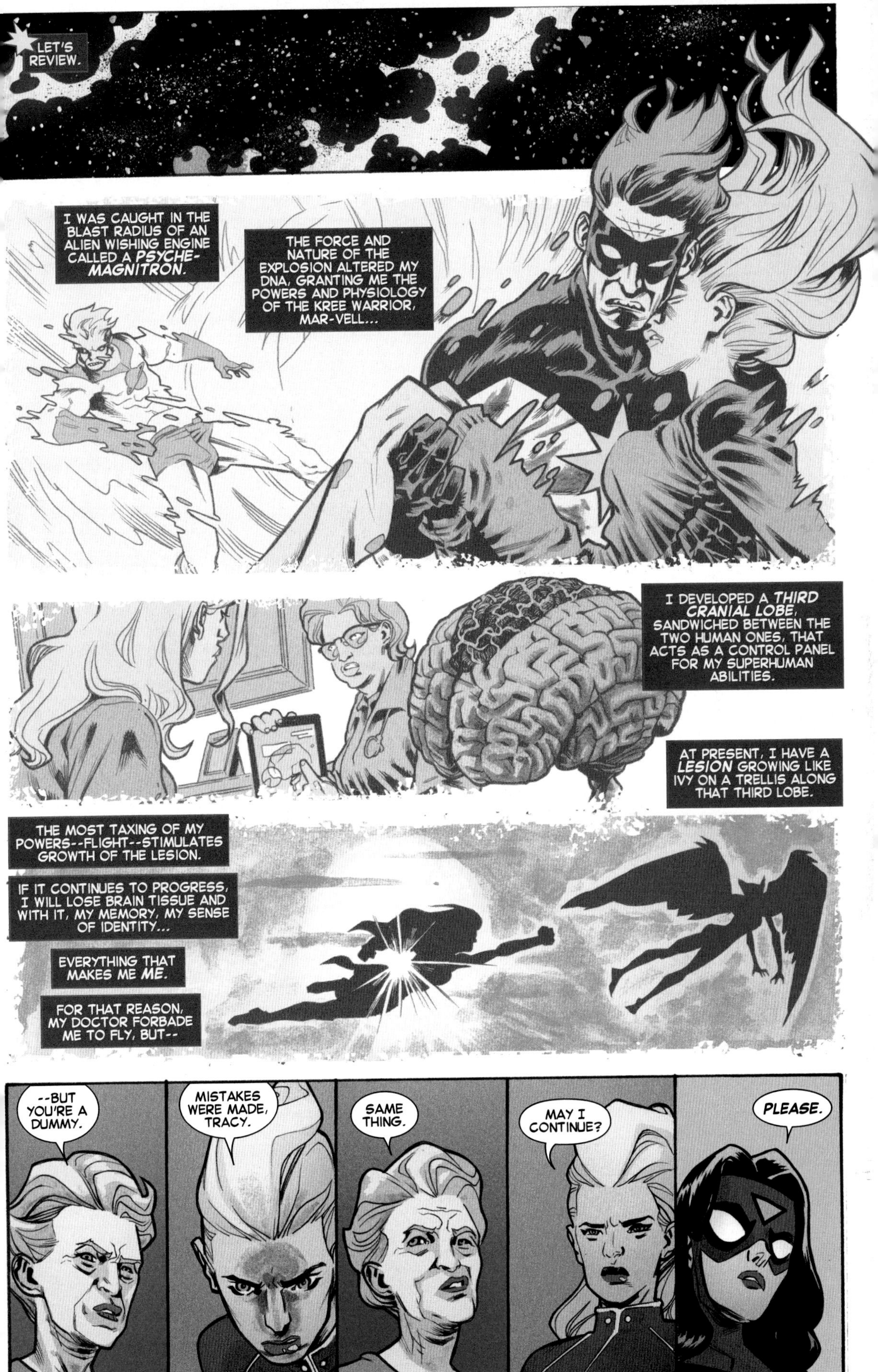
LET'S REVIEW.
I WAS CAUGHT IN THE BLAST RADIUS OF AN ALIEN WISHING ENGINE CALLED A PSYCHE-MAGNITRON.
THE FORCE AND NATURE OF THE EXPLOSION ALTERED MY DNA, GRANTING ME THE POWERS AND PHYSIOLOGY OF THE KREE WARRIOR, MAR-VELL...
I DEVELOPED A THIRD CRANIAL LOBE, SANDWICHED BETWEEN THE TWO HUMAN ONES, THAT ACTS AS A CONTROL PANEL FOR MY SUPERHUMAN ABILITIES.
AT PRESENT, I HAVE A LESION GROWING LIKE IVY ON A TRELLIS ALONG THAT THIRD LOBE.
THE MOST TAXING OF MY POWERS--FLIGHT--STIMULATES GROWTH OF THE LESION.
IF IT CONTINUES TO PROGRESS, I WILL LOSE BRAIN TISSUE AND WITH IT, MY MEMORY, MY SENSE OF IDENTITY...
EVERYTHING THAT MAKES ME ME.
FOR THAT REASON, MY DOCTOR FORBADE ME TO FLY, BUT--
--BUT YOU'RE A DUMMY.
MISTAKES WERE MADE, TRACY.
SAME THING.
MAY I CONTINUE?
PLEASE.

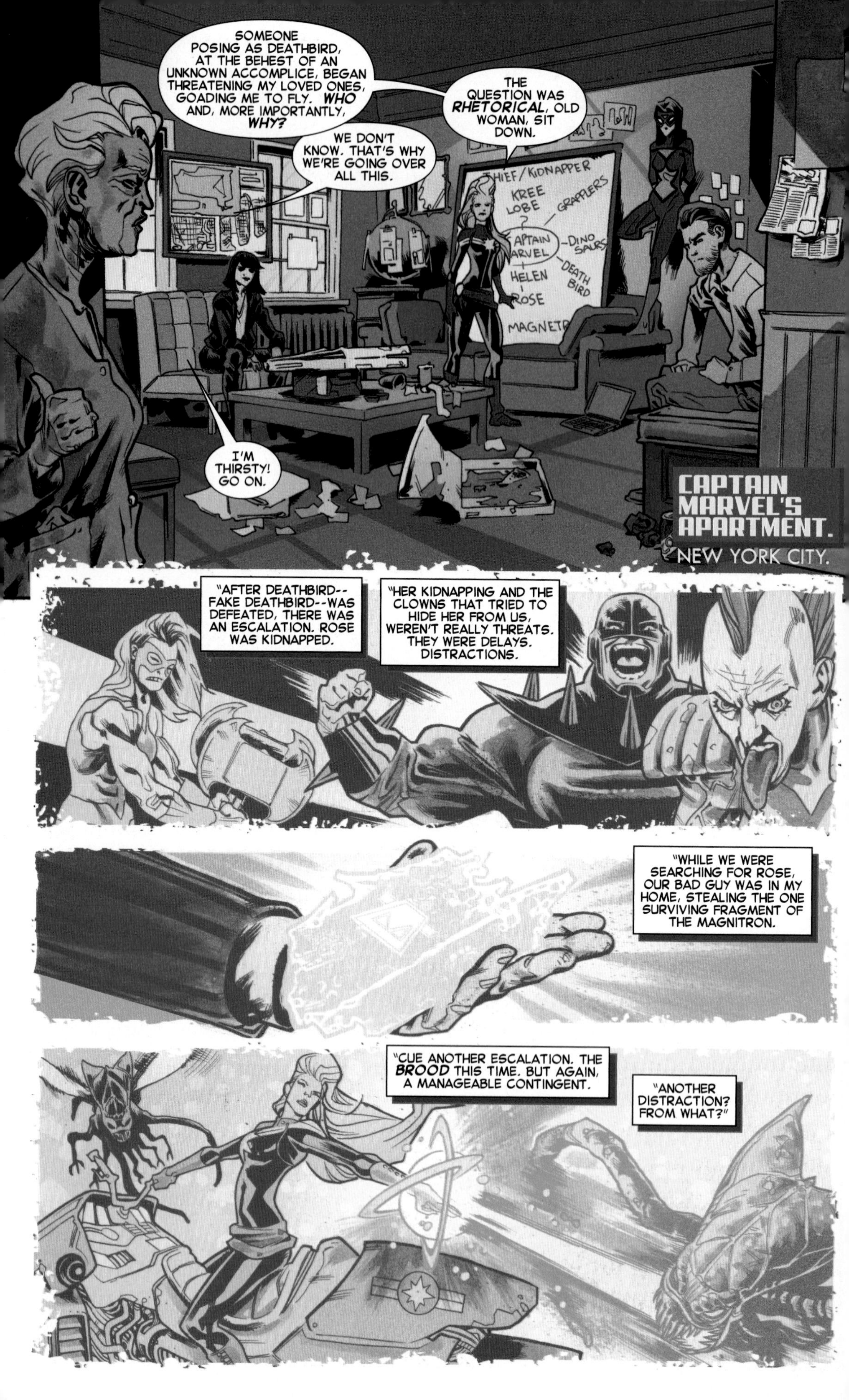

SOMEONE POSING AS DEATHBIRD, AT THE BEHEST OF AN UNKNOWN ACCOMPLICE, BEGAN THREATENING MY LOVED ONES, GOADING ME TO FLY. WHO AND, MORE IMPORTANTLY, WHY?
THE QUESTION WAS RHETORICAL, OLD WOMAN, SIT DOWN.
WE DON'T KNOW. THAT'S WHY WE'RE GOING OVER ALL THIS.
KREE LOBE
GRAPPLERS
CAPTAIN MARVEL
DINO SAURS
DEATH BIRD
HELEN
ROSE
I'M THIRSTY! GO ON.
CAPTAIN MARVEL'S APARTMENT.
NEW YORK CITY.
"AFTER DEATHBIRD--FAKE DEATHBIRD--WAS DEFEATED, THERE WAS AN ESCALATION. ROSE WAS KIDNAPPED.
"HER KIDNAPPING AND THE CLOWNS THAT TRIED TO HIDE HER FROM US, WEREN'T REALLY THREATS. THEY WERE DELAYS. DISTRACTIONS.
"WHILE WE WERE SEARCHING FOR ROSE, OUR BAD GUY WAS IN MY HOME, STEALING THE ONE SURVIVING FRAGMENT OF THE MAGNITRON.
"CUE ANOTHER ESCALATION. THE BROOD THIS TIME. BUT AGAIN, A MANAGEABLE CONTINGENT.
"ANOTHER DISTRACTION? FROM WHAT?"

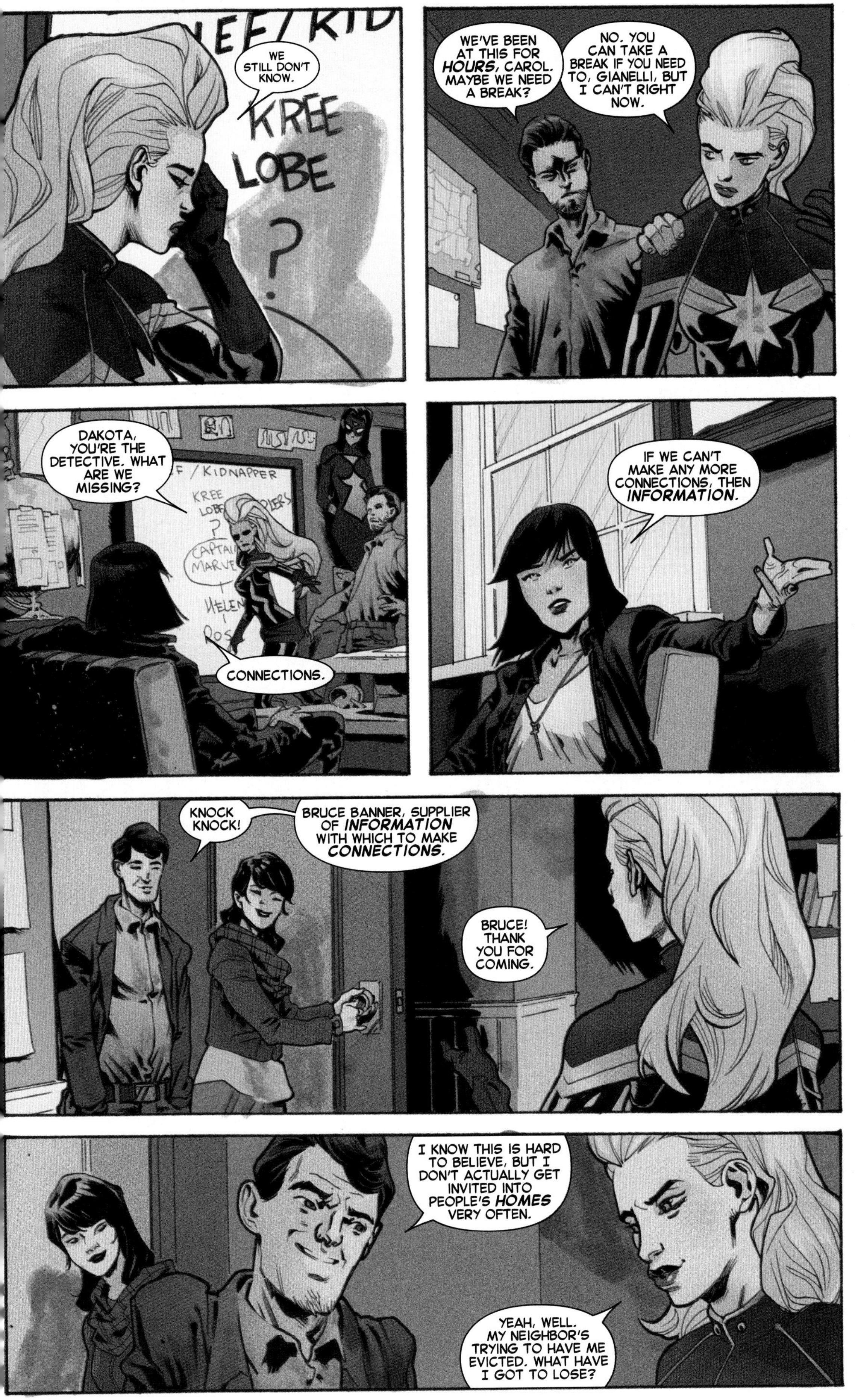
EF / KID
KREE
LOBE
?
WE STILL DON'T KNOW.
WE'VE BEEN AT THIS FOR HOURS, CAROL. MAYBE WE NEED A BREAK?
NO. YOU CAN TAKE A BREAK IF YOU NEED TO, GIANELLI, BUT I CAN'T RIGHT NOW.
DAKOTA, YOU'RE THE DETECTIVE. WHAT ARE WE MISSING?
CONNECTIONS.
IF WE CAN'T MAKE ANY MORE CONNECTIONS, THEN INFORMATION.
KNOCK KNOCK!
BRUCE BANNER, SUPPLIER OF INFORMATION WITH WHICH TO MAKE CONNECTIONS.
BRUCE! THANK YOU FOR COMING.
I KNOW THIS IS HARD TO BELIEVE, BUT I DON'T ACTUALLY GET INVITED INTO PEOPLE'S HOMES VERY OFTEN.
YEAH, WELL. MY NEIGHBOR'S TRYING TO HAVE ME EVICTED. WHAT HAVE I GOT TO LOSE?

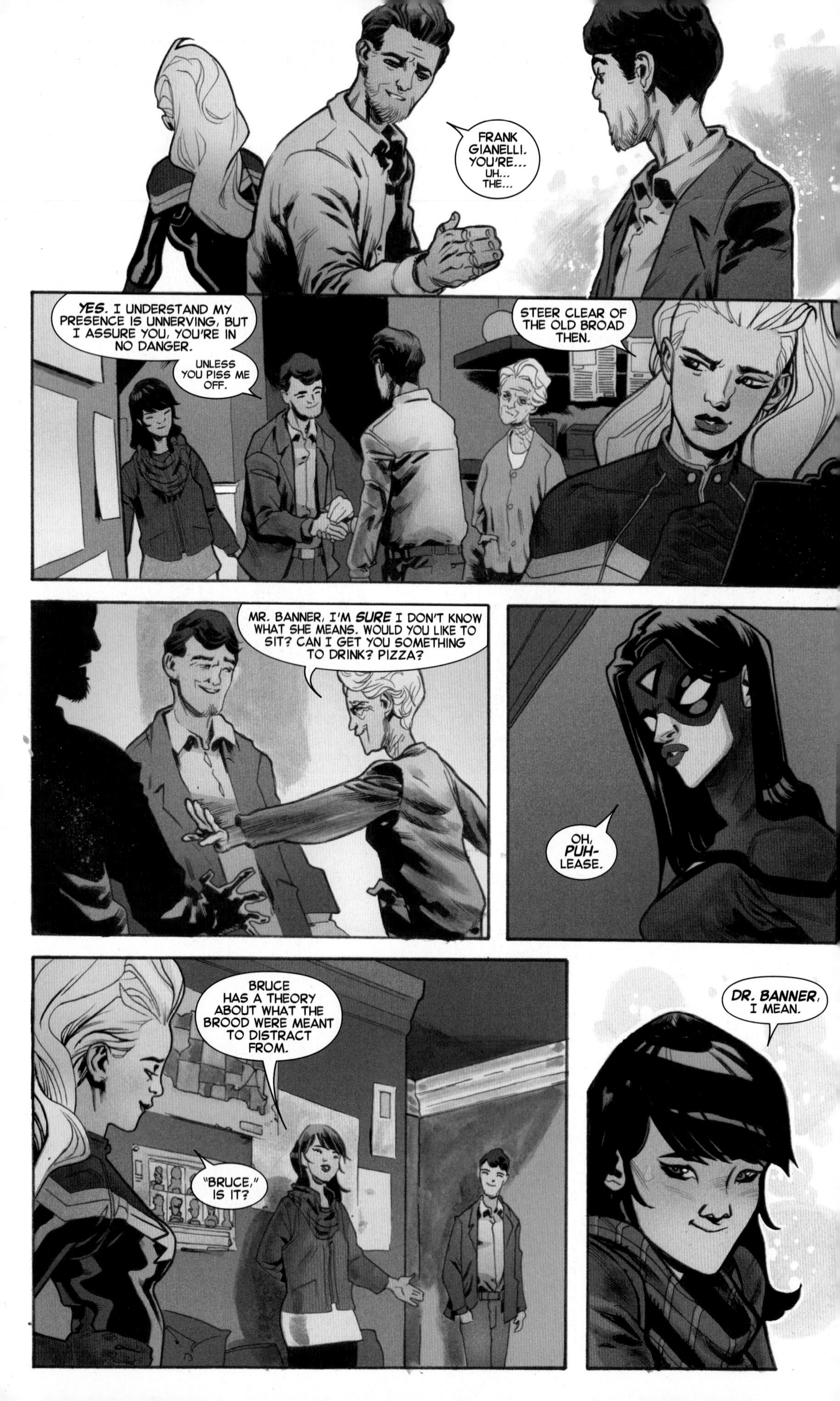
FRANK GIANELLI. YOU'RE... UH... THE...
YES. I UNDERSTAND MY PRESENCE IS UNNERVING, BUT I ASSURE YOU, YOU'RE IN NO DANGER.
UNLESS YOU PISS ME OFF.
STEER CLEAR OF THE OLD BROAD THEN.
MR. BANNER, I'M SURE I DON'T KNOW WHAT SHE MEANS. WOULD YOU LIKE TO SIT? CAN I GET YOU SOMETHING TO DRINK? PIZZA?
OH, PUH-LEASE.
BRUCE HAS A THEORY ABOUT WHAT THE BROOD WERE MEANT TO DISTRACT FROM.
"BRUCE," IS IT?
DR. BANNER, I MEAN.

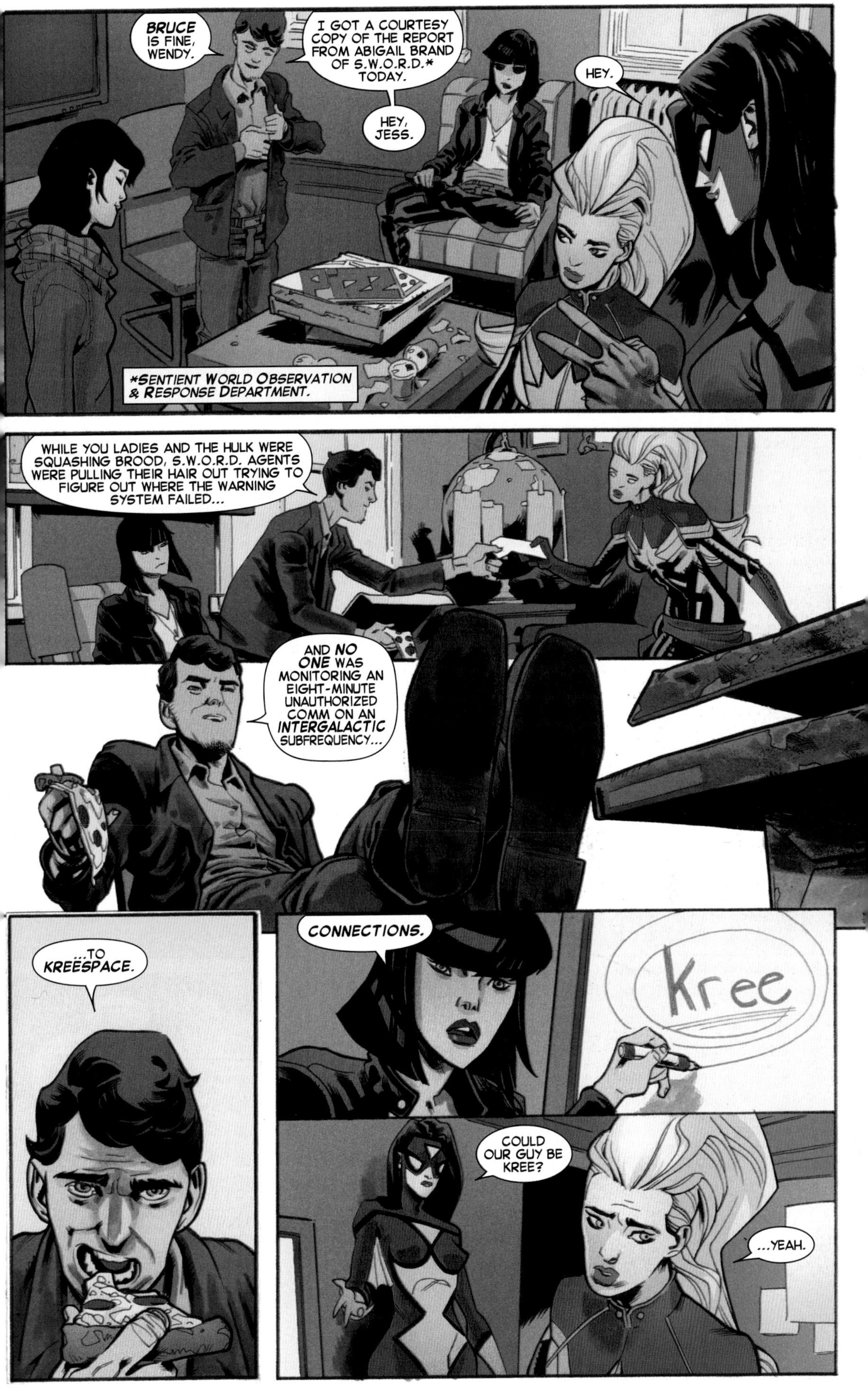
BRUCE IS FINE, WENDY.
I GOT A COURTESY COPY OF THE REPORT FROM ABIGAIL BRAND OF S.W.O.R.D.* TODAY.
HEY, JESS.
HEY.
*SENTIENT WORLD OBSERVATION & RESPONSE DEPARTMENT.
WHILE YOU LADIES AND THE HULK WERE SQUASHING BROOD, S.W.O.R.D. AGENTS WERE PULLING THEIR HAIR OUT TRYING TO FIGURE OUT WHERE THE WARNING SYSTEM FAILED...
AND NO ONE WAS MONITORING AN EIGHT-MINUTE UNAUTHORIZED COMM ON AN INTERGALACTIC SUBFREQUENCY...
...TO KREESPACE.
CONNECTIONS.
Kree
COULD OUR GUY BE KREE?
...YEAH.

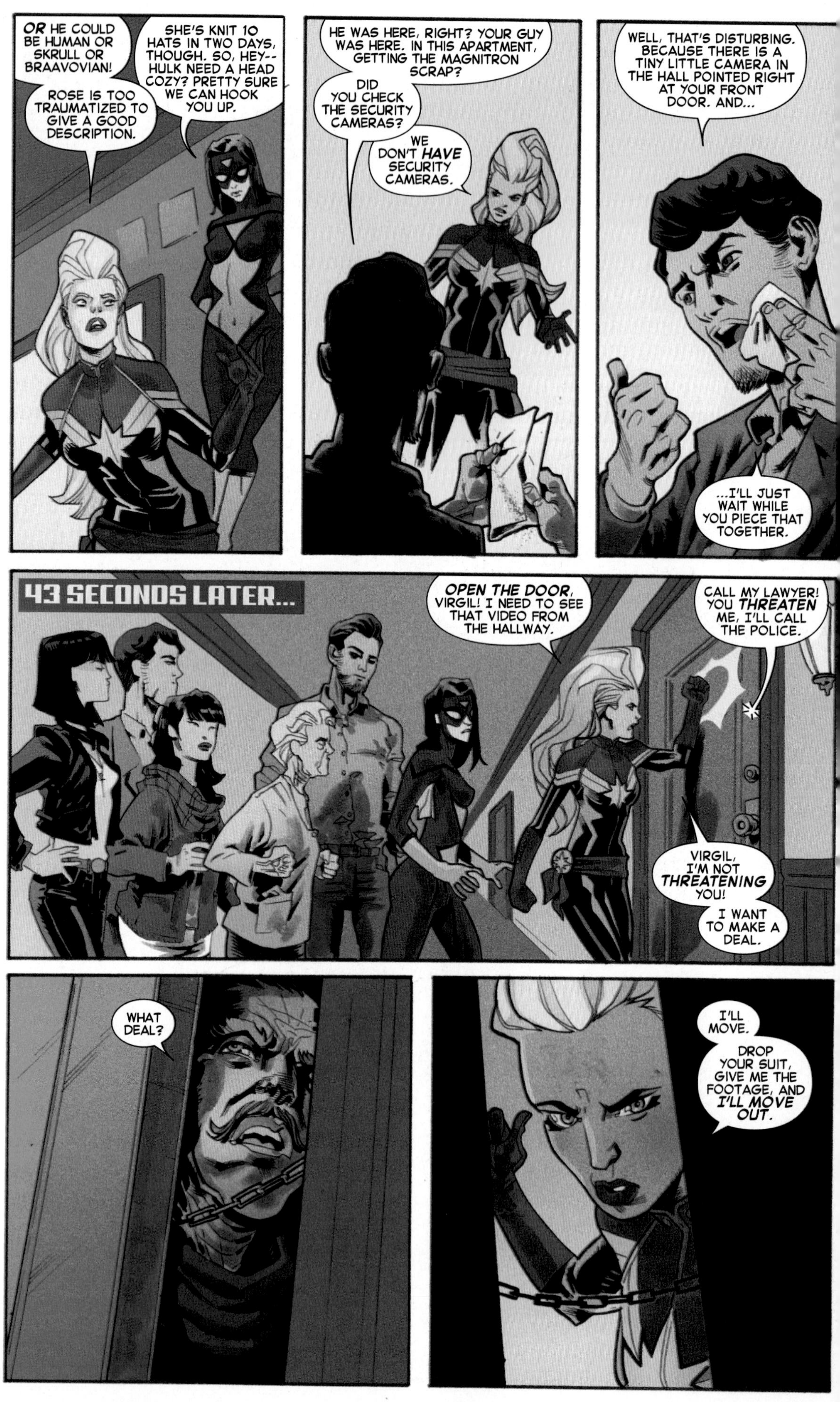
OR HE COULD BE HUMAN OR SKRULL OR BRAAVOVIAN!
ROSE IS TOO TRAUMATIZED TO GIVE A GOOD DESCRIPTION.
SHE'S KNIT 10 HATS IN TWO DAYS, THOUGH. SO, HEY-- HULK NEED A HEAD COZY? PRETTY SURE WE CAN HOOK YOU UP.
HE WAS HERE, RIGHT? YOUR GUY WAS HERE. IN THIS APARTMENT, GETTING THE MAGNITRON SCRAP?
DID YOU CHECK THE SECURITY CAMERAS?
WE DON'T HAVE SECURITY CAMERAS.
WELL, THAT'S DISTURBING. BECAUSE THERE IS A TINY LITTLE CAMERA IN THE HALL POINTED RIGHT AT YOUR FRONT DOOR. AND...
...I'LL JUST WAIT WHILE YOU PIECE THAT TOGETHER.
43 SECONDS LATER...
OPEN THE DOOR, VIRGIL! I NEED TO SEE THAT VIDEO FROM THE HALLWAY.
CALL MY LAWYER! YOU THREATEN ME, I'LL CALL THE POLICE.
VIRGIL, I'M NOT THREATENING YOU!
I WANT TO MAKE A DEAL.
WHAT DEAL?
I'LL MOVE.
DROP YOUR SUIT, GIVE ME THE FOOTAGE, AND I'LL MOVE OUT.

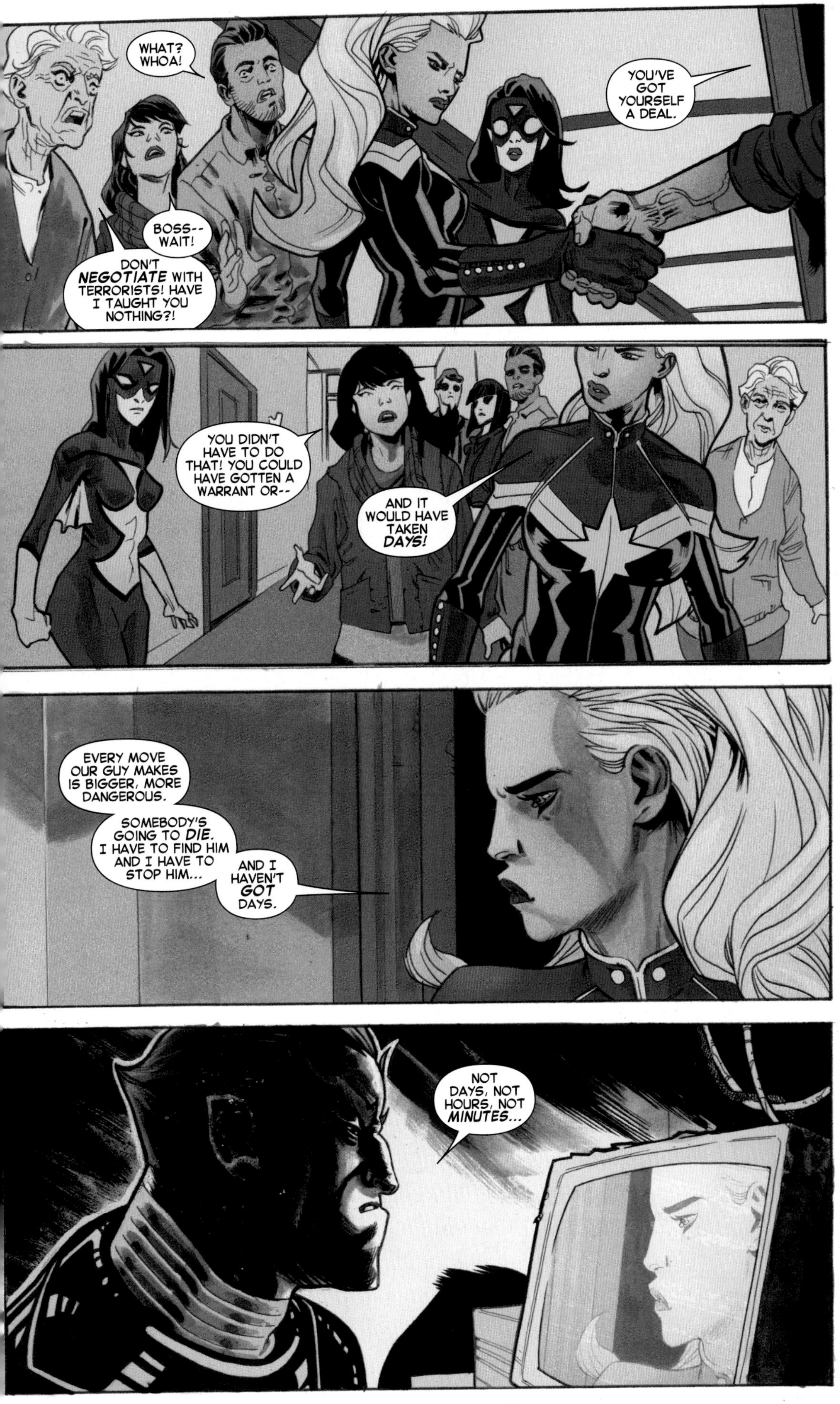

WHAT? WHOA!
YOU'VE GOT YOURSELF A DEAL.
BOSS-- WAIT!
DON'T NEGOTIATE WITH TERRORISTS! HAVE I TAUGHT YOU NOTHING?!
YOU DIDN'T HAVE TO DO THAT! YOU COULD HAVE GOTTEN A WARRANT OR--
AND IT WOULD HAVE TAKEN DAYS!
EVERY MOVE OUR GUY MAKES IS BIGGER, MORE DANGEROUS.
SOMEBODY'S GOING TO DIE. I HAVE TO FIND HIM AND I HAVE TO STOP HIM...
AND I HAVEN'T GOT DAYS.
NOT DAYS, NOT HOURS, NOT MINUTES...

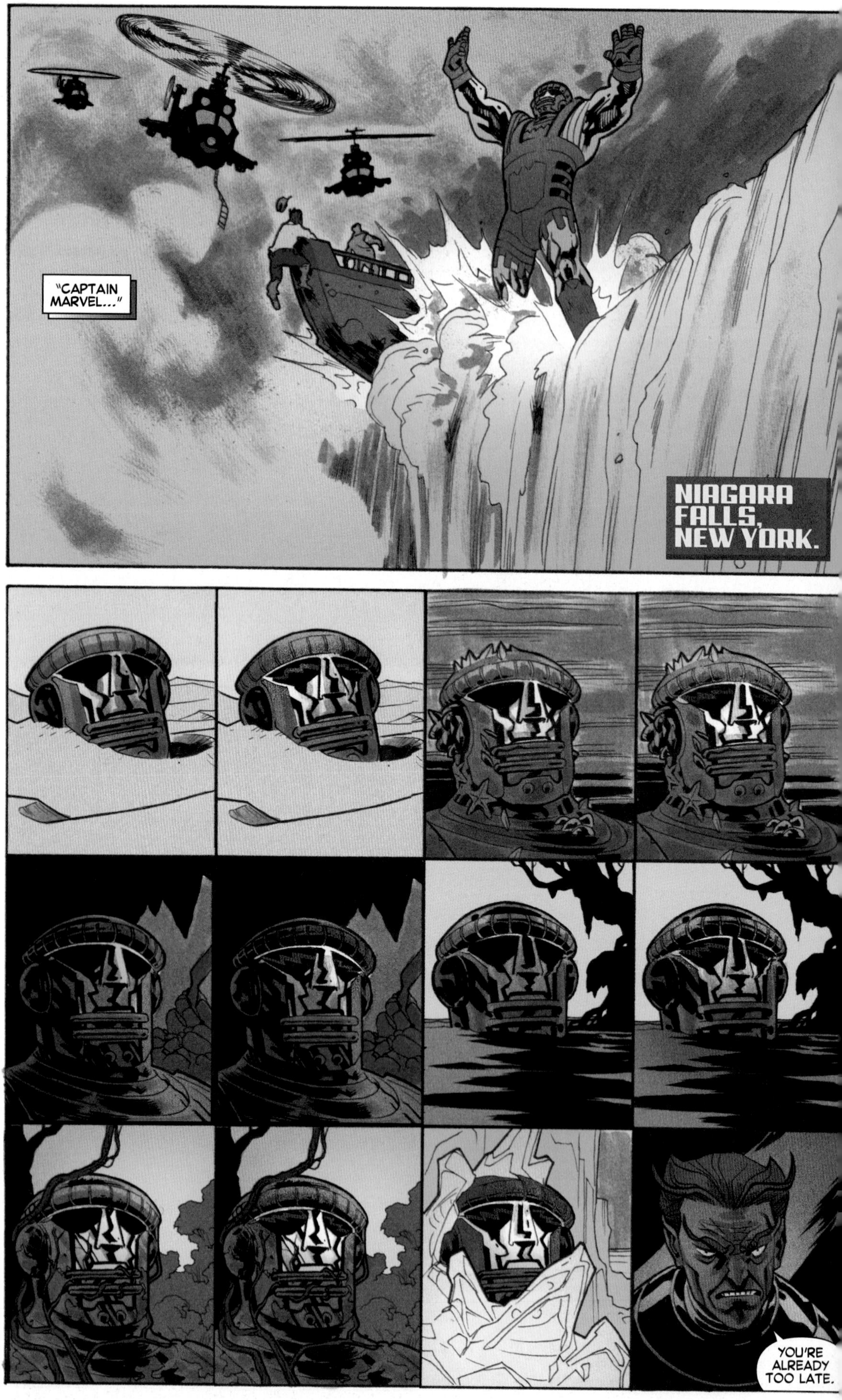
"CAPTAIN MARVEL..."
NIAGARA FALLS, NEW YORK.
YOU'RE ALREADY TOO LATE.

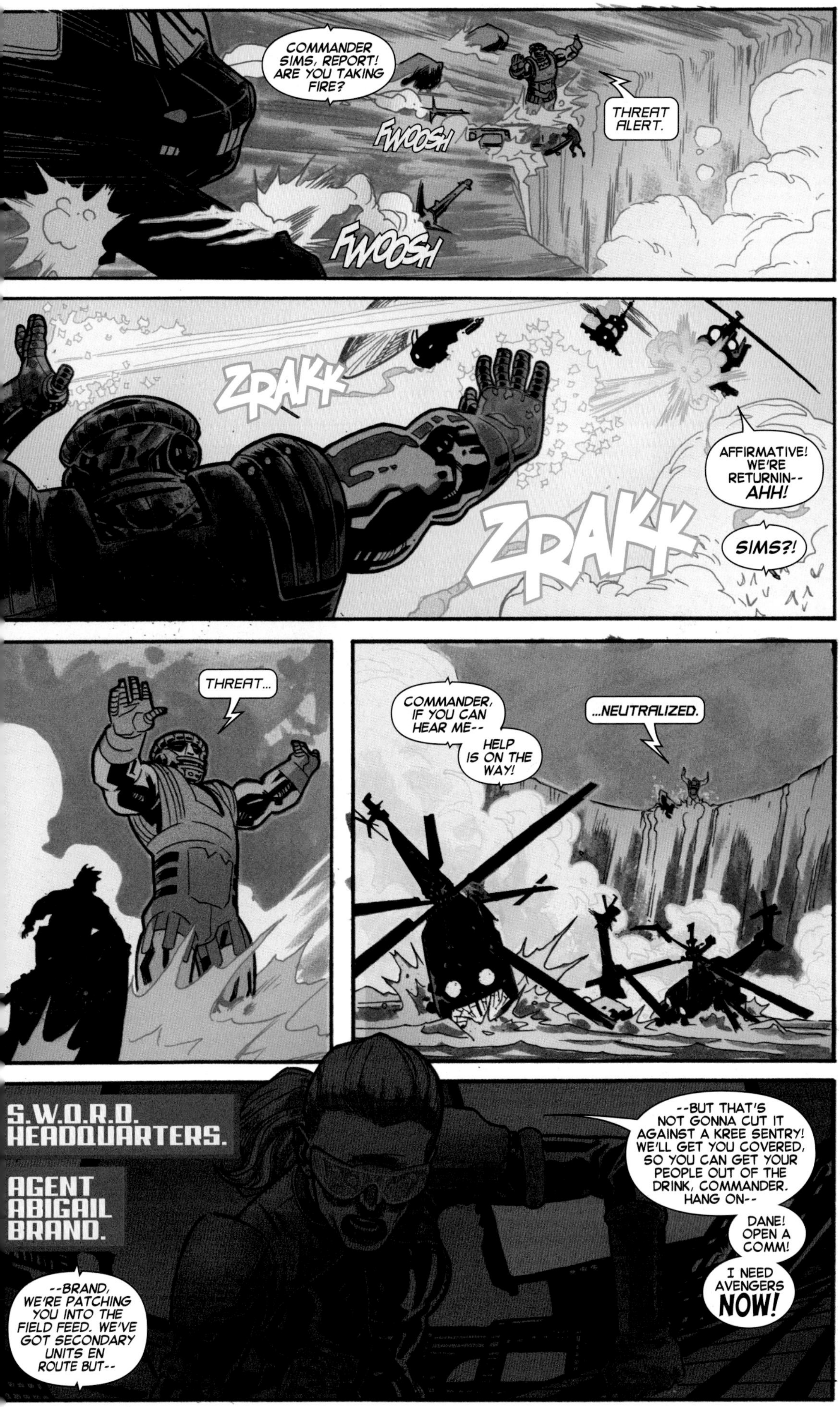

COMMANDER SIMS, REPORT! ARE YOU TAKING FIRE?
THREAT ALERT.
FWOOSH
FWOOSH
ZRAKK
AFFIRMATIVE! WE'RE RETURNIN-- AHH!
ZRAKK
SIMS?!
THREAT...
COMMANDER, IF YOU CAN HEAR ME--
HELP IS ON THE WAY!
...NEUTRALIZED.
S.W.O.R.D. HEADQUARTERS.
AGENT ABIGAIL BRAND.
--BRAND, WE'RE PATCHING YOU INTO THE FIELD FEED. WE'VE GOT SECONDARY UNITS EN ROUTE BUT--
--BUT THAT'S NOT GONNA CUT IT AGAINST A KREE SENTRY! WE'LL GET YOU COVERED, SO YOU CAN GET YOUR PEOPLE OUT OF THE DRINK, COMMANDER. HANG ON--
DANE! OPEN A COMM!
I NEED AVENGERS NOW!

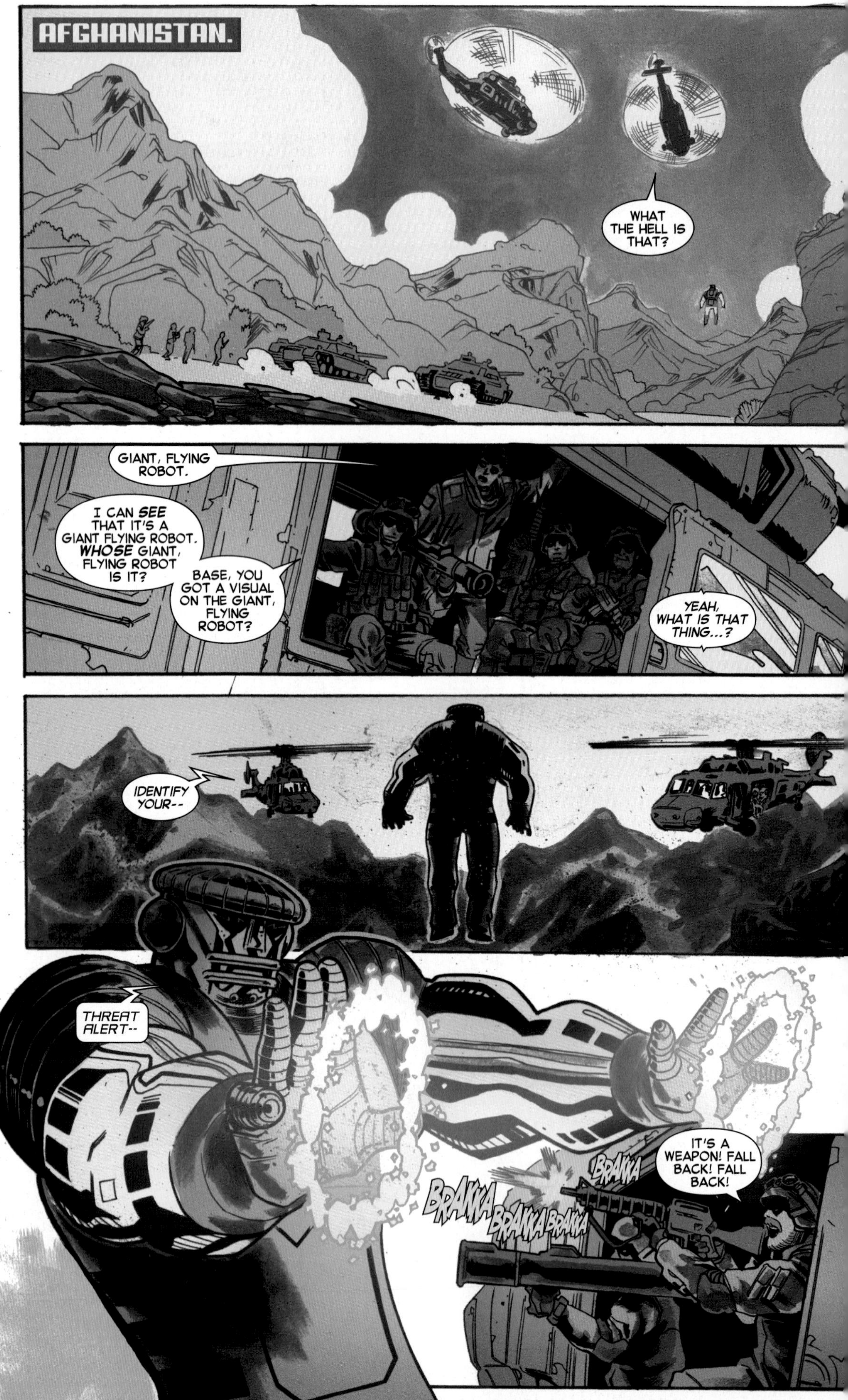
AFGHANISTAN.
WHAT THE HELL IS THAT?
GIANT, FLYING ROBOT.
I CAN SEE THAT IT'S A GIANT FLYING ROBOT. WHOSE GIANT, FLYING ROBOT IS IT?
BASE, YOU GOT A VISUAL ON THE GIANT, FLYING ROBOT?
YEAH, WHAT IS THAT THING...?
IDENTIFY YOUR--
THREAT ALERT--
BRAKKA
BRAKKA BRAKKA BRAKKA
IT'S A WEAPON! FALL BACK! FALL BACK!

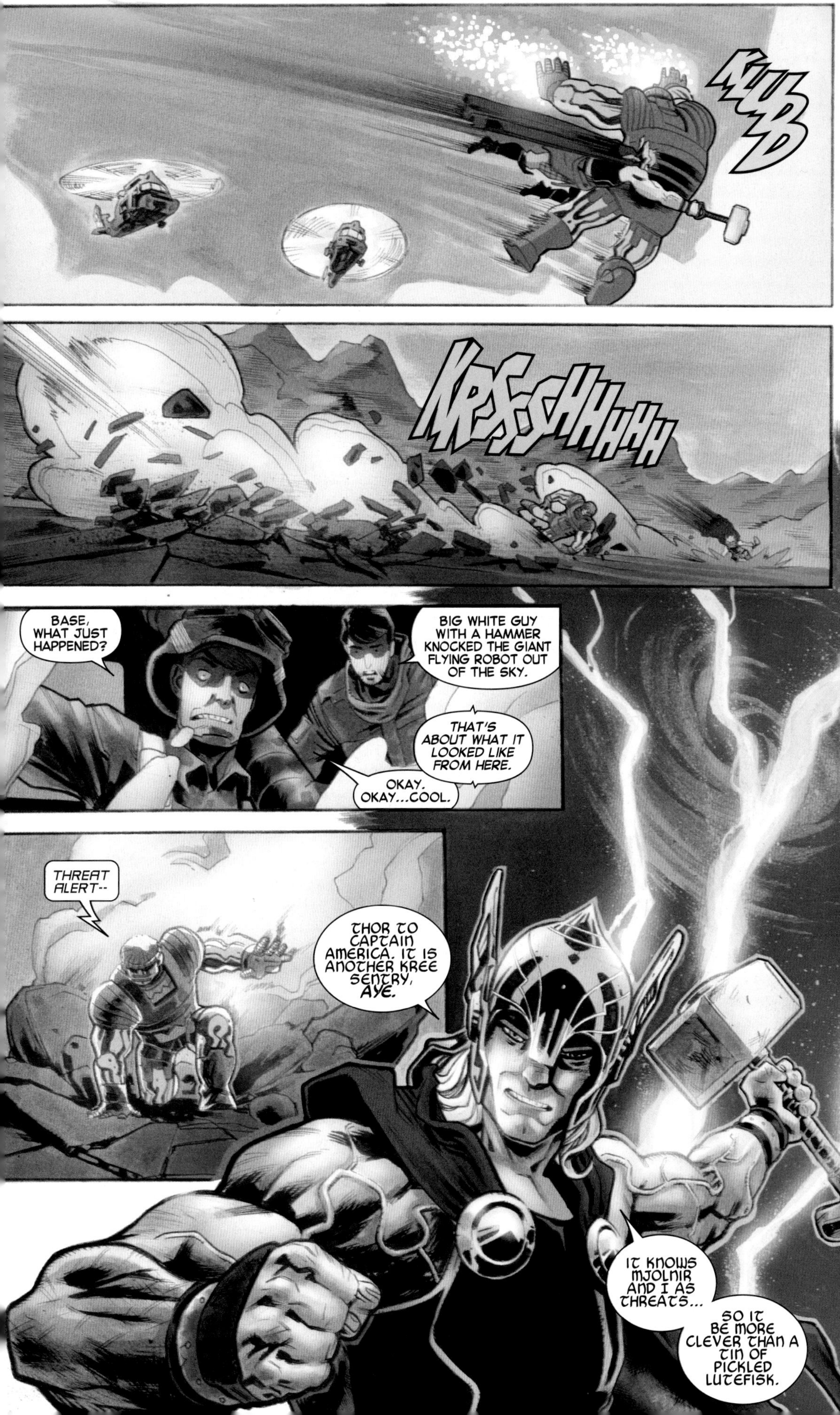
KLUB
KRSSSCHHHHH
BASE, WHAT JUST HAPPENED?
BIG WHITE GUY WITH A HAMMER KNOCKED THE GIANT FLYING ROBOT OUT OF THE SKY.
THAT'S ABOUT WHAT IT LOOKED LIKE FROM HERE.
OKAY. OKAY...COOL.
THREAT ALERT--
THOR TO CAPTAIN AMERICA. IT IS ANOTHER KREE SENTRY, AYE.
IT KNOWS MJOLNIR AND I AS THREATS...
SO IT BE MORE CLEVER THAN A TIN OF PICKLED LUTEFISK.

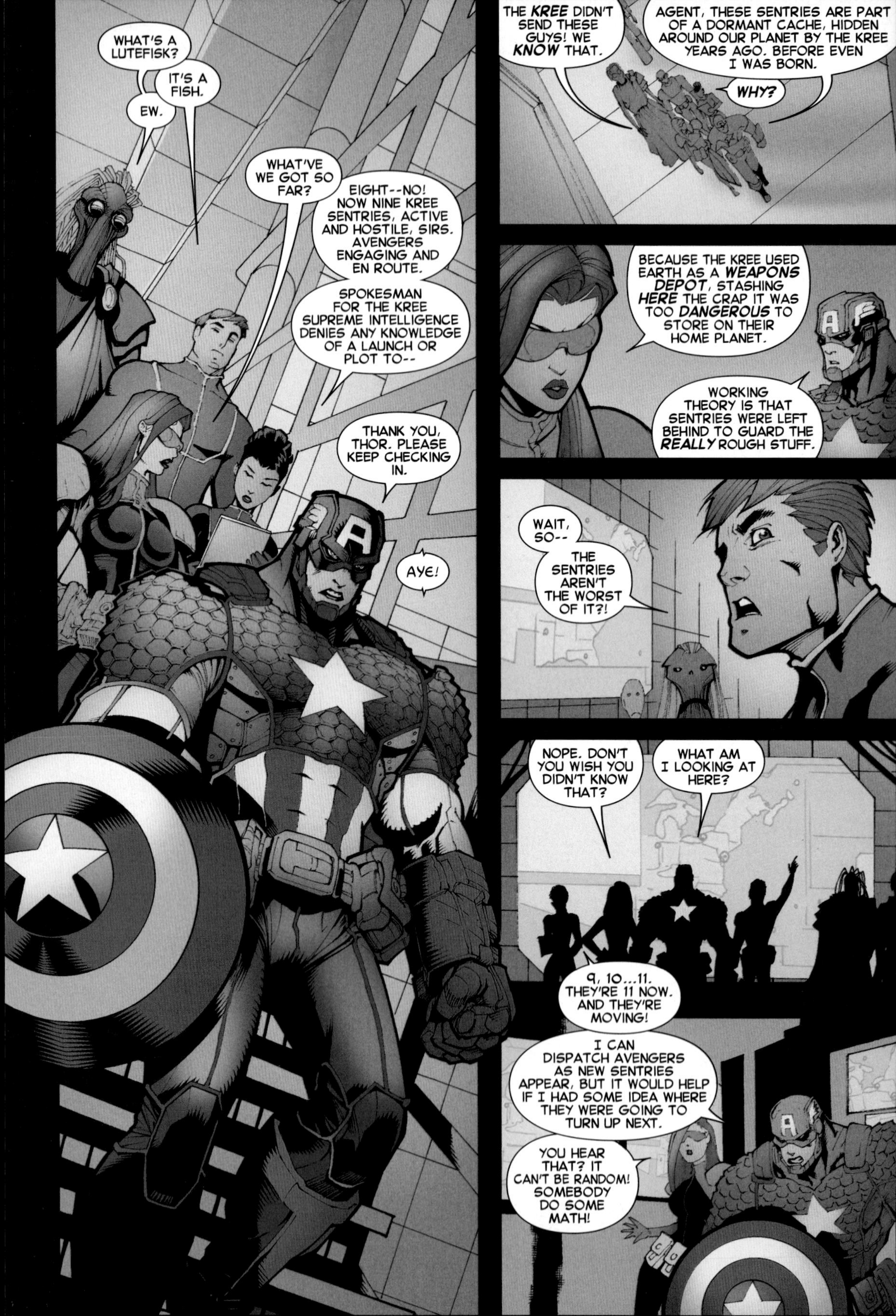
WHAT'S A LUTEFISK?
IT'S A FISH.
EW.
WHAT'VE WE GOT SO FAR?
EIGHT--NO! NOW NINE KREE SENTRIES, ACTIVE AND HOSTILE, SIRS. AVENGERS ENGAGING AND EN ROUTE.
SPOKESMAN FOR THE KREE SUPREME INTELLIGENCE DENIES ANY KNOWLEDGE OF A LAUNCH OR PLOT TO--
THANK YOU, THOR. PLEASE KEEP CHECKING IN.
AYE!
THE KREE DIDN'T SEND THESE GUYS! WE KNOW THAT.
AGENT, THESE SENTRIES ARE PART OF A DORMANT CACHE, HIDDEN AROUND OUR PLANET BY THE KREE YEARS AGO. BEFORE EVEN I WAS BORN.
WHY?
BECAUSE THE KREE USED EARTH AS A WEAPONS DEPOT, STASHING HERE THE CRAP IT WAS TOO DANGEROUS TO STORE ON THEIR HOME PLANET.
WORKING THEORY IS THAT SENTRIES WERE LEFT BEHIND TO GUARD THE REALLY ROUGH STUFF.
WAIT, SO--
THE SENTRIES AREN'T THE WORST OF IT?!
NOPE. DON'T YOU WISH YOU DIDN'T KNOW THAT?
WHAT AM I LOOKING AT HERE?
9, 10...11. THEY'RE 11 NOW. AND THEY'RE MOVING!
I CAN DISPATCH AVENGERS AS NEW SENTRIES APPEAR, BUT IT WOULD HELP IF I HAD SOME IDEA WHERE THEY WERE GOING TO TURN UP NEXT.
YOU HEAR THAT? IT CAN'T BE RANDOM! SOMEBODY DO SOME MATH!

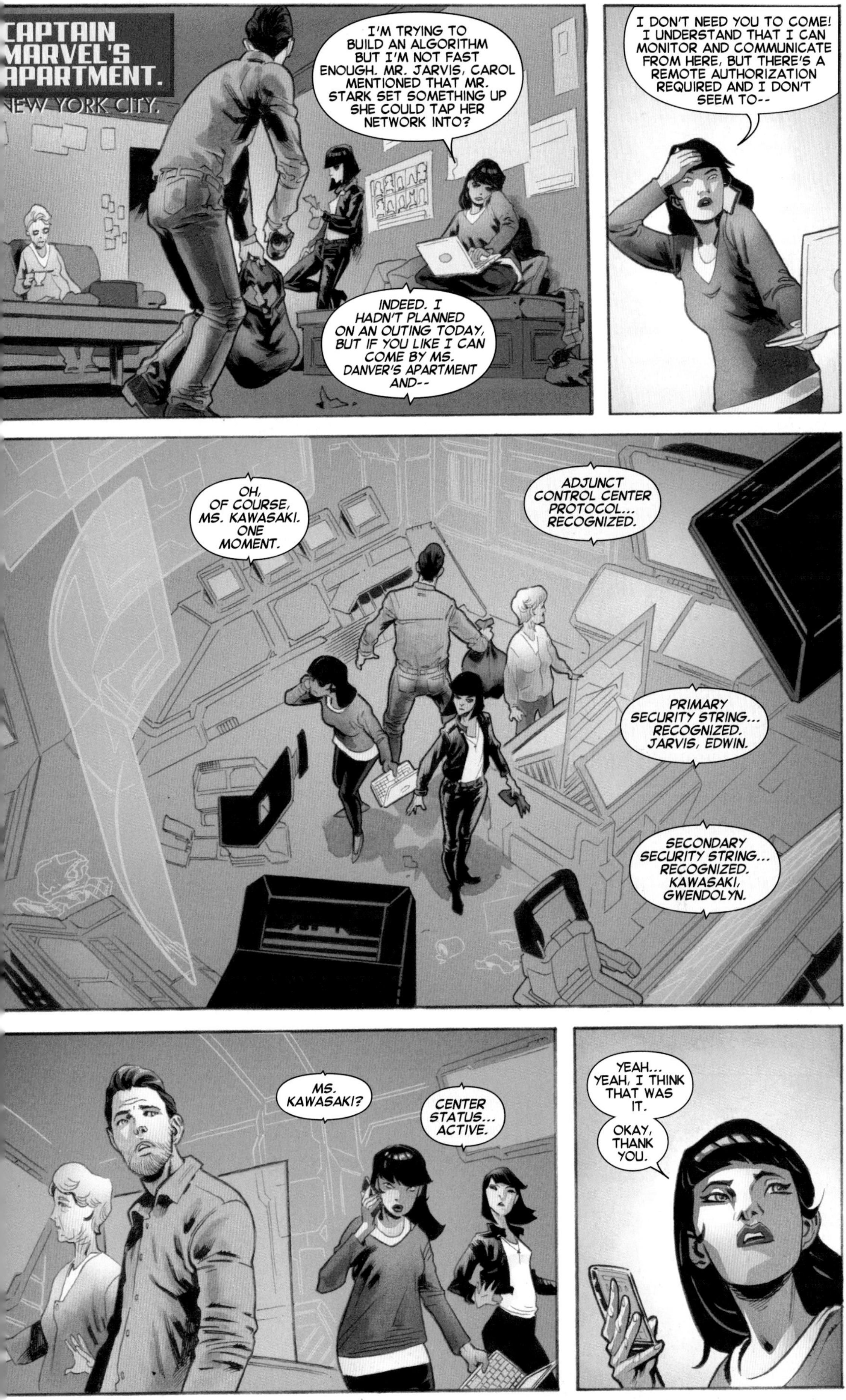
CAPTAIN MARVEL'S APARTMENT.
NEW YORK CITY.
I'M TRYING TO BUILD AN ALGORITHM BUT I'M NOT FAST ENOUGH. MR. JARVIS, CAROL MENTIONED THAT MR. STARK SET SOMETHING UP SHE COULD TAP HER NETWORK INTO?
INDEED. I HADN'T PLANNED ON AN OUTING TODAY, BUT IF YOU LIKE I CAN COME BY MS. DANVER'S APARTMENT AND--
I DON'T NEED YOU TO COME! I UNDERSTAND THAT I CAN MONITOR AND COMMUNICATE FROM HERE, BUT THERE'S A REMOTE AUTHORIZATION REQUIRED AND I DON'T SEEM TO--
OH, OF COURSE, MS. KAWASAKI. ONE MOMENT.
ADJUNCT CONTROL CENTER PROTOCOL... RECOGNIZED.
PRIMARY SECURITY STRING... RECOGNIZED. JARVIS, EDWIN.
SECONDARY SECURITY STRING... RECOGNIZED. KAWASAKI, GWENDOLYN.
MS. KAWASAKI?
CENTER STATUS... ACTIVE.
YEAH... YEAH, I THINK THAT WAS IT.
OKAY, THANK YOU.

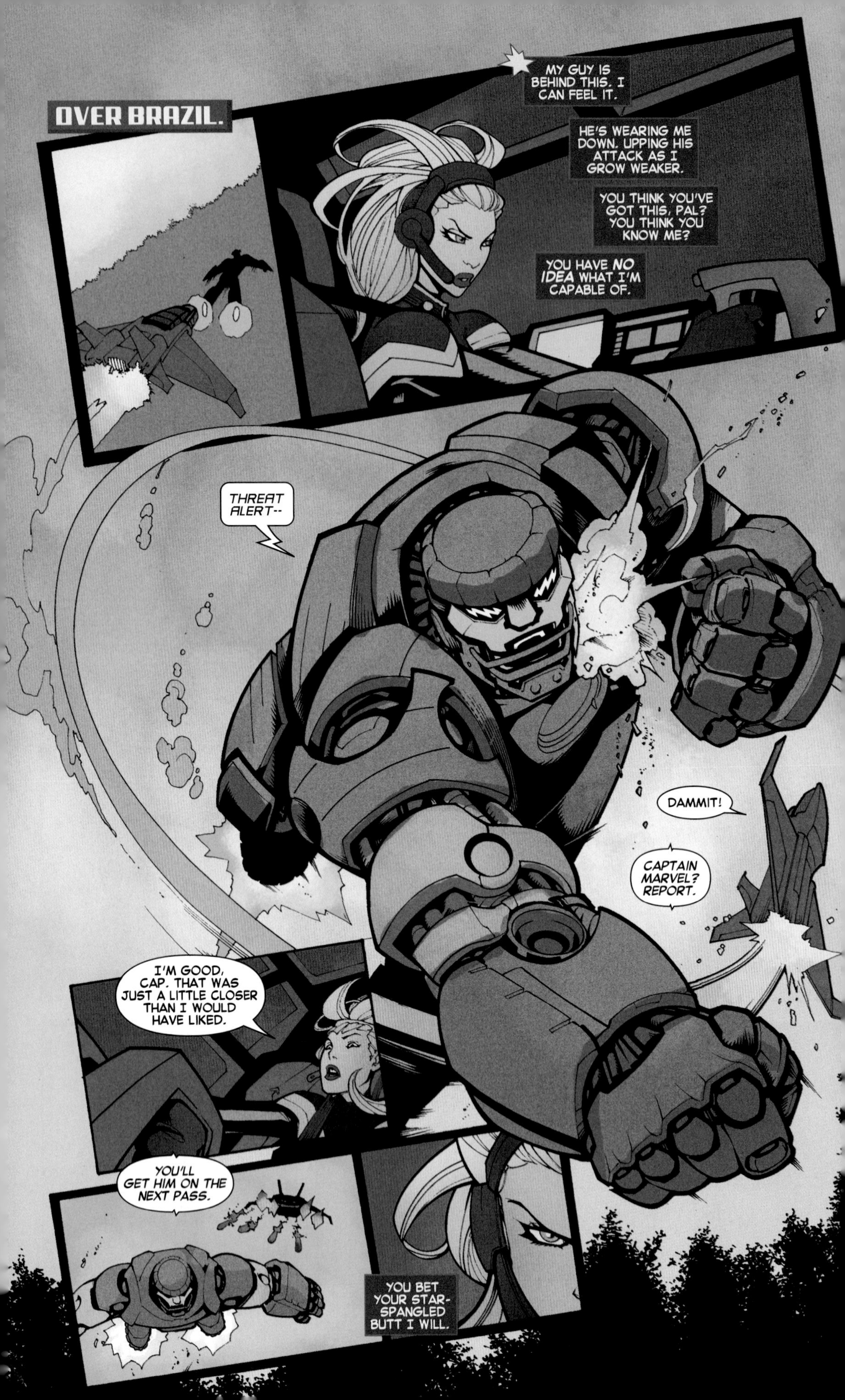
OVER BRAZIL.
MY GUY IS BEHIND THIS. I CAN FEEL IT.
HE'S WEARING ME DOWN. UPPING HIS ATTACK AS I GROW WEAKER.
YOU THINK YOU'VE GOT THIS, PAL? YOU THINK YOU KNOW ME?
YOU HAVE NO IDEA WHAT I'M CAPABLE OF.
THREAT ALERT--
DAMMIT!
CAPTAIN MARVEL? REPORT.
I'M GOOD, CAP. THAT WAS JUST A LITTLE CLOSER THAN I WOULD HAVE LIKED.
YOU'LL GET HIM ON THE NEXT PASS.
YOU BET YOUR STAR-SPANGLED BUTT I WILL.

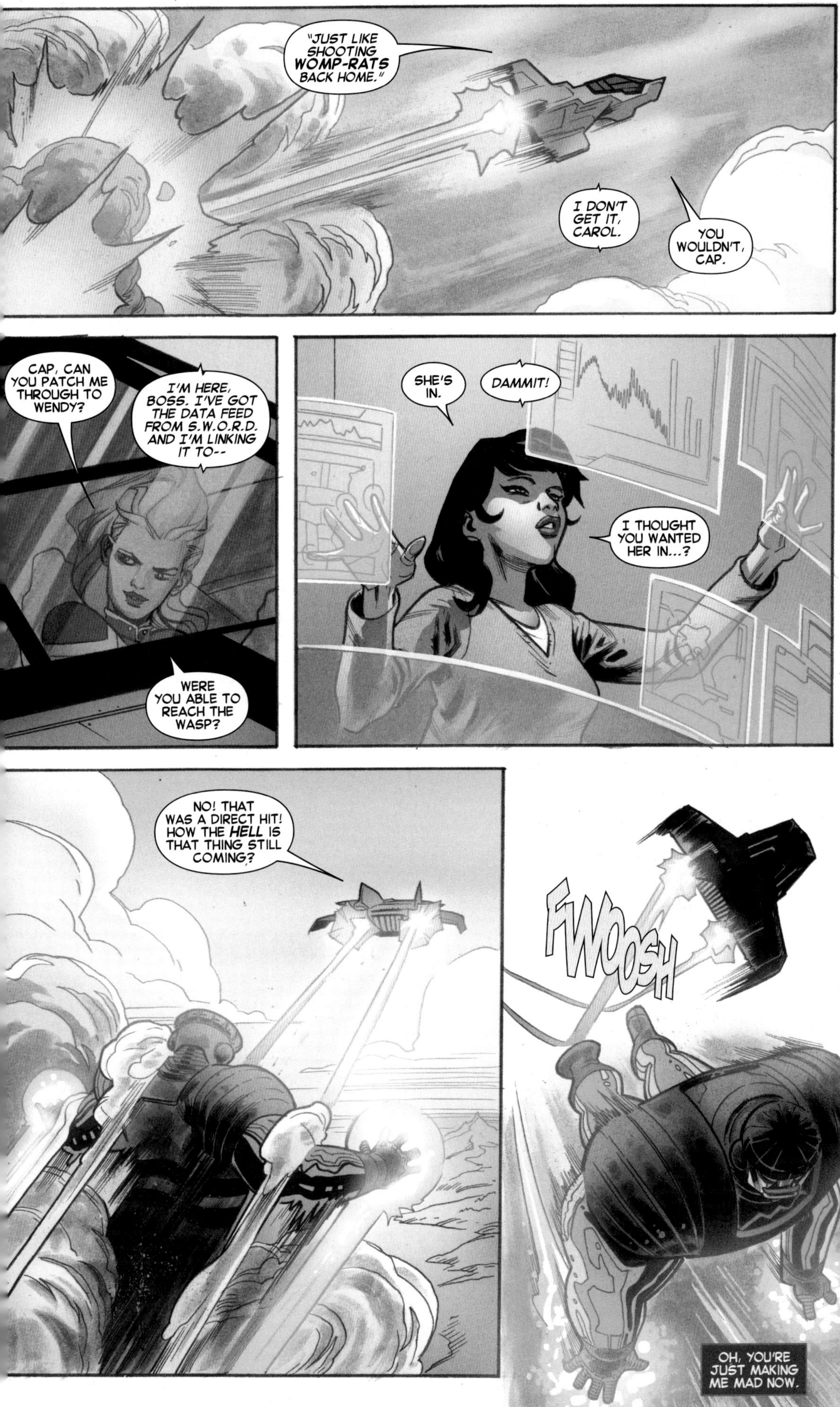
"JUST LIKE SHOOTING WOMP-RATS BACK HOME."
I DON'T GET IT, CAROL.
YOU WOULDN'T, CAP.
CAP, CAN YOU PATCH ME THROUGH TO WENDY?
I'M HERE, BOSS. I'VE GOT THE DATA FEED FROM S.W.O.R.D. AND I'M LINKING IT TO--
WERE YOU ABLE TO REACH THE WASP?
SHE'S IN.
DAMMIT!
I THOUGHT YOU WANTED HER IN...?
NO! THAT WAS A DIRECT HIT! HOW THE HELL IS THAT THING STILL COMING?
FWOOSH
OH, YOU'RE JUST MAKING ME MAD NOW.

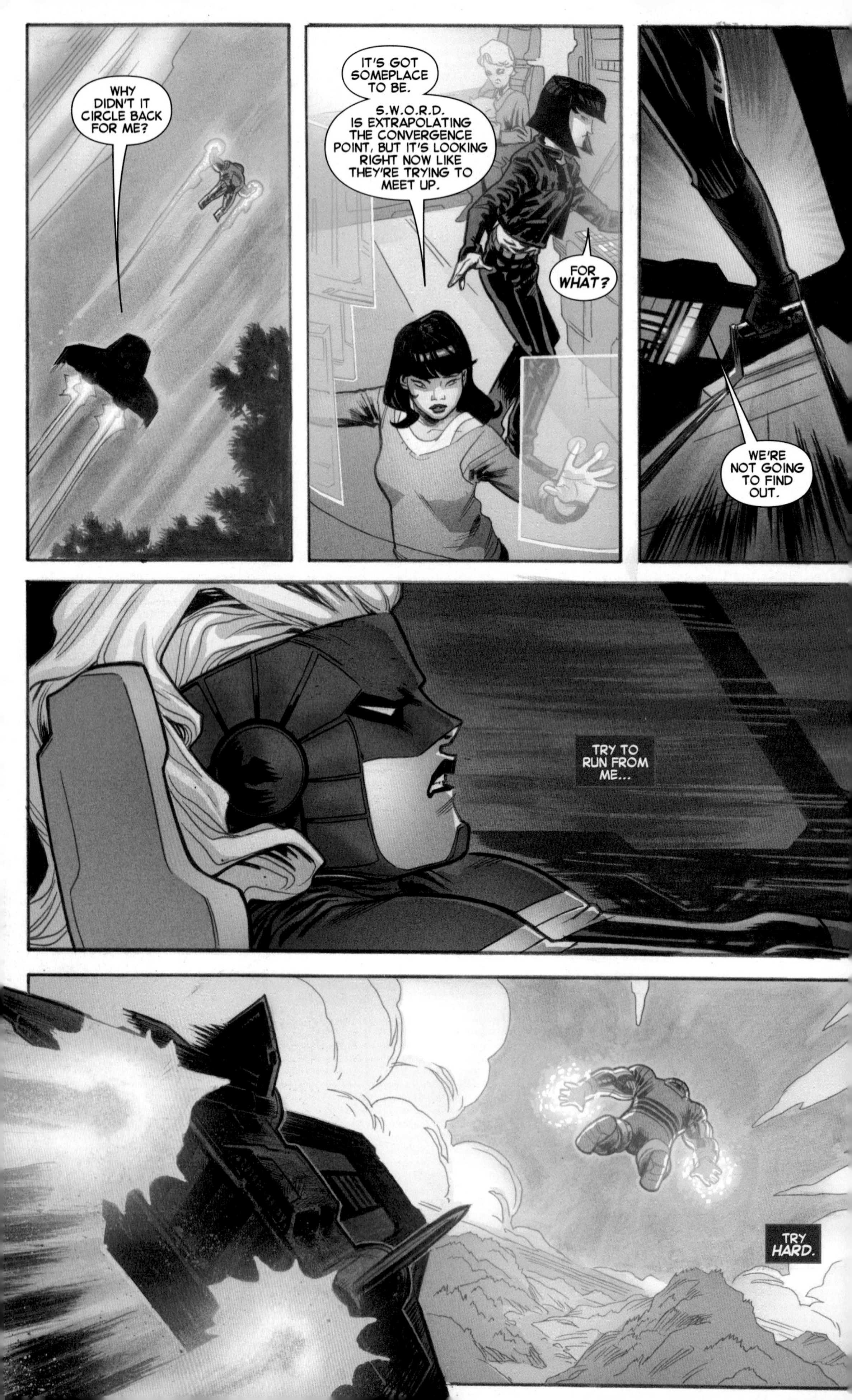
WHY DIDN'T IT CIRCLE BACK FOR ME?
IT'S GOT SOMEPLACE TO BE.
S.W.O.R.D. IS EXTRAPOLATING THE CONVERGENCE POINT, BUT IT'S LOOKING RIGHT NOW LIKE THEY'RE TRYING TO MEET UP.
FOR *WHAT?*
WE'RE NOT GOING TO FIND OUT.
TRY TO RUN FROM ME...
TRY *HARD.*

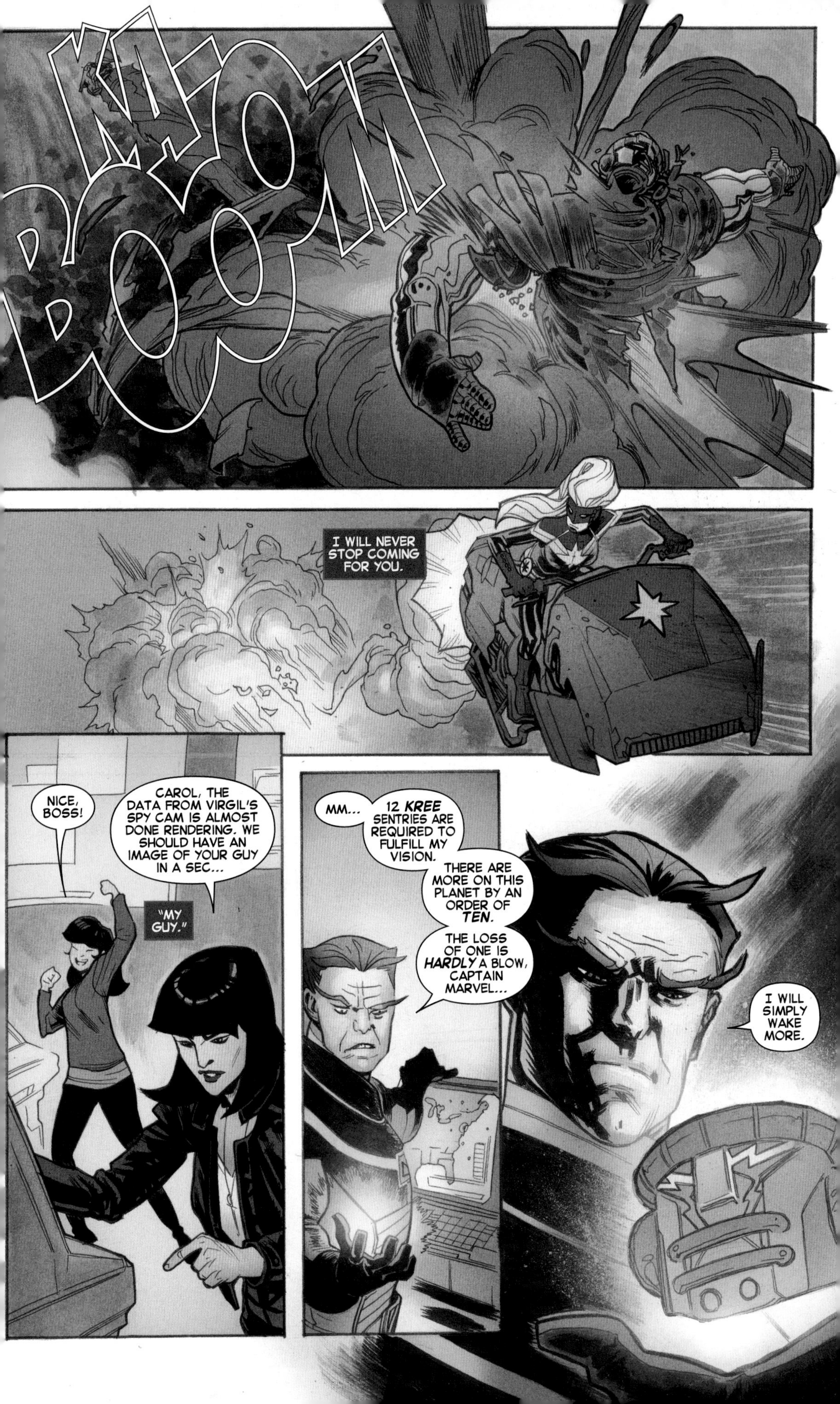
KA-BOOOOM
I WILL NEVER STOP COMING FOR YOU.
NICE, BOSS!
CAROL, THE DATA FROM VIRGIL'S SPY CAM IS ALMOST DONE RENDERING. WE SHOULD HAVE AN IMAGE OF YOUR GUY IN A SEC...
"MY GUY."
MM...
12 KREE SENTRIES ARE REQUIRED TO FULFILL MY VISION.
THERE ARE MORE ON THIS PLANET BY AN ORDER OF TEN.
THE LOSS OF ONE IS HARDLY A BLOW, CAPTAIN MARVEL...
I WILL SIMPLY WAKE MORE.

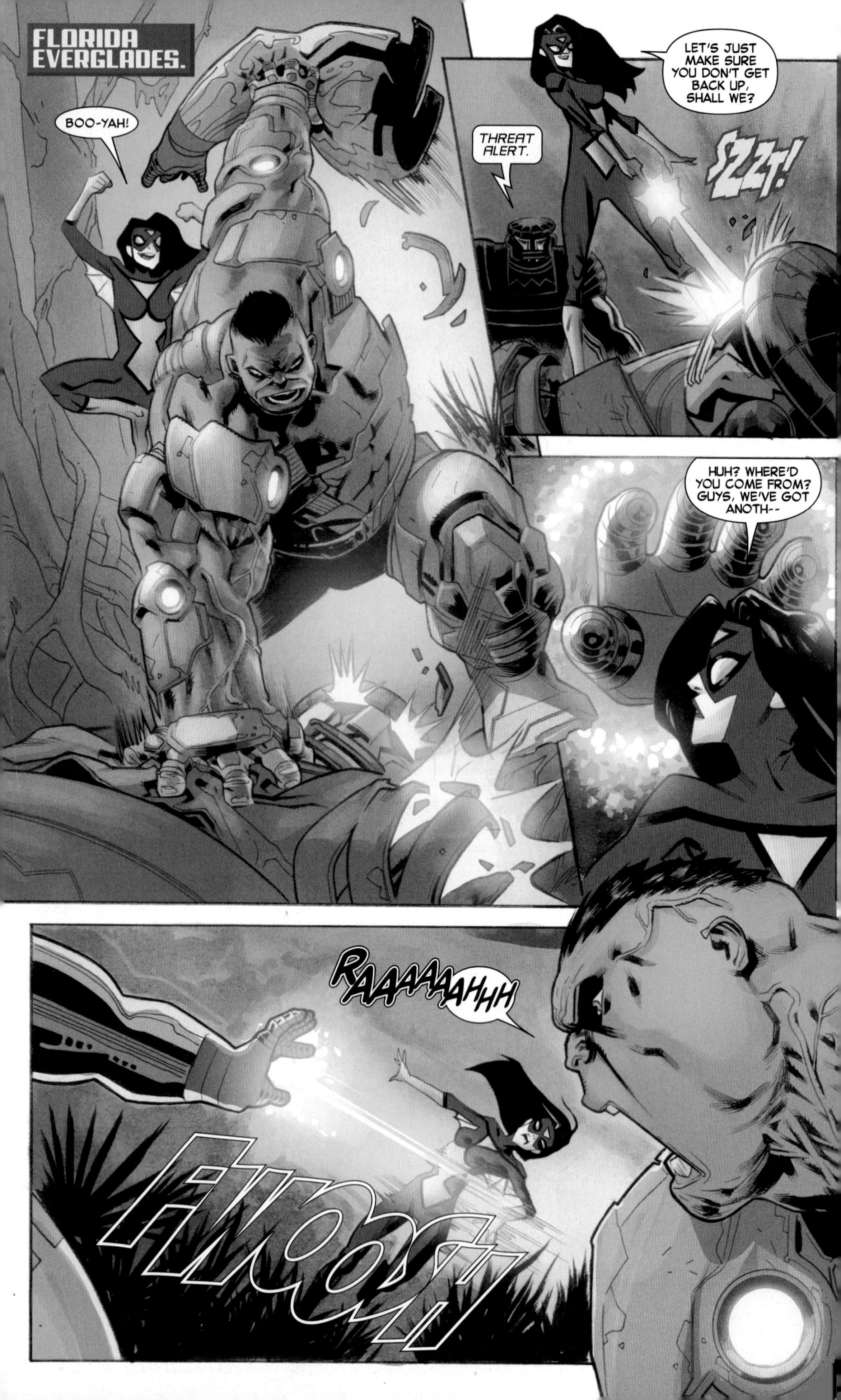

FLORIDA EVERGLADES.
BOO-YAH!
THREAT ALERT.
LET'S JUST MAKE SURE YOU DON'T GET BACK UP, SHALL WE?
SZZT!
HUH? WHERE'D YOU COME FROM? GUYS, WE'VE GOT ANOTH--
RAAAAAAHHH
FWOOSH

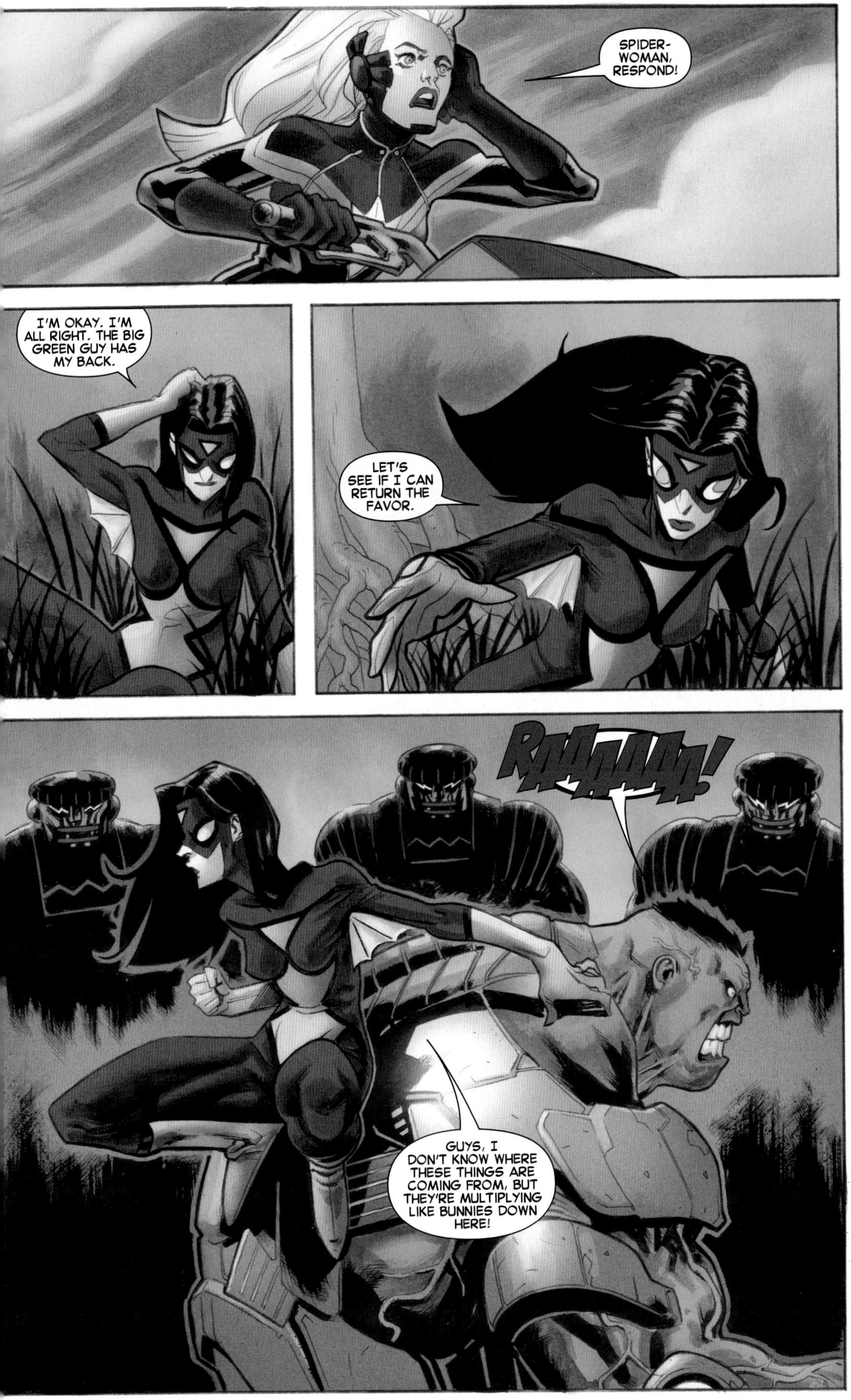
SPIDER-WOMAN, RESPOND!
I'M OKAY. I'M ALL RIGHT. THE BIG GREEN GUY HAS MY BACK.
LET'S SEE IF I CAN RETURN THE FAVOR.
RAAAAAA!
GUYS, I DON'T KNOW WHERE THESE THINGS ARE COMING FROM, BUT THEY'RE MULTIPLYING LIKE BUNNIES DOWN HERE!

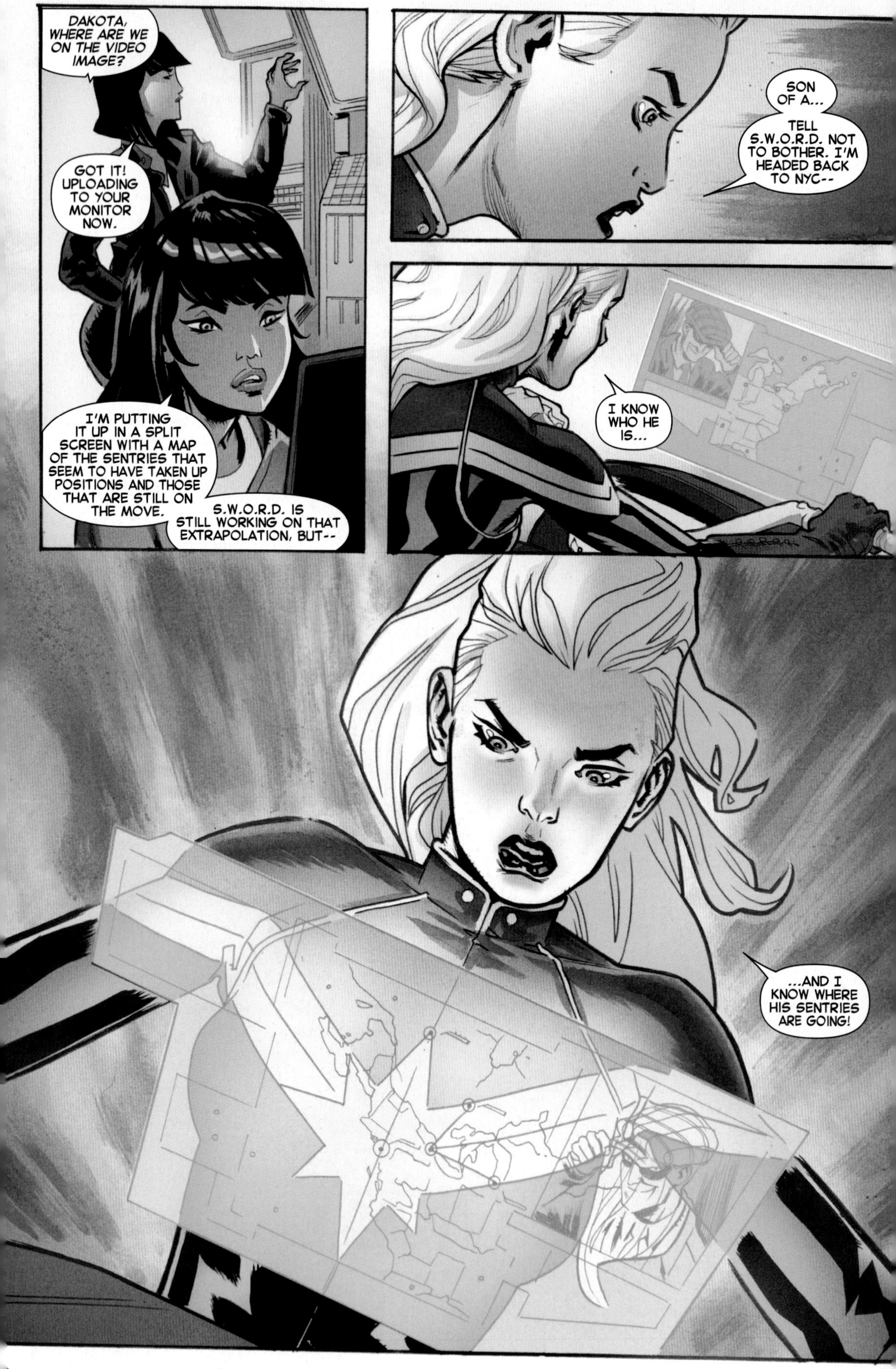
DAKOTA, WHERE ARE WE ON THE VIDEO IMAGE?
GOT IT! UPLOADING TO YOUR MONITOR NOW.
I'M PUTTING IT UP IN A SPLIT SCREEN WITH A MAP OF THE SENTRIES THAT SEEM TO HAVE TAKEN UP POSITIONS AND THOSE THAT ARE STILL ON THE MOVE.
S.W.O.R.D. IS STILL WORKING ON THAT EXTRAPOLATION, BUT--
SON OF A...
TELL S.W.O.R.D. NOT TO BOTHER. I'M HEADED BACK TO NYC--
I KNOW WHO HE IS...
...AND I KNOW WHERE HIS SENTRIES ARE GOING!

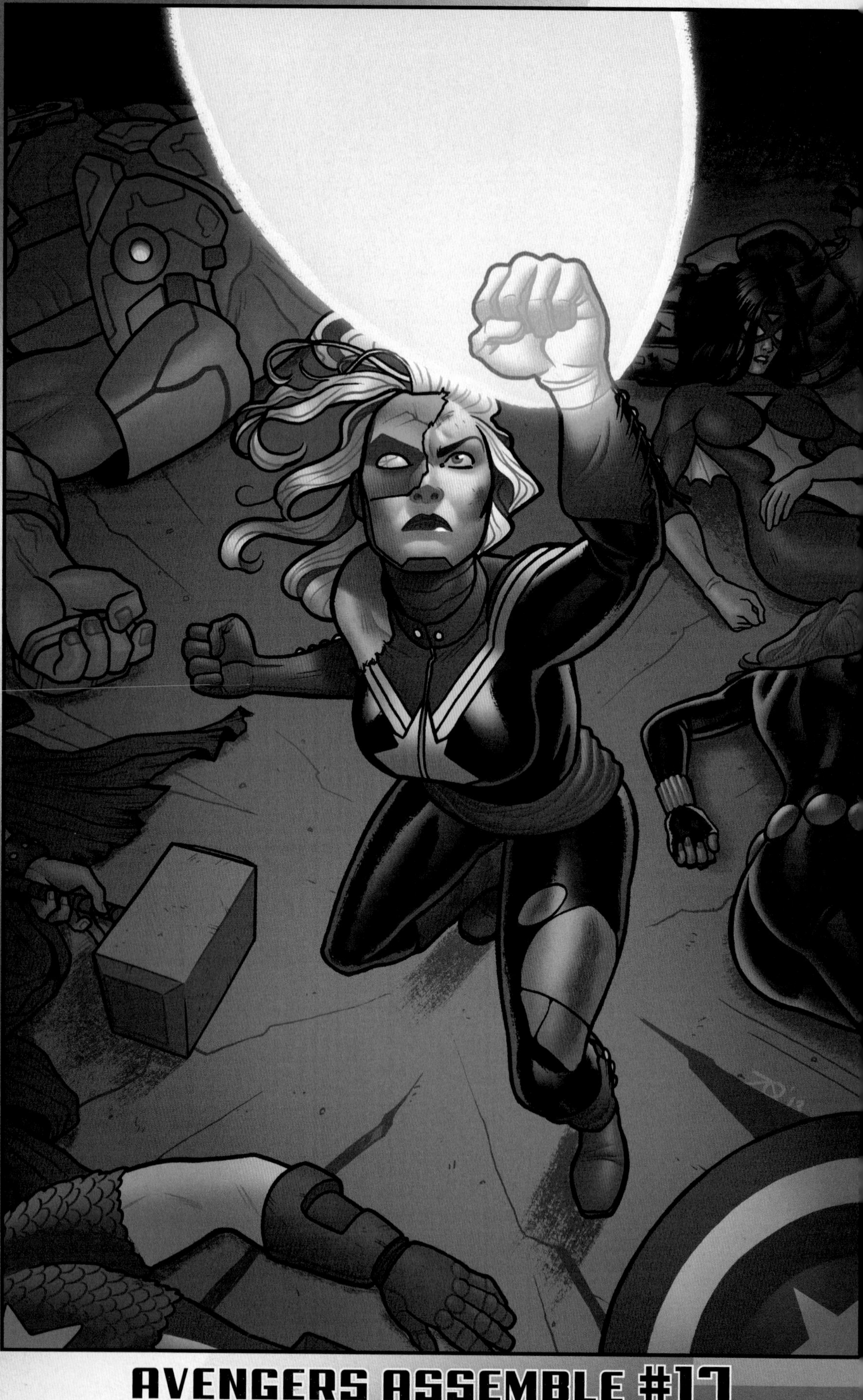

AVENGERS ASSEMBLE #17

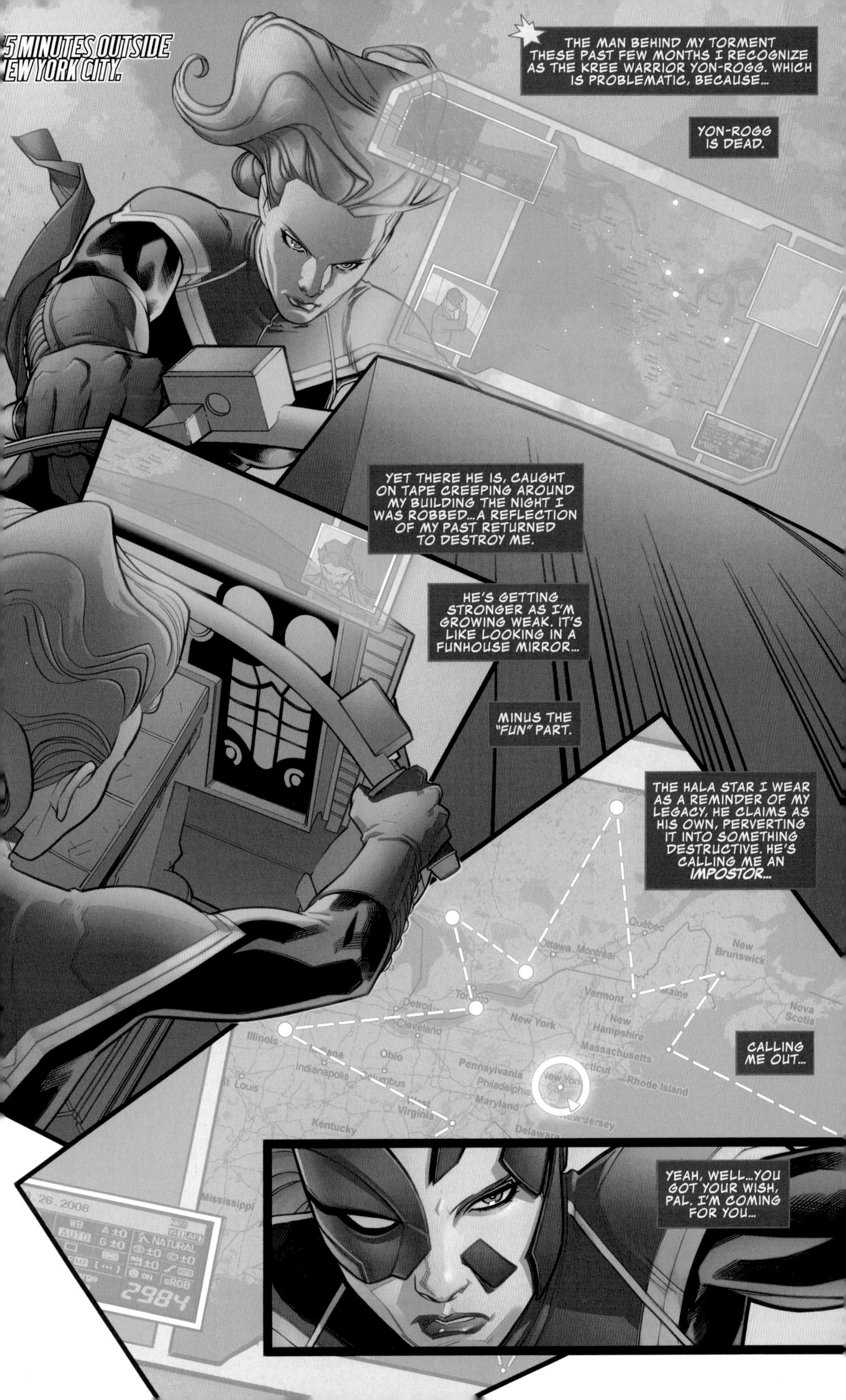
5 MINUTES OUTSIDE
EW YORK CITY.
THE MAN BEHIND MY TORMENT THESE PAST FEW MONTHS I RECOGNIZE AS THE KREE WARRIOR YON-ROGG. WHICH IS PROBLEMATIC, BECAUSE...
YON-ROGG IS DEAD.
YET THERE HE IS, CAUGHT ON TAPE CREEPING AROUND MY BUILDING THE NIGHT I WAS ROBBED...A REFLECTION OF MY PAST RETURNED TO DESTROY ME.
HE'S GETTING STRONGER AS I'M GROWING WEAK. IT'S LIKE LOOKING IN A FUNHOUSE MIRROR...
MINUS THE "FUN" PART.
THE HALA STAR I WEAR AS A REMINDER OF MY LEGACY, HE CLAIMS AS HIS OWN, PERVERTING IT INTO SOMETHING DESTRUCTIVE. HE'S CALLING ME AN IMPOSTOR...
CALLING ME OUT...
YEAH, WELL...YOU GOT YOUR WISH, PAL. I'M COMING FOR YOU...

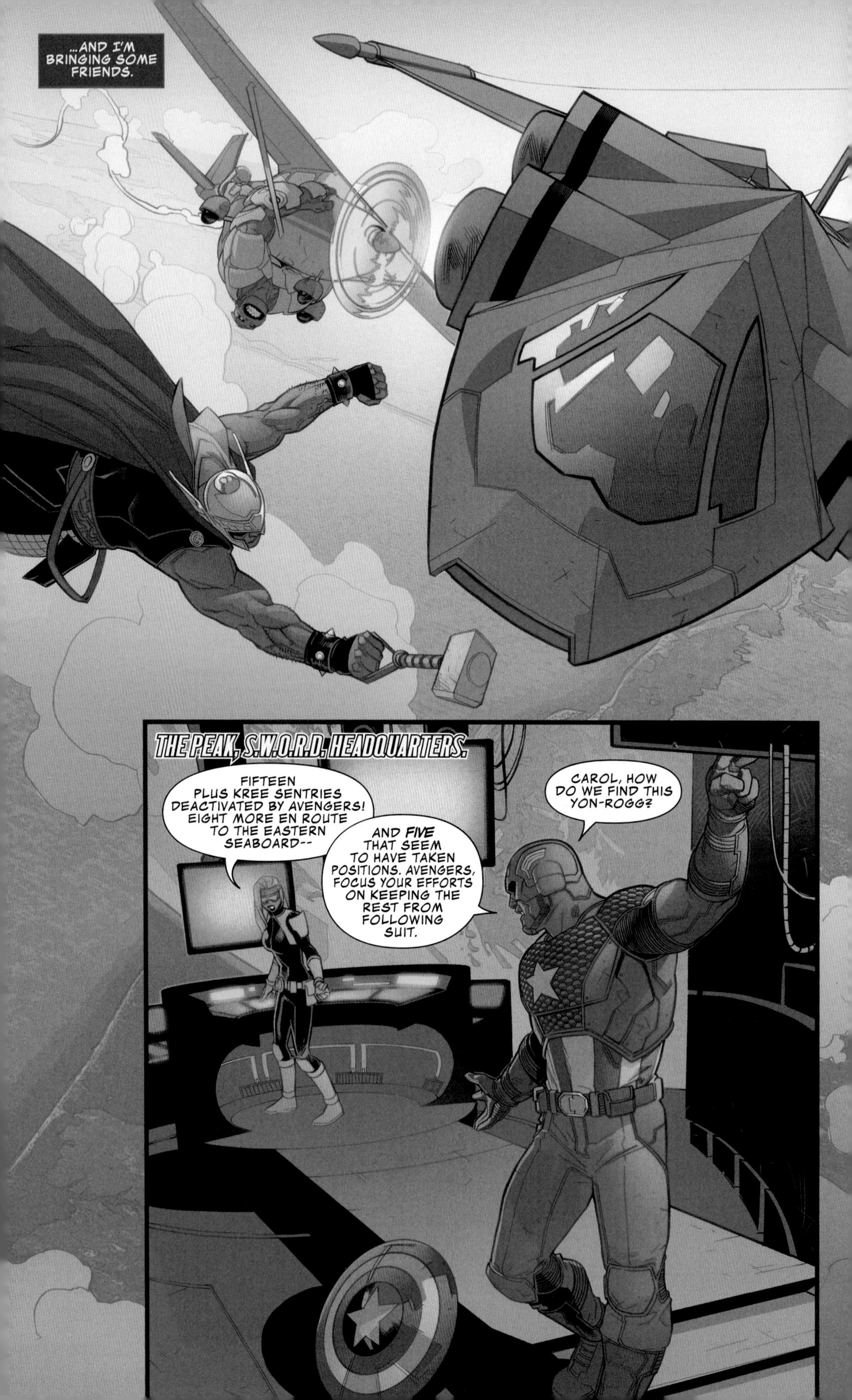
...AND I'M BRINGING SOME FRIENDS.
THE PEAK, S.W.O.R.D. HEADQUARTERS.
FIFTEEN PLUS KREE SENTRIES DEACTIVATED BY AVENGERS! EIGHT MORE EN ROUTE TO THE EASTERN SEABOARD--
AND FIVE THAT SEEM TO HAVE TAKEN POSITIONS. AVENGERS, FOCUS YOUR EFFORTS ON KEEPING THE REST FROM FOLLOWING SUIT.
CAROL, HOW DO WE FIND THIS YON-ROGG?

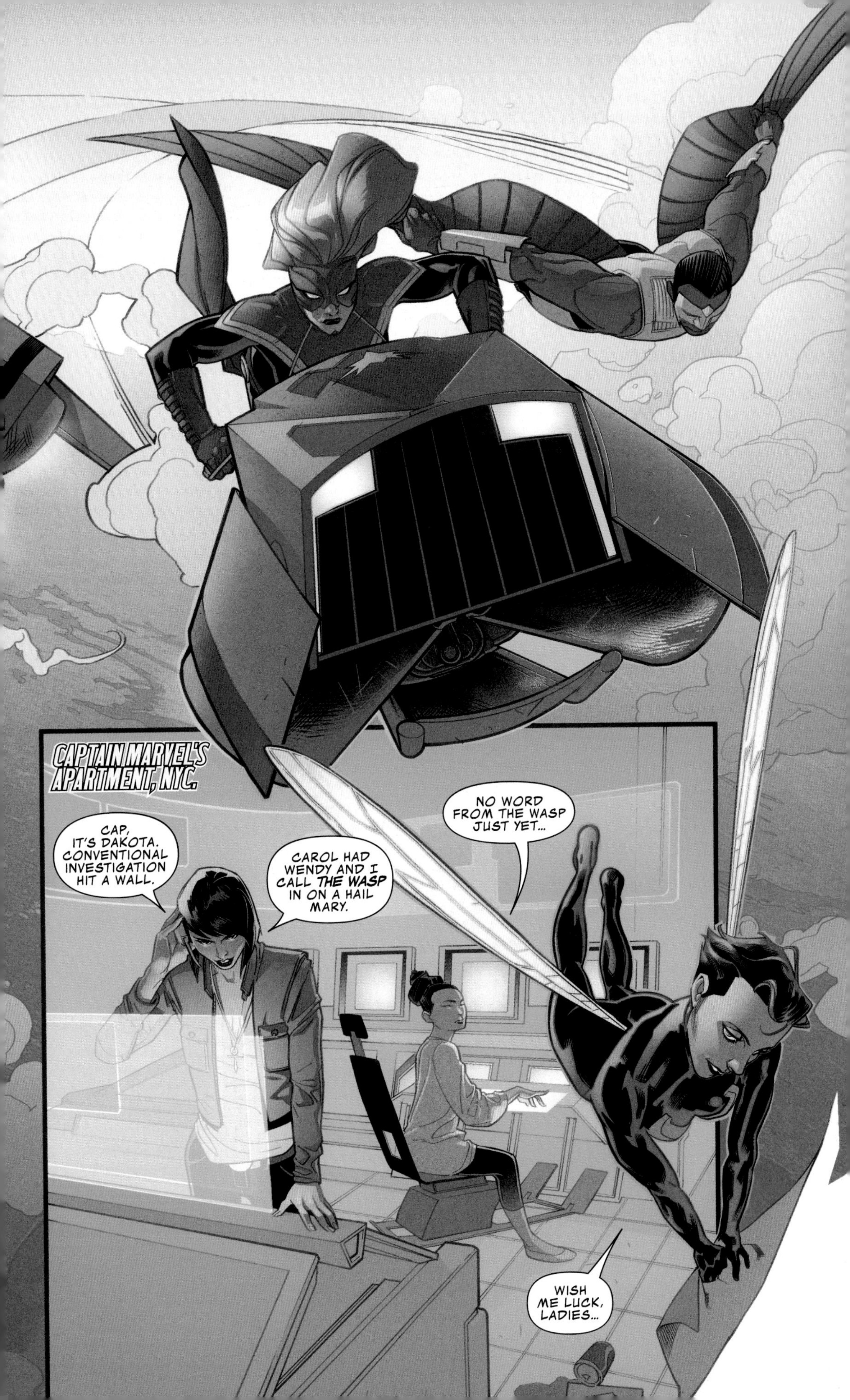
CAPTAIN MARVEL'S APARTMENT, NYC.
CAP, IT'S DAKOTA. CONVENTIONAL INVESTIGATION HIT A WALL.
CAROL HAD WENDY AND I CALL THE WASP IN ON A HAIL MARY.
NO WORD FROM THE WASP JUST YET...
WISH ME LUCK, LADIES...

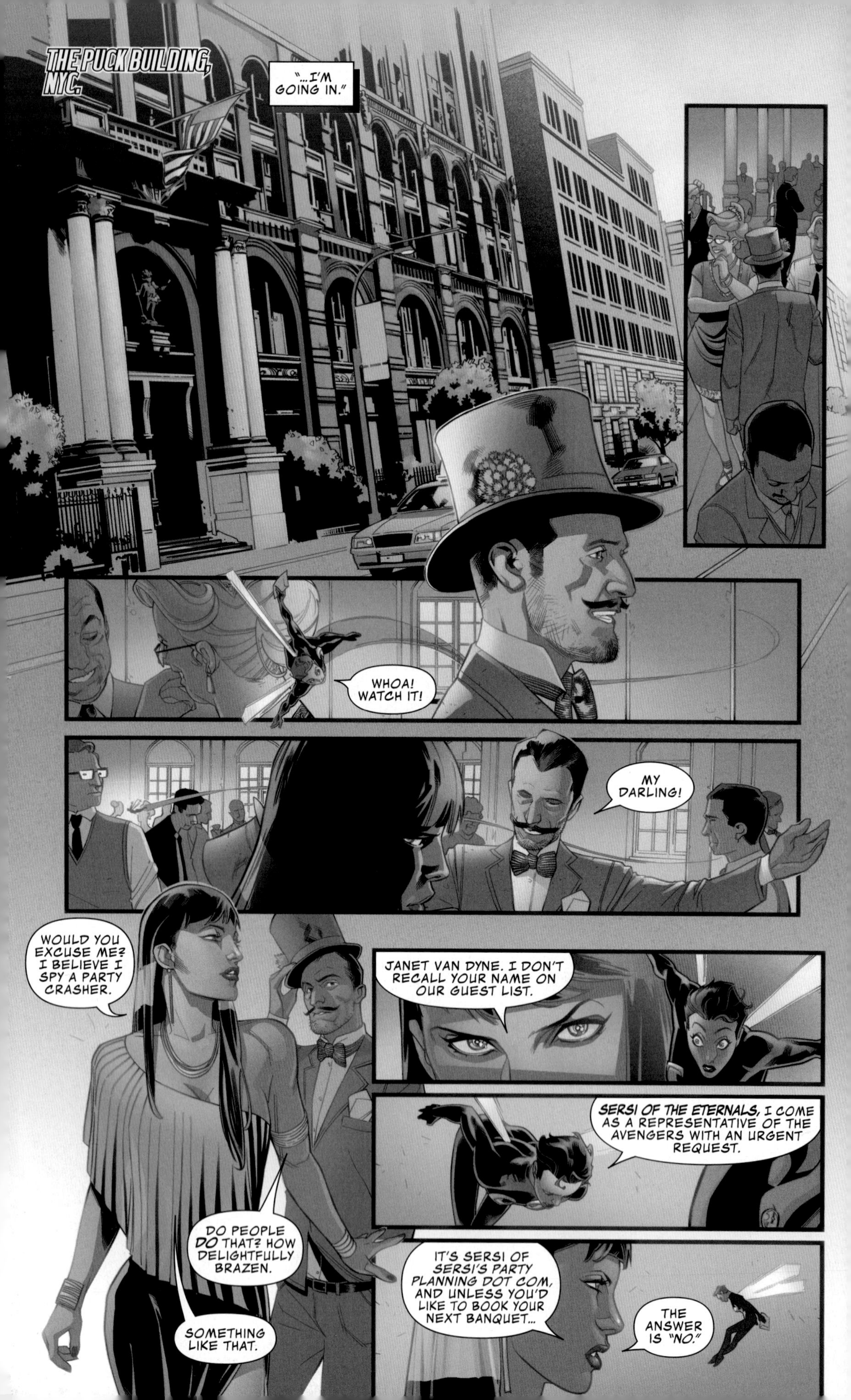
THE PUCK BUILDING, NYC.
"...I'M GOING IN."
WHOA! WATCH IT!
MY DARLING!
WOULD YOU EXCUSE ME? I BELIEVE I SPY A PARTY CRASHER.
DO PEOPLE DO THAT? HOW DELIGHTFULLY BRAZEN.
SOMETHING LIKE THAT.
JANET VAN DYNE. I DON'T RECALL YOUR NAME ON OUR GUEST LIST.
SERSI OF THE ETERNALS, I COME AS A REPRESENTATIVE OF THE AVENGERS WITH AN URGENT REQUEST.
IT'S SERSI OF SERSI'S PARTY PLANNING DOT COM, AND UNLESS YOU'D LIKE TO BOOK YOUR NEXT BANQUET...
THE ANSWER IS "NO."

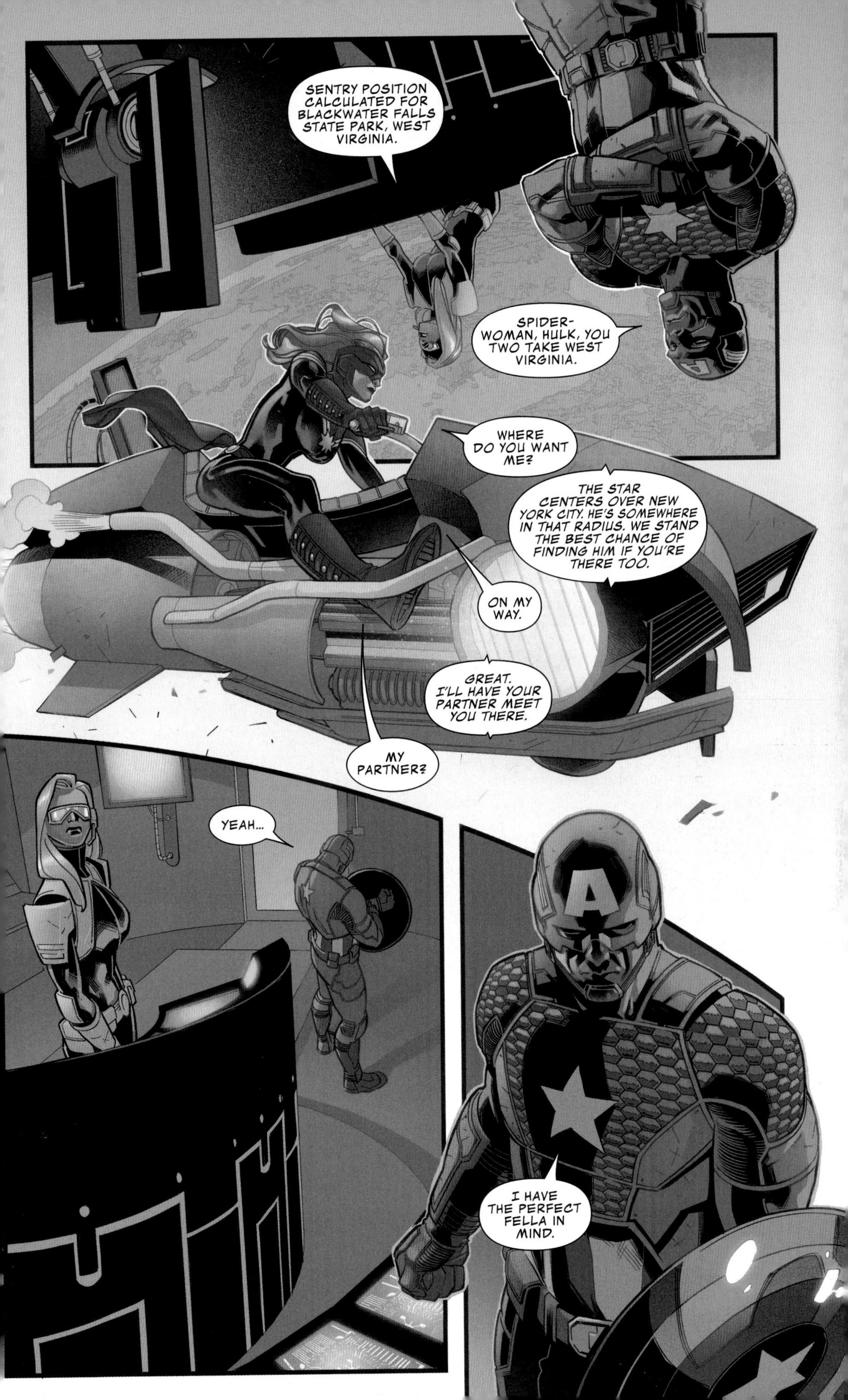
SENTRY POSITION CALCULATED FOR BLACKWATER FALLS STATE PARK, WEST VIRGINIA.
SPIDER-WOMAN, HULK, YOU TWO TAKE WEST VIRGINIA.
WHERE DO YOU WANT ME?
THE STAR CENTERS OVER NEW YORK CITY. HE'S SOMEWHERE IN THAT RADIUS. WE STAND THE BEST CHANCE OF FINDING HIM IF YOU'RE THERE TOO.
ON MY WAY.
GREAT. I'LL HAVE YOUR PARTNER MEET YOU THERE.
MY PARTNER?
YEAH...
I HAVE THE PERFECT FELLA IN MIND.

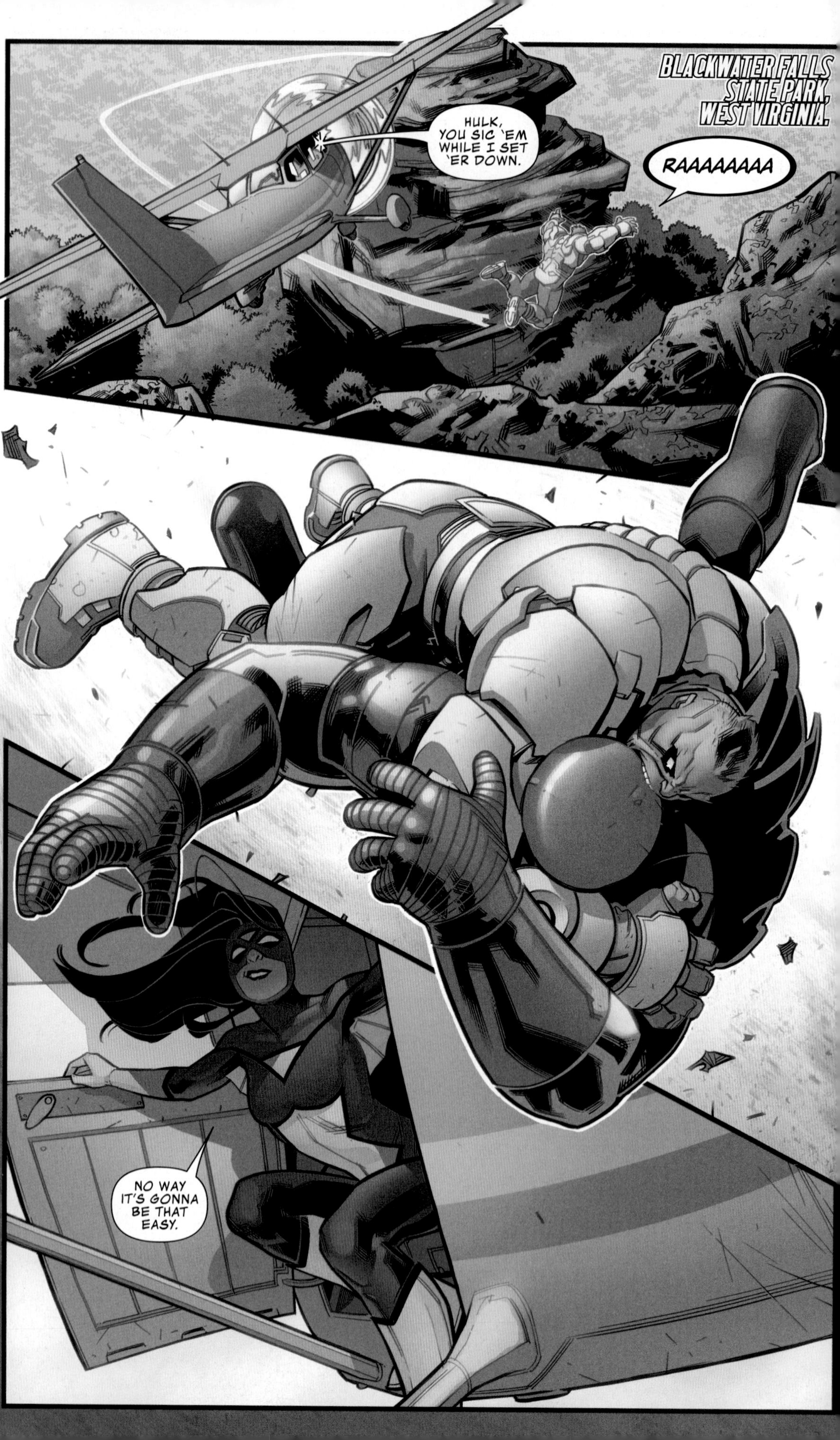
BLACKWATER FALLS STATE PARK, WEST VIRGINIA.
HULK, YOU SIC 'EM WHILE I SET 'ER DOWN.
RAAAAAAAA
NO WAY IT'S GONNA BE THAT EASY.

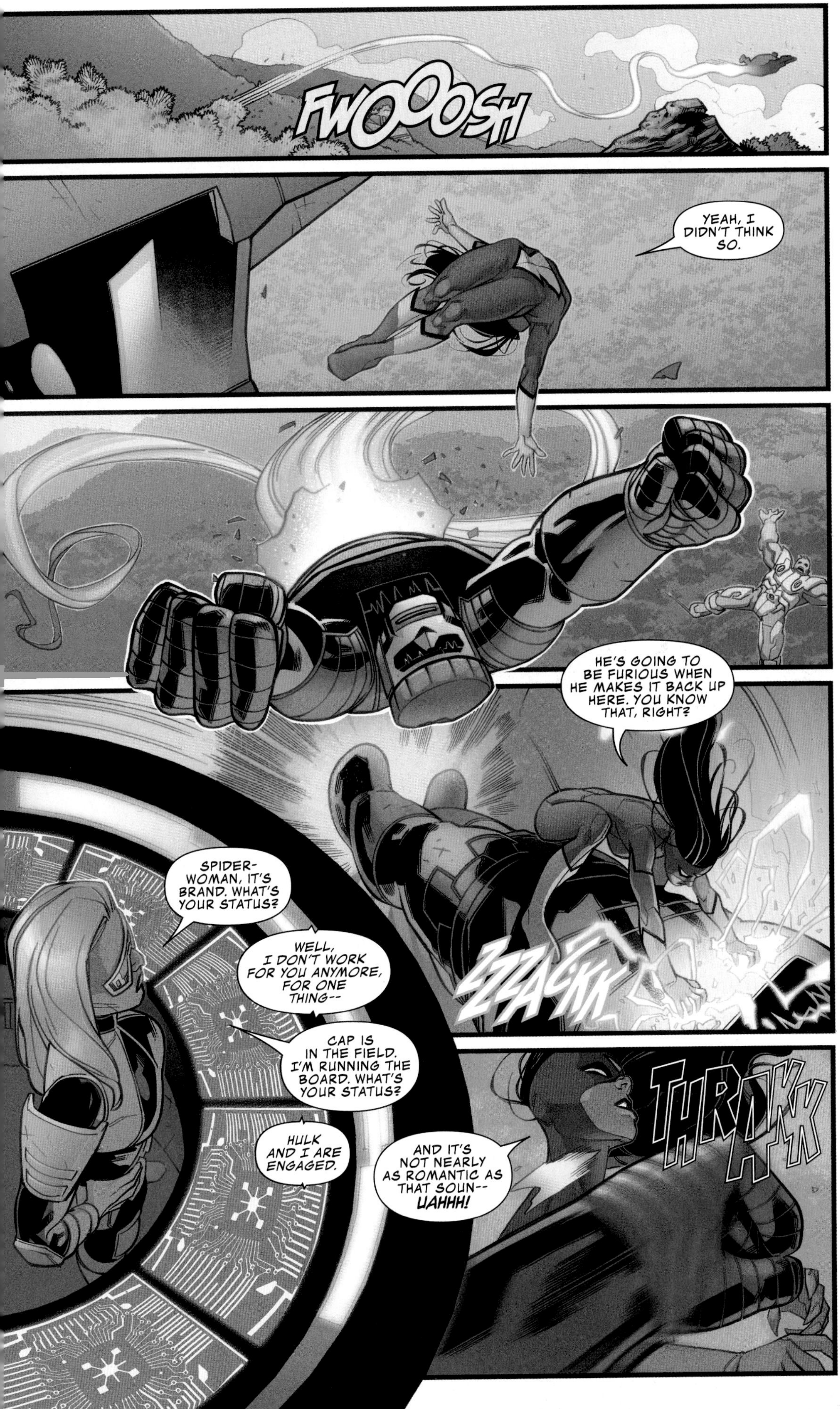
FWOOOSH
YEAH, I DIDN'T THINK SO.
HE'S GOING TO BE FURIOUS WHEN HE MAKES IT BACK UP HERE. YOU KNOW THAT, RIGHT?
ZZZACKK
SPIDER-WOMAN, IT'S BRAND. WHAT'S YOUR STATUS?
WELL, I DON'T WORK FOR YOU ANYMORE, FOR ONE THING--
CAP IS IN THE FIELD. I'M RUNNING THE BOARD. WHAT'S YOUR STATUS?
HULK AND I ARE ENGAGED.
AND IT'S NOT NEARLY AS ROMANTIC AS THAT SOUN-- UAHHH!
THRAKK

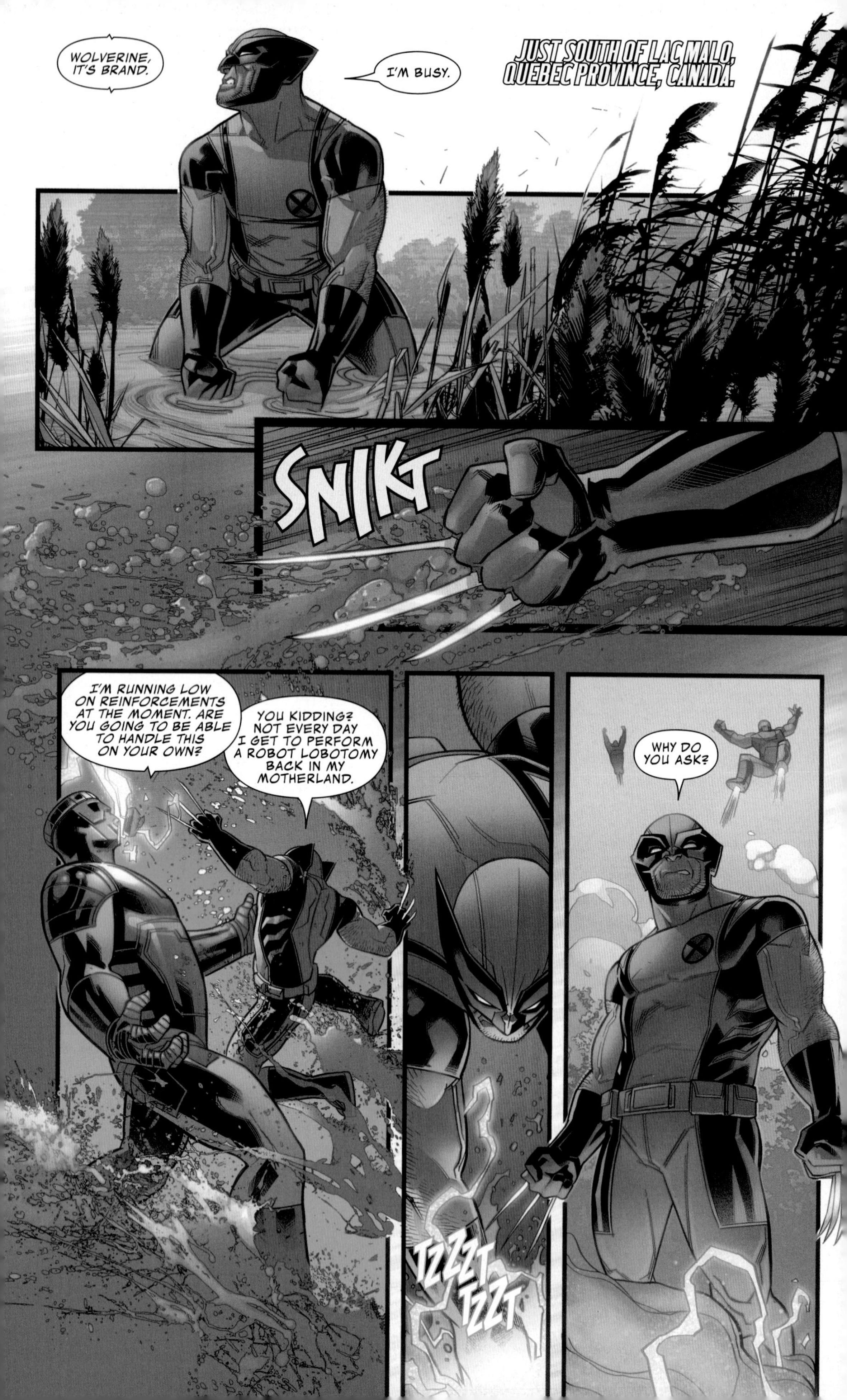
JUST SOUTH OF LAC MALO, QUEBEC PROVINCE, CANADA.
WOLVERINE, IT'S BRAND.
I'M BUSY.
SNIKT
I'M RUNNING LOW ON REINFORCEMENTS AT THE MOMENT. ARE YOU GOING TO BE ABLE TO HANDLE THIS ON YOUR OWN?
YOU KIDDING? NOT EVERY DAY I GET TO PERFORM A ROBOT LOBOTOMY BACK IN MY MOTHERLAND.
TZZZT
TZZT
WHY DO YOU ASK?

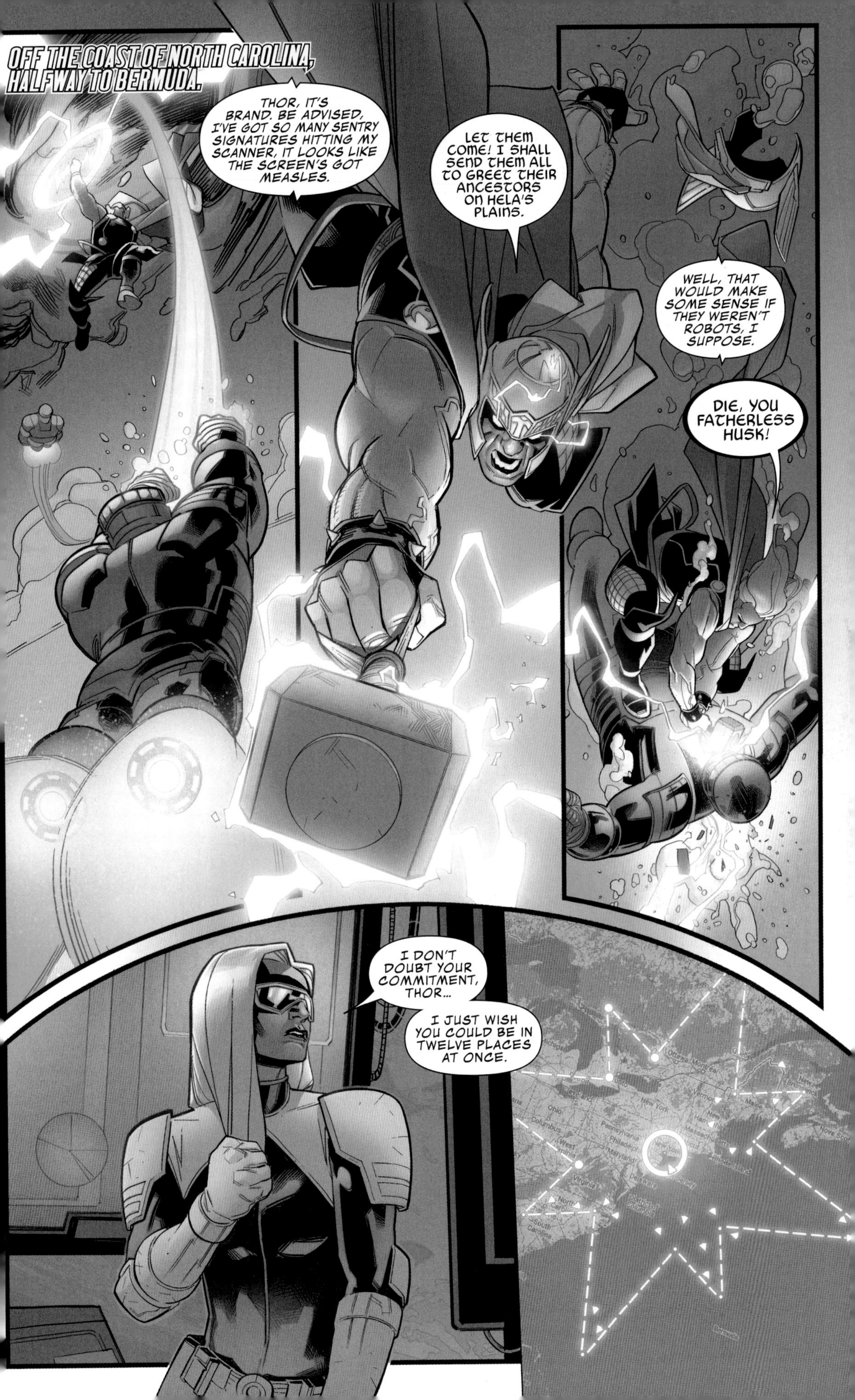
OFF THE COAST OF NORTH CAROLINA, HALFWAY TO BERMUDA.
THOR, IT'S BRAND. BE ADVISED, I'VE GOT SO MANY SENTRY SIGNATURES HITTING MY SCANNER, IT LOOKS LIKE THE SCREEN'S GOT MEASLES.
LET THEM COME! I SHALL SEND THEM ALL TO GREET THEIR ANCESTORS ON HELA'S PLAINS.
WELL, THAT WOULD MAKE SOME SENSE IF THEY WEREN'T ROBOTS, I SUPPOSE.
DIE, YOU FATHERLESS HUSK!
I DON'T DOUBT YOUR COMMITMENT, THOR...
I JUST WISH YOU COULD BE IN TWELVE PLACES AT ONCE.

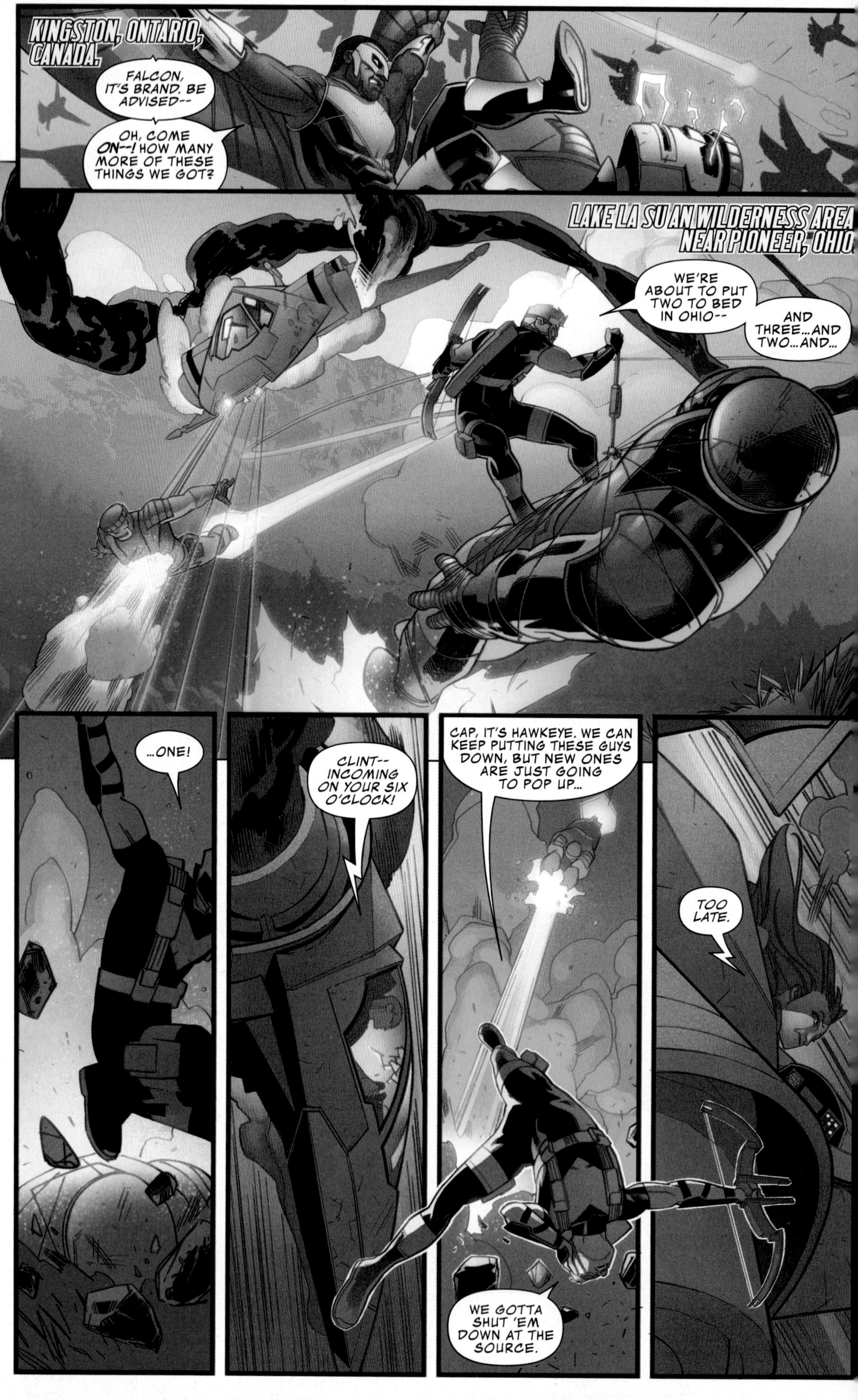
KINGSTON, ONTARIO, CANADA.
FALCON, IT'S BRAND. BE ADVISED--
OH, COME ON--! HOW MANY MORE OF THESE THINGS WE GOT?
LAKE LA SU AN WILDERNESS AREA NEAR PIONEER, OHIO
WE'RE ABOUT TO PUT TWO TO BED IN OHIO--
AND THREE...AND TWO...AND...
...ONE!
CLINT-- INCOMING ON YOUR SIX O'CLOCK!
CAP, IT'S HAWKEYE. WE CAN KEEP PUTTING THESE GUYS DOWN, BUT NEW ONES ARE JUST GOING TO POP UP...
WE GOTTA SHUT 'EM DOWN AT THE SOURCE.
TOO LATE.

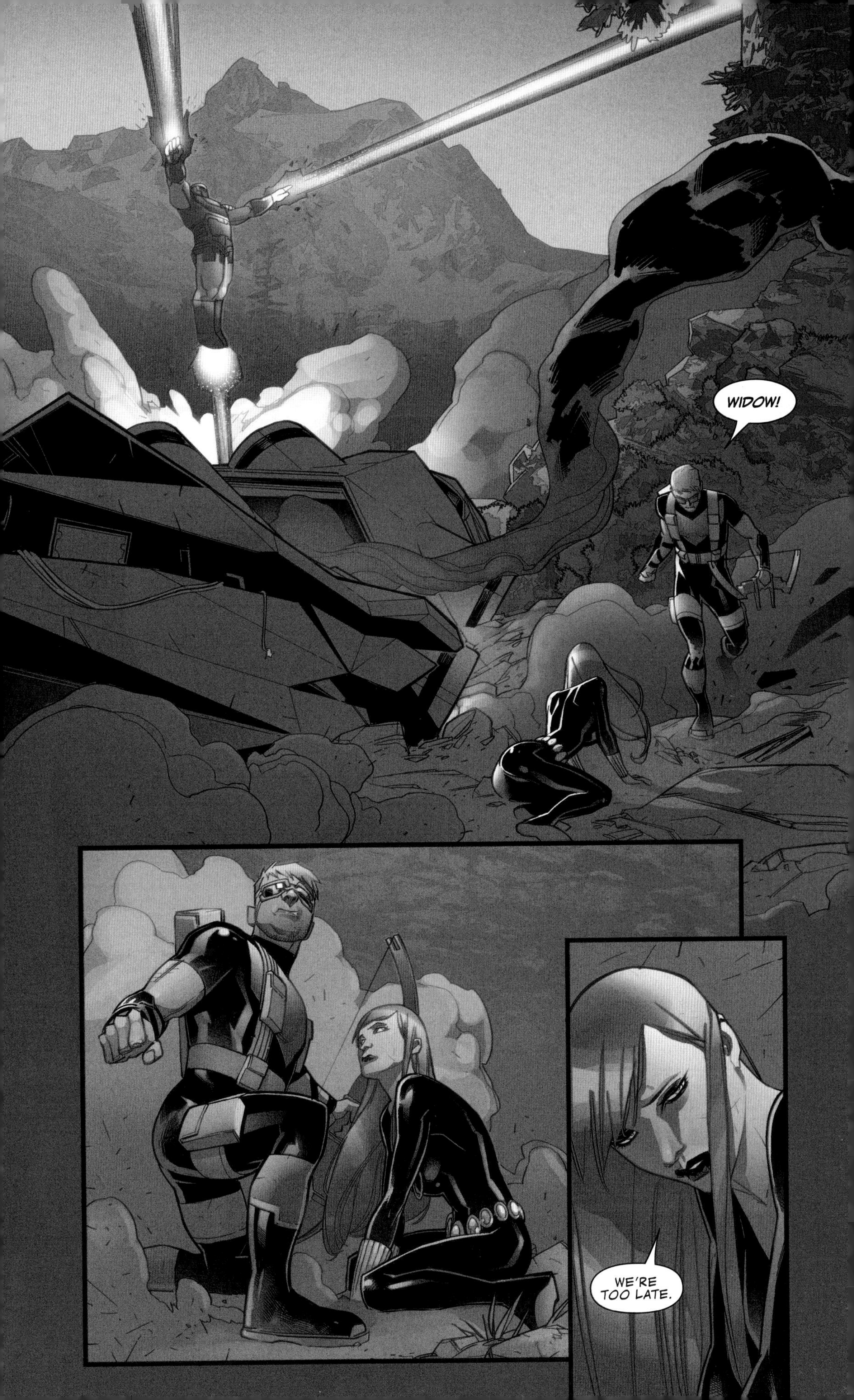
WIDOW!
WE'RE TOO LATE.

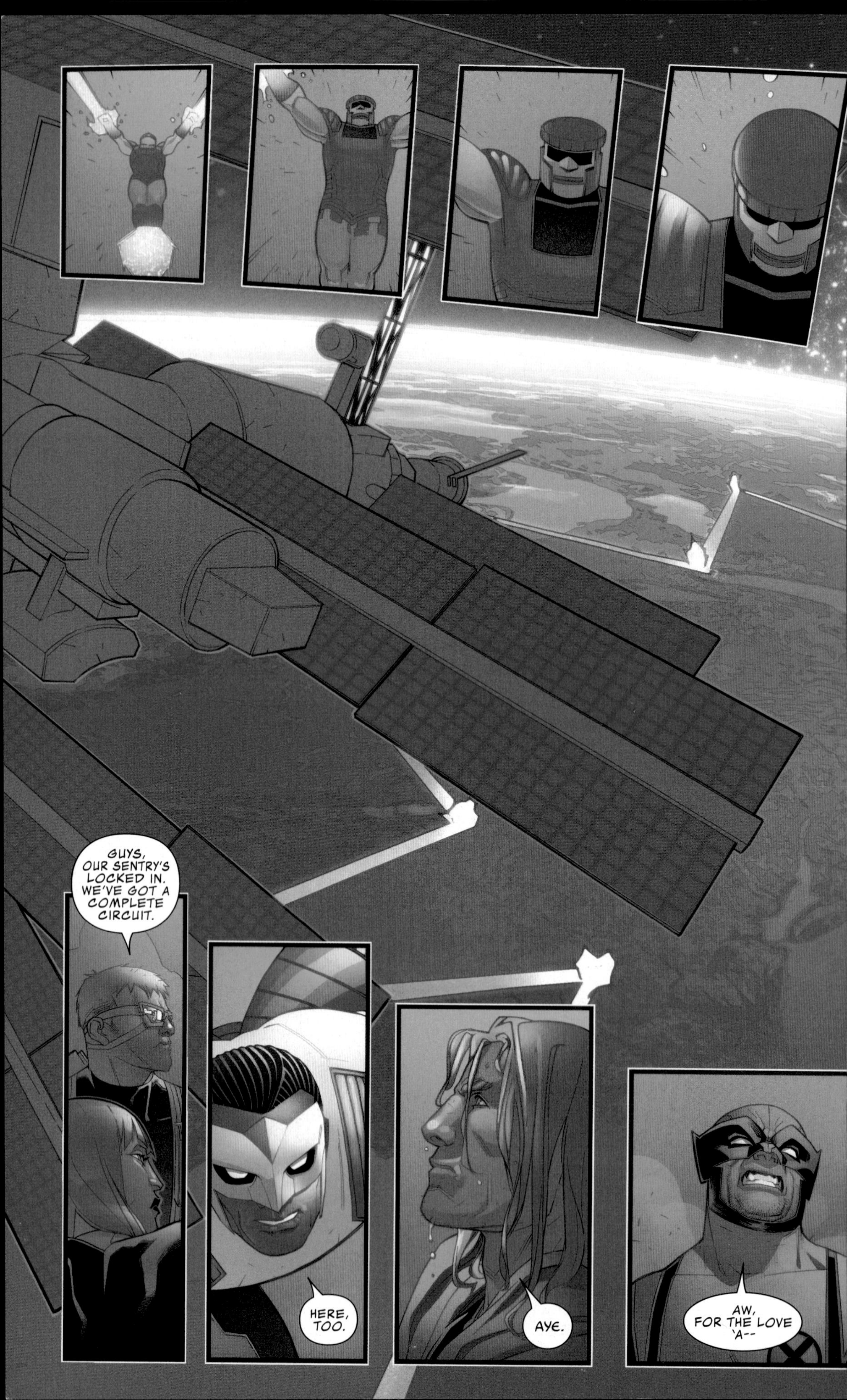
GUYS, OUR SENTRY'S LOCKED IN. WE'VE GOT A COMPLETE CIRCUIT.
HERE, TOO.
AYE.
AW, FOR THE LOVE 'A--

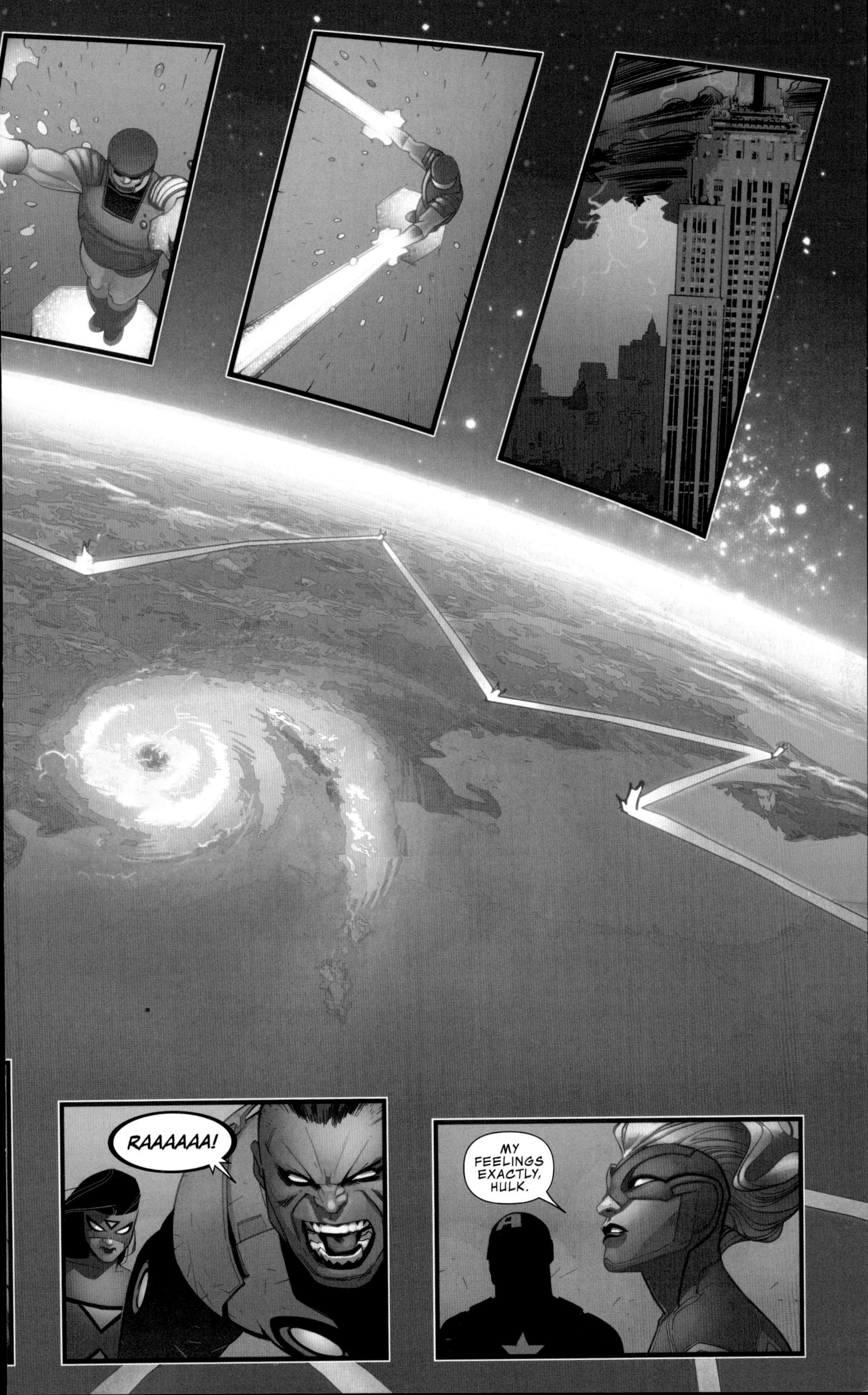
RAAAAAA!
MY FEELINGS EXACTLY, HULK.

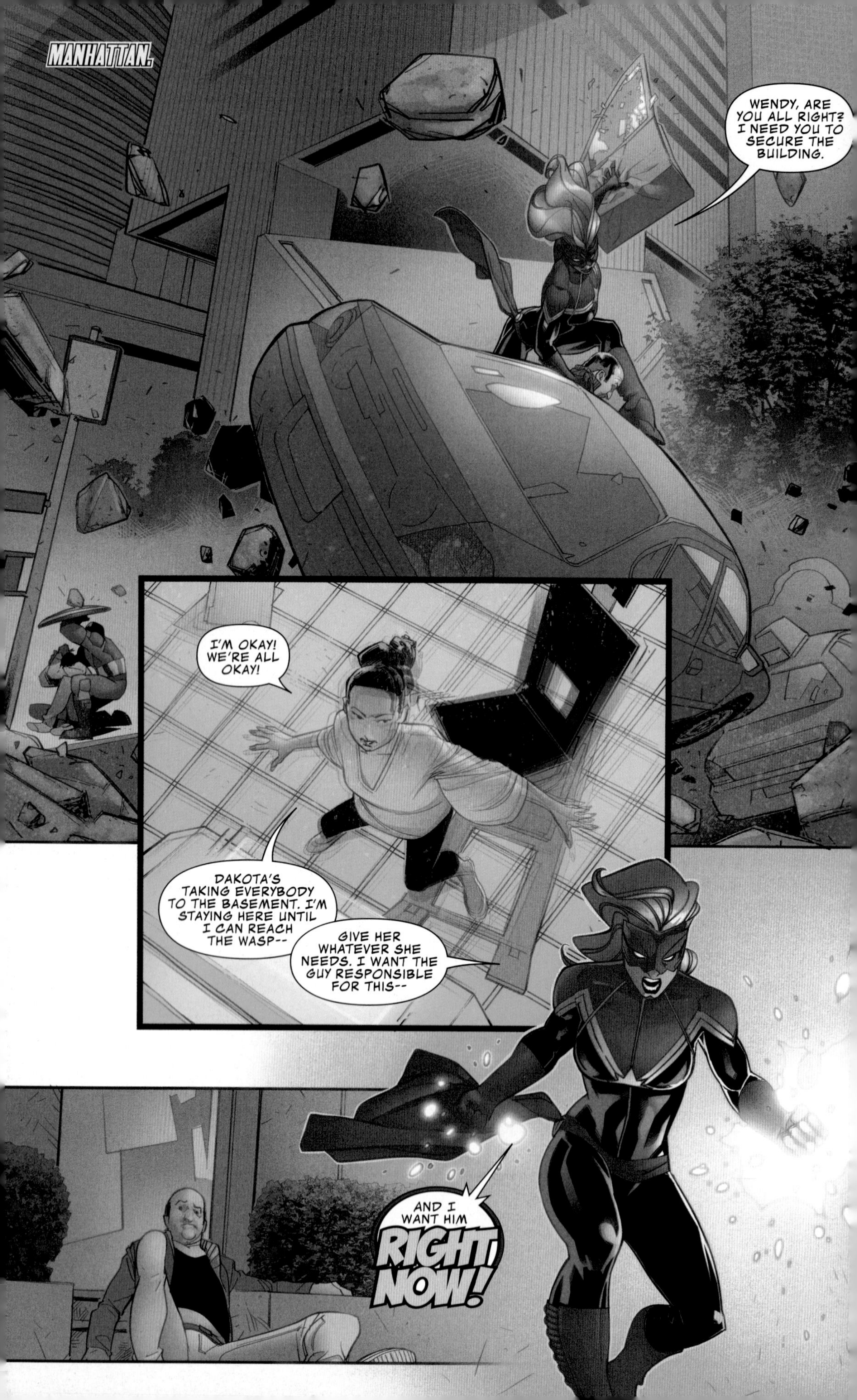
MANHATTAN.
WENDY, ARE YOU ALL RIGHT? I NEED YOU TO SECURE THE BUILDING.
I'M OKAY! WE'RE ALL OKAY!
DAKOTA'S TAKING EVERYBODY TO THE BASEMENT. I'M STAYING HERE UNTIL I CAN REACH THE WASP--
GIVE HER WHATEVER SHE NEEDS. I WANT THE GUY RESPONSIBLE FOR THIS--
AND I WANT HIM RIGHT NOW!

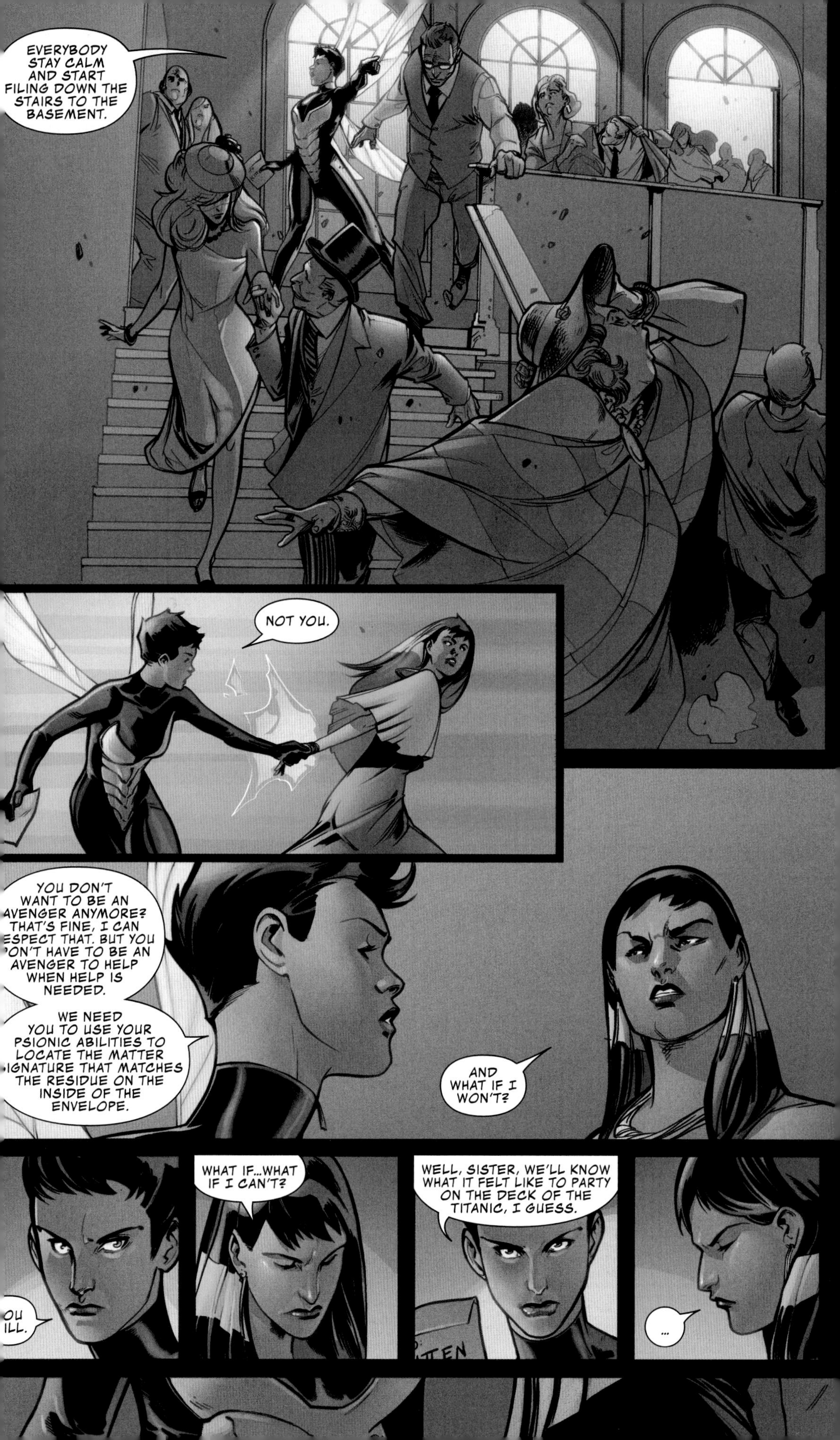
EVERYBODY STAY CALM AND START FILING DOWN THE STAIRS TO THE BASEMENT.
NOT YOU.
YOU DON'T WANT TO BE AN AVENGER ANYMORE? THAT'S FINE, I CAN ESPECT THAT. BUT YOU 'ON'T HAVE TO BE AN AVENGER TO HELP WHEN HELP IS NEEDED.
WE NEED YOU TO USE YOUR PSIONIC ABILITIES TO LOCATE THE MATTER IGNATURE THAT MATCHES THE RESIDUE ON THE INSIDE OF THE ENVELOPE.
AND WHAT IF I WON'T?
OU ILL.
WHAT IF...WHAT IF I CAN'T?
WELL, SISTER, WE'LL KNOW WHAT IT FELT LIKE TO PARTY ON THE DECK OF THE TITANIC, I GUESS.
...

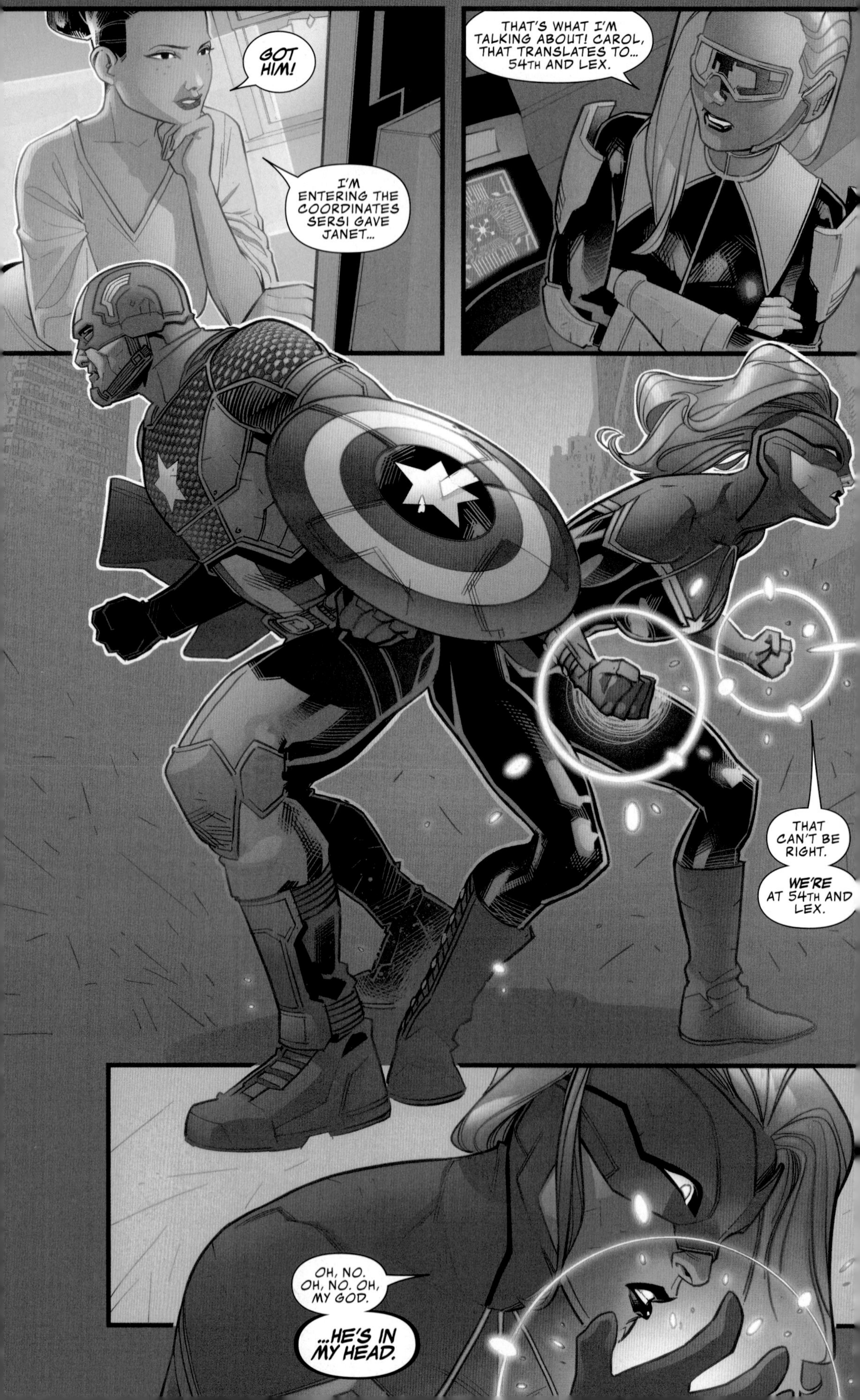
GOT HIM!
I'M ENTERING THE COORDINATES SERSI GAVE JANET...
THAT'S WHAT I'M TALKING ABOUT! CAROL, THAT TRANSLATES TO... 54TH AND LEX.
THAT CAN'T BE RIGHT.
WE'RE AT 54TH AND LEX.
OH, NO. OH, NO. OH, MY GOD.
...HE'S IN MY HEAD.

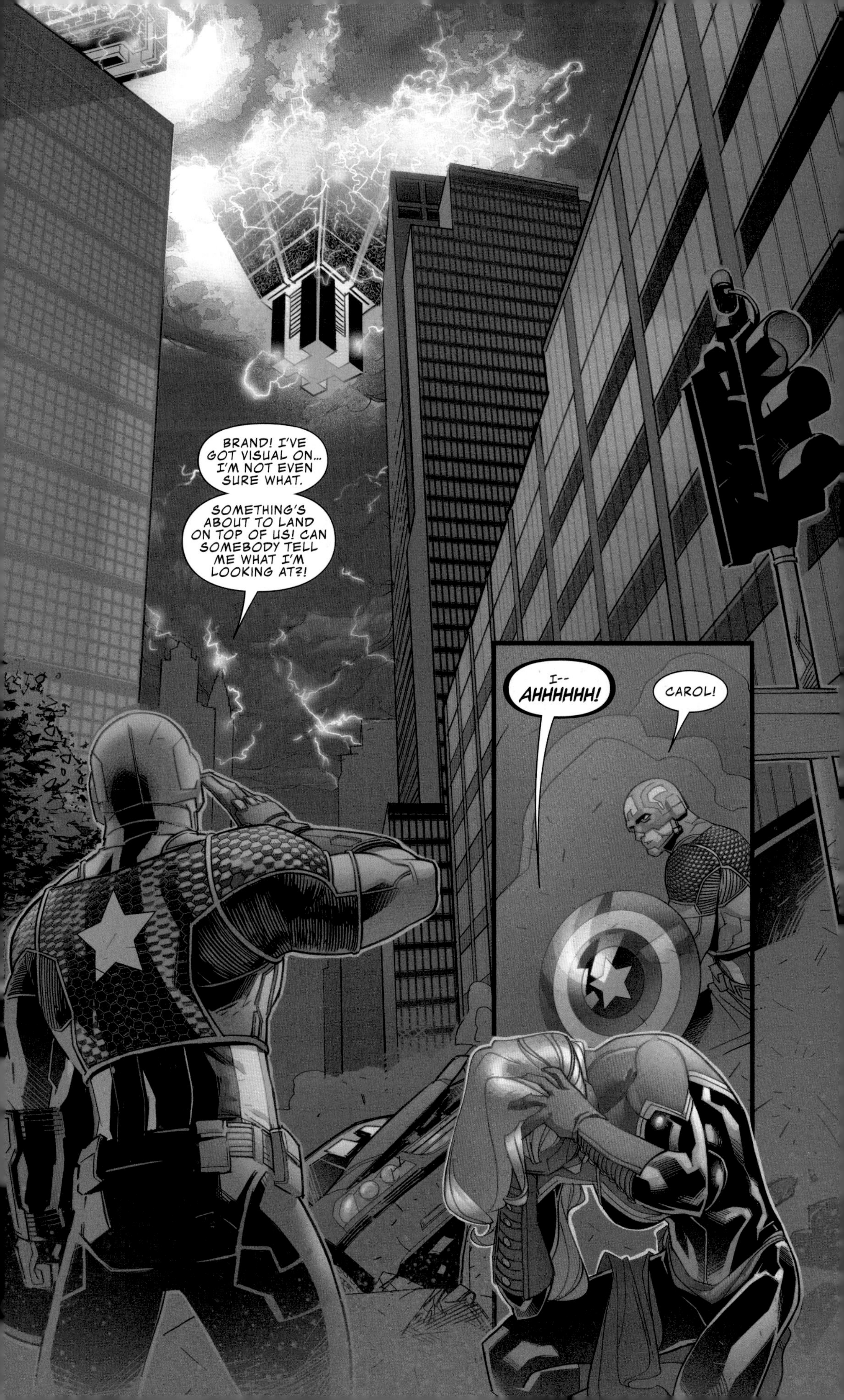
BRAND! I'VE GOT VISUAL ON... I'M NOT EVEN SURE WHAT.
SOMETHING'S ABOUT TO LAND ON TOP OF US! CAN SOMEBODY TELL ME WHAT I'M LOOKING AT?!
I-- AHHHHHH!
CAROL!

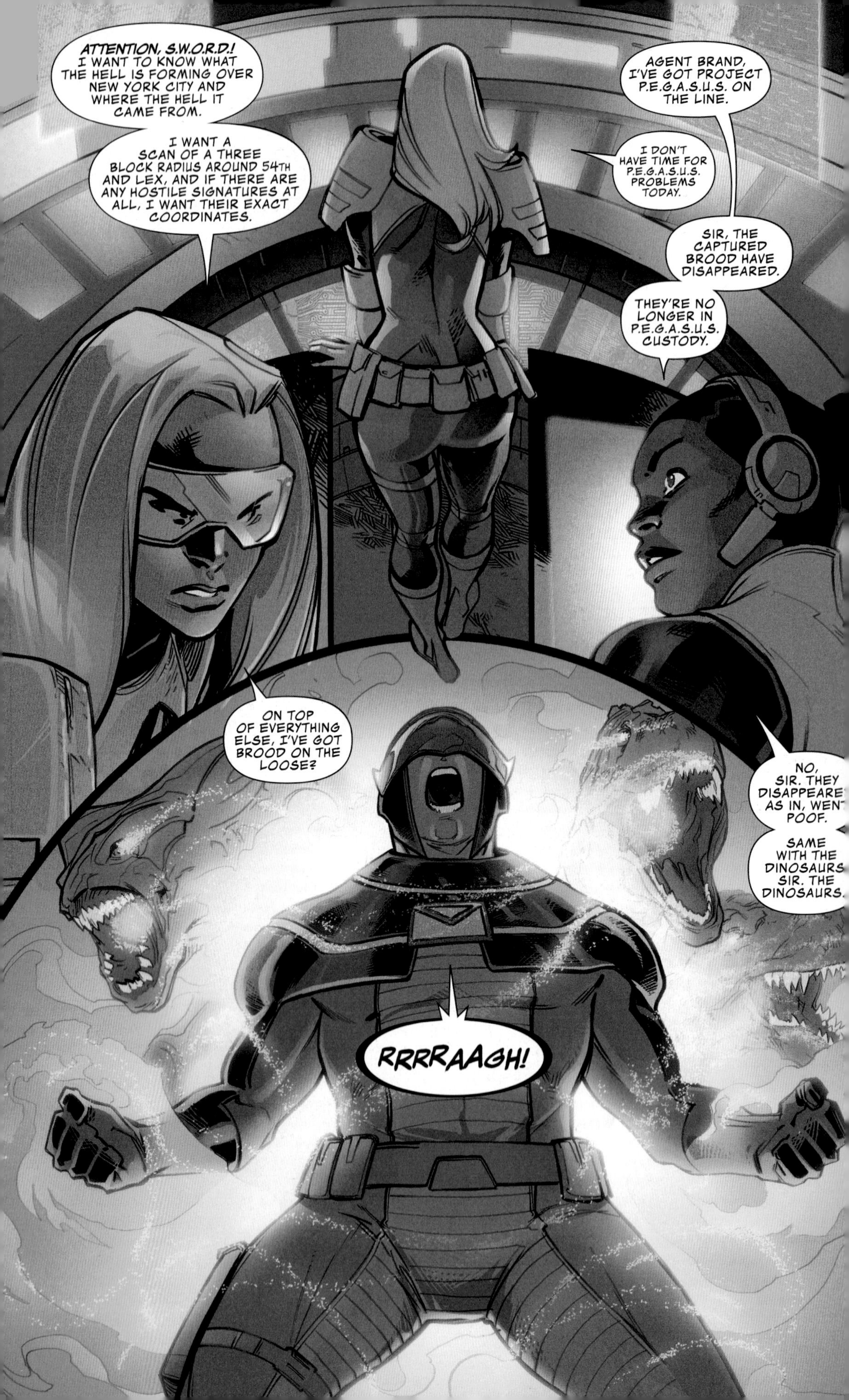

ATTENTION, S.W.O.R.D.! I WANT TO KNOW WHAT THE HELL IS FORMING OVER NEW YORK CITY AND WHERE THE HELL IT CAME FROM.
I WANT A SCAN OF A THREE BLOCK RADIUS AROUND 54TH AND LEX, AND IF THERE ARE ANY HOSTILE SIGNATURES AT ALL, I WANT THEIR EXACT COORDINATES.
AGENT BRAND, I'VE GOT PROJECT P.E.G.A.S.U.S. ON THE LINE.
I DON'T HAVE TIME FOR P.E.G.A.S.U.S. PROBLEMS TODAY.
SIR, THE CAPTURED BROOD HAVE DISAPPEARED.
THEY'RE NO LONGER IN P.E.G.A.S.U.S. CUSTODY.
ON TOP OF EVERYTHING ELSE, I'VE GOT BROOD ON THE LOOSE?
NO, SIR. THEY DISAPPEARE AS IN, WENT POOF.
SAME WITH THE DINOSAURS SIR. THE DINOSAURS.
RRRRAAGH!

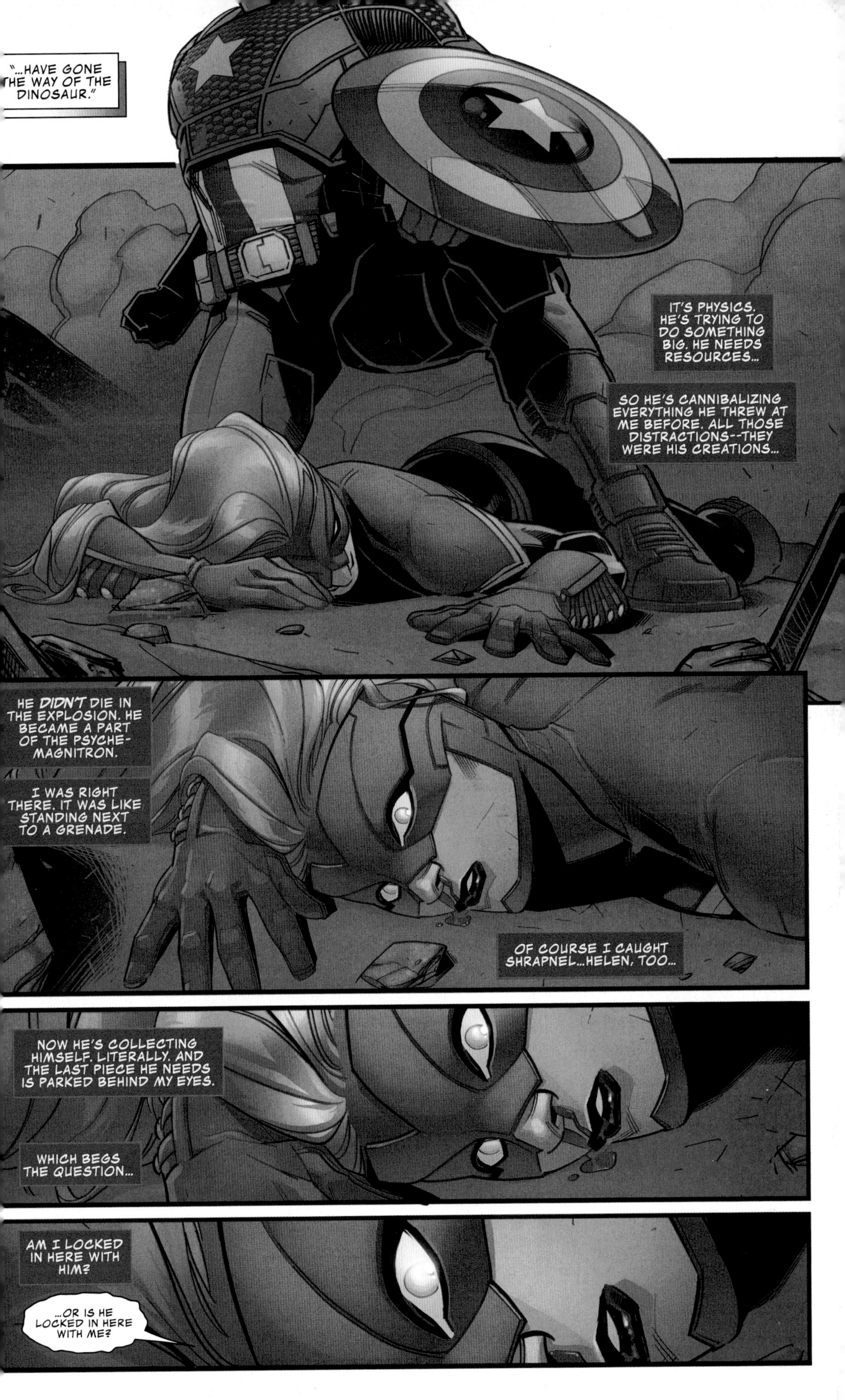
"...HAVE GONE THE WAY OF THE DINOSAUR."
IT'S PHYSICS. HE'S TRYING TO DO SOMETHING BIG. HE NEEDS RESOURCES...
SO HE'S CANNIBALIZING EVERYTHING HE THREW AT ME BEFORE. ALL THOSE DISTRACTIONS--THEY WERE HIS CREATIONS...
HE DIDN'T DIE IN THE EXPLOSION. HE BECAME A PART OF THE PSYCHE-MAGNITRON.
I WAS RIGHT THERE. IT WAS LIKE STANDING NEXT TO A GRENADE.
OF COURSE I CAUGHT SHRAPNEL...HELEN, TOO...
NOW HE'S COLLECTING HIMSELF. LITERALLY. AND THE LAST PIECE HE NEEDS IS PARKED BEHIND MY EYES.
WHICH BEGS THE QUESTION...
AM I LOCKED IN HERE WITH HIM?
...OR IS HE LOCKED IN HERE WITH ME?

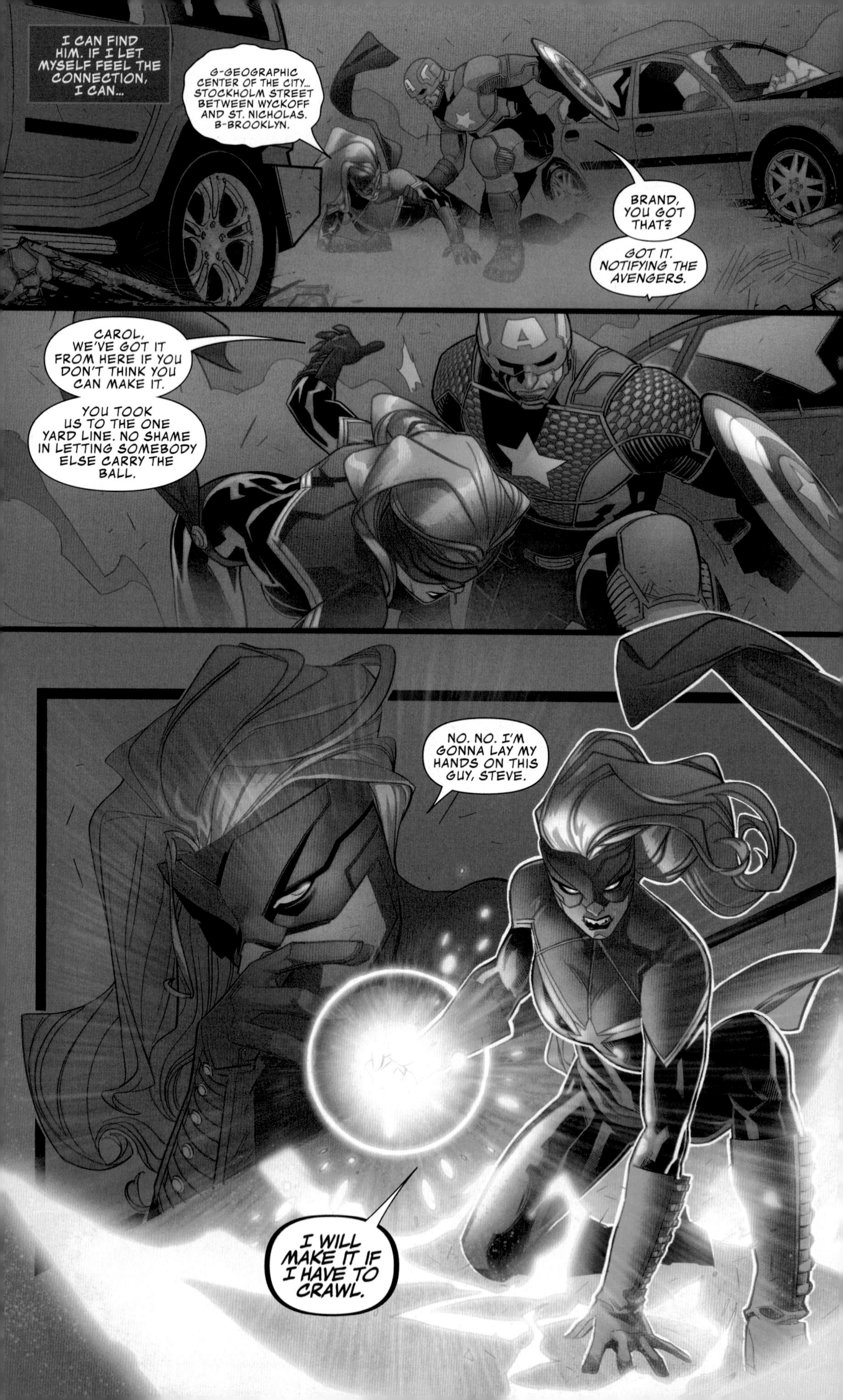

I CAN FIND HIM. IF I LET MYSELF FEEL THE CONNECTION, I CAN...
G-GEOGRAPHIC CENTER OF THE CITY... STOCKHOLM STREET BETWEEN WYCKOFF AND ST. NICHOLAS. B-BROOKLYN.
BRAND, YOU GOT THAT?
GOT IT. NOTIFYING THE AVENGERS.
CAROL, WE'VE GOT IT FROM HERE IF YOU DON'T THINK YOU CAN MAKE IT.
YOU TOOK US TO THE ONE YARD LINE. NO SHAME IN LETTING SOMEBODY ELSE CARRY THE BALL.
NO. NO. I'M GONNA LAY MY HANDS ON THIS GUY, STEVE.
I WILL MAKE IT IF I HAVE TO CRAWL.

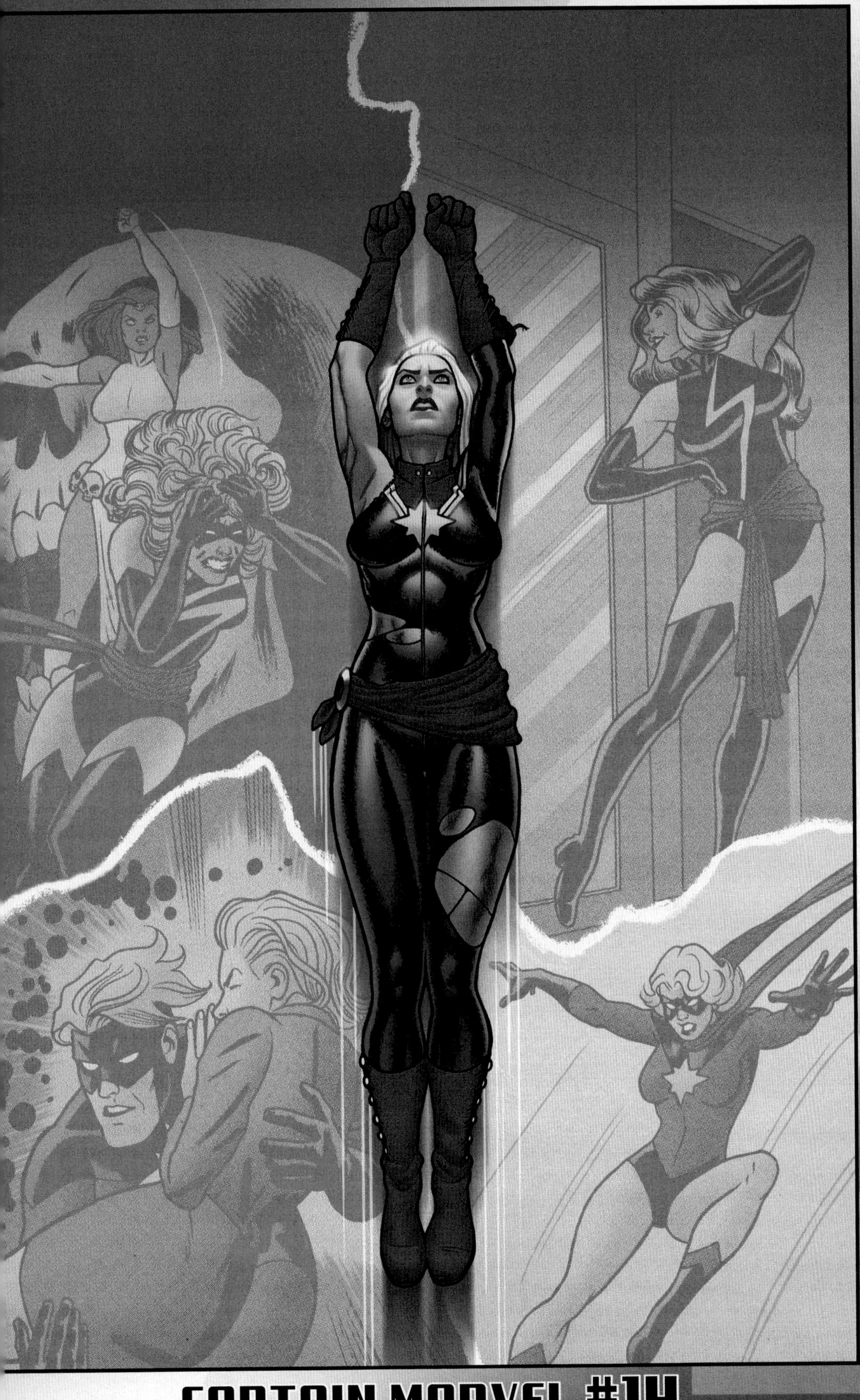

CAPTAIN MARVEL #14

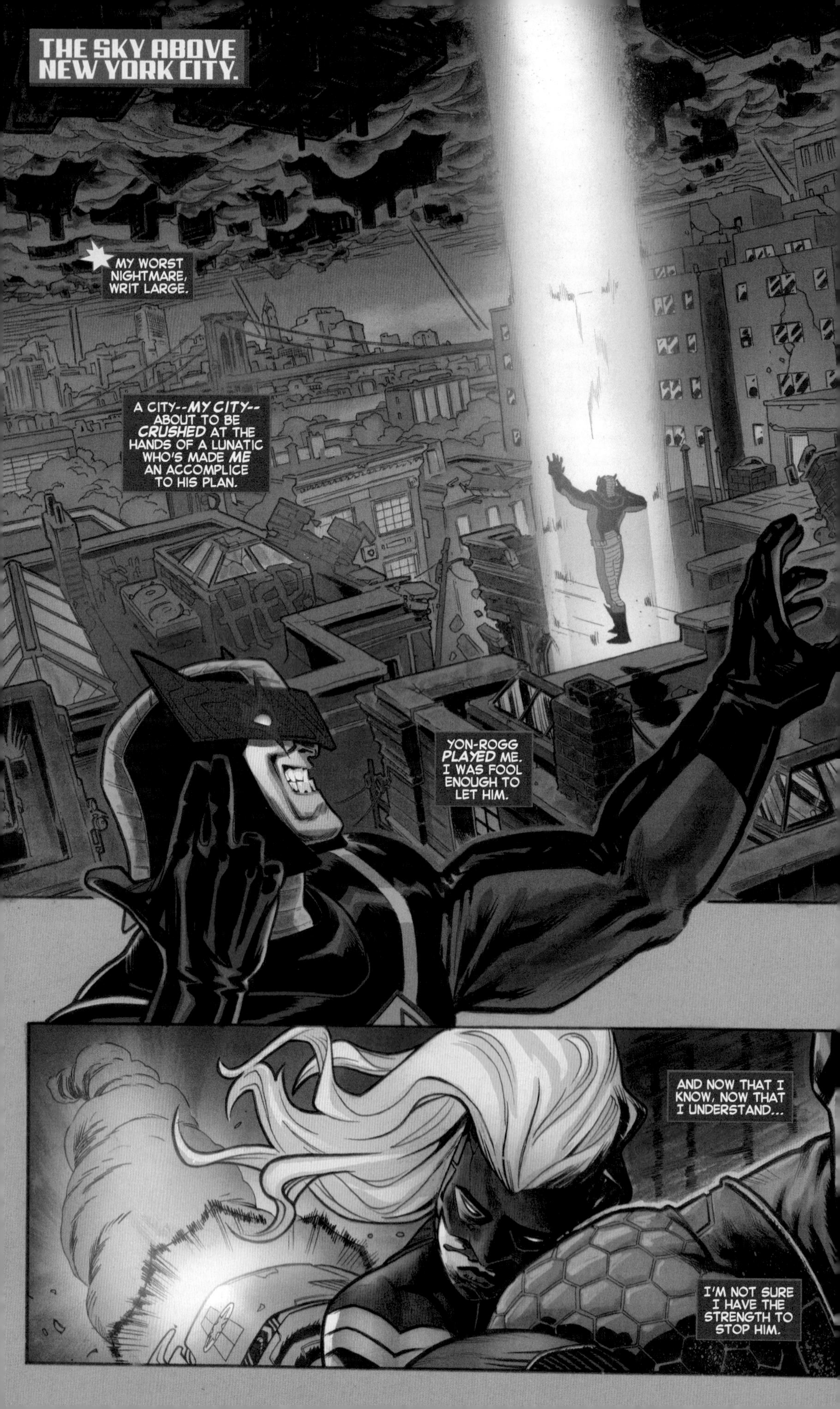
THE SKY ABOVE NEW YORK CITY.
MY WORST NIGHTMARE, WRIT LARGE.
A CITY--MY CITY--ABOUT TO BE CRUSHED AT THE HANDS OF A LUNATIC WHO'S MADE ME AN ACCOMPLICE TO HIS PLAN.
YON-ROGG PLAYED ME. I WAS FOOL ENOUGH TO LET HIM.
AND NOW THAT I KNOW, NOW THAT I UNDERSTAND...
I'M NOT SURE I HAVE THE STRENGTH TO STOP HIM.

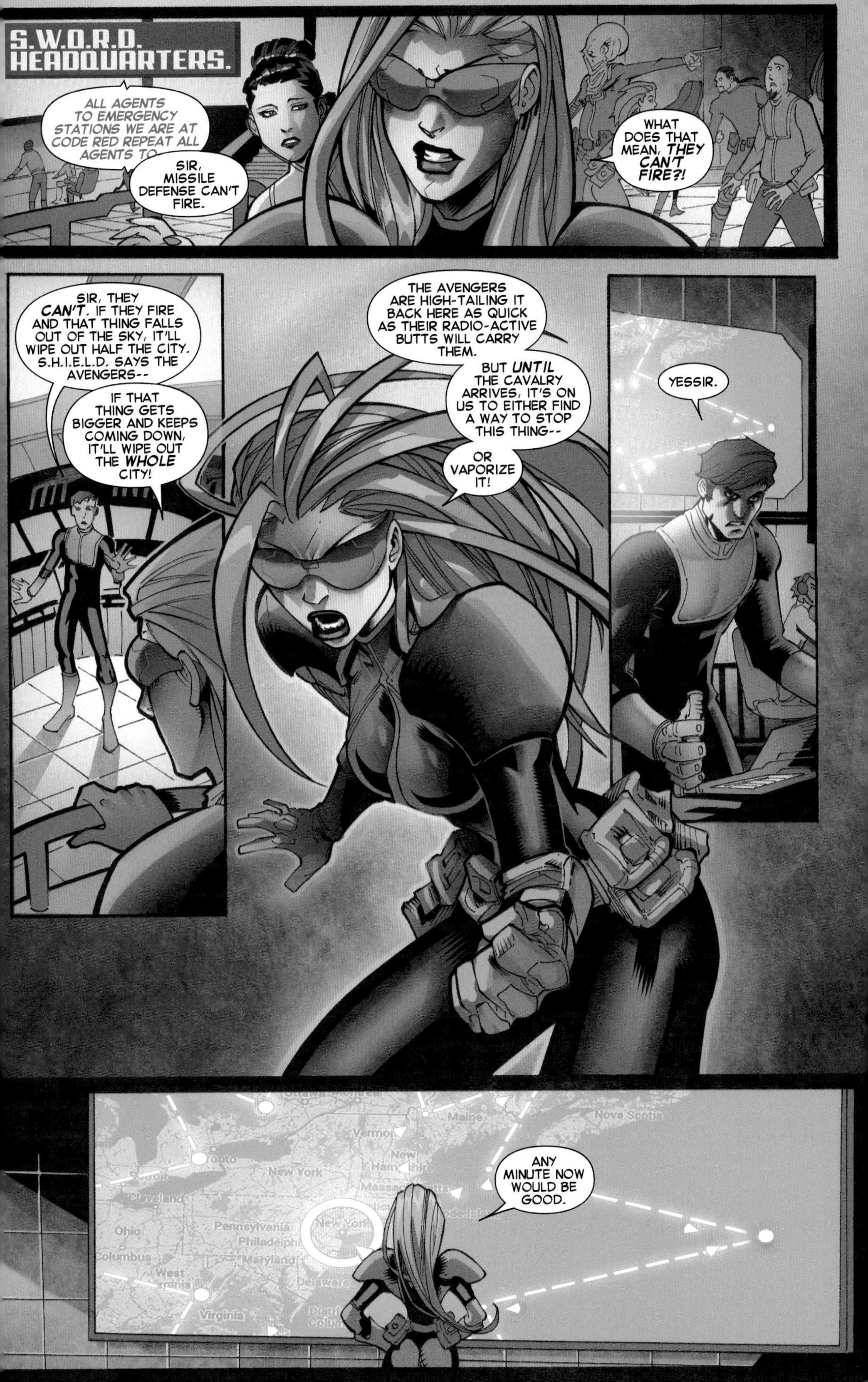
S.W.O.R.D. HEADQUARTERS.
ALL AGENTS TO EMERGENCY STATIONS WE ARE AT CODE RED REPEAT ALL AGENTS TO
SIR, MISSILE DEFENSE CAN'T FIRE.
WHAT DOES THAT MEAN, THEY CAN'T FIRE?!
SIR, THEY CAN'T. IF THEY FIRE AND THAT THING FALLS OUT OF THE SKY, IT'LL WIPE OUT HALF THE CITY. S.H.I.E.L.D. SAYS THE AVENGERS--
IF THAT THING GETS BIGGER AND KEEPS COMING DOWN, IT'LL WIPE OUT THE WHOLE CITY!
THE AVENGERS ARE HIGH-TAILING IT BACK HERE AS QUICK AS THEIR RADIO-ACTIVE BUTTS WILL CARRY THEM.
BUT UNTIL THE CAVALRY ARRIVES, IT'S ON US TO EITHER FIND A WAY TO STOP THIS THING--
OR VAPORIZE IT!
YESSIR.
Maine
New York
Cleveland
Ohio
Pennsylvania
Maryland
Columbus
Delaware
Virginia
ANY MINUTE NOW WOULD BE GOOD.

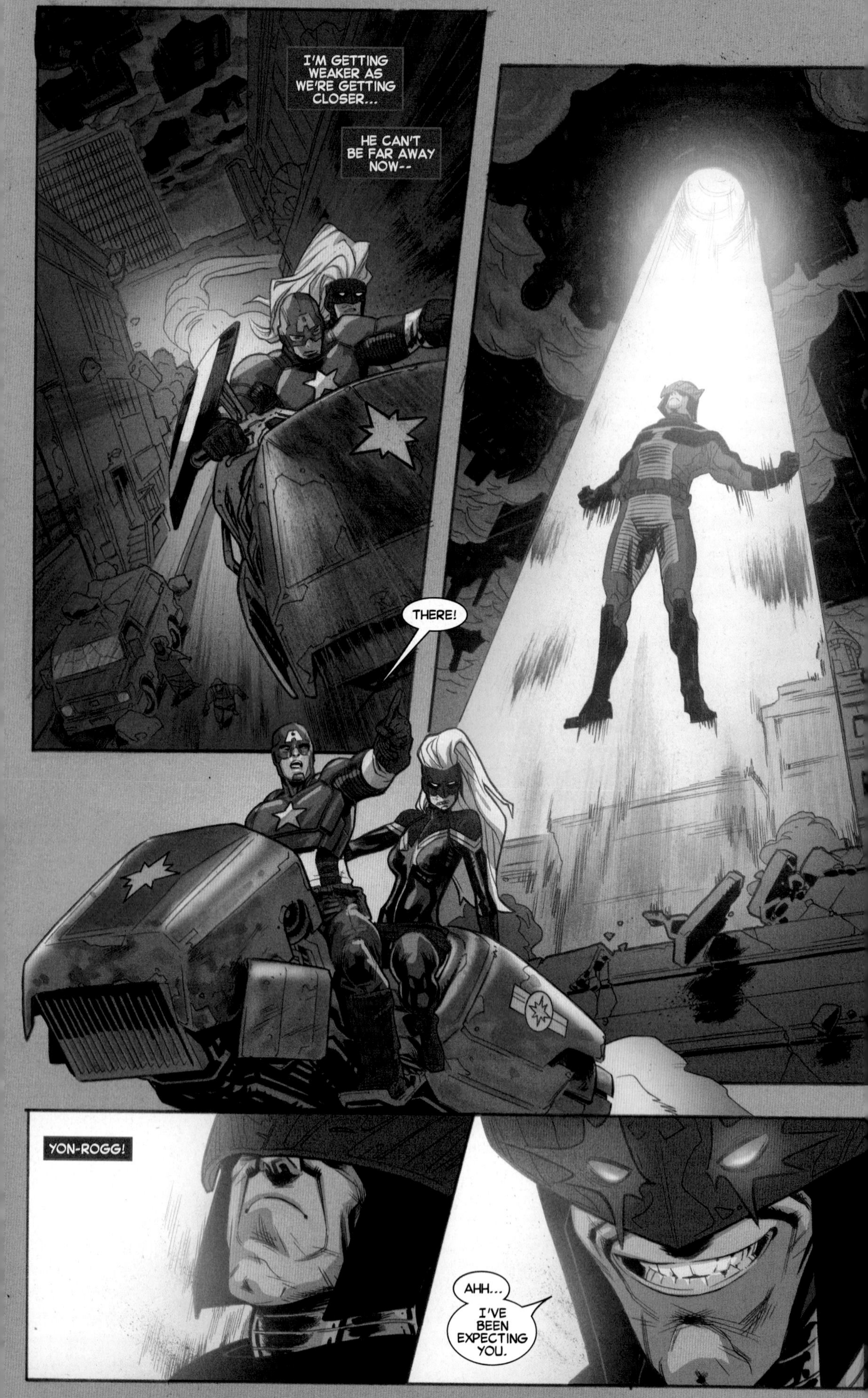
I'M GETTING WEAKER AS WE'RE GETTING CLOSER...
HE CAN'T BE FAR AWAY NOW--
THERE!
YON-ROGG!
AHH...
I'VE BEEN EXPECTING YOU.

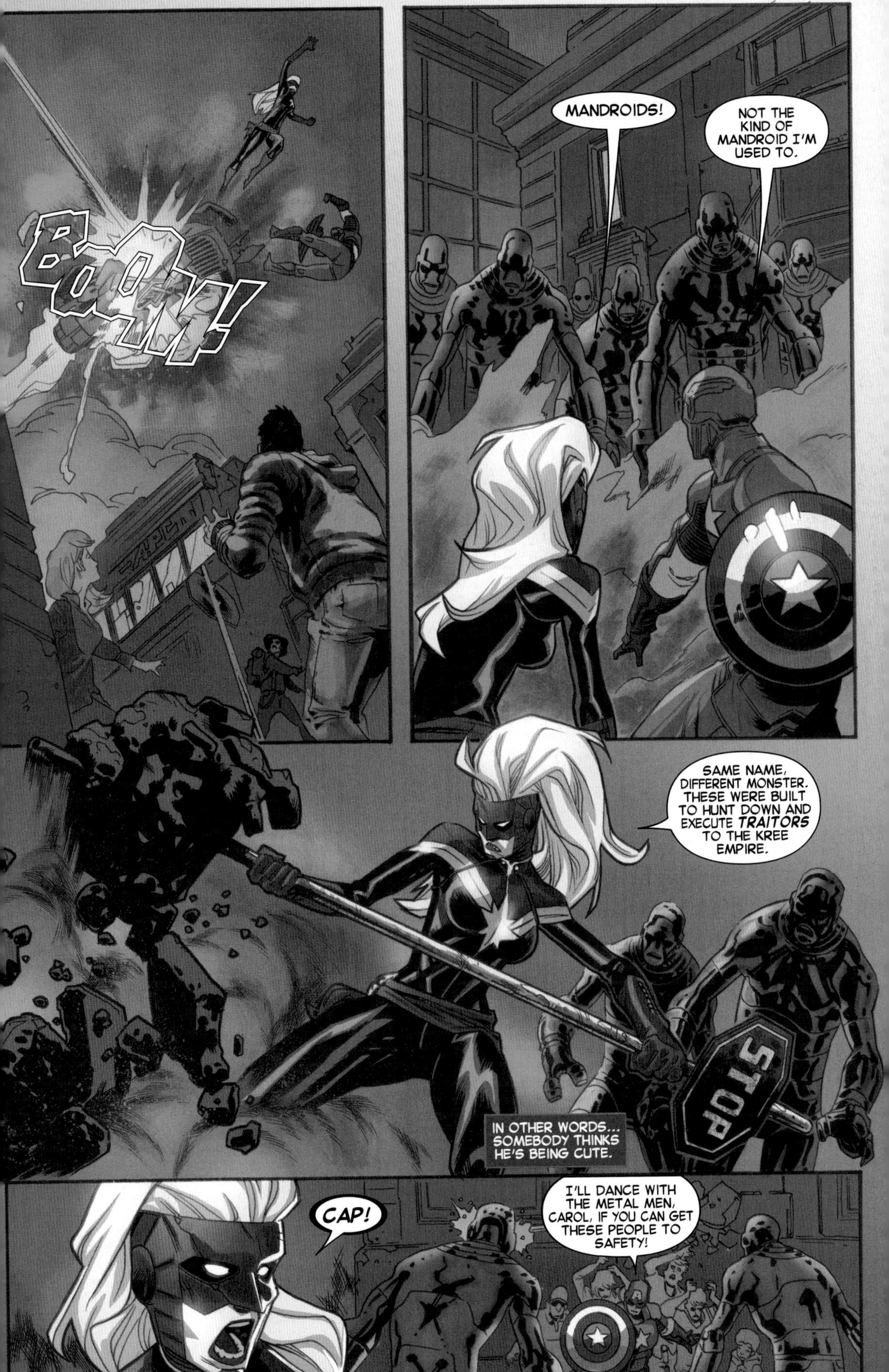
BOOM!
MANDROIDS!
NOT THE KIND OF MANDROID I'M USED TO.
SAME NAME, DIFFERENT MONSTER. THESE WERE BUILT TO HUNT DOWN AND EXECUTE TRAITORS TO THE KREE EMPIRE.
IN OTHER WORDS... SOMEBODY THINKS HE'S BEING CUTE.
STOP
CAP!
I'LL DANCE WITH THE METAL MEN, CAROL, IF YOU CAN GET THESE PEOPLE TO SAFETY!

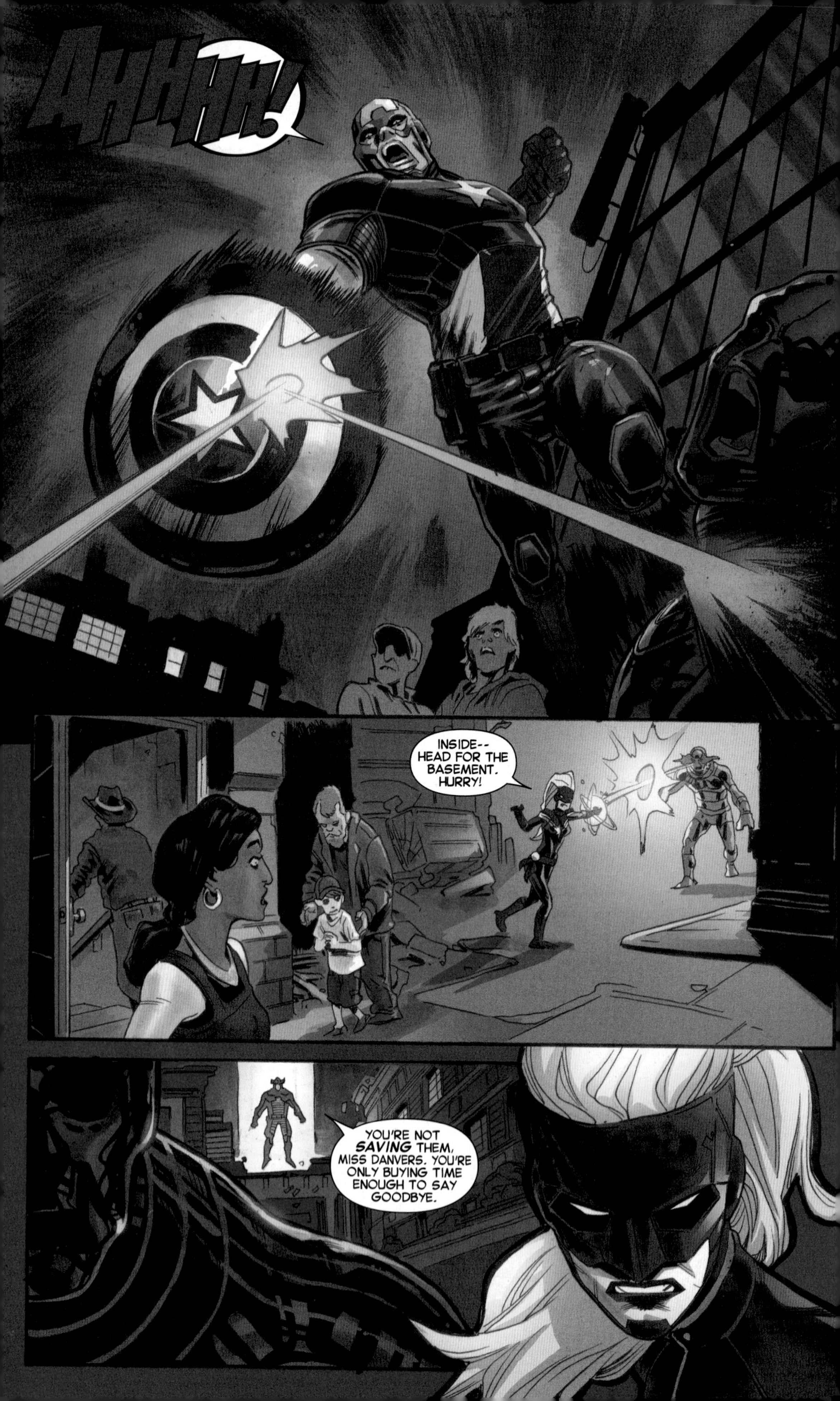
AHHHH!
INSIDE-- HEAD FOR THE BASEMENT. HURRY!
YOU'RE NOT SAVING THEM, MISS DANVERS. YOU'RE ONLY BUYING TIME ENOUGH TO SAY GOODBYE.

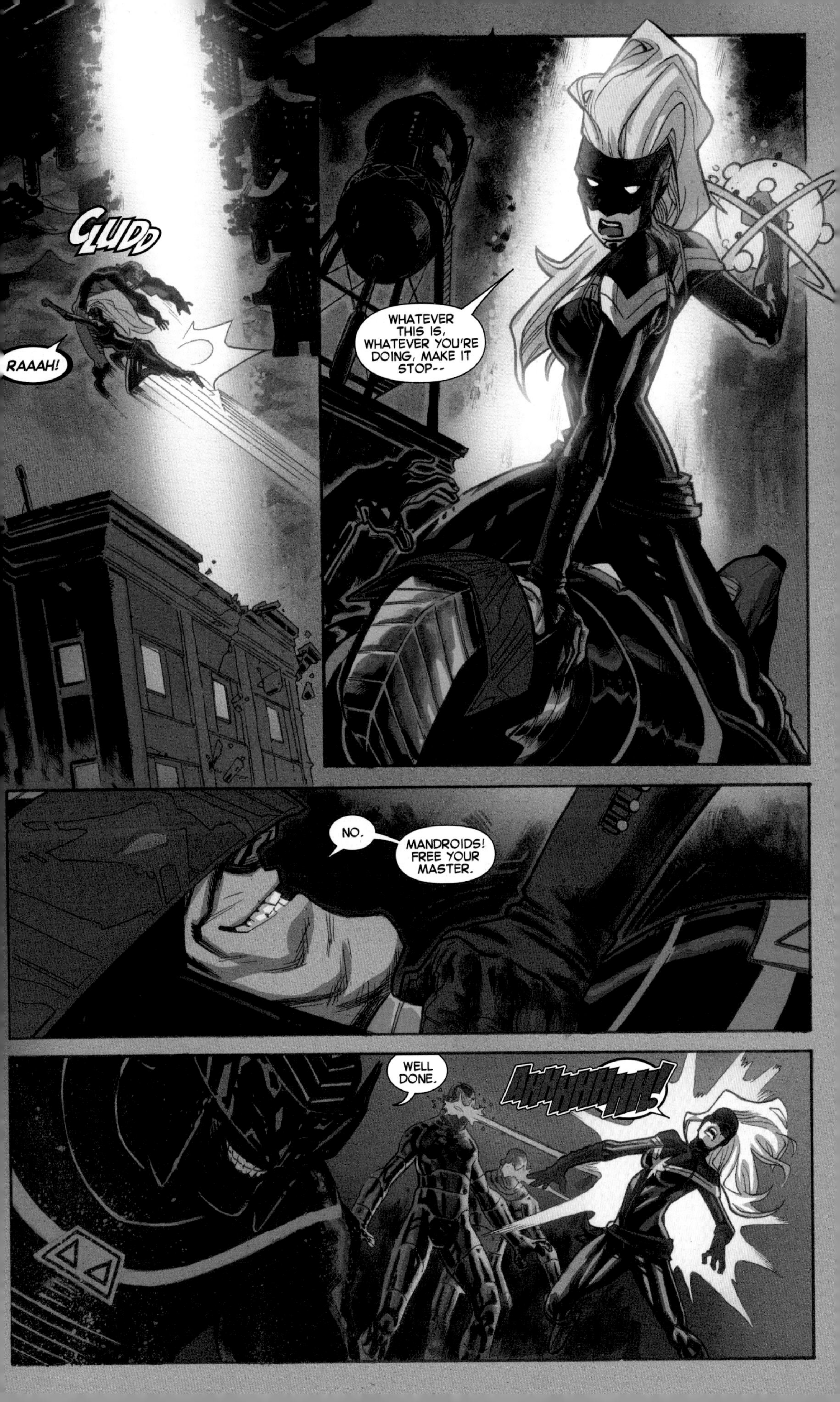
CLUDD
RAAAH!
WHATEVER THIS IS, WHATEVER YOU'RE DOING, MAKE IT STOP--
NO.
MANDROIDS! FREE YOUR MASTER.
WELL DONE.
AHHHHHHH!

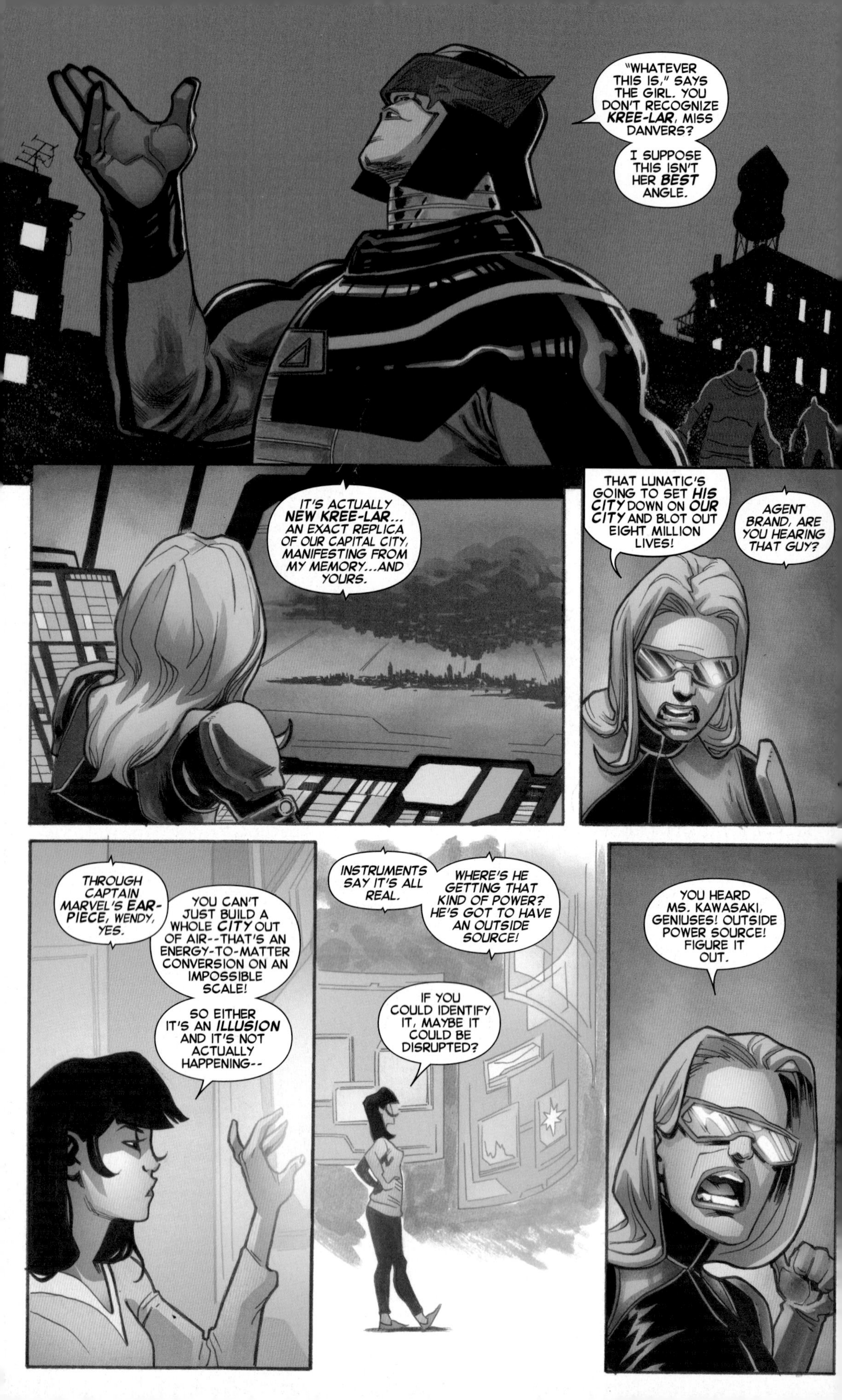
"WHATEVER THIS IS," SAYS THE GIRL. YOU DON'T RECOGNIZE KREE-LAR, MISS DANVERS?
I SUPPOSE THIS ISN'T HER BEST ANGLE.
IT'S ACTUALLY NEW KREE-LAR... AN EXACT REPLICA OF OUR CAPITAL CITY, MANIFESTING FROM MY MEMORY...AND YOURS.
THAT LUNATIC'S GOING TO SET HIS CITY DOWN ON OUR CITY AND BLOT OUT EIGHT MILLION LIVES!
AGENT BRAND, ARE YOU HEARING THAT GUY?
THROUGH CAPTAIN MARVEL'S EAR-PIECE, WENDY, YES.
YOU CAN'T JUST BUILD A WHOLE CITY OUT OF AIR--THAT'S AN ENERGY-TO-MATTER CONVERSION ON AN IMPOSSIBLE SCALE!
SO EITHER IT'S AN ILLUSION AND IT'S NOT ACTUALLY HAPPENING--
INSTRUMENTS SAY IT'S ALL REAL.
WHERE'S HE GETTING THAT KIND OF POWER? HE'S GOT TO HAVE AN OUTSIDE SOURCE!
IF YOU COULD IDENTIFY IT, MAYBE IT COULD BE DISRUPTED?
YOU HEARD MS. KAWASAKI, GENIUSES! OUTSIDE POWER SOURCE! FIGURE IT OUT.

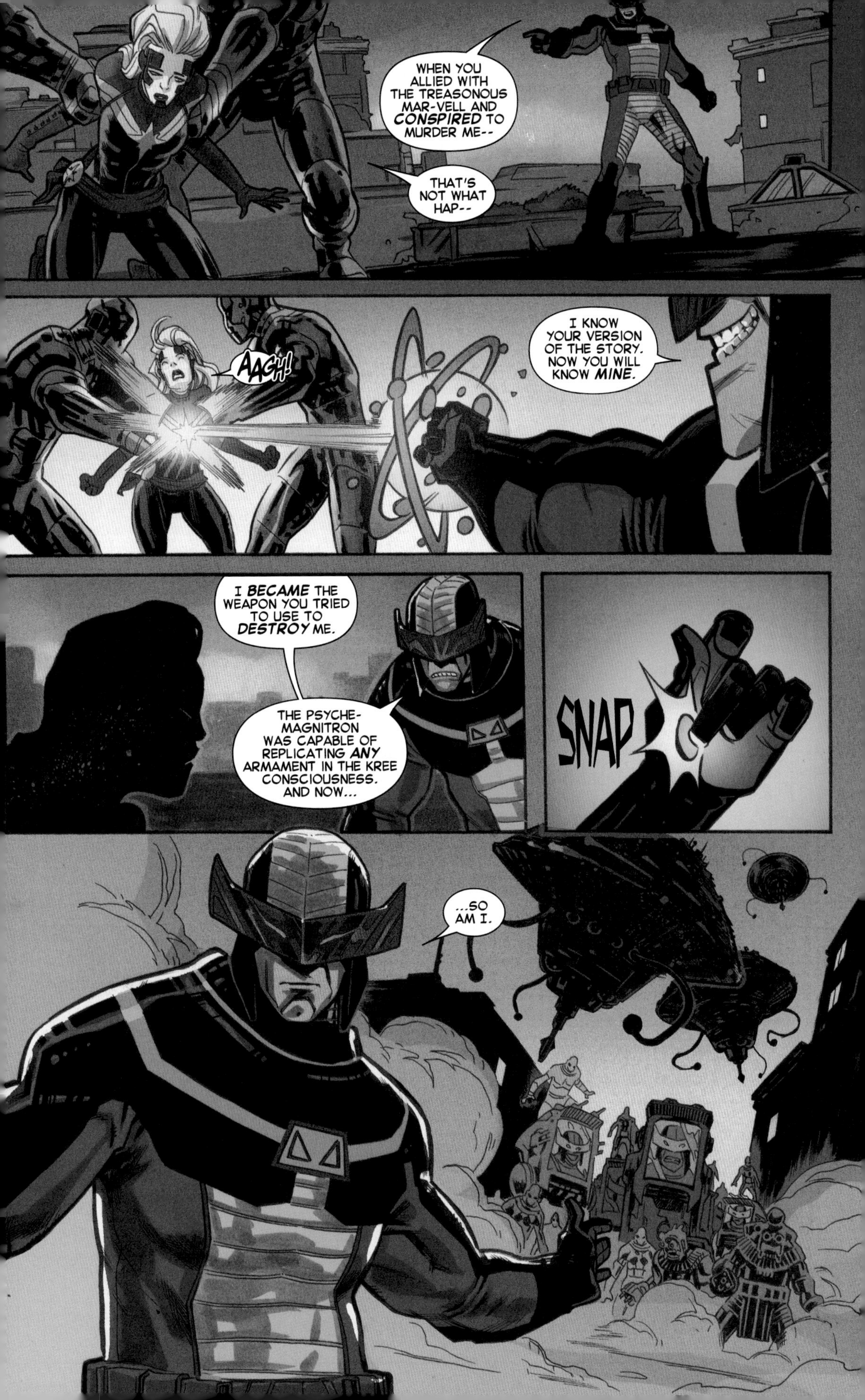
WHEN YOU ALLIED WITH THE TREASONOUS MAR-VELL AND CONSPIRED TO MURDER ME--
THAT'S NOT WHAT HAP--
AAGH!
I KNOW YOUR VERSION OF THE STORY. NOW YOU WILL KNOW MINE.
I BECAME THE WEAPON YOU TRIED TO USE TO DESTROY ME.
THE PSYCHE-MAGNITRON WAS CAPABLE OF REPLICATING ANY ARMAMENT IN THE KREE CONSCIOUSNESS. AND NOW...
SNAP
...SO AM I.

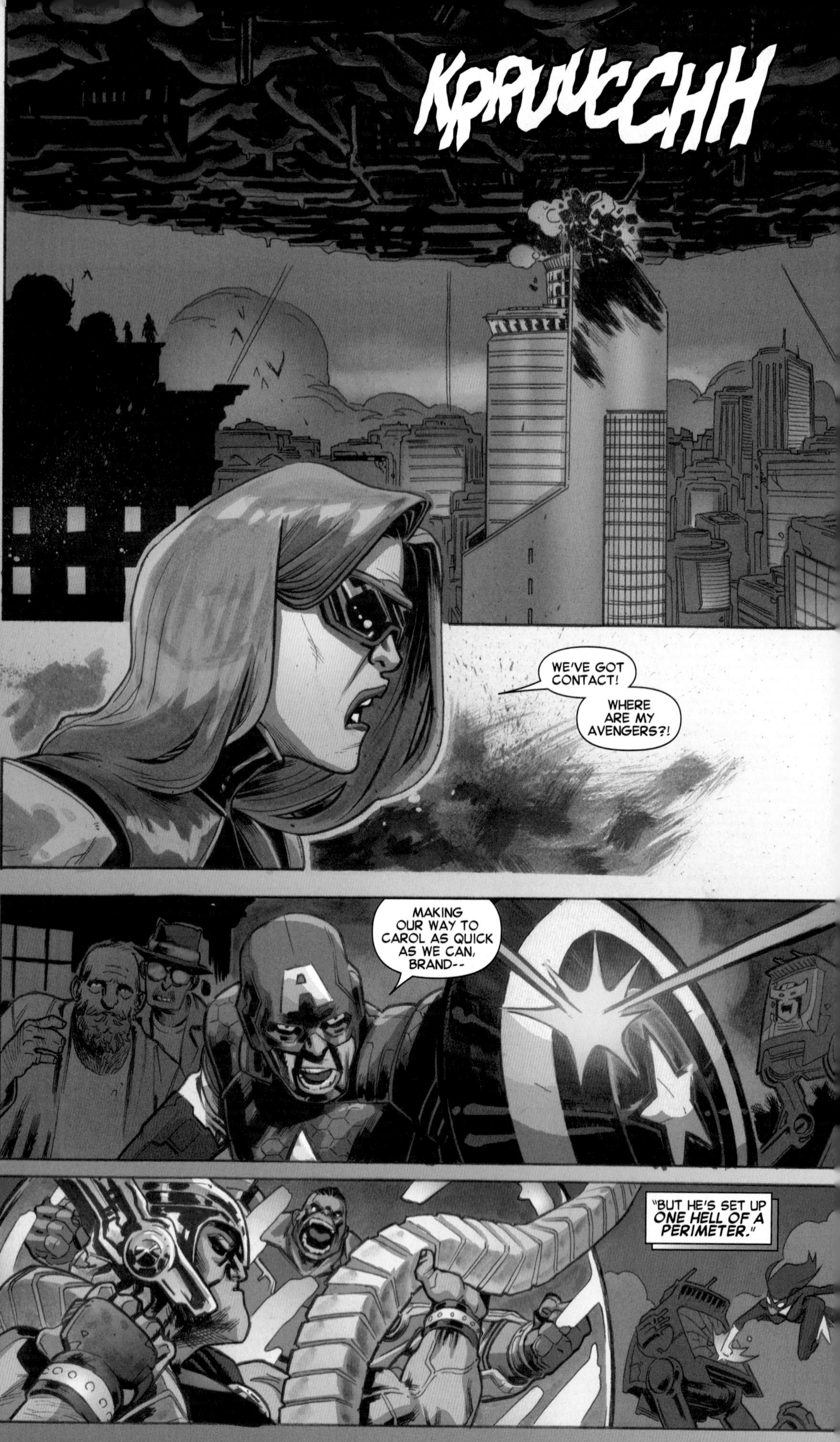
KRRUUCCHH
WE'VE GOT CONTACT!
WHERE ARE MY AVENGERS?!
MAKING OUR WAY TO CAROL AS QUICK AS WE CAN, BRAND--
"BUT HE'S SET UP ONE HELL OF A PERIMETER."

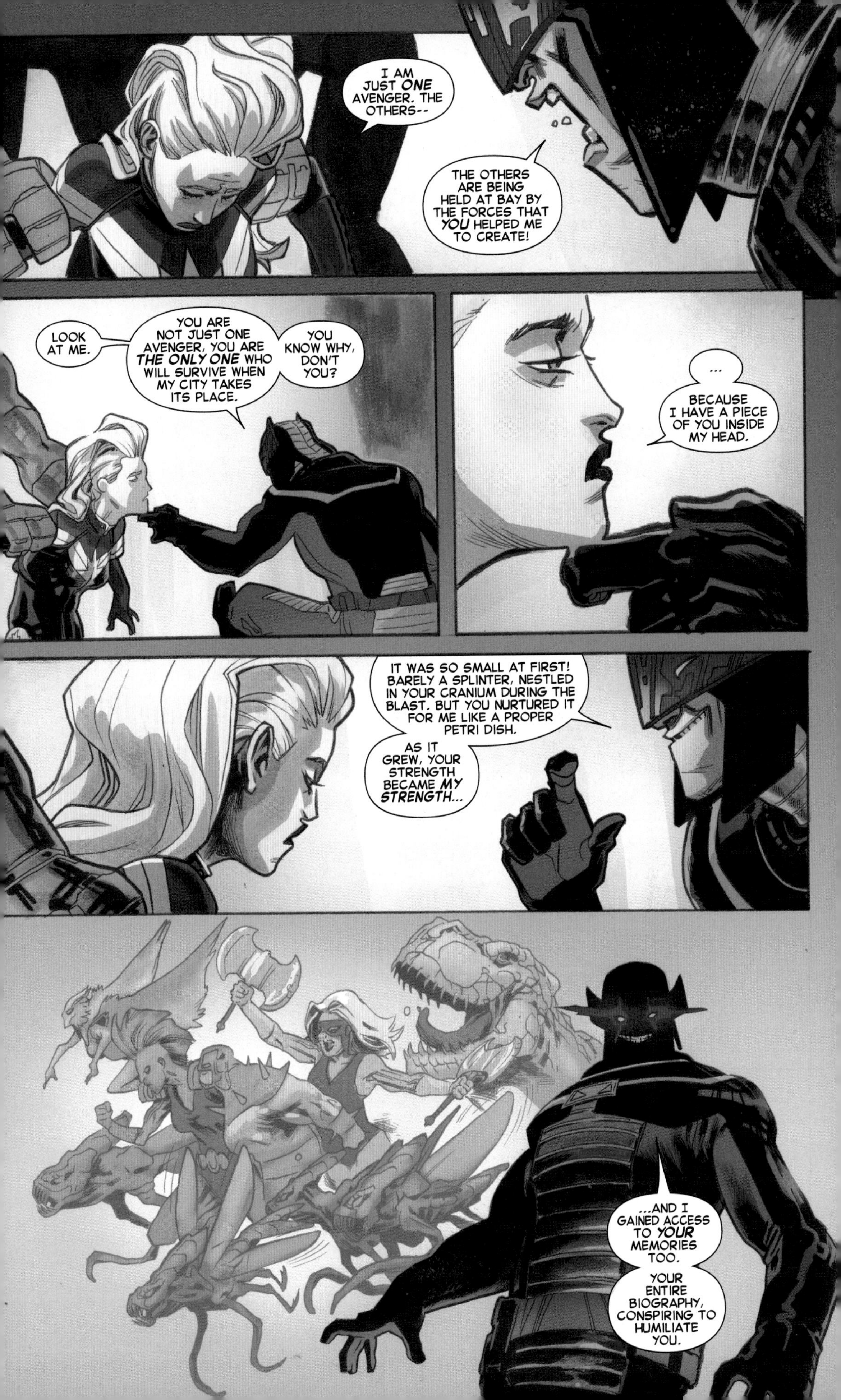
I AM JUST ONE AVENGER. THE OTHERS--
THE OTHERS ARE BEING HELD AT BAY BY THE FORCES THAT YOU HELPED ME TO CREATE!
LOOK AT ME.
YOU ARE NOT JUST ONE AVENGER, YOU ARE THE ONLY ONE WHO WILL SURVIVE WHEN MY CITY TAKES ITS PLACE.
YOU KNOW WHY, DON'T YOU?
...
BECAUSE I HAVE A PIECE OF YOU INSIDE MY HEAD.
IT WAS SO SMALL AT FIRST! BARELY A SPLINTER, NESTLED IN YOUR CRANIUM DURING THE BLAST. BUT YOU NURTURED IT FOR ME LIKE A PROPER PETRI DISH.
AS IT GREW, YOUR STRENGTH BECAME MY STRENGTH...
...AND I GAINED ACCESS TO YOUR MEMORIES TOO.
YOUR ENTIRE BIOGRAPHY, CONSPIRING TO HUMILIATE YOU.

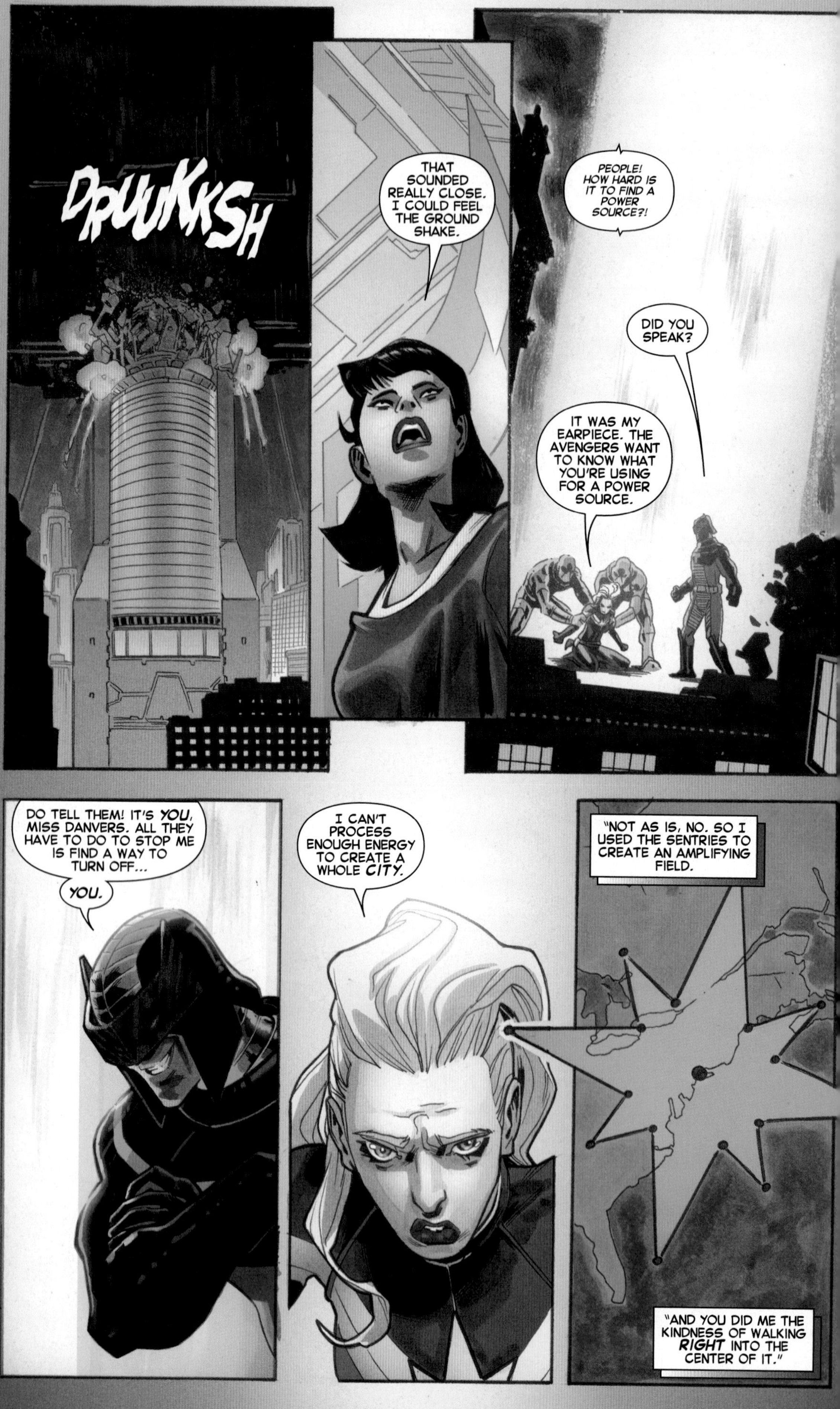
DRUUKKSH
THAT SOUNDED REALLY CLOSE. I COULD FEEL THE GROUND SHAKE.
PEOPLE! HOW HARD IS IT TO FIND A POWER SOURCE?!
DID YOU SPEAK?
IT WAS MY EARPIECE. THE AVENGERS WANT TO KNOW WHAT YOU'RE USING FOR A POWER SOURCE.
DO TELL THEM! IT'S YOU, MISS DANVERS. ALL THEY HAVE TO DO TO STOP ME IS FIND A WAY TO TURN OFF...
YOU.
I CAN'T PROCESS ENOUGH ENERGY TO CREATE A WHOLE CITY.
"NOT AS IS, NO. SO I USED THE SENTRIES TO CREATE AN AMPLIFYING FIELD.
"AND YOU DID ME THE KINDNESS OF WALKING RIGHT INTO THE CENTER OF IT."

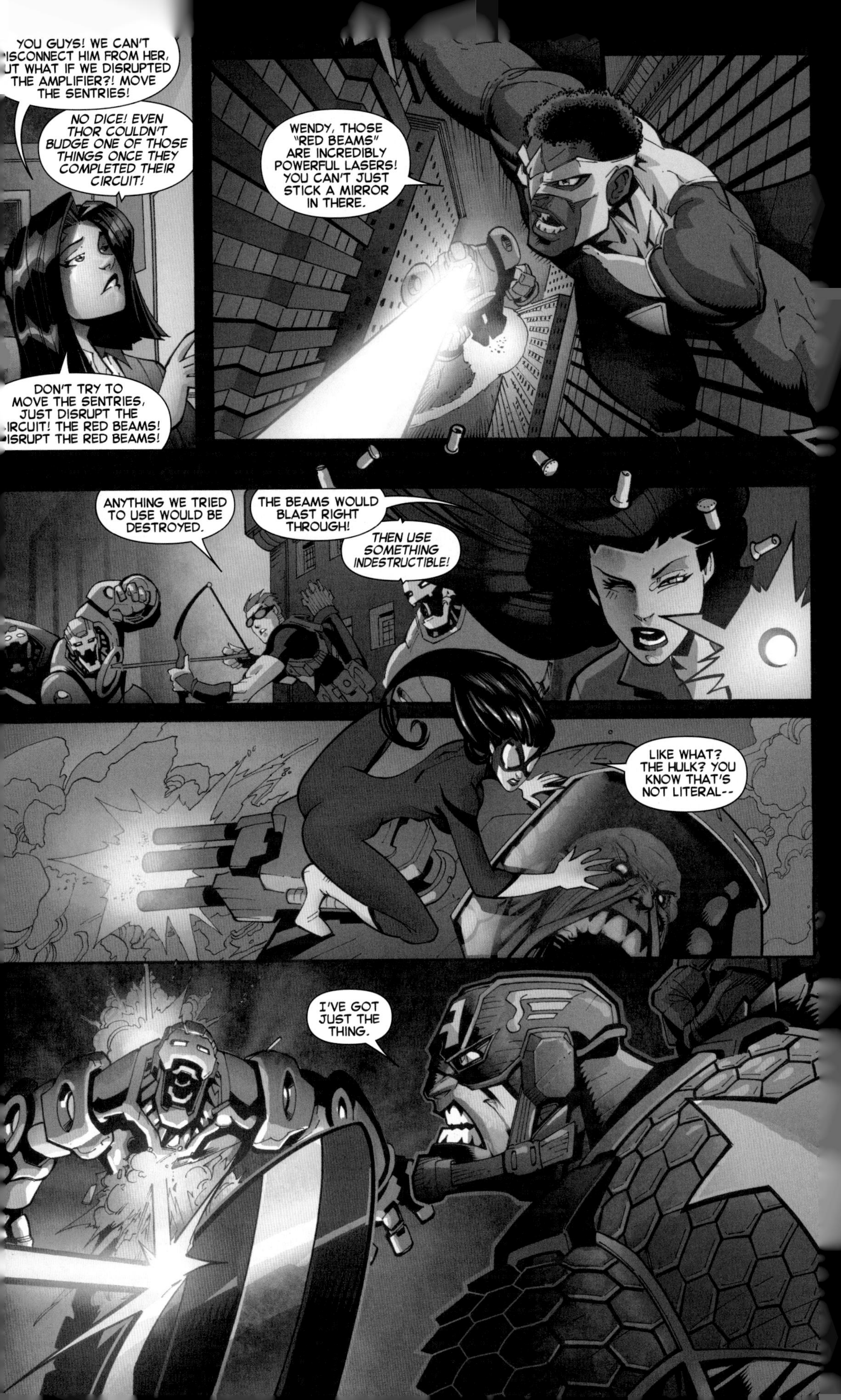

YOU GUYS! WE CAN'T DISCONNECT HIM FROM HER, BUT WHAT IF WE DISRUPTED THE AMPLIFIER?! MOVE THE SENTRIES!
NO DICE! EVEN THOR COULDN'T BUDGE ONE OF THOSE THINGS ONCE THEY COMPLETED THEIR CIRCUIT!
DON'T TRY TO MOVE THE SENTRIES, JUST DISRUPT THE CIRCUIT! THE RED BEAMS! DISRUPT THE RED BEAMS!
WENDY, THOSE "RED BEAMS" ARE INCREDIBLY POWERFUL LASERS! YOU CAN'T JUST STICK A MIRROR IN THERE.
ANYTHING WE TRIED TO USE WOULD BE DESTROYED.
THE BEAMS WOULD BLAST RIGHT THROUGH!
THEN USE SOMETHING INDESTRUCTIBLE!
LIKE WHAT? THE HULK? YOU KNOW THAT'S NOT LITERAL--
I'VE GOT JUST THE THING.

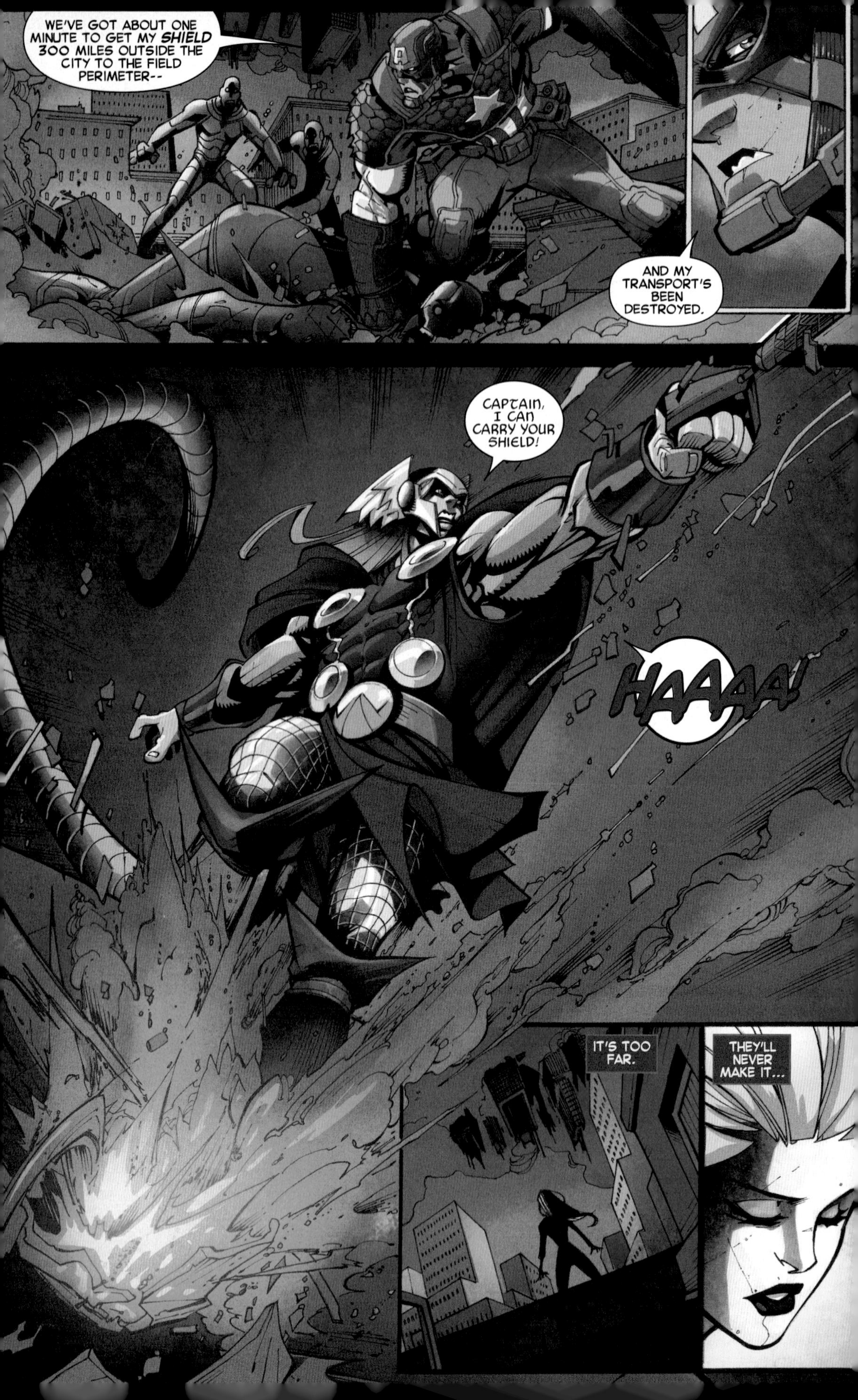
WE'VE GOT ABOUT ONE MINUTE TO GET MY SHIELD 300 MILES OUTSIDE THE CITY TO THE FIELD PERIMETER--
AND MY TRANSPORT'S BEEN DESTROYED.
CAPTAIN, I CAN CARRY YOUR SHIELD!
HAAAA!
IT'S TOO FAR.
THEY'LL NEVER MAKE IT...

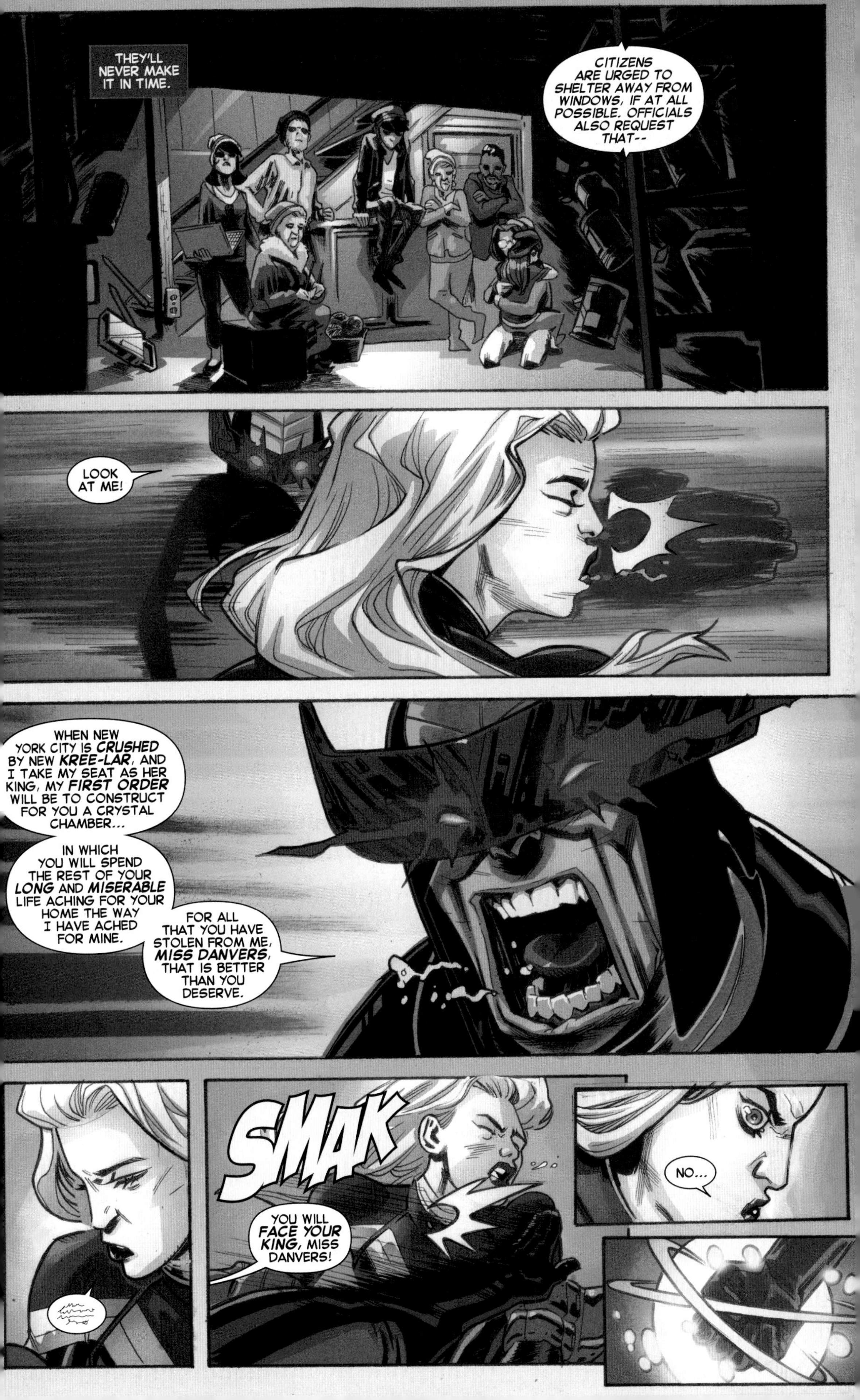
THEY'LL NEVER MAKE IT IN TIME.
CITIZENS ARE URGED TO SHELTER AWAY FROM WINDOWS, IF AT ALL POSSIBLE. OFFICIALS ALSO REQUEST THAT--
LOOK AT ME!
WHEN NEW YORK CITY IS CRUSHED BY NEW KREE-LAR, AND I TAKE MY SEAT AS HER KING, MY FIRST ORDER WILL BE TO CONSTRUCT FOR YOU A CRYSTAL CHAMBER...
IN WHICH YOU WILL SPEND THE REST OF YOUR LONG AND MISERABLE LIFE ACHING FOR YOUR HOME THE WAY I HAVE ACHED FOR MINE.
FOR ALL THAT YOU HAVE STOLEN FROM ME, MISS DANVERS, THAT IS BETTER THAN YOU DESERVE.
SMAK
YOU WILL FACE YOUR KING, MISS DANVERS!
NO...

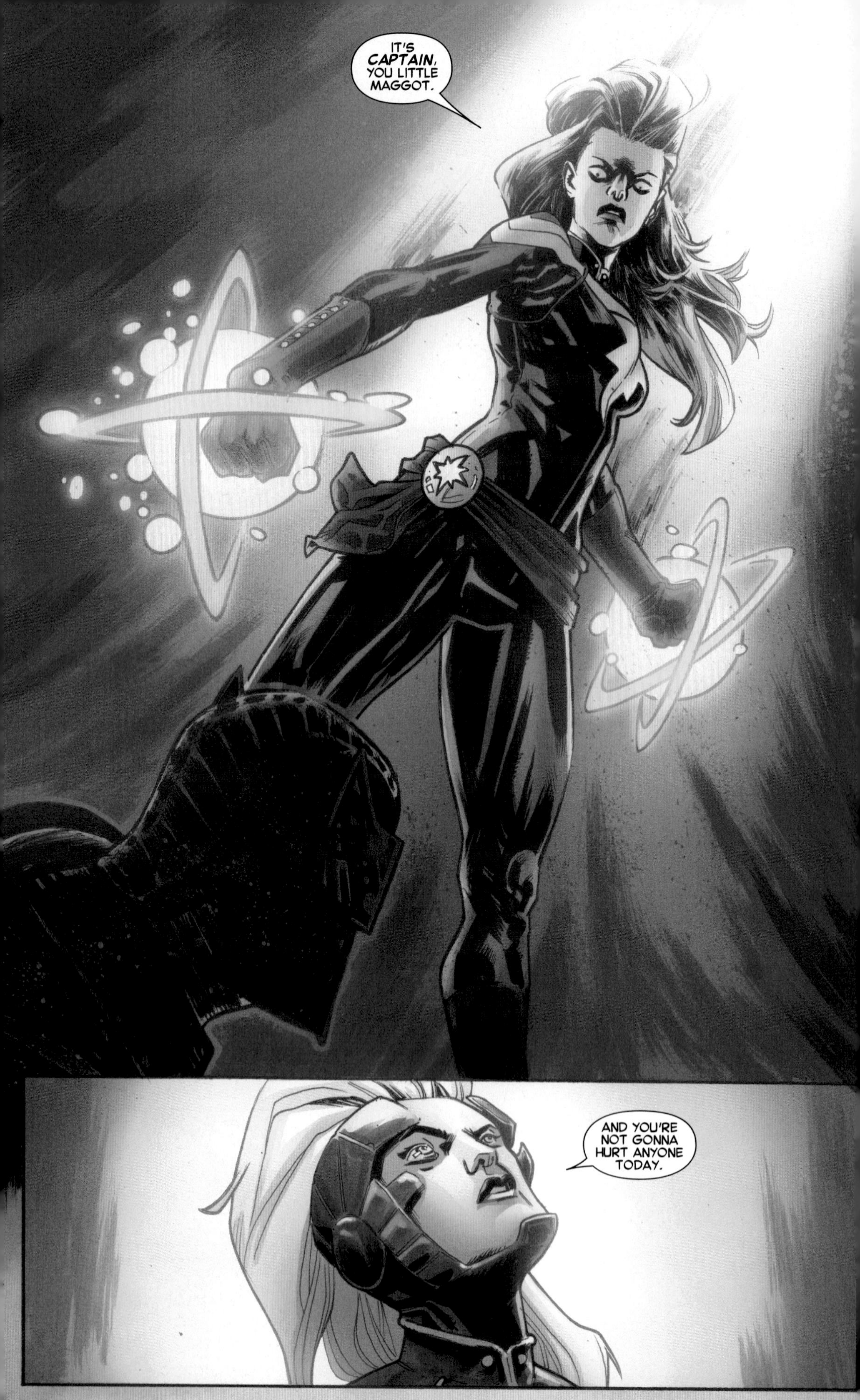
IT'S CAPTAIN, YOU LITTLE MAGGOT.
AND YOU'RE NOT GONNA HURT ANYONE TODAY.

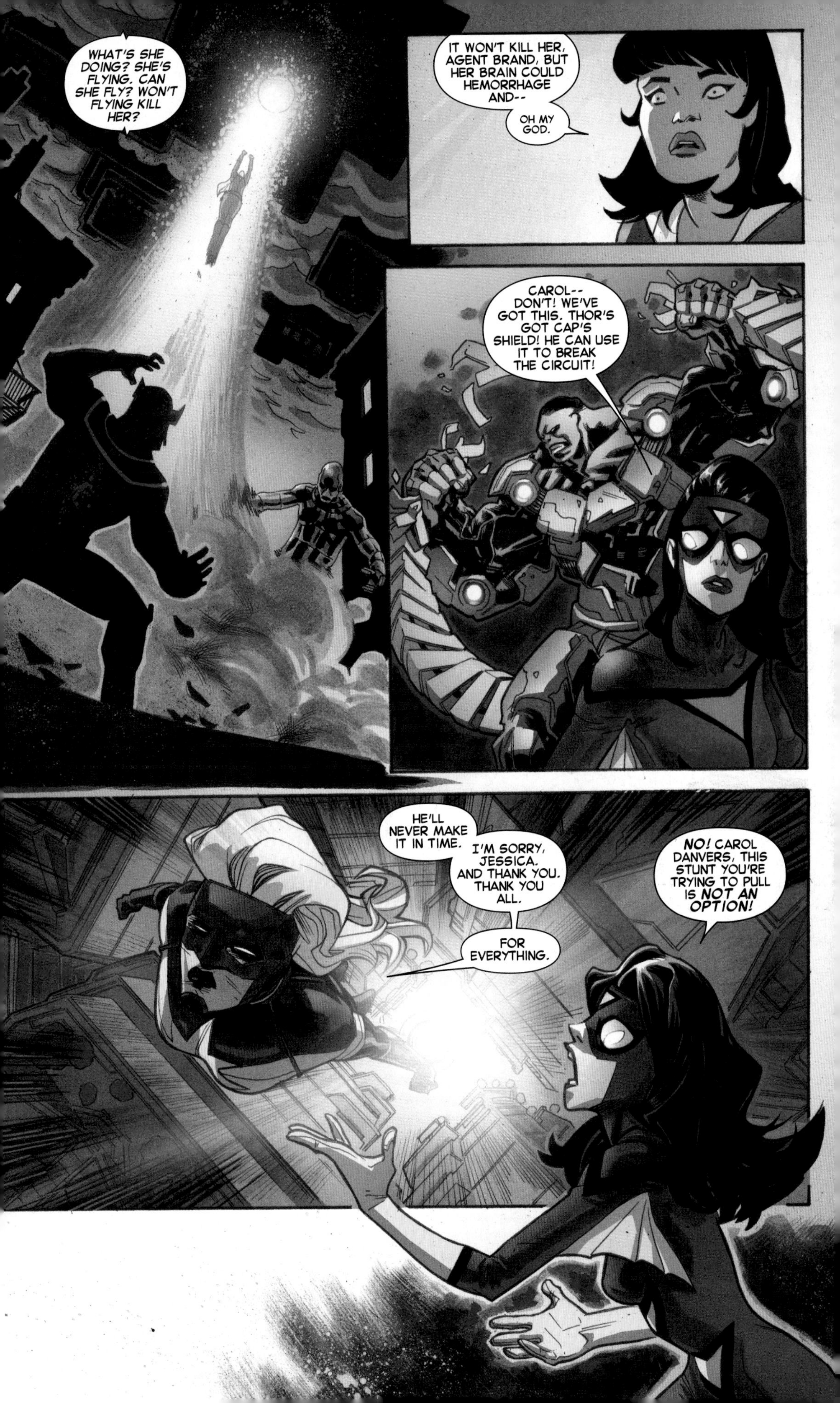
WHAT'S SHE DOING? SHE'S FLYING. CAN SHE FLY? WON'T FLYING KILL HER?
IT WON'T KILL HER, AGENT BRAND, BUT HER BRAIN COULD HEMORRHAGE AND--
OH MY GOD.
CAROL-- DON'T! WE'VE GOT THIS. THOR'S GOT CAP'S SHIELD! HE CAN USE IT TO BREAK THE CIRCUIT!
HE'LL NEVER MAKE IT IN TIME.
I'M SORRY, JESSICA. AND THANK YOU. THANK YOU ALL.
FOR EVERYTHING.
NO! CAROL DANVERS, THIS STUNT YOU'RE TRYING TO PULL IS NOT AN OPTION!

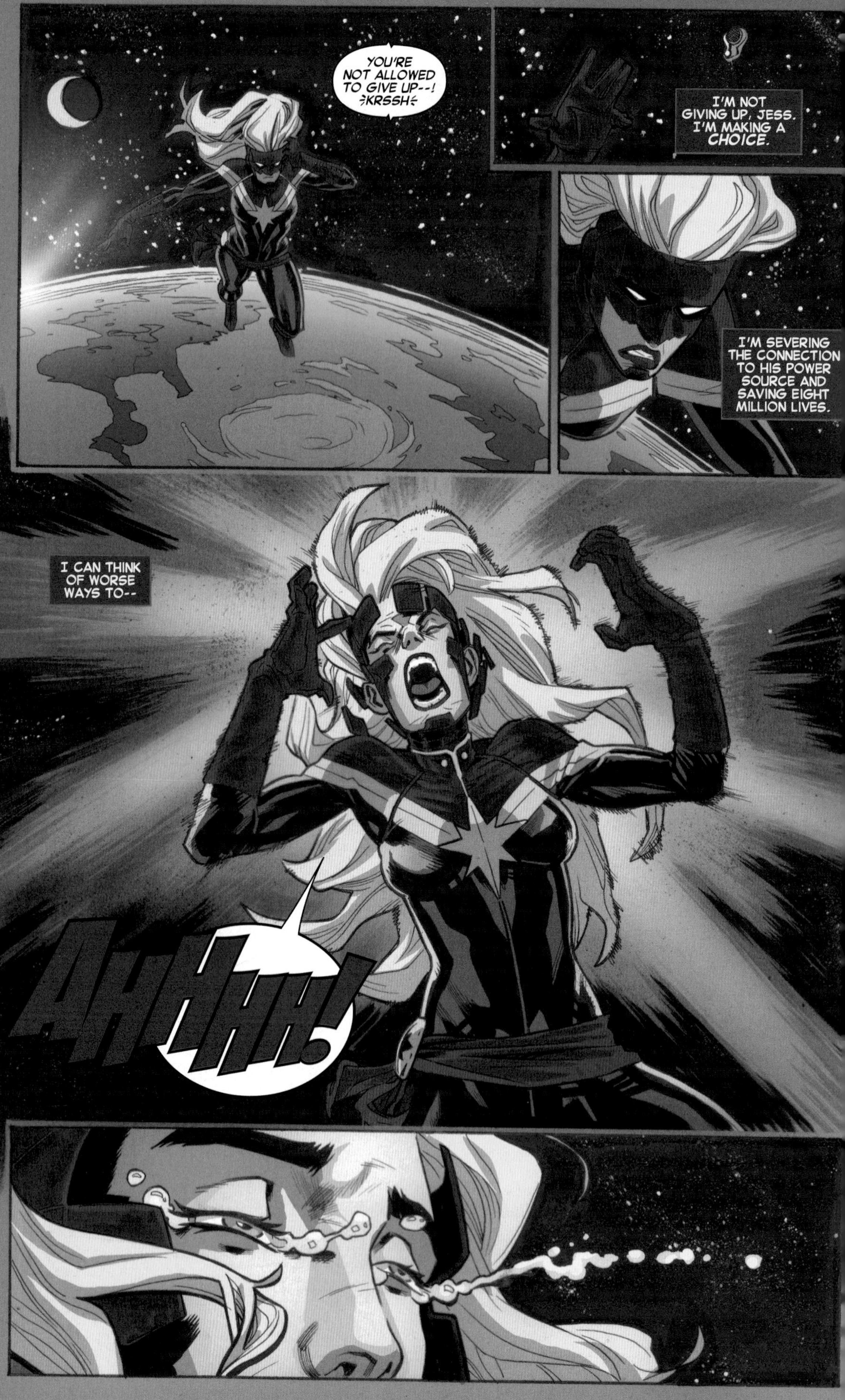

YOU'RE NOT ALLOWED TO GIVE UP--! ⚡KRSSH⚡
I'M NOT GIVING UP, JESS. I'M MAKING A CHOICE.
I'M SEVERING THE CONNECTION TO HIS POWER SOURCE AND SAVING EIGHT MILLION LIVES.
I CAN THINK OF WORSE WAYS TO--
AHHHH!

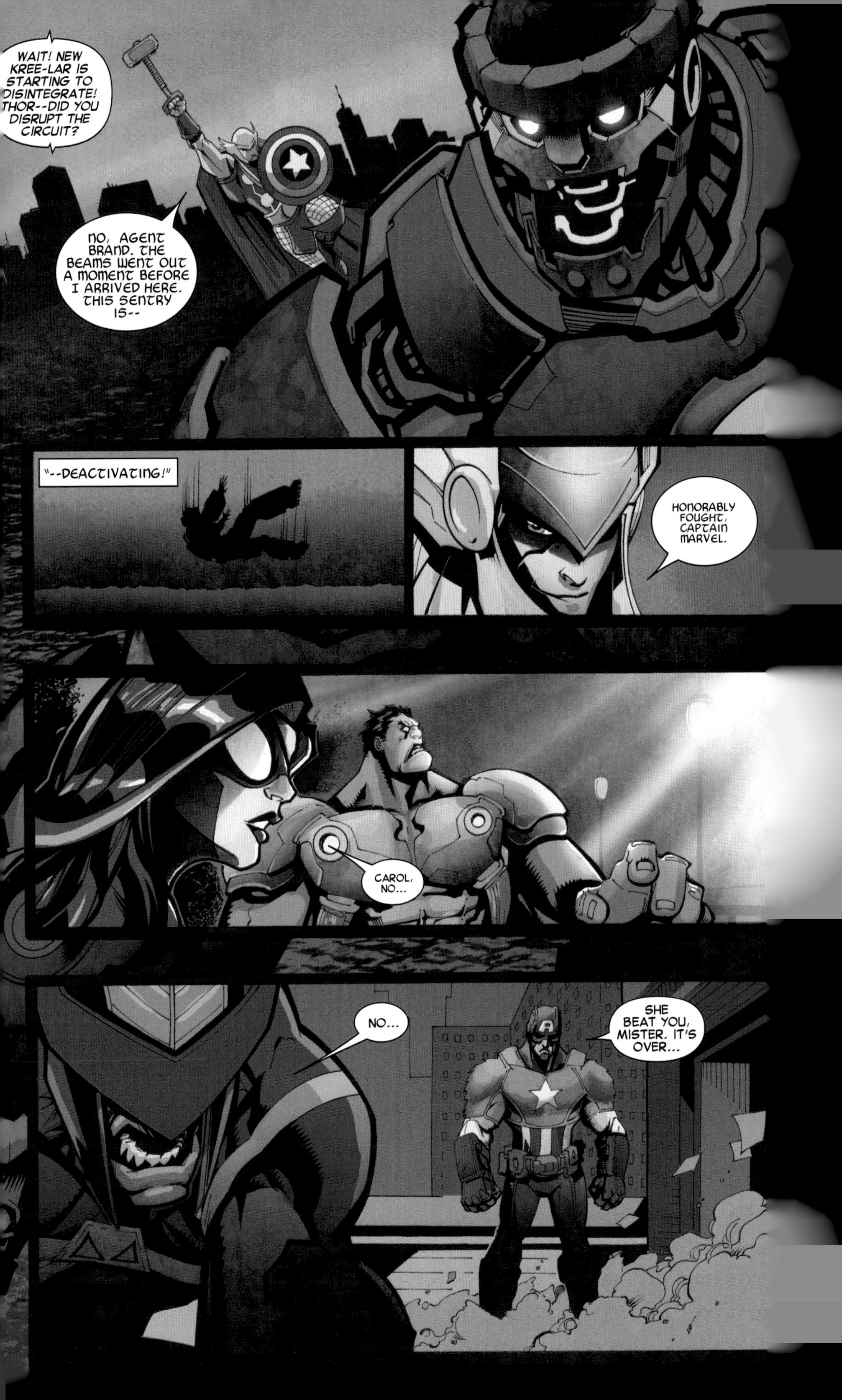
WAIT! NEW KREE-LAR IS STARTING TO DISINTEGRATE! THOR--DID YOU DISRUPT THE CIRCUIT?
NO, AGENT BRAND. THE BEAMS WENT OUT A MOMENT BEFORE I ARRIVED HERE. THIS SENTRY IS--
"--DEACTIVATING!"
HONORABLY FOUGHT, CAPTAIN MARVEL.
CAROL, NO...
NO...
SHE BEAT YOU, MISTER. IT'S OVER...

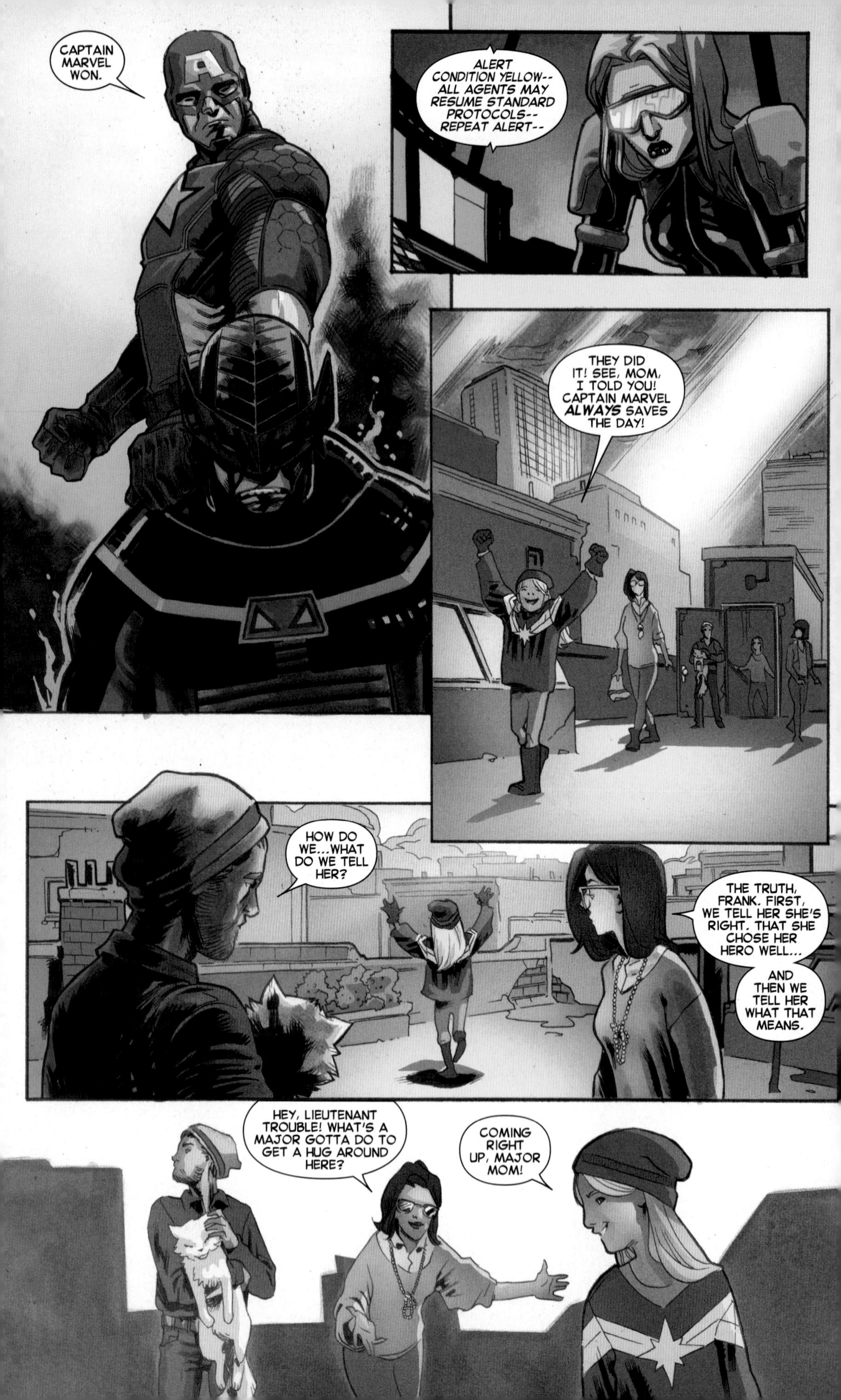
CAPTAIN MARVEL WON.
ALERT CONDITION YELLOW-- ALL AGENTS MAY RESUME STANDARD PROTOCOLS-- REPEAT ALERT--
THEY DID IT! SEE, MOM, I TOLD YOU! CAPTAIN MARVEL ALWAYS SAVES THE DAY!
HOW DO WE...WHAT DO WE TELL HER?
THE TRUTH, FRANK. FIRST, WE TELL HER SHE'S RIGHT. THAT SHE CHOSE HER HERO WELL...
AND THEN WE TELL HER WHAT THAT MEANS.
HEY, LIEUTENANT TROUBLE! WHAT'S A MAJOR GOTTA DO TO GET A HUG AROUND HERE?
COMING RIGHT UP, MAJOR MOM!

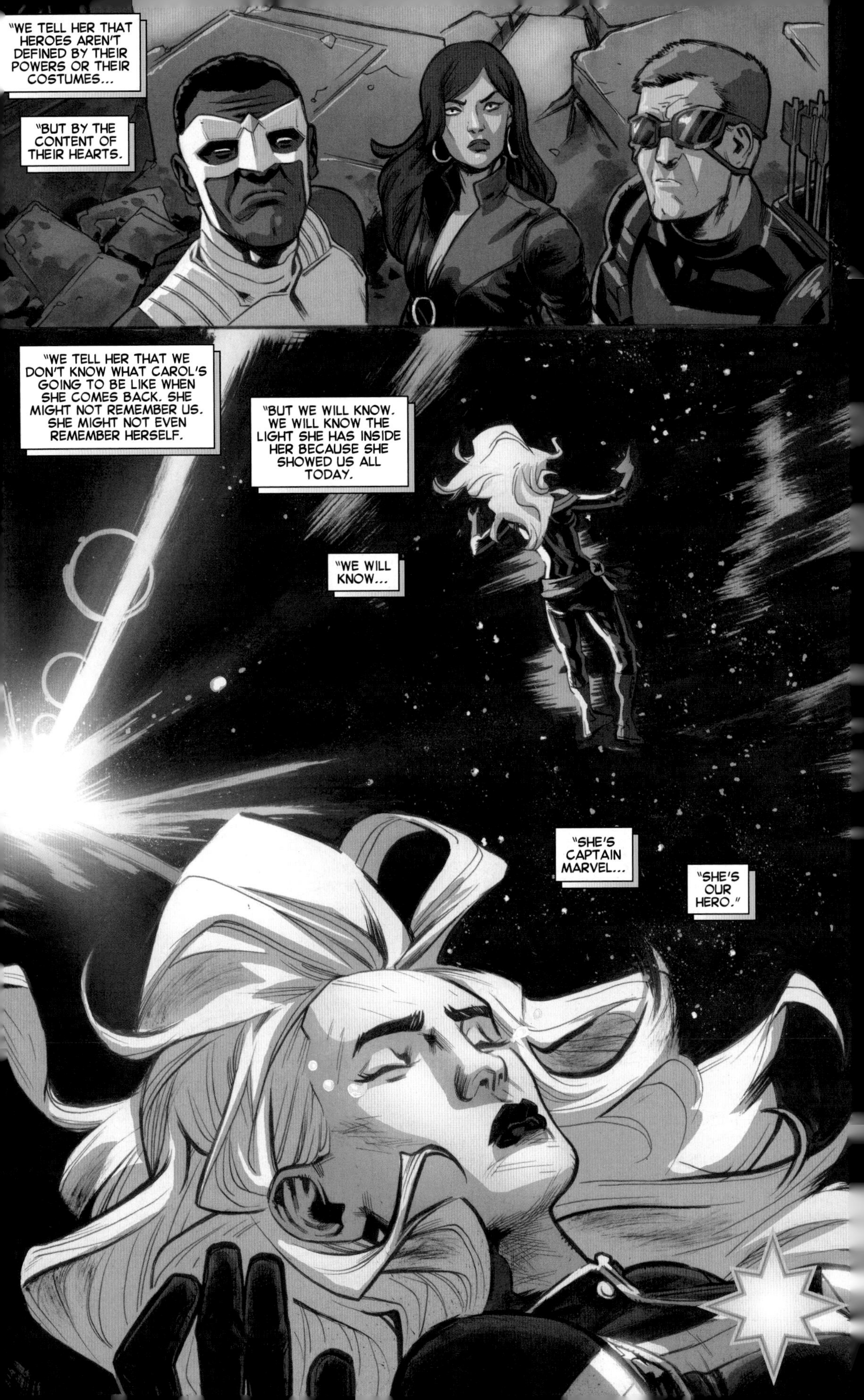
"WE TELL HER THAT HEROES AREN'T DEFINED BY THEIR POWERS OR THEIR COSTUMES...
"BUT BY THE CONTENT OF THEIR HEARTS.
"WE TELL HER THAT WE DON'T KNOW WHAT CAROL'S GOING TO BE LIKE WHEN SHE COMES BACK. SHE MIGHT NOT REMEMBER US. SHE MIGHT NOT EVEN REMEMBER HERSELF.
"BUT WE WILL KNOW. WE WILL KNOW THE LIGHT SHE HAS INSIDE HER BECAUSE SHE SHOWED US ALL TODAY.
"WE WILL KNOW...
"SHE'S CAPTAIN MARVEL...
"SHE'S OUR HERO."

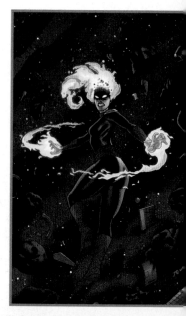

LET'S RAP WITH CAP

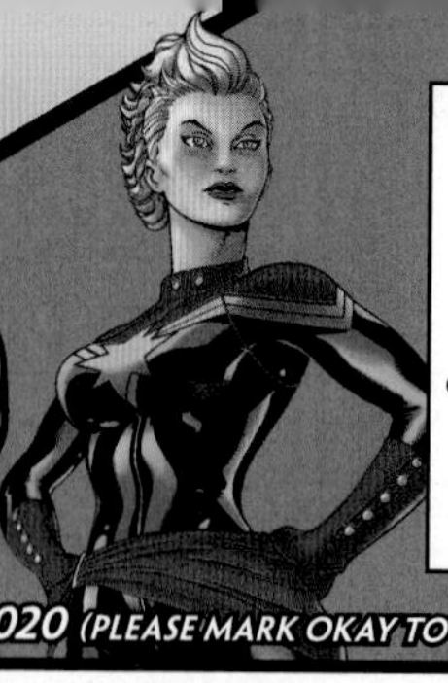

SANA AMANAT
EDITOR
STEPHEN WACKE
SENIOR EDITOR
AXEL ALONSO
EDITOR-IN-CHIEF
JOE QUESADA
CHIEF CREATIVE OFFIC
DAN BUCKLEY
PUBLISHER
ALAN FINE
EXECUTIVE PRODUCE

Send letters to:
mheroes@marvel.com • 135 W 50TH ST, 7TH FLOOR, NEW YORK, NY 10020 (PLEASE MARK OKAY TO PRINT)

Didn't think we'd end it like that, did ya? Don't worry we did NOT kill Captain Marvel. If you missed the previews, Carol's about to jump into an Infinity adventure next month. However, she will be slightly different the next time you see her. That's all I'm sharing for now–even if you try to bribe me with cookies or chocolate covered strawberries or something–I'll never tell! But I mean, no harm in *trying* (strawberries are in season, bt-dubs).

I think that Carol's strength as a hero has little to do with her actual powers and more to do with what she chooses to do with them—protect those she loves. As her little protégé Kit stood by and watched her beloved champion beat the bad guy once again, I started wondering what it actually meant to be someone's hero. Recently, my niece Zayna made my heart melt when she named me her hero for a school project and presented me with this swanky award:

HILLDALE HERO
this certificate is awarded to:
SANA AMANAT
in honor of

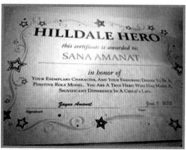

Usually this is where I'd turn into a braggart, but I was honestly so touched by the gesture—and confused as to why she picked me—that I was tearing throughout the ceremony. It dawned on me then that I actually have a lot of responsibility on my hands to *not screw it all up!* I have a nine-year-old niece who actually thinks I'm worthy--so now I've got to live up to that image and make sure that everything I do is a positive example for her. Until, of course, she's old enough to realize I'm a farce! (Kidding, ZZ, thanks for picking me, I love you!)

We've all got our heroes in the real world. Whether they're people who actually save lives, or people who teach you how to ride a bike—they're the ones who make you want to be a better person, too. So in the effort to honor our real life heroes, I asked the rest of the Captain Marvel team who they'd name as theirs...

I've been blessed with so many. On my mind right now, my great aunt who we call "Gamma Polly." Heroes are defined by their courage and nobility. I could spend all day telling you stories of Polly's noble acts, but it's her courage in the face of her cancer struggle that moves me to name her. She's modeling a kind of grace and compassion that doesn't just put me in awe of her, but of what we as human beings are capable of.

–Kelly Sue DeConnick

My dearest personal hero is my Dad for his constant selfless acts of kindness.

–Jordie Bellaire

I'm inspired by teachers who wake up every morning and prepare my kids for the future. With little pay and no fame, they are some of the most important people in our society.

–Steve Wacker

Jim Troy, my dad. The most intelligent person I know. My entire life, he's never answered my questions with "I don't know." Through peaks and valleys, he's always been there for me. He handles any situation, no matter how adverse, with such grace. Plus, he's extremely handsome!

–Andy Troy

When my dad came to this country at 16-years-old, his family didn't have much money and he didn't speak a word of English. Even though he was almost finished with school back in Sicily, he enrolled in high school as a freshman here in New Jersey. Four years later he went to college on a scholarship and by the time he was 35, own and operated two businesses th he'd have for 30 years. Today, h a councilman in the town he liv in. His story proves that we can anything we set our minds to if work hard, believe in ourselves a never give up!

–Joe Caramag

And mine? Well I'm bless with a lot, but I've got two amazi forces in my life—my mom a dad. They came here from Pakist in the `60s broke and alone. years later they've helped mo people financially and emotiona than I will probably ever know my life. My mother texts me poen of love every day, and my dad, no diagnosed with cancer, still wak up every morning with a smile his face and asks, "How are *you?*"

So with that, this issue dedicated to all of the heroes in o lives—thanks for making us want be the best version of ourselves.

Your turn, Carol Corps, fin someone to be an inspiration for.

Love, peace and spande
San

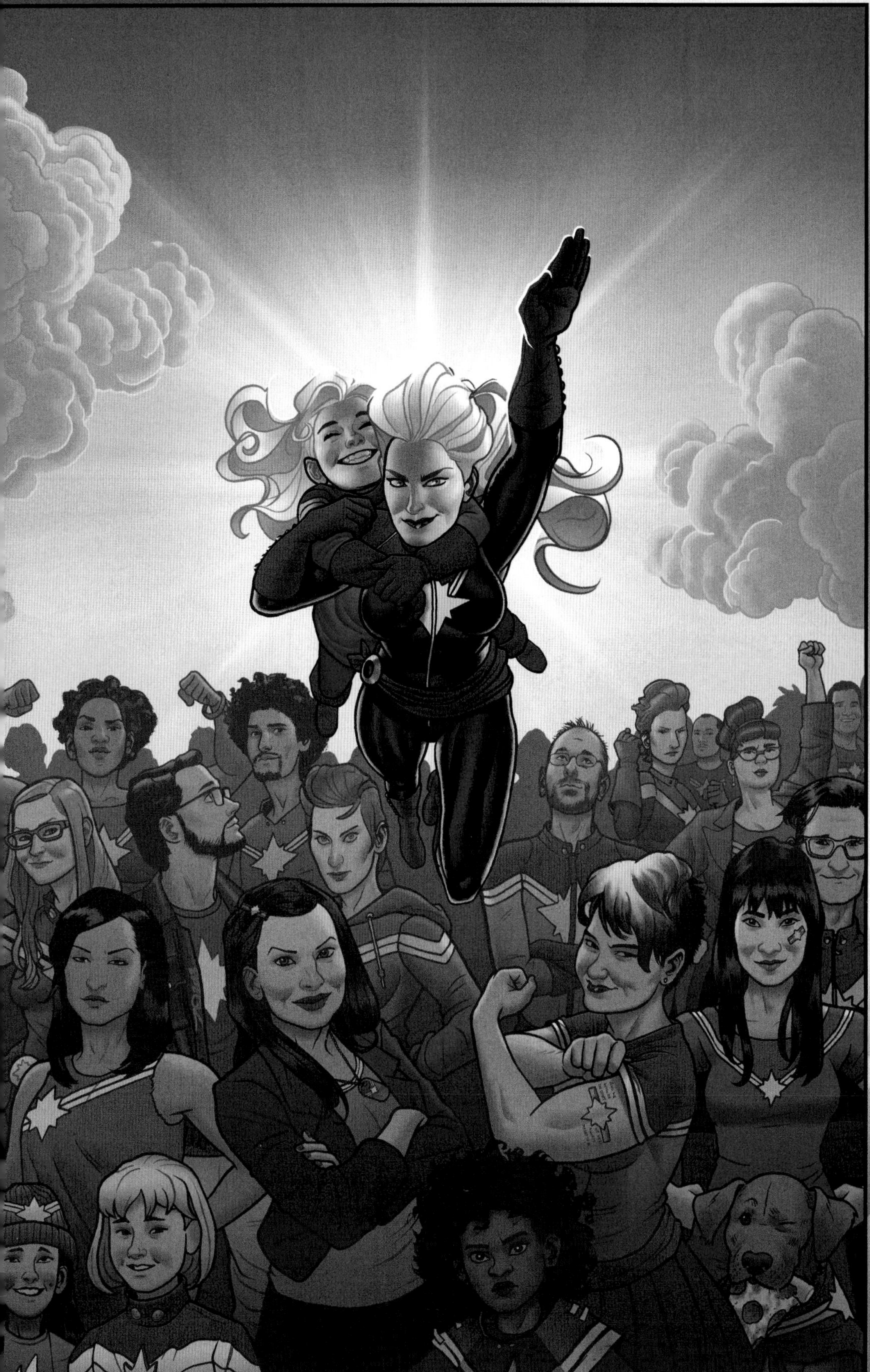

CAPTAIN MARVEL #17

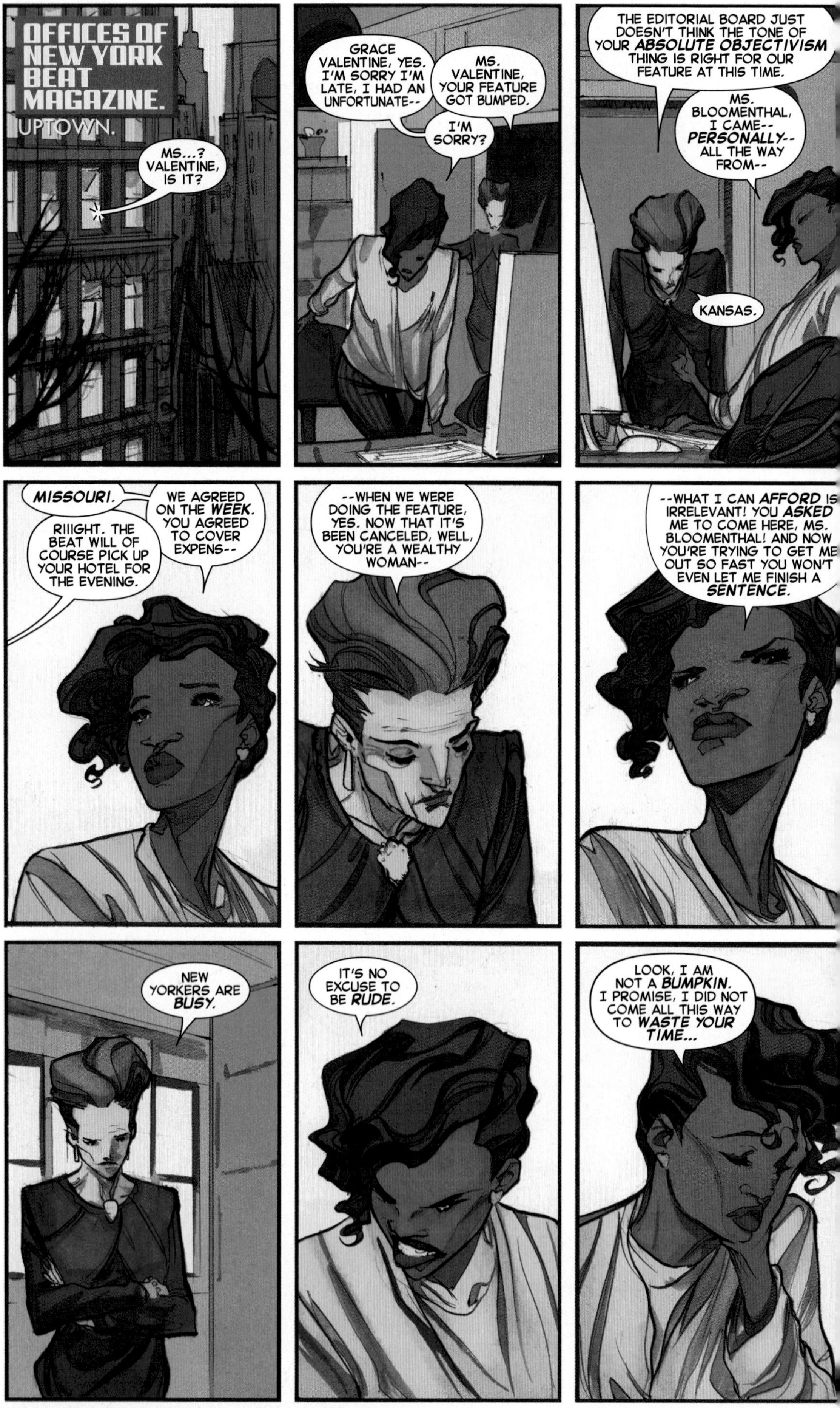
OFFICES OF NEW YORK BEAT MAGAZINE.
UPTOWN.
MS...? VALENTINE, IS IT?
GRACE VALENTINE, YES. I'M SORRY I'M LATE, I HAD AN UNFORTUNATE--
MS. VALENTINE, YOUR FEATURE GOT BUMPED.
I'M SORRY?
THE EDITORIAL BOARD JUST DOESN'T THINK THE TONE OF YOUR ABSOLUTE OBJECTIVISM THING IS RIGHT FOR OUR FEATURE AT THIS TIME.
MS. BLOOMENTHAL, I CAME-- PERSONALLY-- ALL THE WAY FROM--
KANSAS.
MISSOURI.
RIIIGHT. THE BEAT WILL OF COURSE PICK UP YOUR HOTEL FOR THE EVENING.
WE AGREED ON THE WEEK. YOU AGREED TO COVER EXPENS--
--WHEN WE WERE DOING THE FEATURE, YES. NOW THAT IT'S BEEN CANCELED, WELL, YOU'RE A WEALTHY WOMAN--
--WHAT I CAN AFFORD IS IRRELEVANT! YOU ASKED ME TO COME HERE, MS. BLOOMENTHAL! AND NOW YOU'RE TRYING TO GET ME OUT SO FAST YOU WON'T EVEN LET ME FINISH A SENTENCE.
NEW YORKERS ARE BUSY.
IT'S NO EXCUSE TO BE RUDE.
LOOK, I AM NOT A BUMPKIN. I PROMISE, I DID NOT COME ALL THIS WAY TO WASTE YOUR TIME...

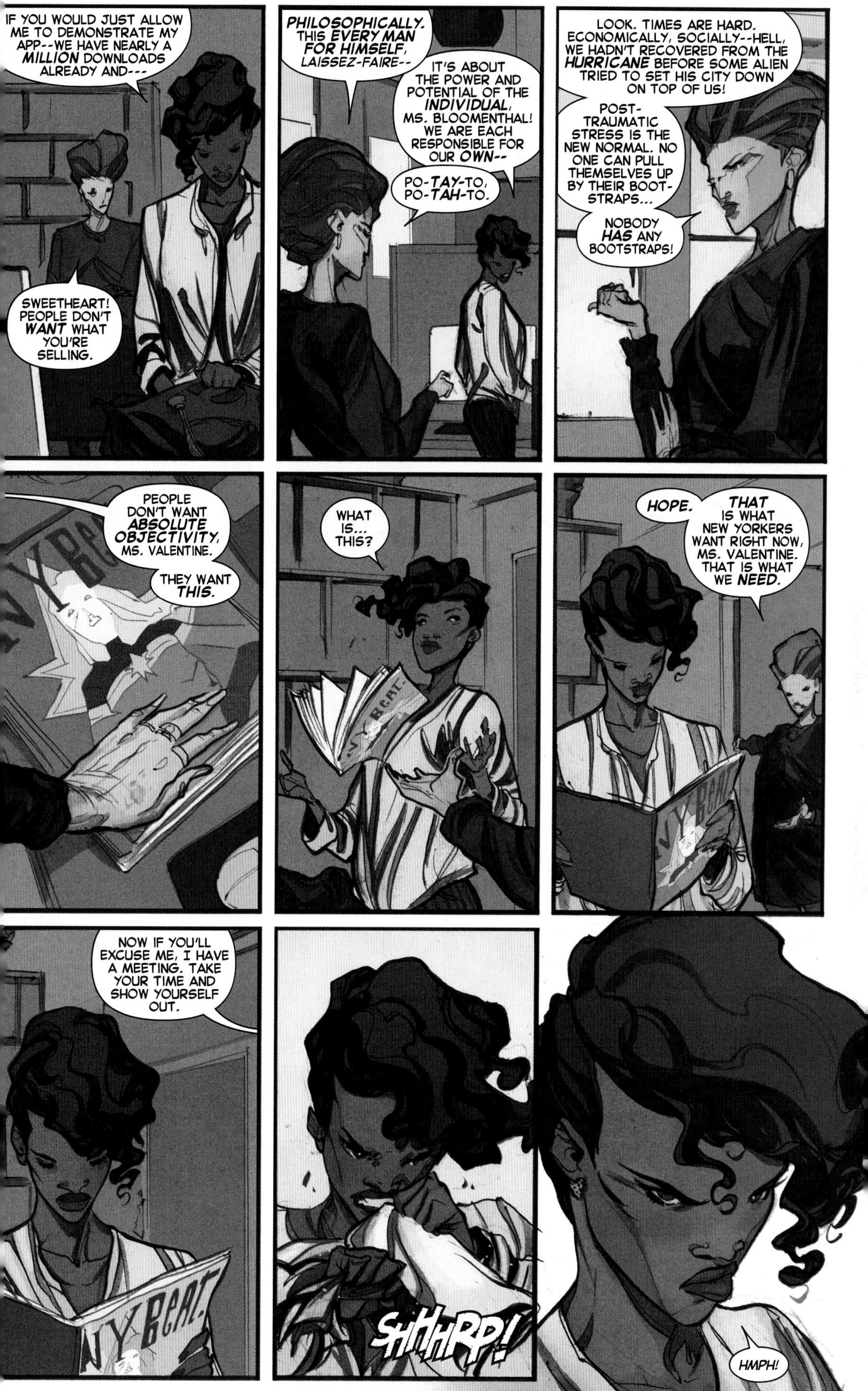
IF YOU WOULD JUST ALLOW ME TO DEMONSTRATE MY APP--WE HAVE NEARLY A MILLION DOWNLOADS ALREADY AND---
SWEETHEART! PEOPLE DON'T WANT WHAT YOU'RE SELLING.
PHILOSOPHICALLY. THIS EVERY MAN FOR HIMSELF, LAISSEZ-FAIRE--
IT'S ABOUT THE POWER AND POTENTIAL OF THE INDIVIDUAL, MS. BLOOMENTHAL! WE ARE EACH RESPONSIBLE FOR OUR OWN--
PO-TAY-TO, PO-TAH-TO.
LOOK. TIMES ARE HARD. ECONOMICALLY, SOCIALLY--HELL, WE HADN'T RECOVERED FROM THE HURRICANE BEFORE SOME ALIEN TRIED TO SET HIS CITY DOWN ON TOP OF US!
POST-TRAUMATIC STRESS IS THE NEW NORMAL. NO ONE CAN PULL THEMSELVES UP BY THEIR BOOT-STRAPS...
NOBODY HAS ANY BOOTSTRAPS!
PEOPLE DON'T WANT ABSOLUTE OBJECTIVITY, MS. VALENTINE.
THEY WANT THIS.
WHAT IS... THIS?
HOPE.
THAT IS WHAT NEW YORKERS WANT RIGHT NOW, MS. VALENTINE. THAT IS WHAT WE NEED.
NOW IF YOU'LL EXCUSE ME, I HAVE A MEETING. TAKE YOUR TIME AND SHOW YOURSELF OUT.
SHHHRP!
HMPH!

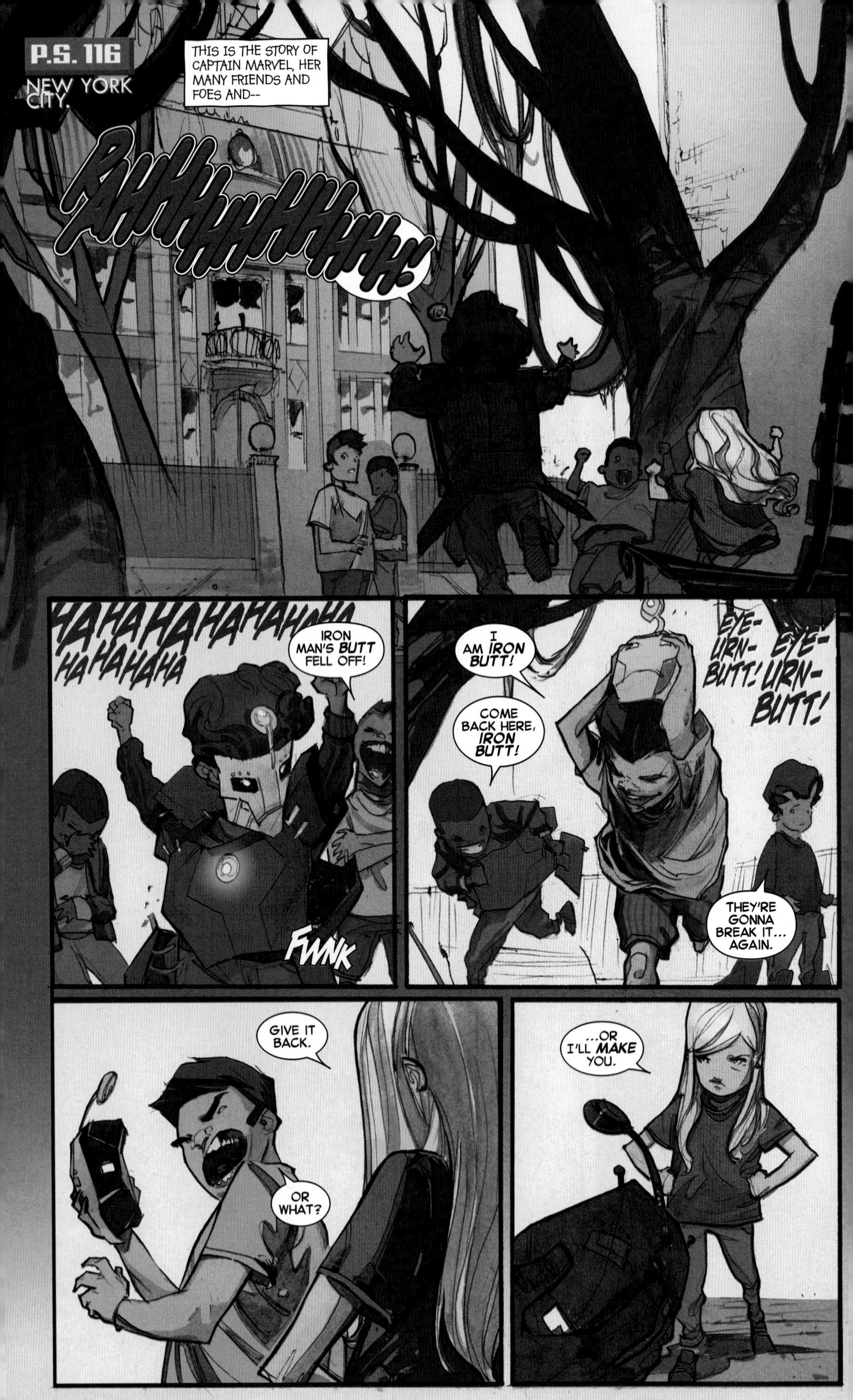
P.S. 116
NEW YORK CITY.
THIS IS THE STORY OF CAPTAIN MARVEL, HER MANY FRIENDS AND FOES AND--
HAHAHAHAHAHAHAHA HAHAHAHA
IRON MAN'S BUTT FELL OFF!
FWNK
I AM IRON BUTT!
COME BACK HERE, IRON BUTT!
EYE-URN-BUTT! EYE-URN-BUTT!
THEY'RE GONNA BREAK IT... AGAIN.
GIVE IT BACK.
OR WHAT?
...OR I'LL MAKE YOU.

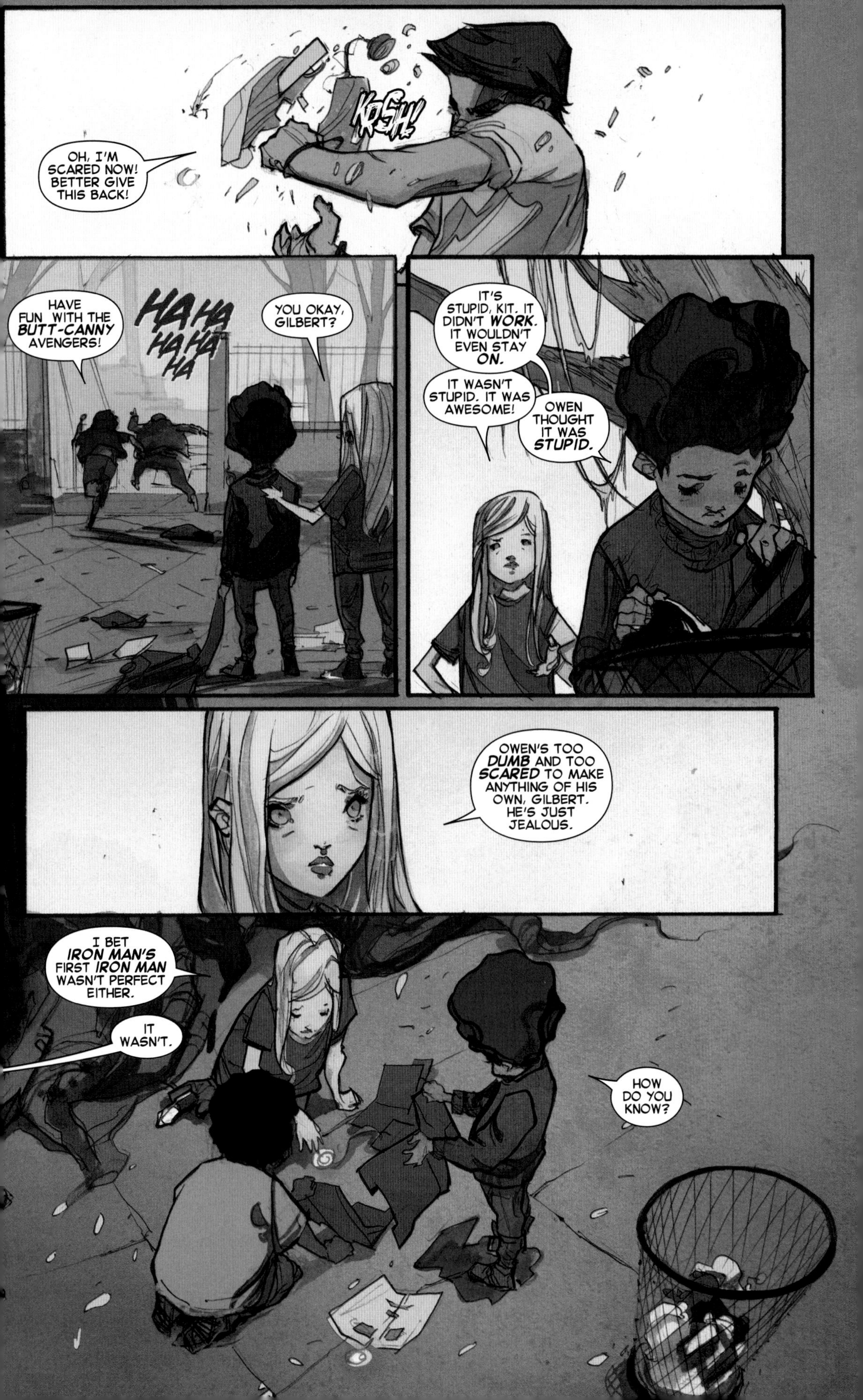
KRSH!
OH, I'M SCARED NOW! BETTER GIVE THIS BACK!
HAVE FUN WITH THE BUTT-CANNY AVENGERS!
HA HA HA HA HA
YOU OKAY, GILBERT?
IT'S STUPID, KIT. IT DIDN'T WORK. IT WOULDN'T EVEN STAY ON.
IT WASN'T STUPID. IT WAS AWESOME!
OWEN THOUGHT IT WAS STUPID.
OWEN'S TOO DUMB AND TOO SCARED TO MAKE ANYTHING OF HIS OWN, GILBERT. HE'S JUST JEALOUS.
I BET IRON MAN'S FIRST IRON MAN WASN'T PERFECT EITHER.
IT WASN'T.
HOW DO YOU KNOW?

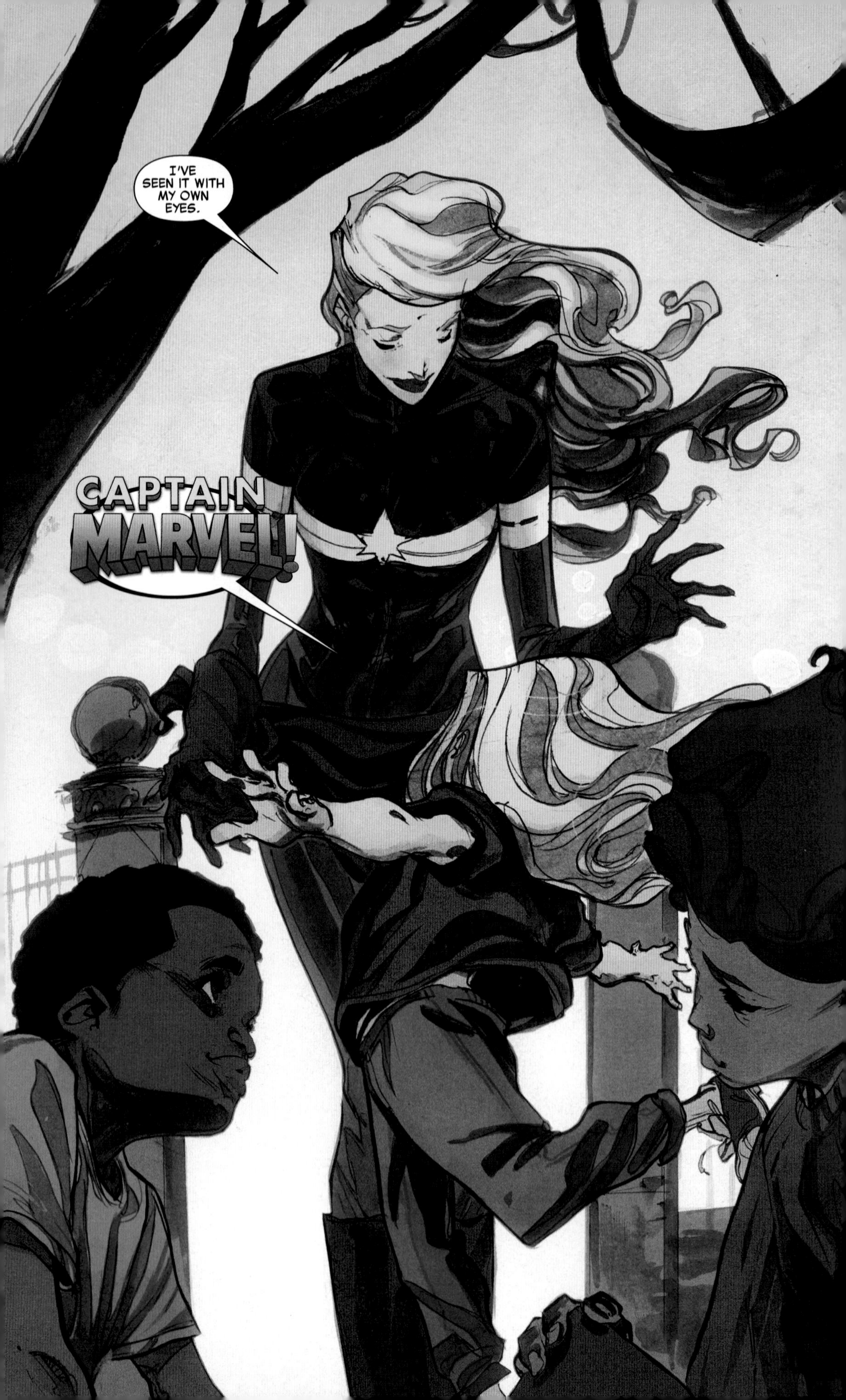
I'VE SEEN IT WITH MY OWN EYES.
CAPTAIN MARVEL!

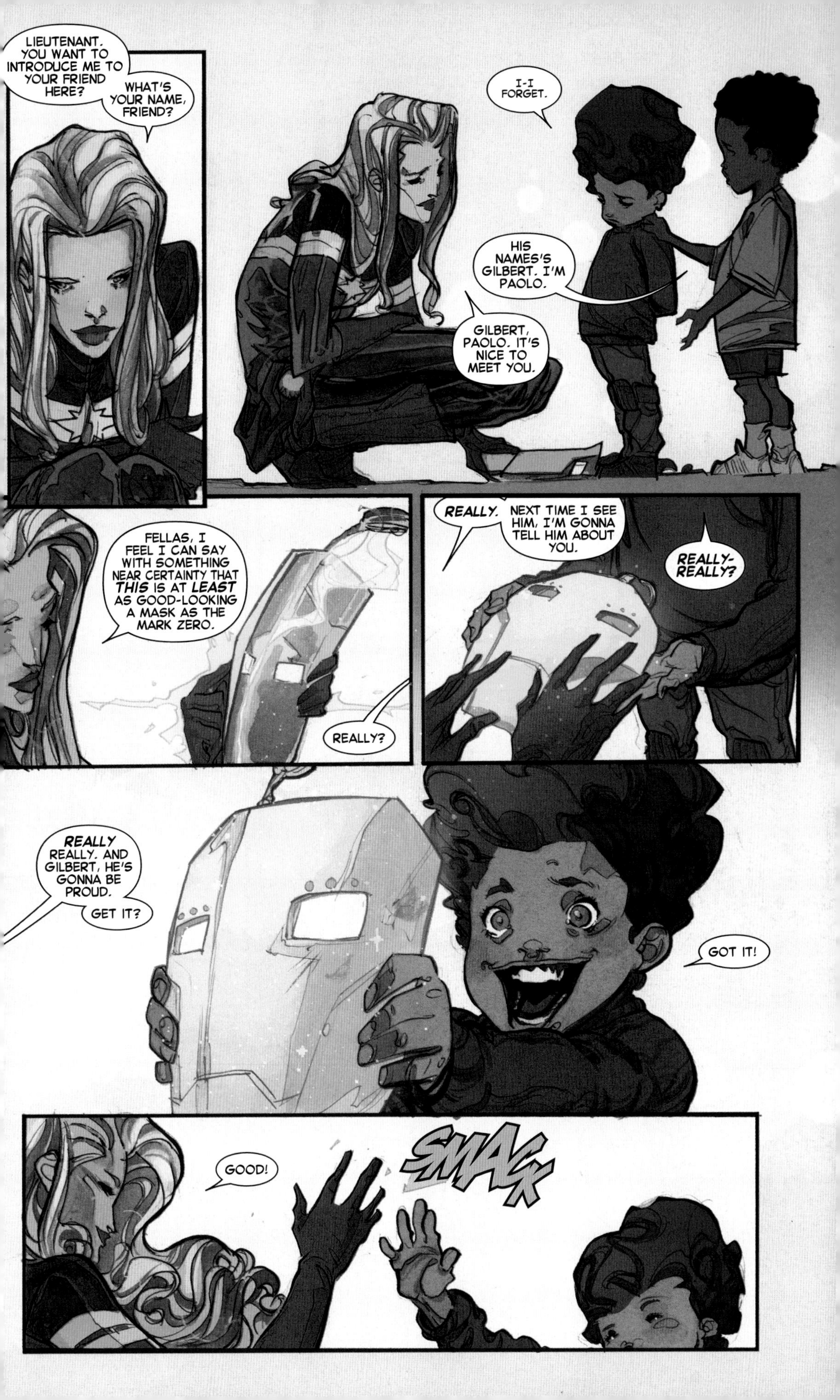
LIEUTENANT. YOU WANT TO INTRODUCE ME TO YOUR FRIEND HERE?
WHAT'S YOUR NAME, FRIEND?
I-I FORGET.
HIS NAMES'S GILBERT. I'M PAOLO.
GILBERT, PAOLO. IT'S NICE TO MEET YOU.
FELLAS, I FEEL I CAN SAY WITH SOMETHING NEAR CERTAINTY THAT *THIS* IS AT *LEAST* AS GOOD-LOOKING A MASK AS THE MARK ZERO.
REALLY?
REALLY.
NEXT TIME I SEE HIM, I'M GONNA TELL HIM ABOUT YOU.
REALLY-REALLY?
REALLY REALLY. AND GILBERT, HE'S GONNA BE PROUD.
GET IT?
GOT IT!
GOOD!
SMACK

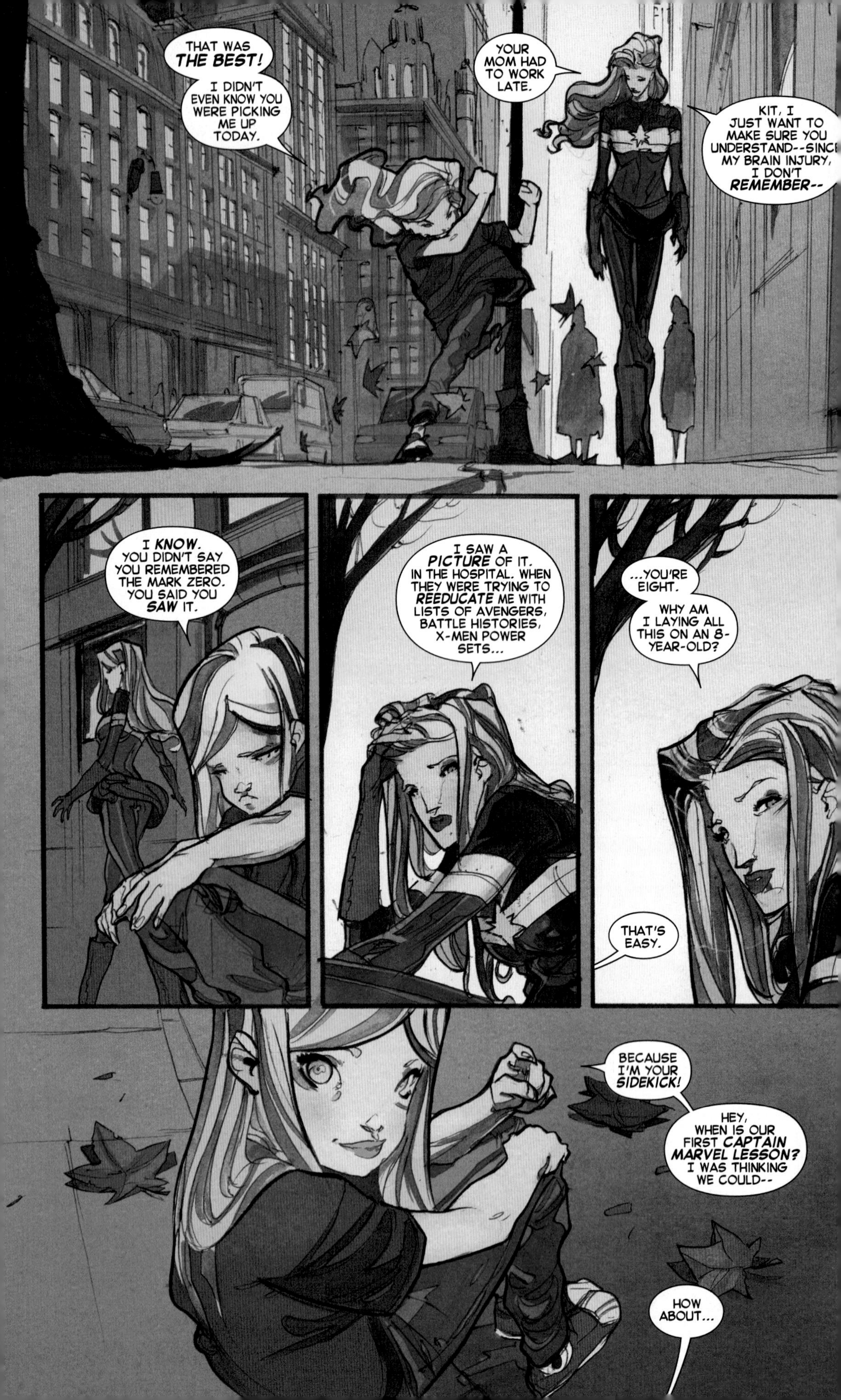

THAT WAS THE BEST!
I DIDN'T EVEN KNOW YOU WERE PICKING ME UP TODAY.
YOUR MOM HAD TO WORK LATE.
KIT, I JUST WANT TO MAKE SURE YOU UNDERSTAND--SINCE MY BRAIN INJURY, I DON'T REMEMBER--
I KNOW. YOU DIDN'T SAY YOU REMEMBERED THE MARK ZERO. YOU SAID YOU SAW IT.
I SAW A PICTURE OF IT. IN THE HOSPITAL. WHEN THEY WERE TRYING TO REEDUCATE ME WITH LISTS OF AVENGERS, BATTLE HISTORIES, X-MEN POWER SETS...
...YOU'RE EIGHT.
WHY AM I LAYING ALL THIS ON AN 8-YEAR-OLD?
THAT'S EASY.
BECAUSE I'M YOUR SIDEKICK!
HEY, WHEN IS OUR FIRST CAPTAIN MARVEL LESSON? I WAS THINKING WE COULD--
HOW ABOUT...

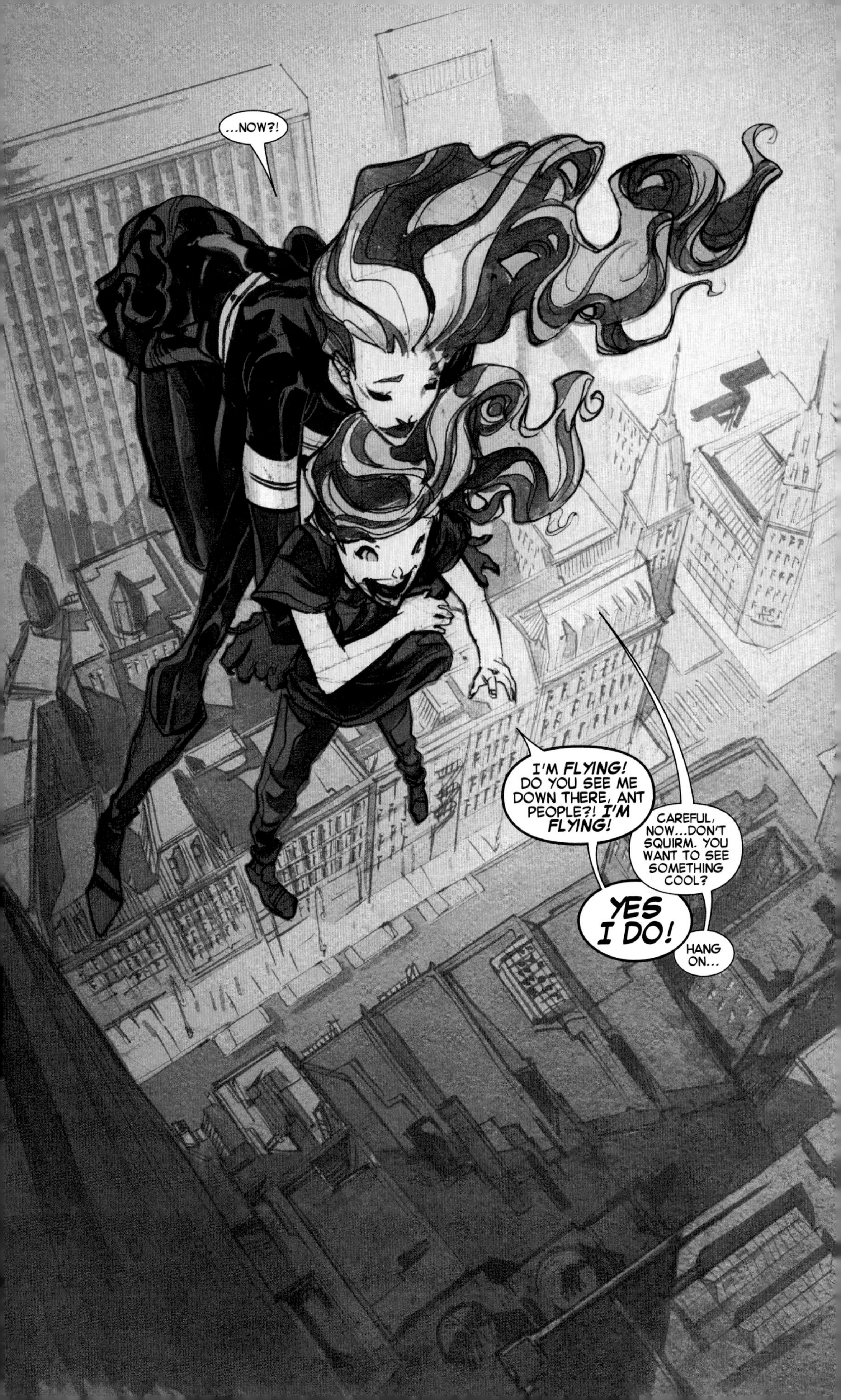
...NOW?!
I'M FLYING! DO YOU SEE ME DOWN THERE, ANT PEOPLE?! I'M FLYING!
CAREFUL, NOW...DON'T SQUIRM. YOU WANT TO SEE SOMETHING COOL?
YES I DO!
HANG ON...

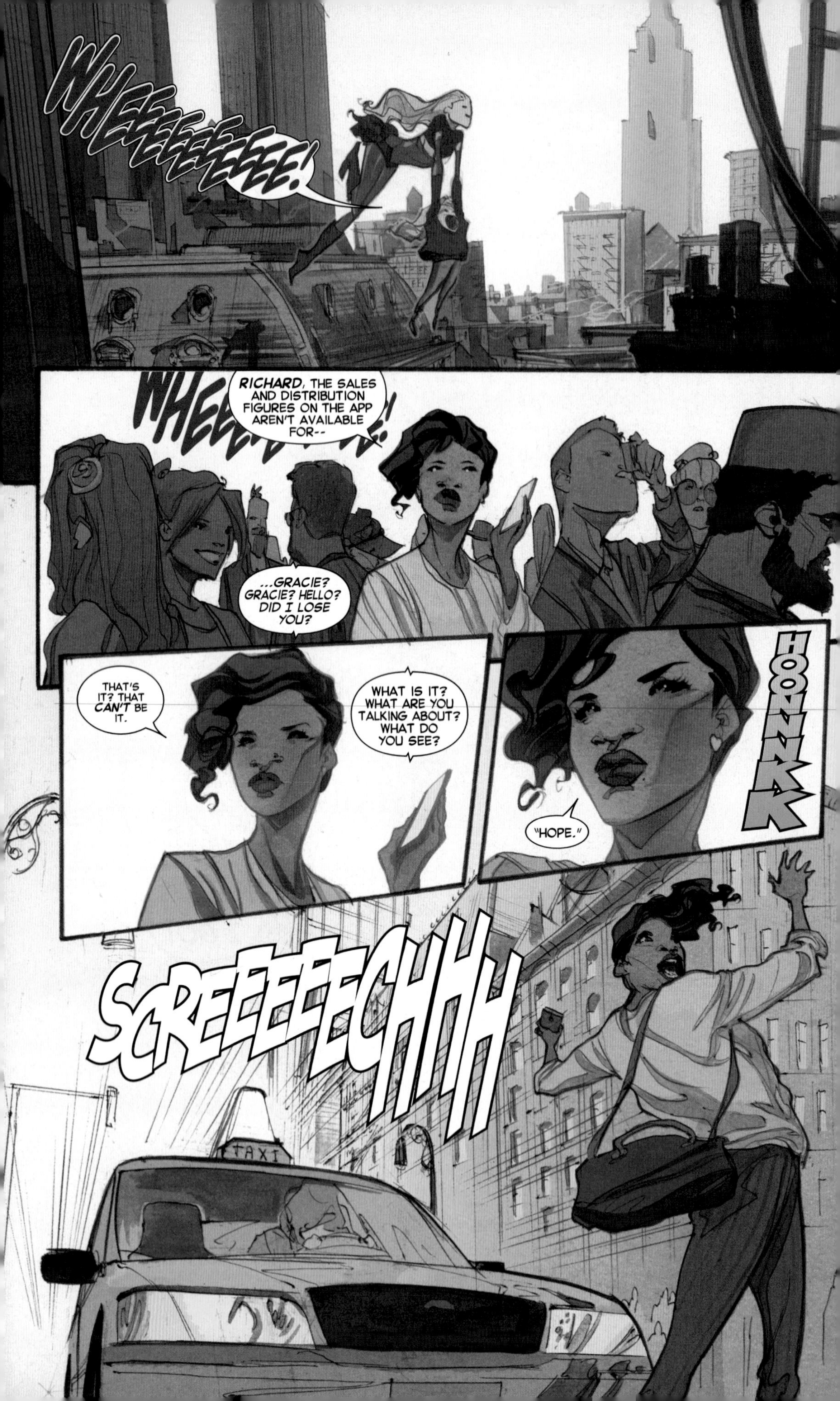
WHEEEEEEEEEEEE!
WHEEEEEEE!
RICHARD, THE SALES AND DISTRIBUTION FIGURES ON THE APP AREN'T AVAILABLE FOR--
...GRACIE? GRACIE? HELLO? DID I LOSE YOU?
THAT'S IT? THAT CAN'T BE IT.
WHAT IS IT? WHAT ARE YOU TALKING ABOUT? WHAT DO YOU SEE?
"HOPE."
HOONNKK
SCREEEEEECHHH
TAXI

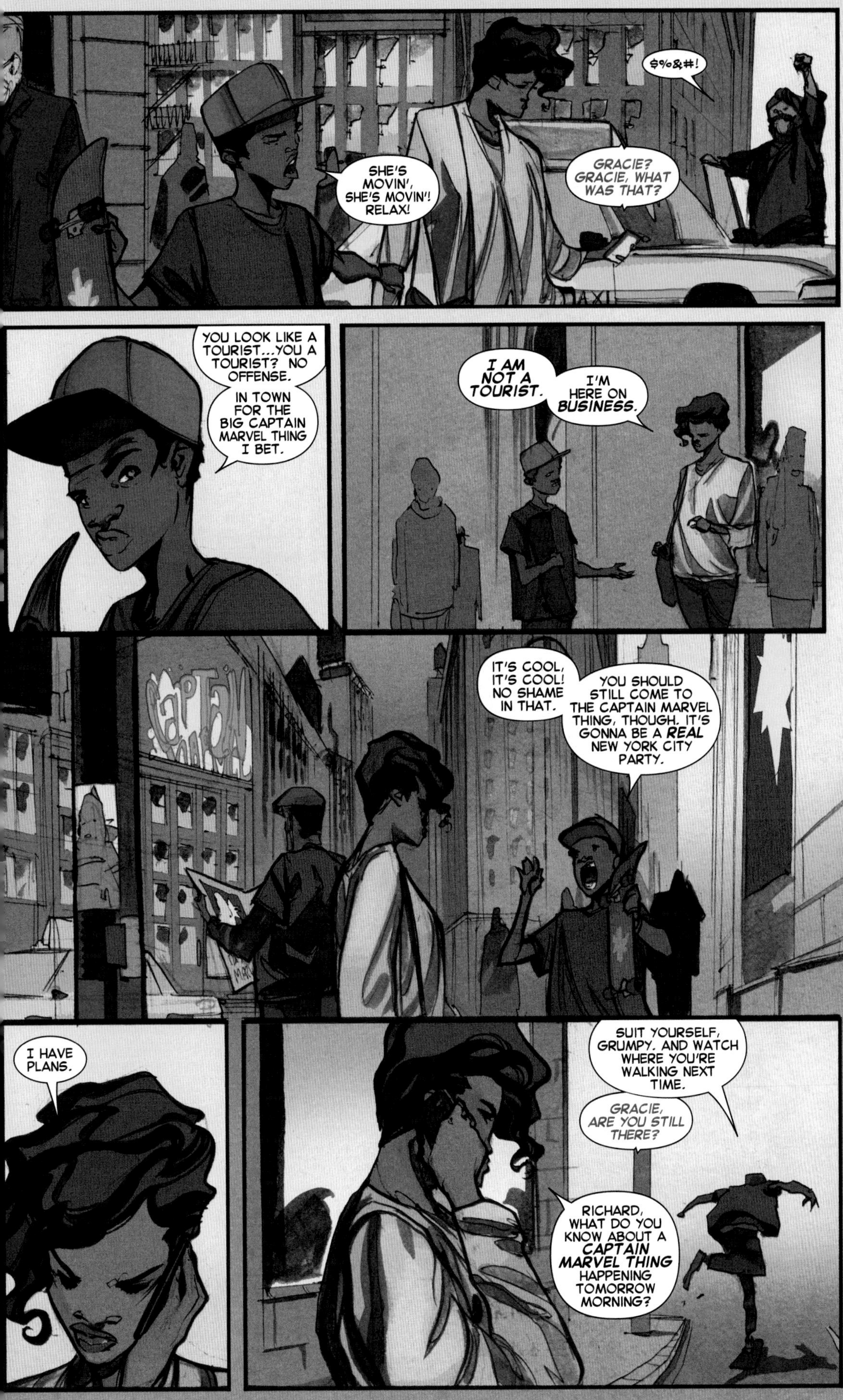

SHE'S MOVIN', SHE'S MOVIN'! RELAX!
GRACIE? GRACIE, WHAT WAS THAT?
$%&#!
YOU LOOK LIKE A TOURIST...YOU A TOURIST? NO OFFENSE.
IN TOWN FOR THE BIG CAPTAIN MARVEL THING I BET.
I AM NOT A TOURIST.
I'M HERE ON BUSINESS.
IT'S COOL, IT'S COOL! NO SHAME IN THAT.
YOU SHOULD STILL COME TO THE CAPTAIN MARVEL THING, THOUGH. IT'S GONNA BE A REAL NEW YORK CITY PARTY.
I HAVE PLANS.
SUIT YOURSELF, GRUMPY. AND WATCH WHERE YOU'RE WALKING NEXT TIME.
GRACIE, ARE YOU STILL THERE?
RICHARD, WHAT DO YOU KNOW ABOUT A CAPTAIN MARVEL THING HAPPENING TOMORROW MORNING?

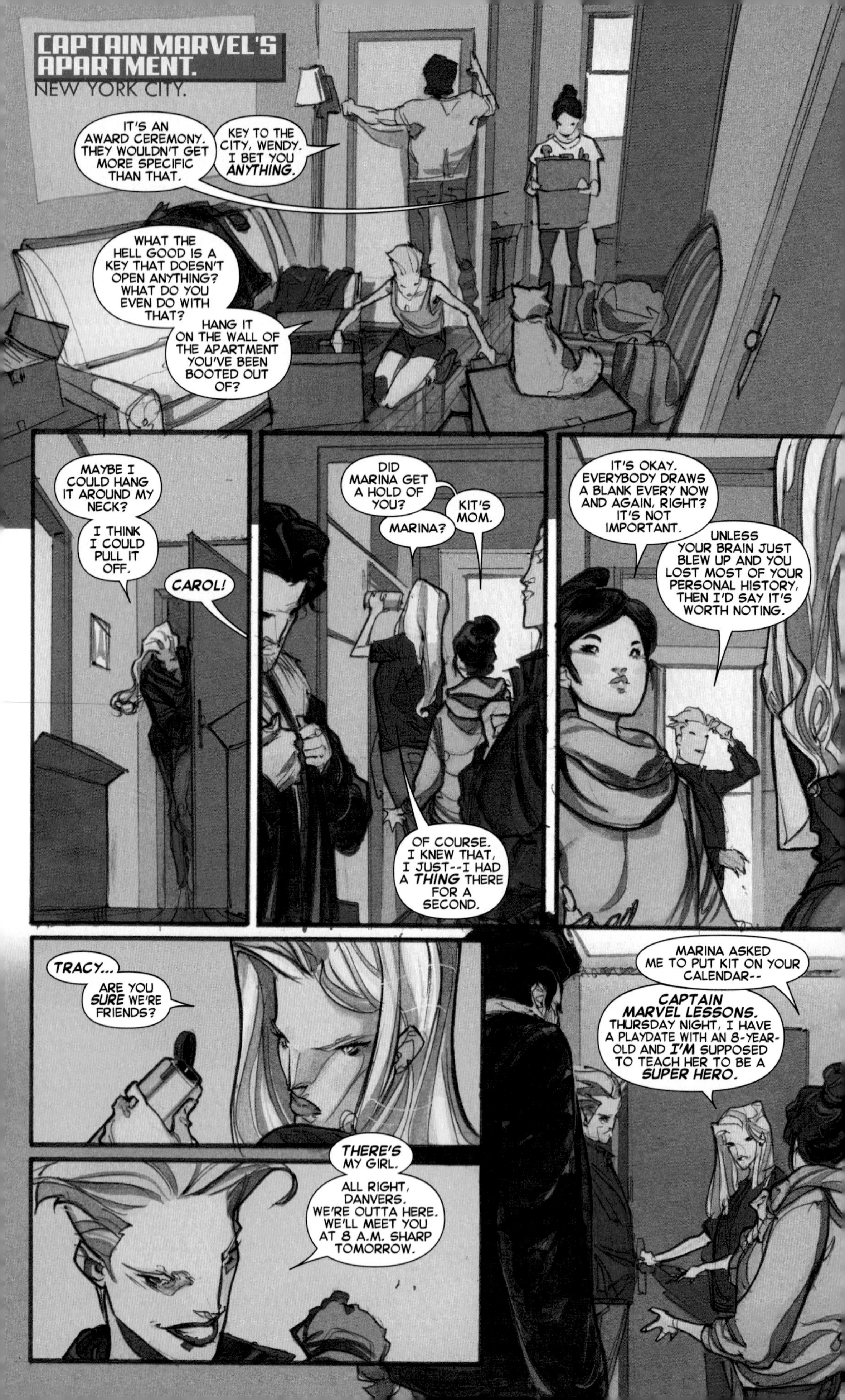
CAPTAIN MARVEL'S APARTMENT.
NEW YORK CITY.
IT'S AN AWARD CEREMONY. THEY WOULDN'T GET MORE SPECIFIC THAN THAT.
KEY TO THE CITY, WENDY. I BET YOU ANYTHING.
WHAT THE HELL GOOD IS A KEY THAT DOESN'T OPEN ANYTHING? WHAT DO YOU EVEN DO WITH THAT?
HANG IT ON THE WALL OF THE APARTMENT YOU'VE BEEN BOOTED OUT OF?
MAYBE I COULD HANG IT AROUND MY NECK?
I THINK I COULD PULL IT OFF.
CAROL!
DID MARINA GET A HOLD OF YOU?
MARINA?
KIT'S MOM.
OF COURSE. I KNEW THAT, I JUST--I HAD A THING THERE FOR A SECOND.
IT'S OKAY. EVERYBODY DRAWS A BLANK EVERY NOW AND AGAIN, RIGHT? IT'S NOT IMPORTANT.
UNLESS YOUR BRAIN JUST BLEW UP AND YOU LOST MOST OF YOUR PERSONAL HISTORY, THEN I'D SAY IT'S WORTH NOTING.
TRACY...
ARE YOU SURE WE'RE FRIENDS?
MARINA ASKED ME TO PUT KIT ON YOUR CALENDAR--
CAPTAIN MARVEL LESSONS. THURSDAY NIGHT, I HAVE A PLAYDATE WITH AN 8-YEAR-OLD AND I'M SUPPOSED TO TEACH HER TO BE A SUPER HERO.
THERE'S MY GIRL.
ALL RIGHT, DANVERS. WE'RE OUTTA HERE. WE'LL MEET YOU AT 8 A.M. SHARP TOMORROW.

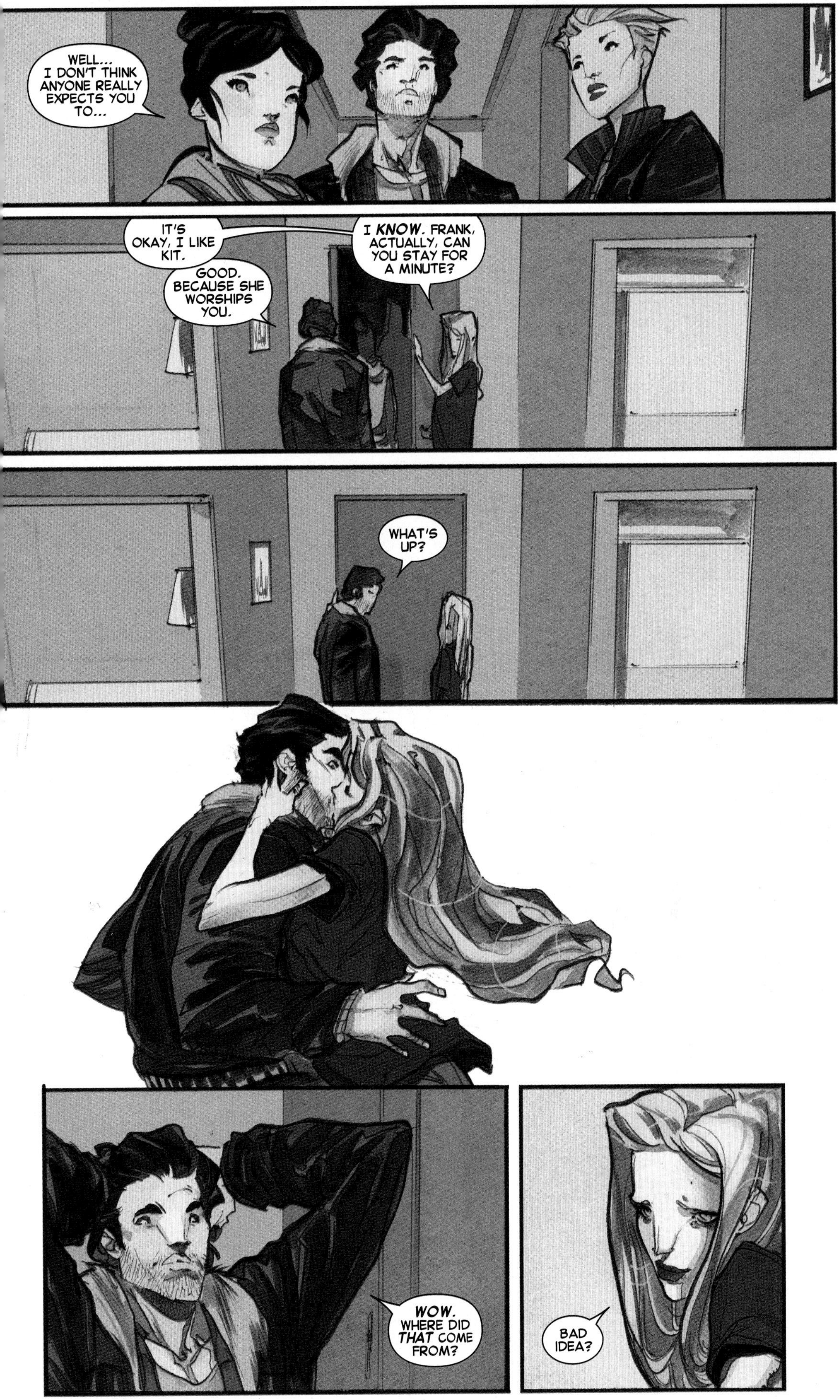
WELL... I DON'T THINK ANYONE REALLY EXPECTS YOU TO...
IT'S OKAY, I LIKE KIT.
GOOD. BECAUSE SHE WORSHIPS YOU.
I KNOW. FRANK, ACTUALLY, CAN YOU STAY FOR A MINUTE?
WHAT'S UP?
WOW. WHERE DID THAT COME FROM?
BAD IDEA?

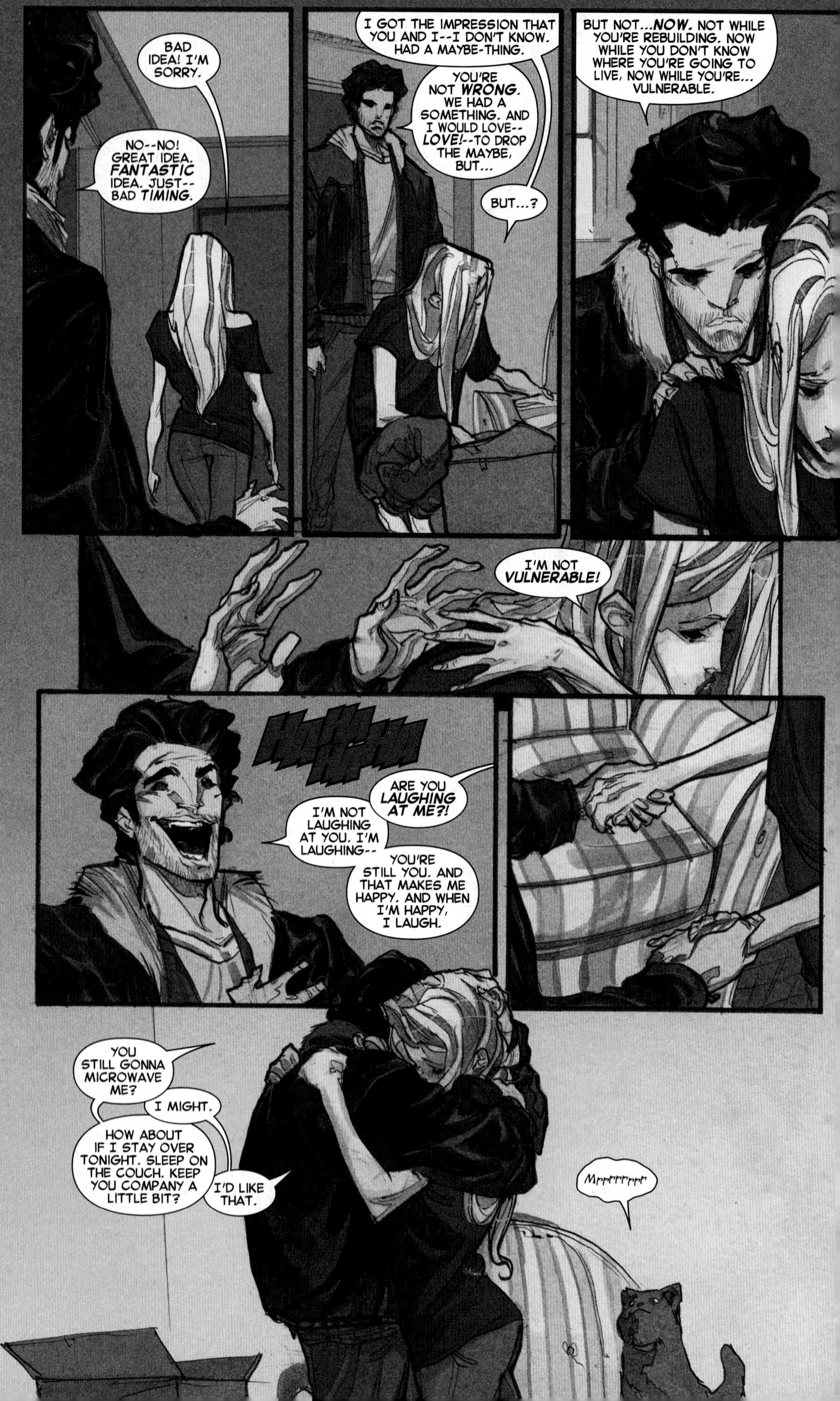
BAD IDEA! I'M SORRY.
NO--NO! GREAT IDEA. *FANTASTIC* IDEA. JUST-- BAD *TIMING*.
I GOT THE IMPRESSION THAT YOU AND I--I DON'T KNOW. HAD A MAYBE-THING.
YOU'RE NOT *WRONG*. WE HAD A SOMETHING. AND I WOULD LOVE-- *LOVE!*--TO DROP THE MAYBE, BUT...
BUT...?
BUT NOT...*NOW*. NOT WHILE YOU'RE REBUILDING. NOW WHILE YOU DON'T KNOW WHERE YOU'RE GOING TO LIVE, NOW WHILE YOU'RE... VULNERABLE.
I'M NOT *VULNERABLE!*
ARE YOU *LAUGHING AT ME?!*
I'M NOT LAUGHING AT YOU. I'M LAUGHING--
YOU'RE STILL YOU. AND THAT MAKES ME HAPPY. AND WHEN I'M HAPPY, I LAUGH.
YOU STILL GONNA MICROWAVE ME?
I MIGHT.
HOW ABOUT IF I STAY OVER TONIGHT. SLEEP ON THE COUCH. KEEP YOU COMPANY A LITTLE BIT?
I'D LIKE THAT.
Mrrrrrrrrr

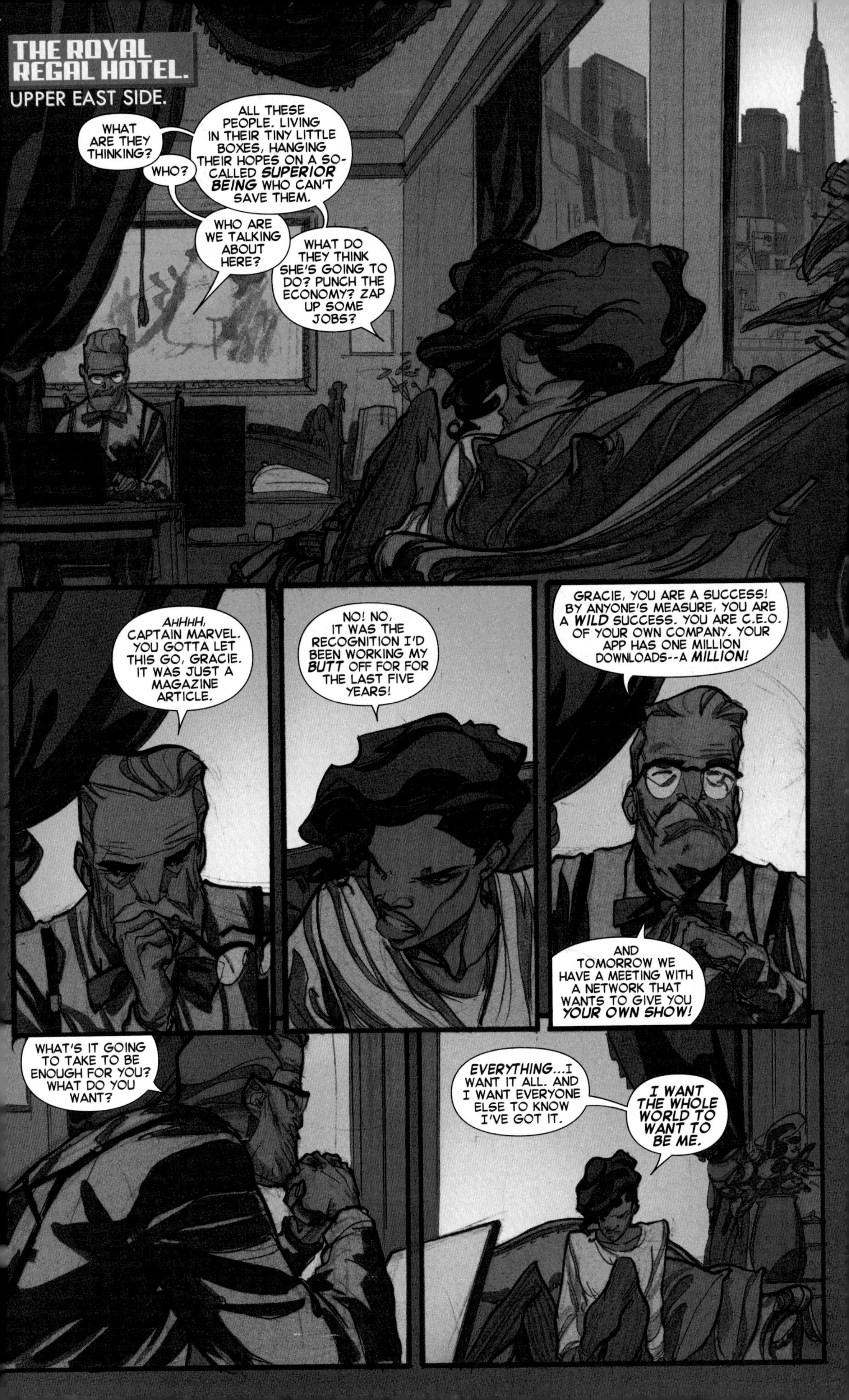
THE ROYAL REGAL HOTEL.
UPPER EAST SIDE.
WHAT ARE THEY THINKING?
ALL THESE PEOPLE. LIVING IN THEIR TINY LITTLE BOXES, HANGING THEIR HOPES ON A SO-CALLED SUPERIOR BEING WHO CAN'T SAVE THEM.
WHO?
WHO ARE WE TALKING ABOUT HERE?
WHAT DO THEY THINK SHE'S GOING TO DO? PUNCH THE ECONOMY? ZAP UP SOME JOBS?
AHHHH, CAPTAIN MARVEL. YOU GOTTA LET THIS GO, GRACIE. IT WAS JUST A MAGAZINE ARTICLE.
NO! NO, IT WAS THE RECOGNITION I'D BEEN WORKING MY BUTT OFF FOR FOR THE LAST FIVE YEARS!
GRACIE, YOU ARE A SUCCESS! BY ANYONE'S MEASURE, YOU ARE A WILD SUCCESS. YOU ARE C.E.O. OF YOUR OWN COMPANY. YOUR APP HAS ONE MILLION DOWNLOADS--A MILLION!
AND TOMORROW WE HAVE A MEETING WITH A NETWORK THAT WANTS TO GIVE YOU YOUR OWN SHOW!
WHAT'S IT GOING TO TAKE TO BE ENOUGH FOR YOU? WHAT DO YOU WANT?
EVERYTHING...I WANT IT ALL. AND I WANT EVERYONE ELSE TO KNOW I'VE GOT IT.
I WANT THE WHOLE WORLD TO WANT TO BE ME.

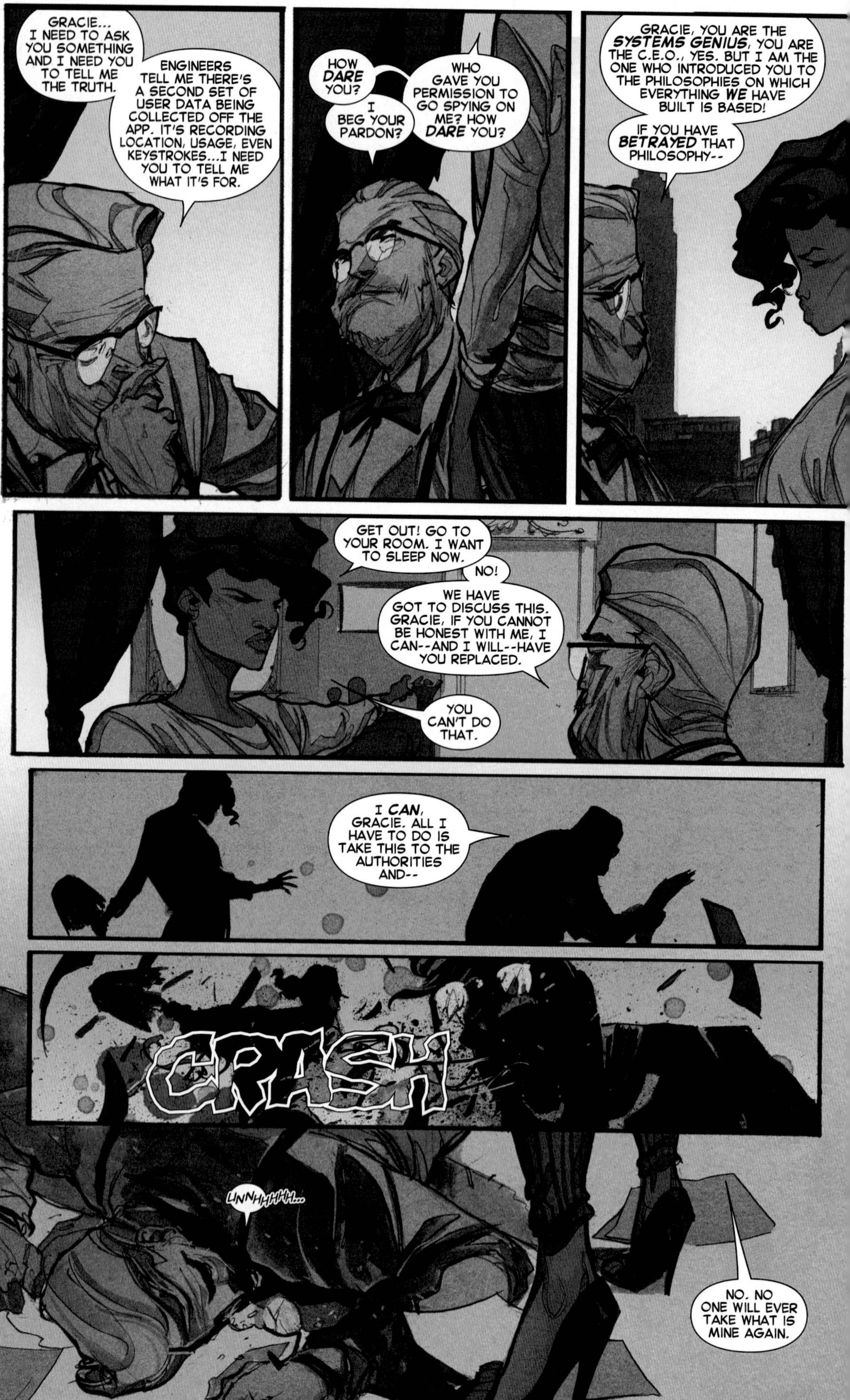
GRACIE... I NEED TO ASK YOU SOMETHING AND I NEED YOU TO TELL ME THE TRUTH.
ENGINEERS TELL ME THERE'S A SECOND SET OF USER DATA BEING COLLECTED OFF THE APP. IT'S RECORDING LOCATION, USAGE, EVEN KEYSTROKES...I NEED YOU TO TELL ME WHAT IT'S FOR.
HOW DARE YOU?
I BEG YOUR PARDON?
WHO GAVE YOU PERMISSION TO GO SPYING ON ME? HOW DARE YOU?
GRACIE, YOU ARE THE SYSTEMS GENIUS, YOU ARE THE C.E.O., YES. BUT I AM THE ONE WHO INTRODUCED YOU TO THE PHILOSOPHIES ON WHICH EVERYTHING WE HAVE BUILT IS BASED!
IF YOU HAVE BETRAYED THAT PHILOSOPHY--
GET OUT! GO TO YOUR ROOM. I WANT TO SLEEP NOW.
NO!
WE HAVE GOT TO DISCUSS THIS. GRACIE, IF YOU CANNOT BE HONEST WITH ME, I CAN--AND I WILL--HAVE YOU REPLACED.
YOU CAN'T DO THAT.
I CAN, GRACIE. ALL I HAVE TO DO IS TAKE THIS TO THE AUTHORITIES AND--
CRASH
UNNHHHHH...
NO. NO ONE WILL EVER TAKE WHAT IS MINE AGAIN.

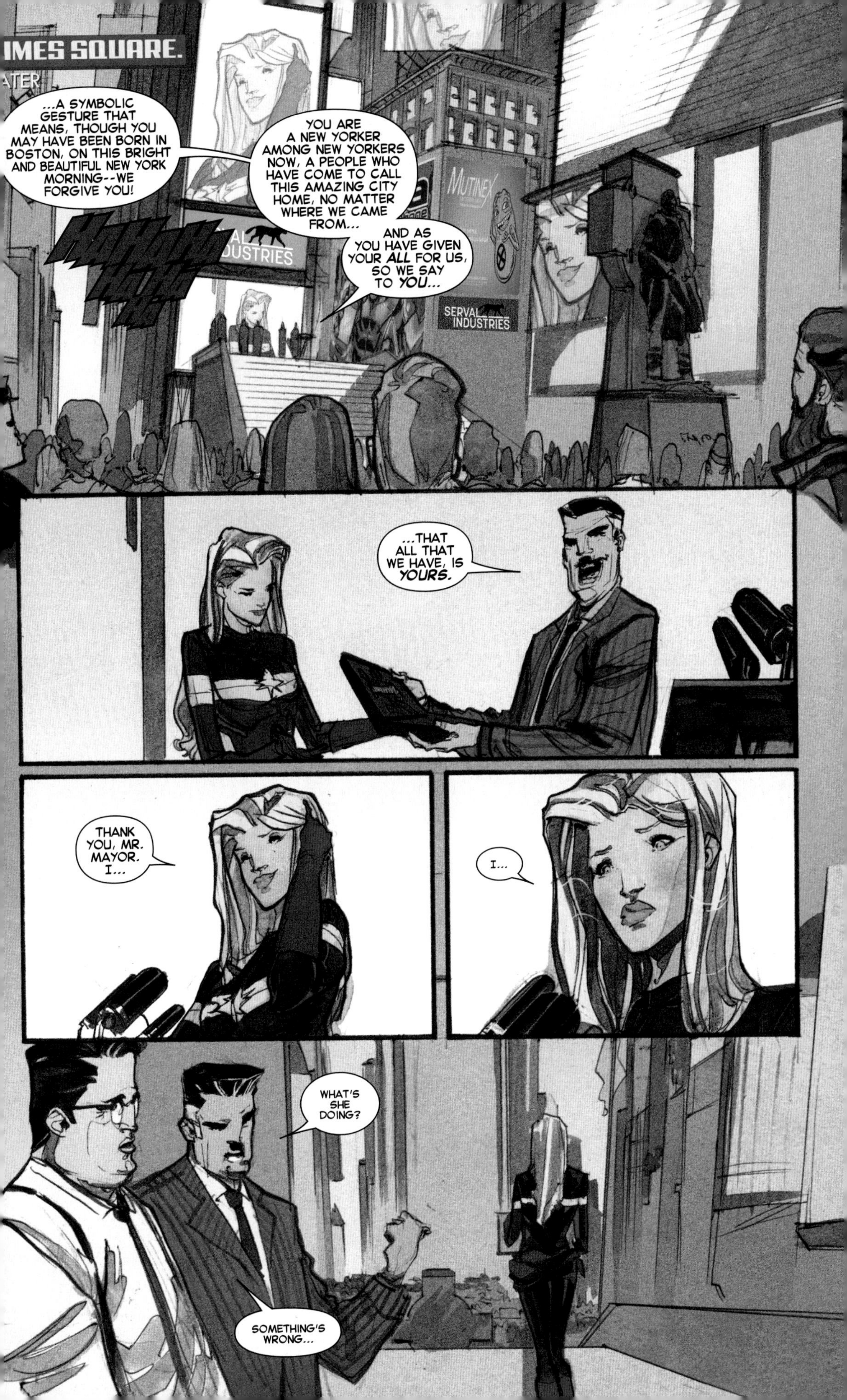
IMES SQUARE.
ATER
...A SYMBOLIC GESTURE THAT MEANS, THOUGH YOU MAY HAVE BEEN BORN IN BOSTON, ON THIS BRIGHT AND BEAUTIFUL NEW YORK MORNING--WE FORGIVE YOU!
YOU ARE A NEW YORKER AMONG NEW YORKERS NOW, A PEOPLE WHO HAVE COME TO CALL THIS AMAZING CITY HOME, NO MATTER WHERE WE CAME FROM...
AND AS YOU HAVE GIVEN YOUR ALL FOR US, SO WE SAY TO YOU...
MUTINEX
SERVAL INDUSTRIES
...THAT ALL THAT WE HAVE, IS YOURS.
THANK YOU, MR. MAYOR. I...
I...
WHAT'S SHE DOING?
SOMETHING'S WRONG...

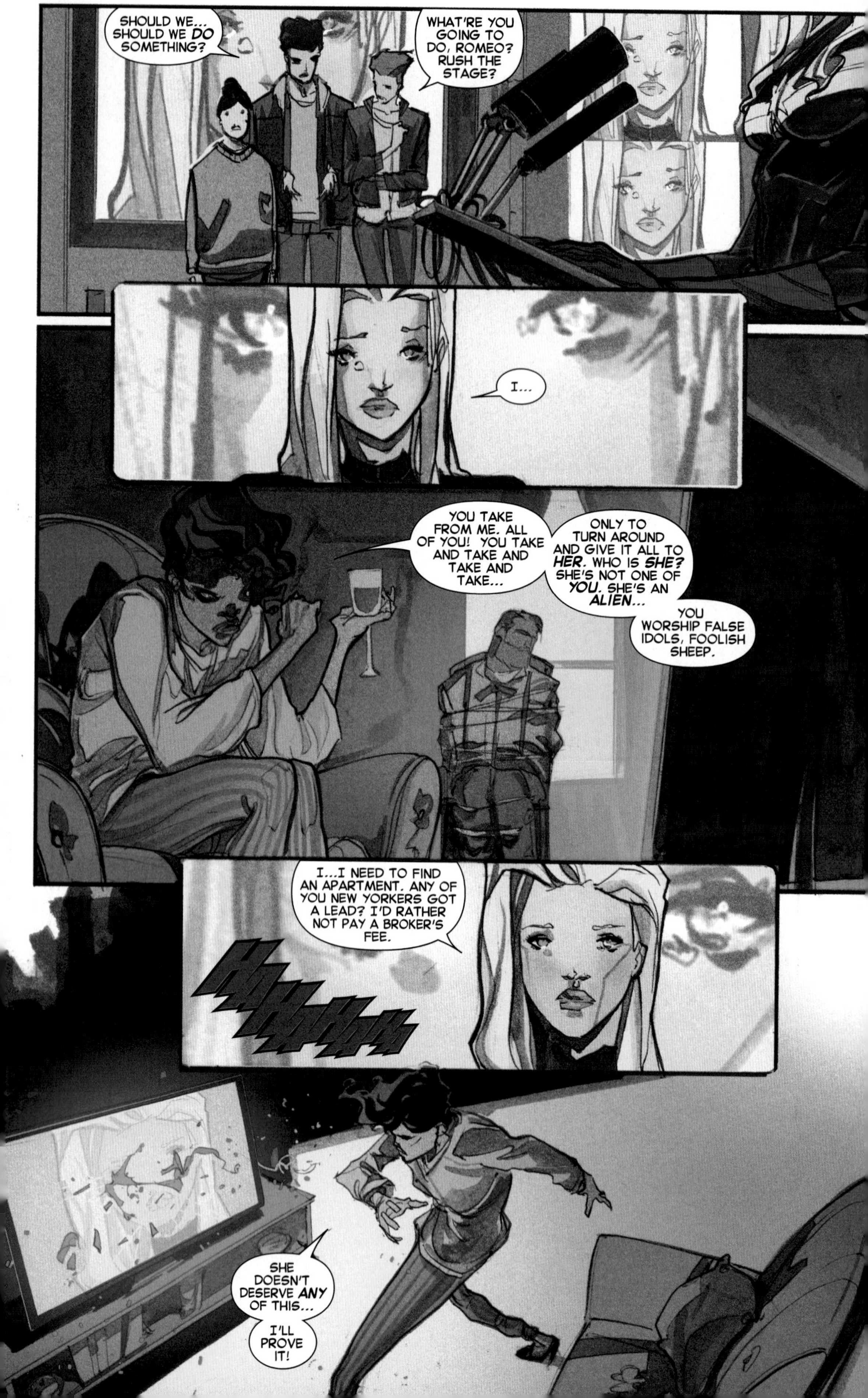
SHOULD WE... SHOULD WE DO SOMETHING?
WHAT'RE YOU GOING TO DO, ROMEO? RUSH THE STAGE?
I...
YOU TAKE FROM ME. ALL OF YOU! YOU TAKE AND TAKE AND TAKE AND TAKE...
ONLY TO TURN AROUND AND GIVE IT ALL TO HER. WHO IS SHE? SHE'S NOT ONE OF YOU. SHE'S AN ALIEN...
YOU WORSHIP FALSE IDOLS, FOOLISH SHEEP.
I...I NEED TO FIND AN APARTMENT. ANY OF YOU NEW YORKERS GOT A LEAD? I'D RATHER NOT PAY A BROKER'S FEE.
HAHAHAHAHA
SHE DOESN'T DESERVE ANY OF THIS...
I'LL PROVE IT!

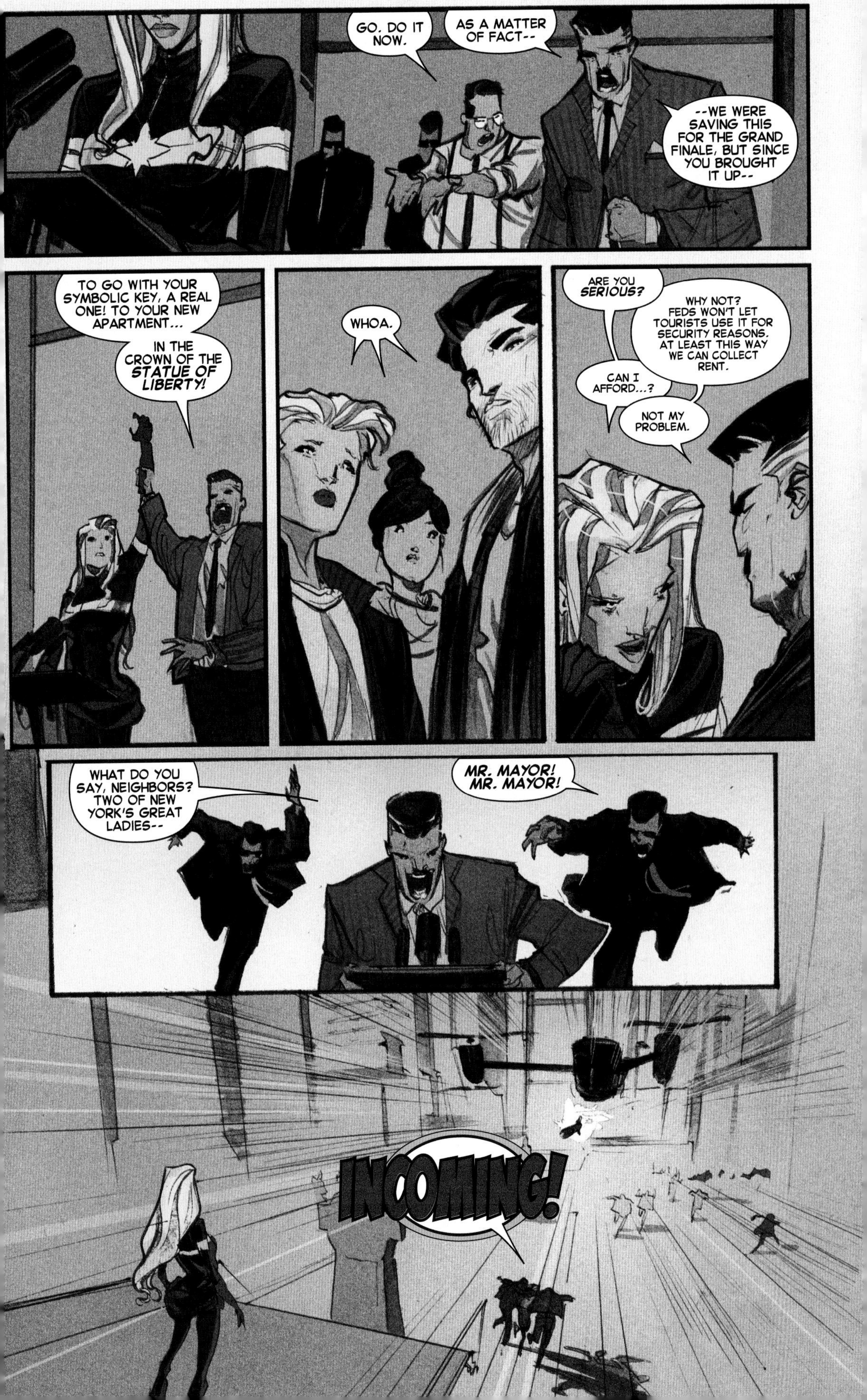
GO. DO IT NOW.
AS A MATTER OF FACT--
--WE WERE SAVING THIS FOR THE GRAND FINALE, BUT SINCE YOU BROUGHT IT UP--
TO GO WITH YOUR SYMBOLIC KEY, A REAL ONE! TO YOUR NEW APARTMENT...
IN THE CROWN OF THE STATUE OF LIBERTY!
WHOA.
ARE YOU SERIOUS?
WHY NOT? FEDS WON'T LET TOURISTS USE IT FOR SECURITY REASONS. AT LEAST THIS WAY WE CAN COLLECT RENT.
CAN I AFFORD...?
NOT MY PROBLEM.
WHAT DO YOU SAY, NEIGHBORS? TWO OF NEW YORK'S GREAT LADIES--
MR. MAYOR! MR. MAYOR!
INCOMING!

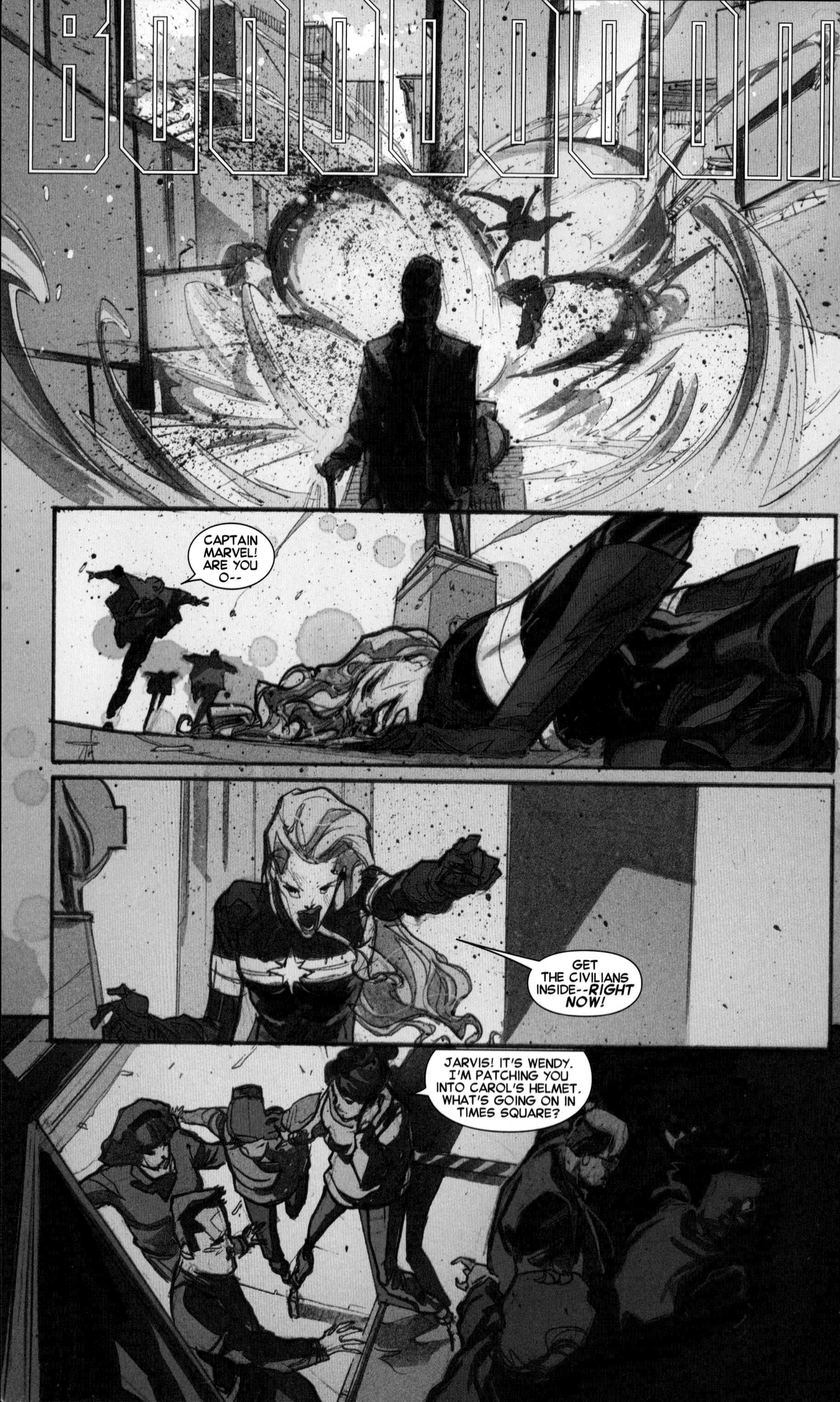
BOOOOOOOOM
CAPTAIN MARVEL! ARE YOU O--
GET THE CIVILIANS INSIDE--*RIGHT NOW!*
JARVIS! IT'S WENDY. I'M PATCHING YOU INTO CAROL'S HELMET. WHAT'S GOING ON IN TIMES SQUARE?

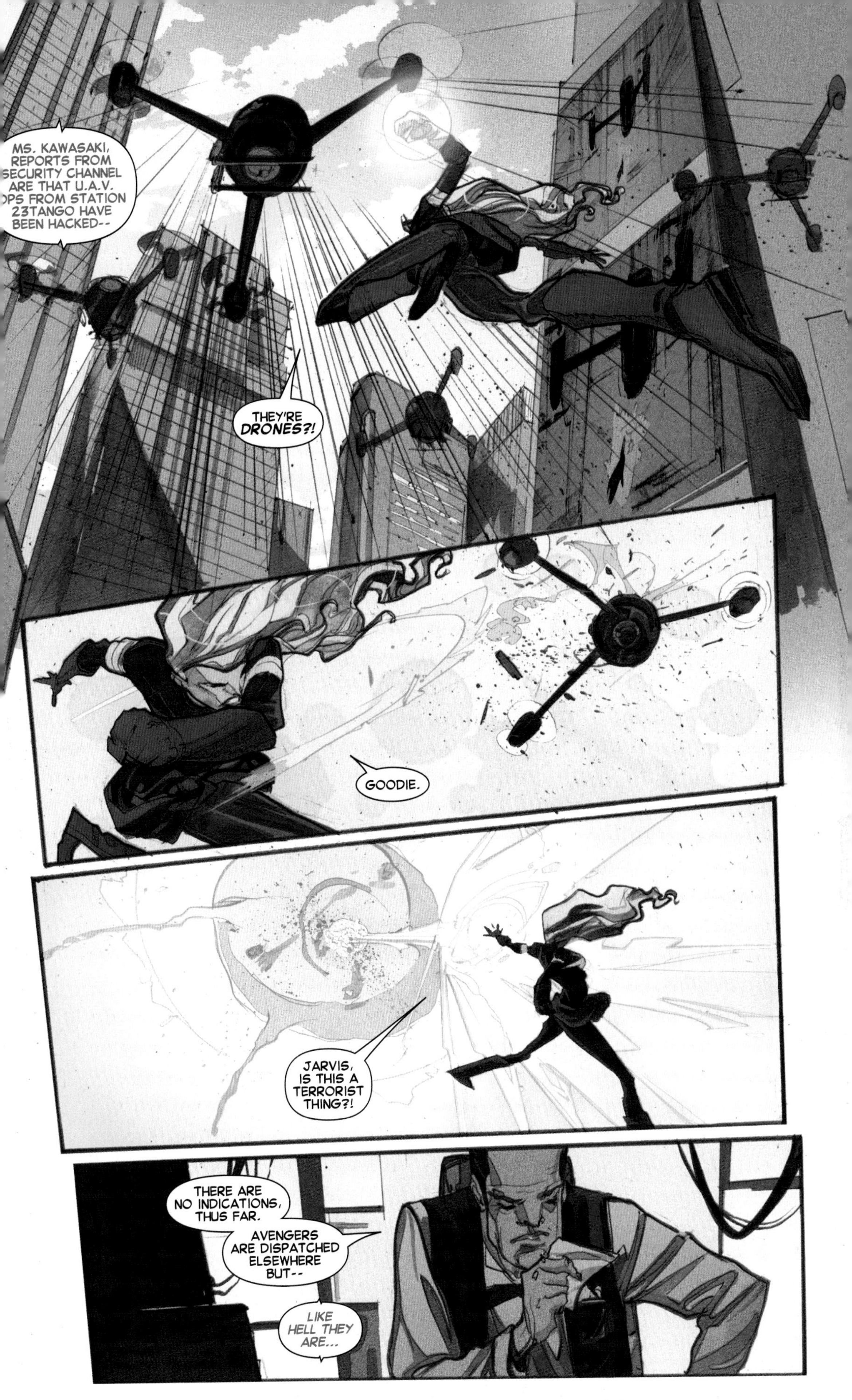
MS. KAWASAKI, REPORTS FROM SECURITY CHANNEL ARE THAT U.A.V. OPS FROM STATION 23TANGO HAVE BEEN HACKED--
THEY'RE DRONES?!
GOODIE.
JARVIS, IS THIS A TERRORIST THING?!
THERE ARE NO INDICATIONS, THUS FAR.
AVENGERS ARE DISPATCHED ELSEWHERE BUT--
LIKE HELL THEY ARE...

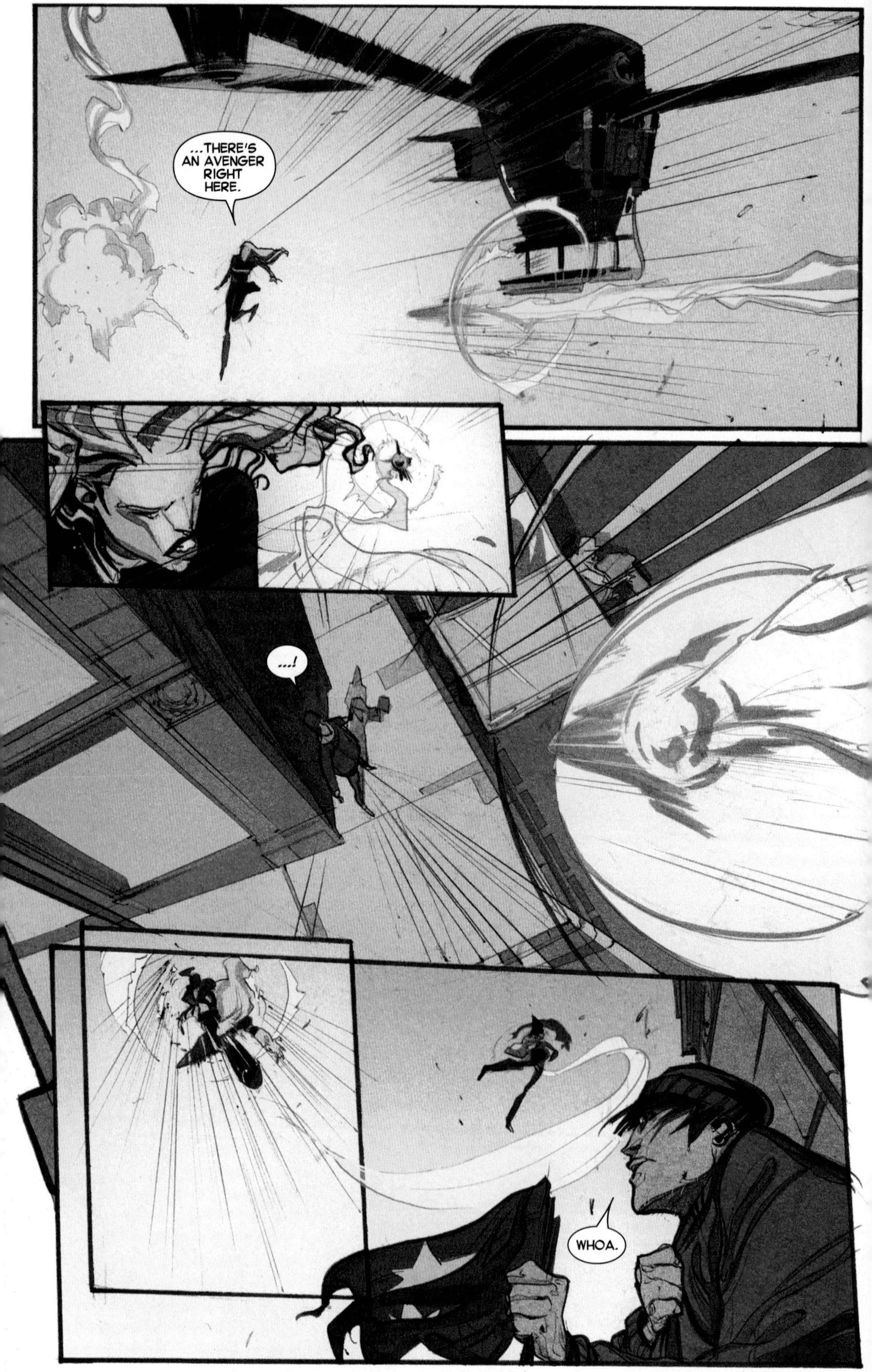
...THERE'S AN AVENGER RIGHT HERE.
...!
WHOA.

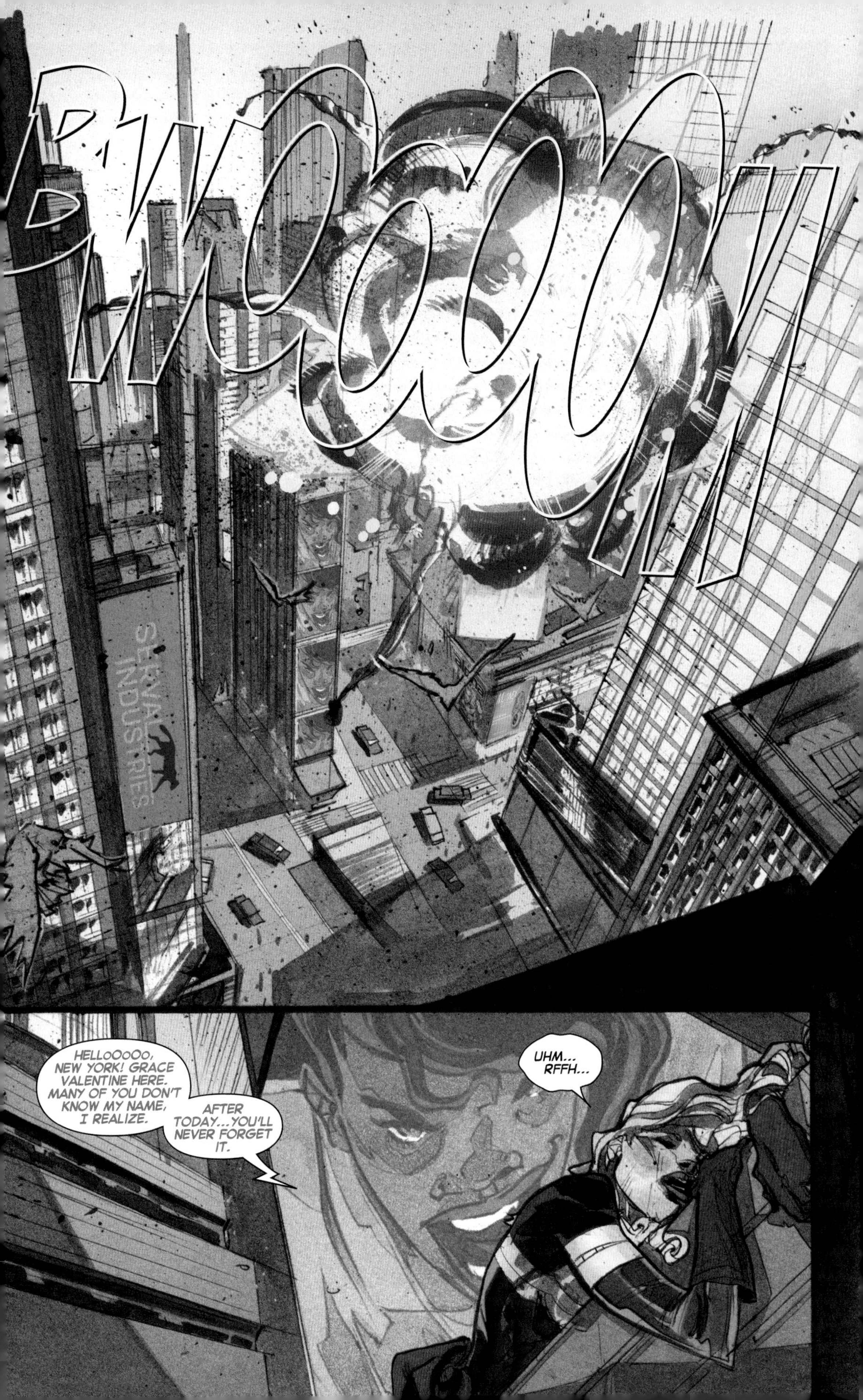

BWOOOM
SERVAL INDUSTRIES
HELLOOOOO, NEW YORK! GRACE VALENTINE HERE. MANY OF YOU DON'T KNOW MY NAME, I REALIZE.
AFTER TODAY... YOU'LL NEVER FORGET IT.
UHM... RFFH...

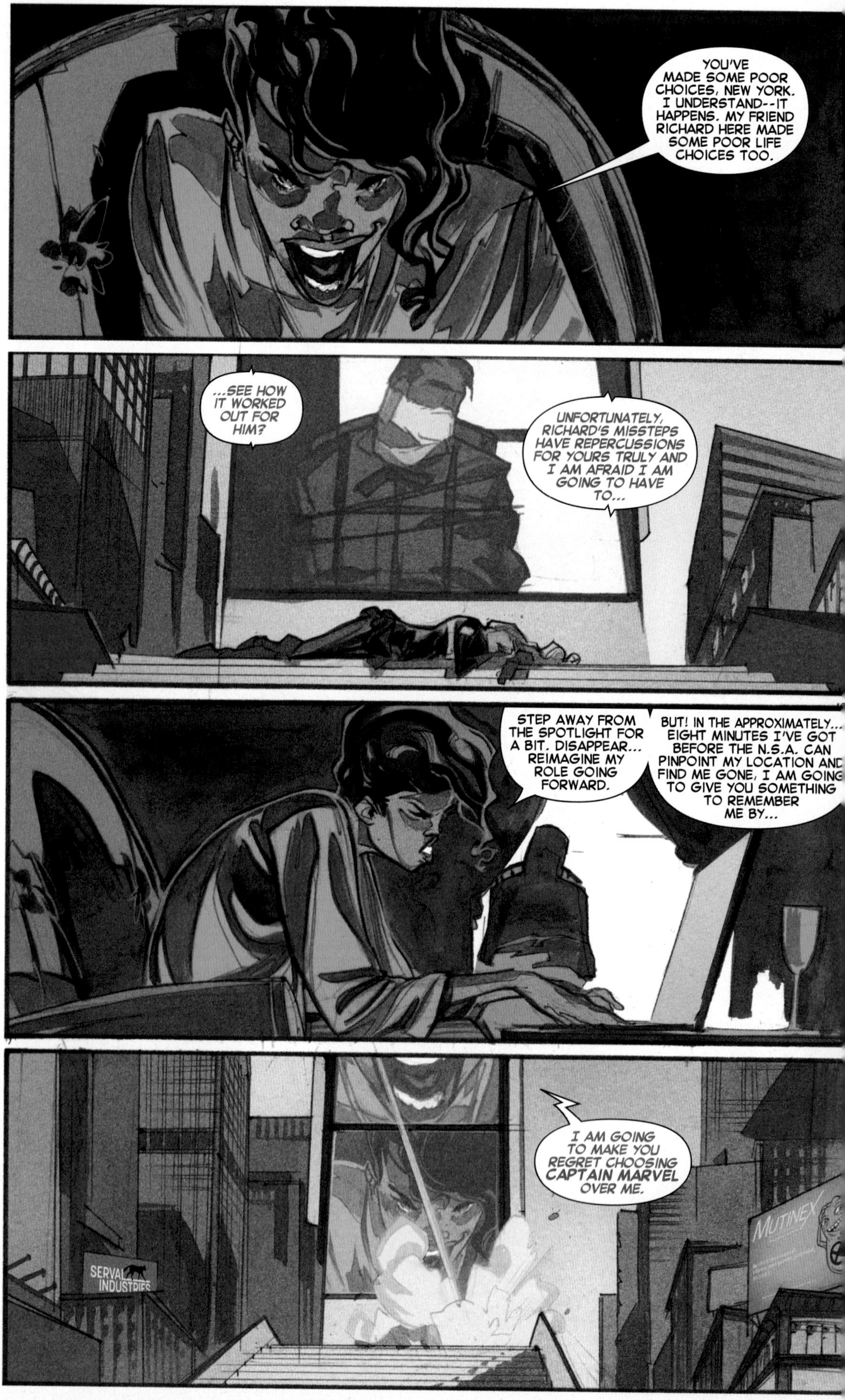
YOU'VE MADE SOME POOR CHOICES, NEW YORK. I UNDERSTAND--IT HAPPENS. MY FRIEND RICHARD HERE MADE SOME POOR LIFE CHOICES TOO.
...SEE HOW IT WORKED OUT FOR HIM?
UNFORTUNATELY, RICHARD'S MISSTEPS HAVE REPERCUSSIONS FOR YOURS TRULY AND I AM AFRAID I AM GOING TO HAVE TO...
STEP AWAY FROM THE SPOTLIGHT FOR A BIT. DISAPPEAR... REIMAGINE MY ROLE GOING FORWARD.
BUT! IN THE APPROXIMATELY... EIGHT MINUTES I'VE GOT BEFORE THE N.S.A. CAN PINPOINT MY LOCATION AND FIND ME GONE, I AM GOING TO GIVE YOU SOMETHING TO REMEMBER ME BY...
I AM GOING TO MAKE YOU REGRET CHOOSING CAPTAIN MARVEL OVER ME.
SERVAL INDUSTRIES
MUTINEX

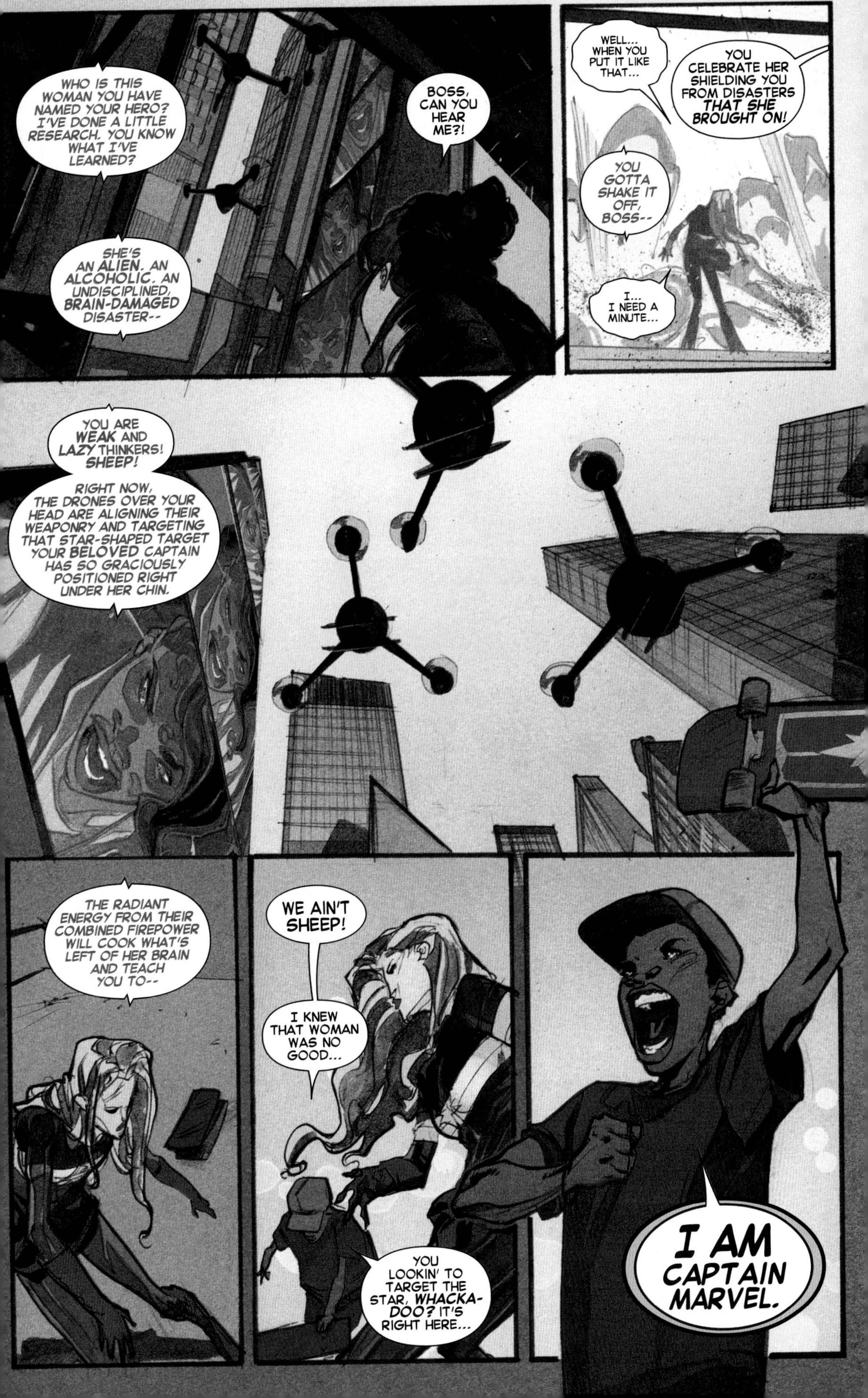
WHO IS THIS WOMAN YOU HAVE NAMED YOUR HERO? I'VE DONE A LITTLE RESEARCH. YOU KNOW WHAT I'VE LEARNED?
BOSS, CAN YOU HEAR ME?!
SHE'S AN ALIEN. AN ALCOHOLIC. AN UNDISCIPLINED, BRAIN-DAMAGED DISASTER--
WELL... WHEN YOU PUT IT LIKE THAT...
YOU CELEBRATE HER SHIELDING YOU FROM DISASTERS THAT SHE BROUGHT ON!
YOU GOTTA SHAKE IT OFF, BOSS--
I... I NEED A MINUTE...
YOU ARE WEAK AND LAZY THINKERS! SHEEP!
RIGHT NOW, THE DRONES OVER YOUR HEAD ARE ALIGNING THEIR WEAPONRY AND TARGETING THAT STAR-SHAPED TARGET YOUR BELOVED CAPTAIN HAS SO GRACIOUSLY POSITIONED RIGHT UNDER HER CHIN.
THE RADIANT ENERGY FROM THEIR COMBINED FIREPOWER WILL COOK WHAT'S LEFT OF HER BRAIN AND TEACH YOU TO--
WE AIN'T SHEEP!
I KNEW THAT WOMAN WAS NO GOOD...
YOU LOOKIN' TO TARGET THE STAR, WHACKA-DOO? IT'S RIGHT HERE...
I AM CAPTAIN MARVEL.

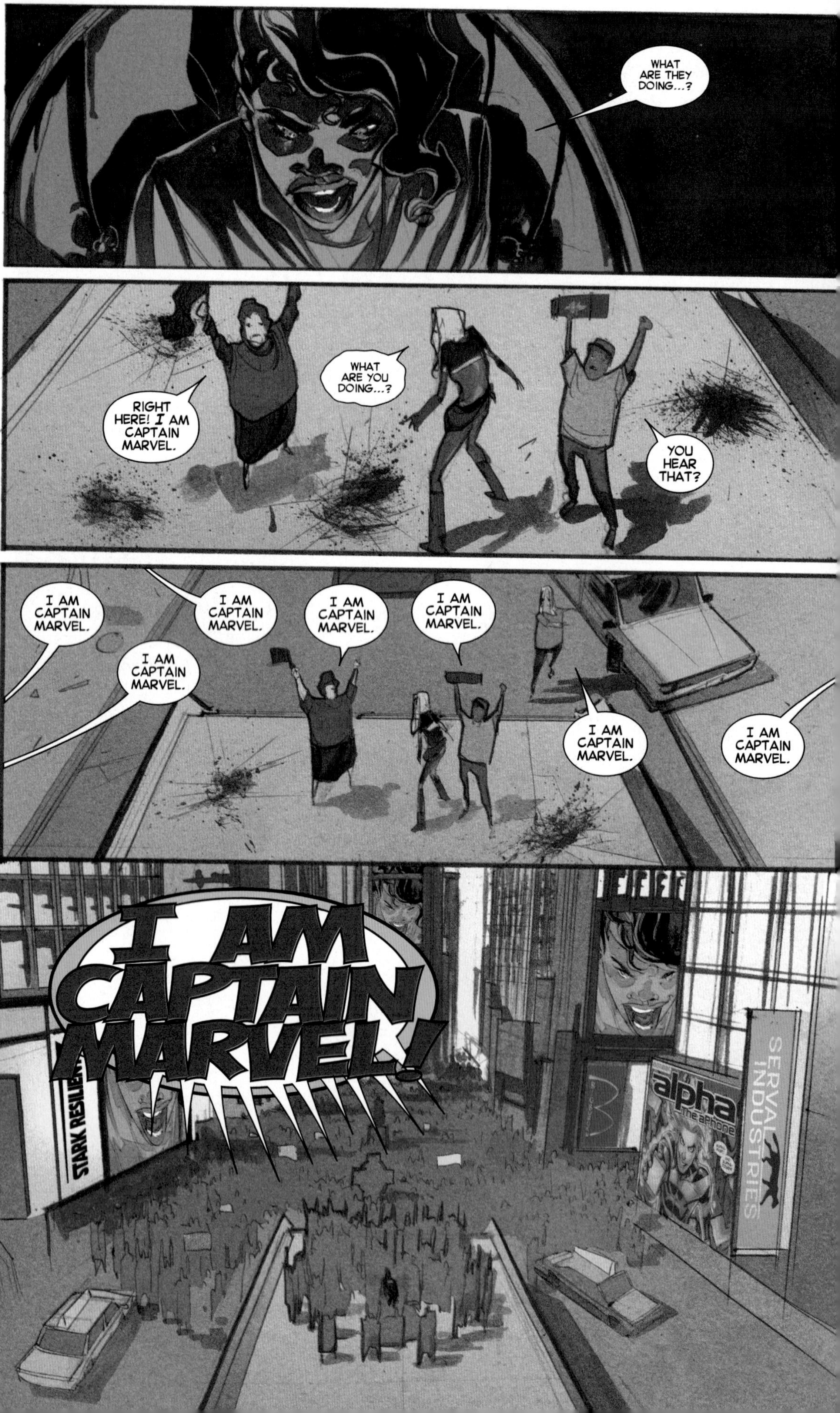
WHAT ARE THEY DOING...?
RIGHT HERE! I AM CAPTAIN MARVEL.
WHAT ARE YOU DOING...?
YOU HEAR THAT?
I AM CAPTAIN MARVEL.
I AM CAPTAIN MARVEL.
I AM CAPTAIN MARVEL.
I AM CAPTAIN MARVEL.
I AM CAPTAIN MARVEL.
I AM CAPTAIN MARVEL.
I AM CAPTAIN MARVEL.
I AM CAPTAIN MARVEL!
STARK RESILIEN
alpha
The aPhone
SERVAL INDUSTRIES

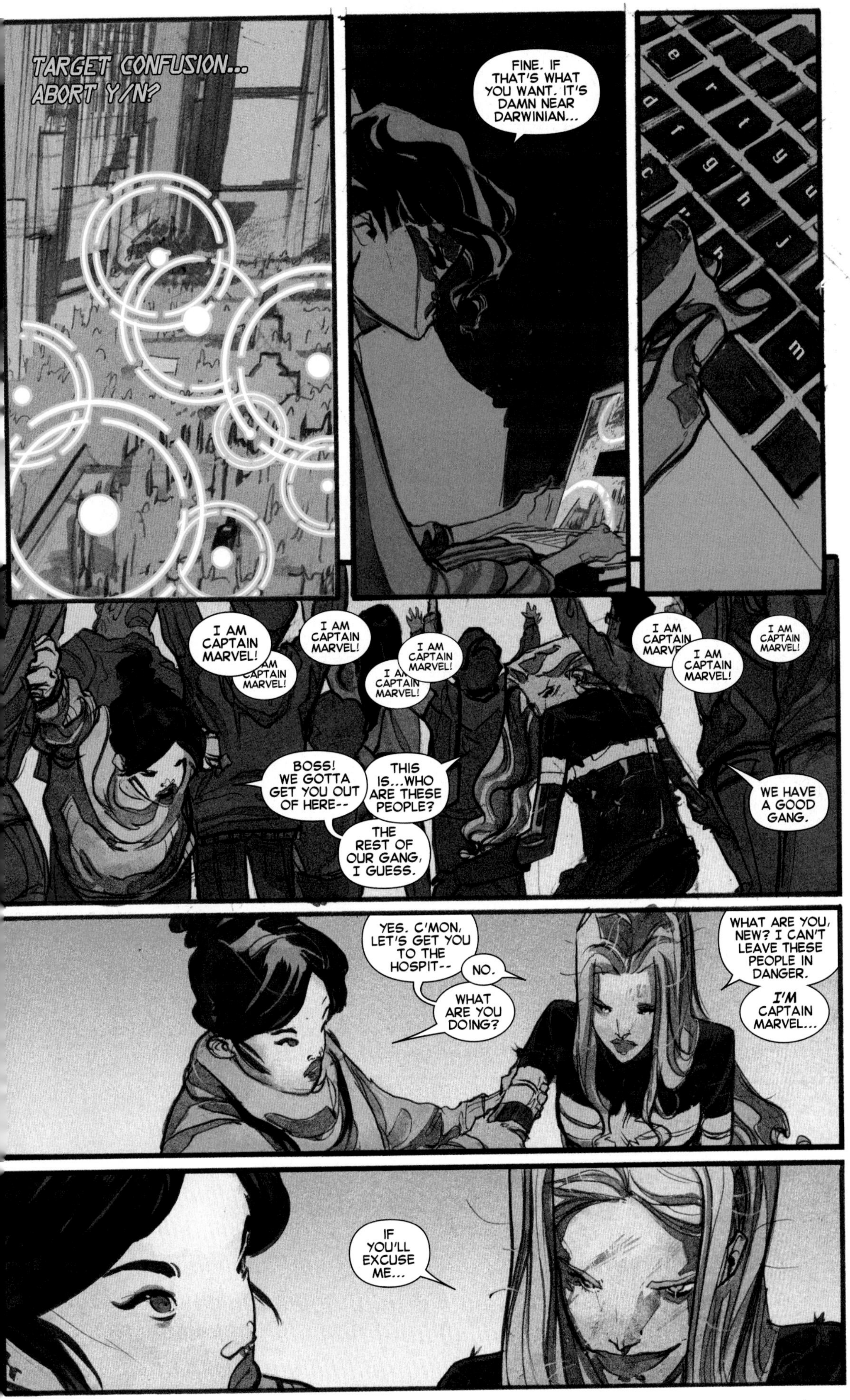
TARGET CONFUSION...
ABORT Y/N?
FINE. IF THAT'S WHAT YOU WANT. IT'S DAMN NEAR DARWINIAN...
I AM CAPTAIN MARVEL!
I AM CAPTAIN MARVEL!
I AM CAPTAIN MARVEL!
I AM CAPTAIN MARVEL!
I AM CAPTAIN MARVEL!
I AM CAPTAIN MARVEL!
I AM CAPTAIN MARVEL!
I AM CAPTAIN MARVEL!
BOSS! WE GOTTA GET YOU OUT OF HERE--
THIS IS...WHO ARE THESE PEOPLE?
THE REST OF OUR GANG, I GUESS.
WE HAVE A GOOD GANG.
YES. C'MON, LET'S GET YOU TO THE HOSPIT--
NO.
WHAT ARE YOU DOING?
WHAT ARE YOU, NEW? I CAN'T LEAVE THESE PEOPLE IN DANGER.
I'M CAPTAIN MARVEL...
IF YOU'LL EXCUSE ME...

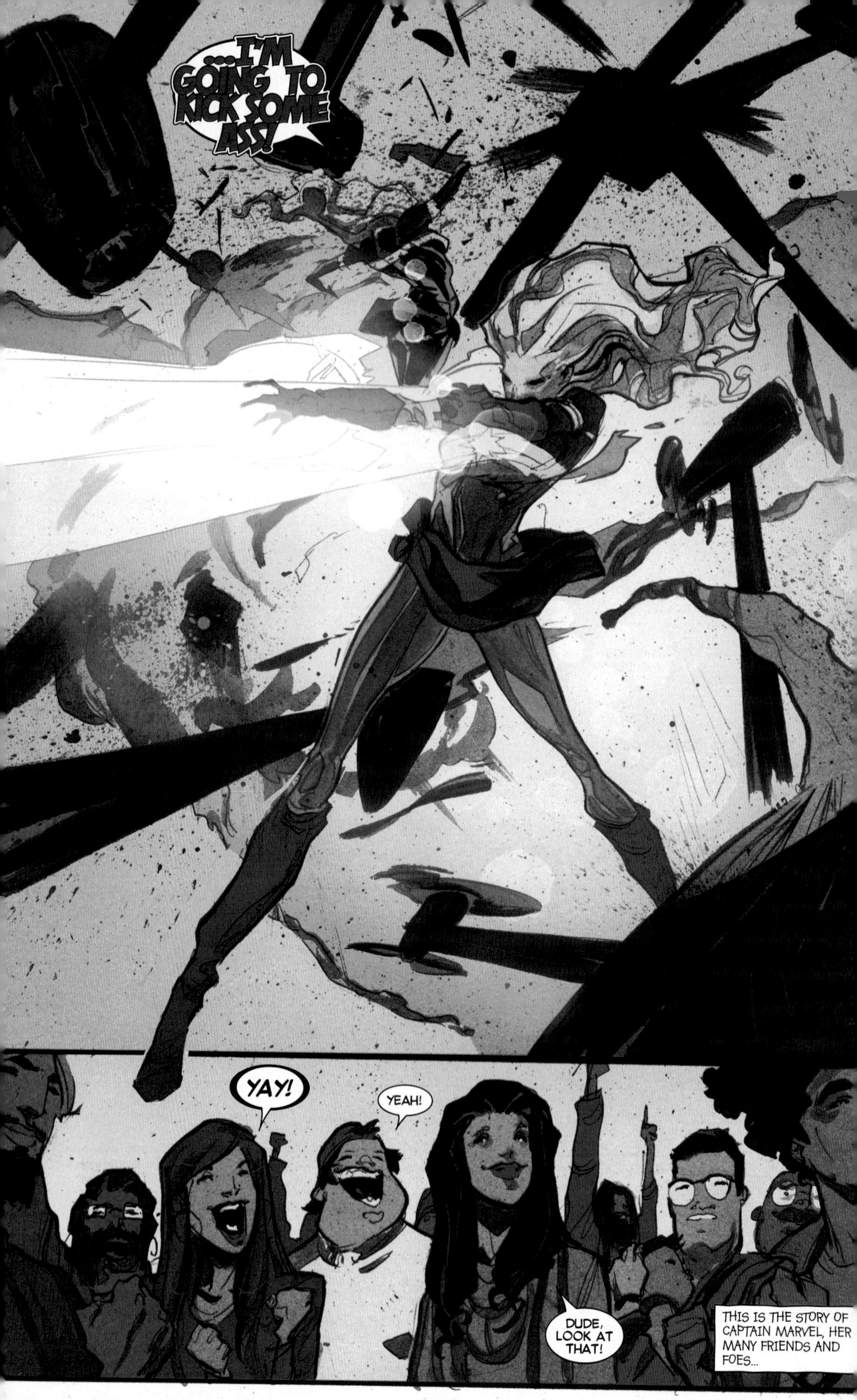
...I'M GOING TO KICK SOME ASS!
YAY!
YEAH!
DUDE, LOOK AT THAT!
THIS IS THE STORY OF CAPTAIN MARVEL, HER MANY FRIENDS AND FOES...

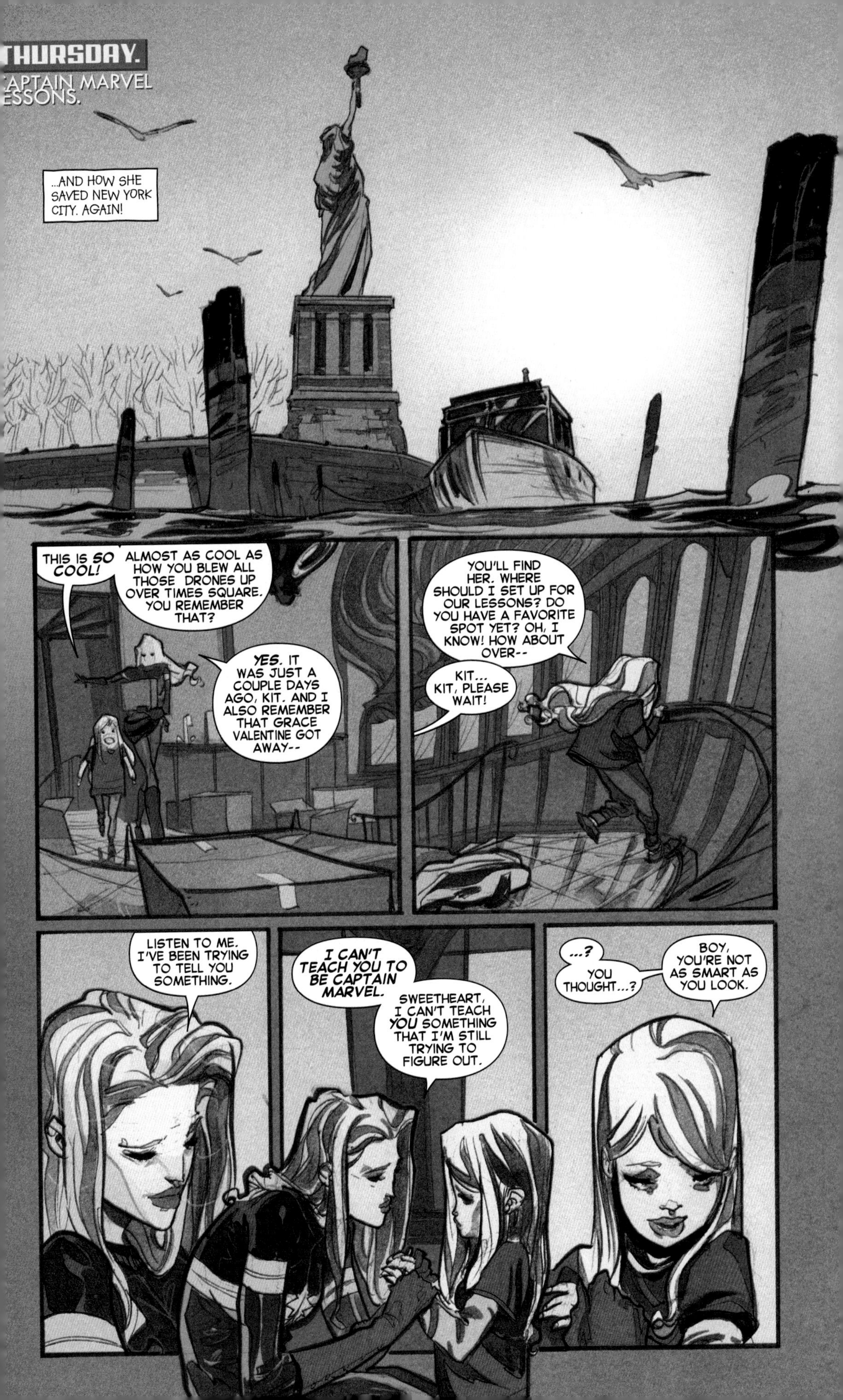

THURSDAY.
CAPTAIN MARVEL LESSONS.
...AND HOW SHE SAVED NEW YORK CITY. AGAIN!
THIS IS SO COOL!
ALMOST AS COOL AS HOW YOU BLEW ALL THOSE DRONES UP OVER TIMES SQUARE. YOU REMEMBER THAT?
YES. IT WAS JUST A COUPLE DAYS AGO, KIT. AND I ALSO REMEMBER THAT GRACE VALENTINE GOT AWAY--
YOU'LL FIND HER. WHERE SHOULD I SET UP FOR OUR LESSONS? DO YOU HAVE A FAVORITE SPOT YET? OH, I KNOW! HOW ABOUT OVER--
KIT... KIT, PLEASE WAIT!
LISTEN TO ME. I'VE BEEN TRYING TO TELL YOU SOMETHING.
I CAN'T TEACH YOU TO BE CAPTAIN MARVEL.
SWEETHEART, I CAN'T TEACH YOU SOMETHING THAT I'M STILL TRYING TO FIGURE OUT.
...?
YOU THOUGHT...?
BOY, YOU'RE NOT AS SMART AS YOU LOOK.

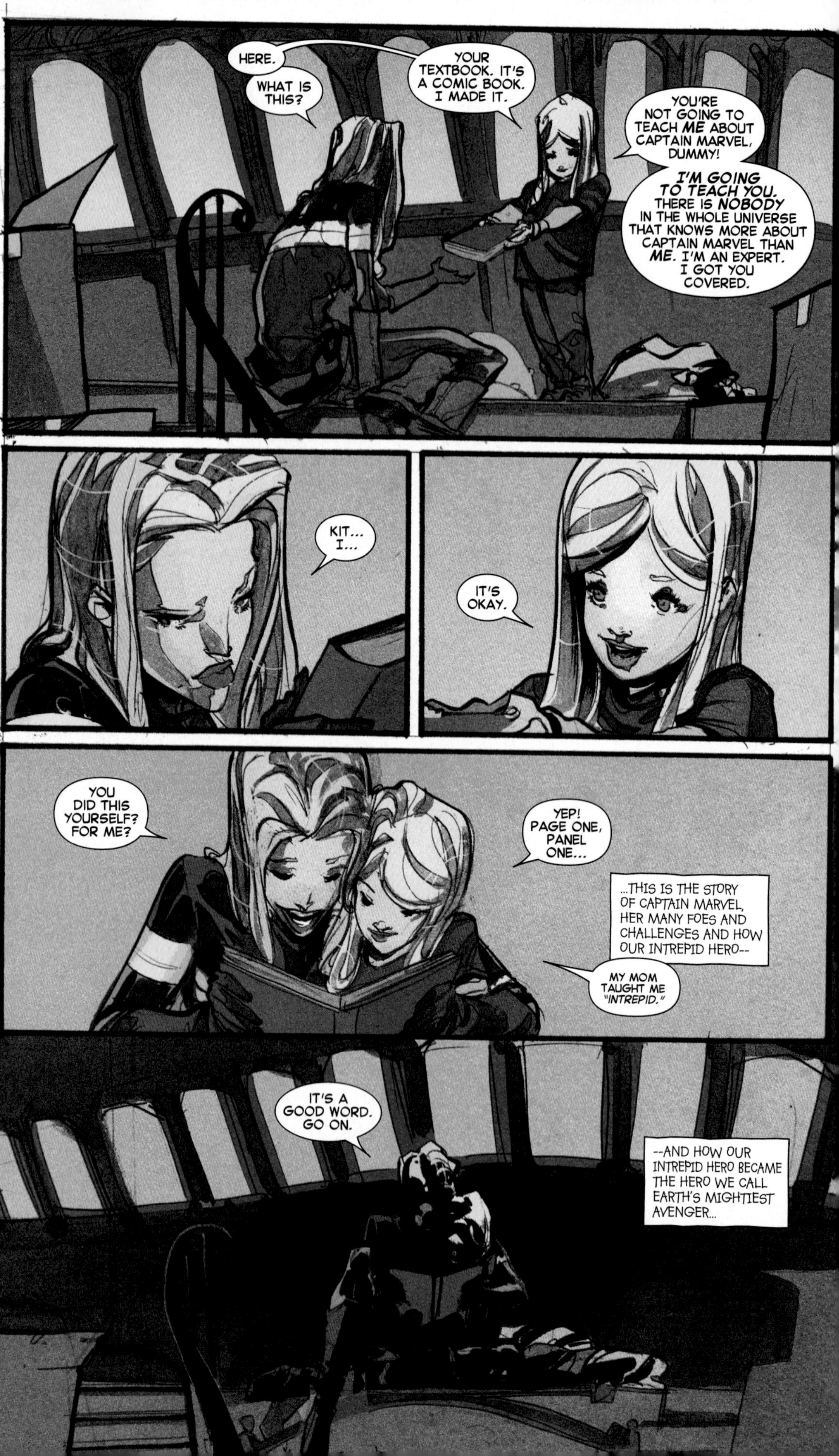
HERE.
WHAT IS THIS?
YOUR TEXTBOOK. IT'S A COMIC BOOK. I MADE IT.
YOU'RE NOT GOING TO TEACH ME ABOUT CAPTAIN MARVEL, DUMMY!
I'M GOING TO TEACH YOU. THERE IS NOBODY IN THE WHOLE UNIVERSE THAT KNOWS MORE ABOUT CAPTAIN MARVEL THAN ME. I'M AN EXPERT. I GOT YOU COVERED.
KIT... I...
IT'S OKAY.
YOU DID THIS YOURSELF? FOR ME?
YEP! PAGE ONE, PANEL ONE...
...THIS IS THE STORY OF CAPTAIN MARVEL, HER MANY FOES AND CHALLENGES AND HOW OUR INTREPID HERO--
MY MOM TAUGHT ME "INTREPID."
IT'S A GOOD WORD. GO ON.
--AND HOW OUR INTREPID HERO BECAME THE HERO WE CALL EARTH'S MIGHTIEST AVENGER...

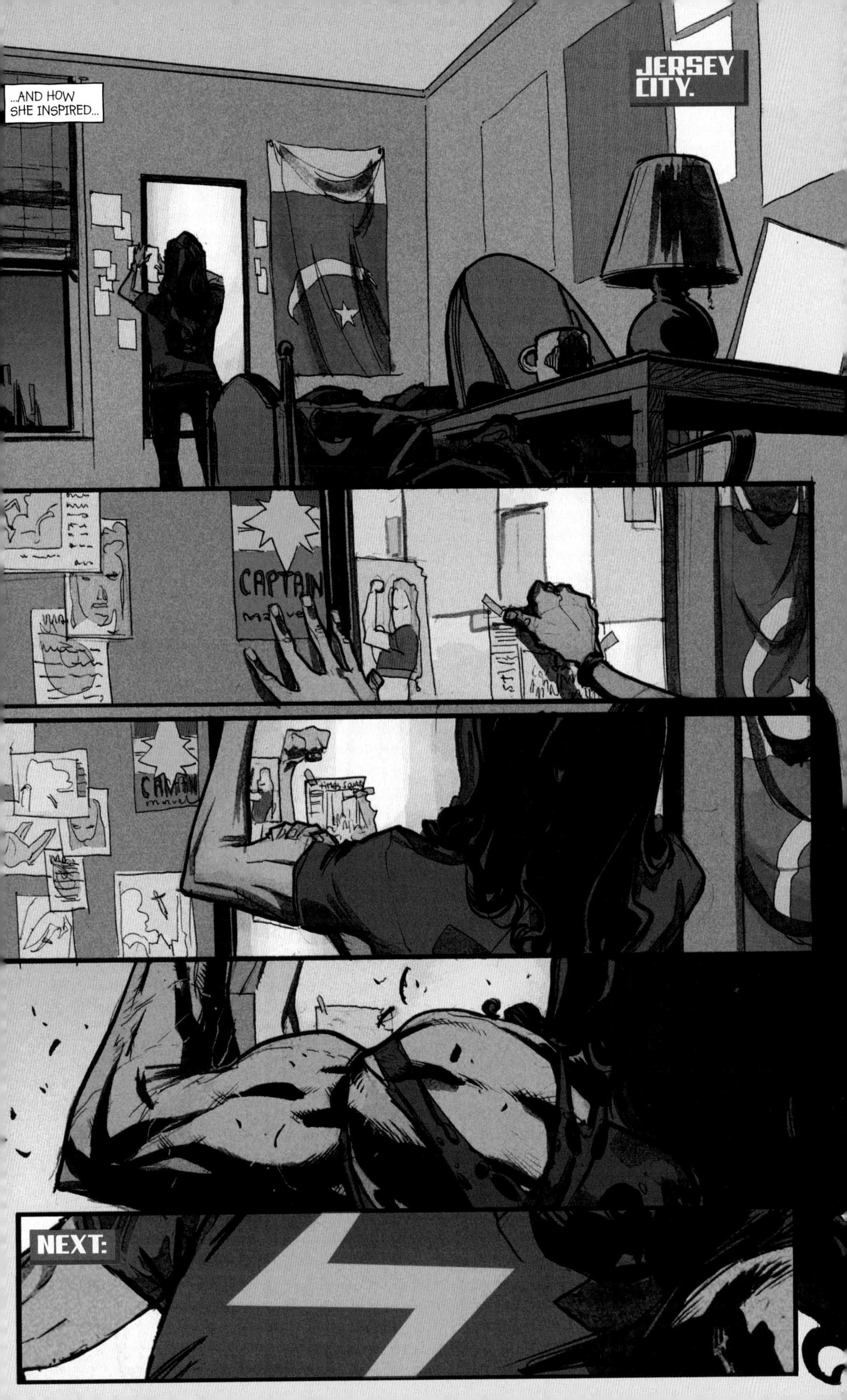
...AND HOW SHE INSPIRED...
JERSEY CITY.
CAPTAIN
NEXT:

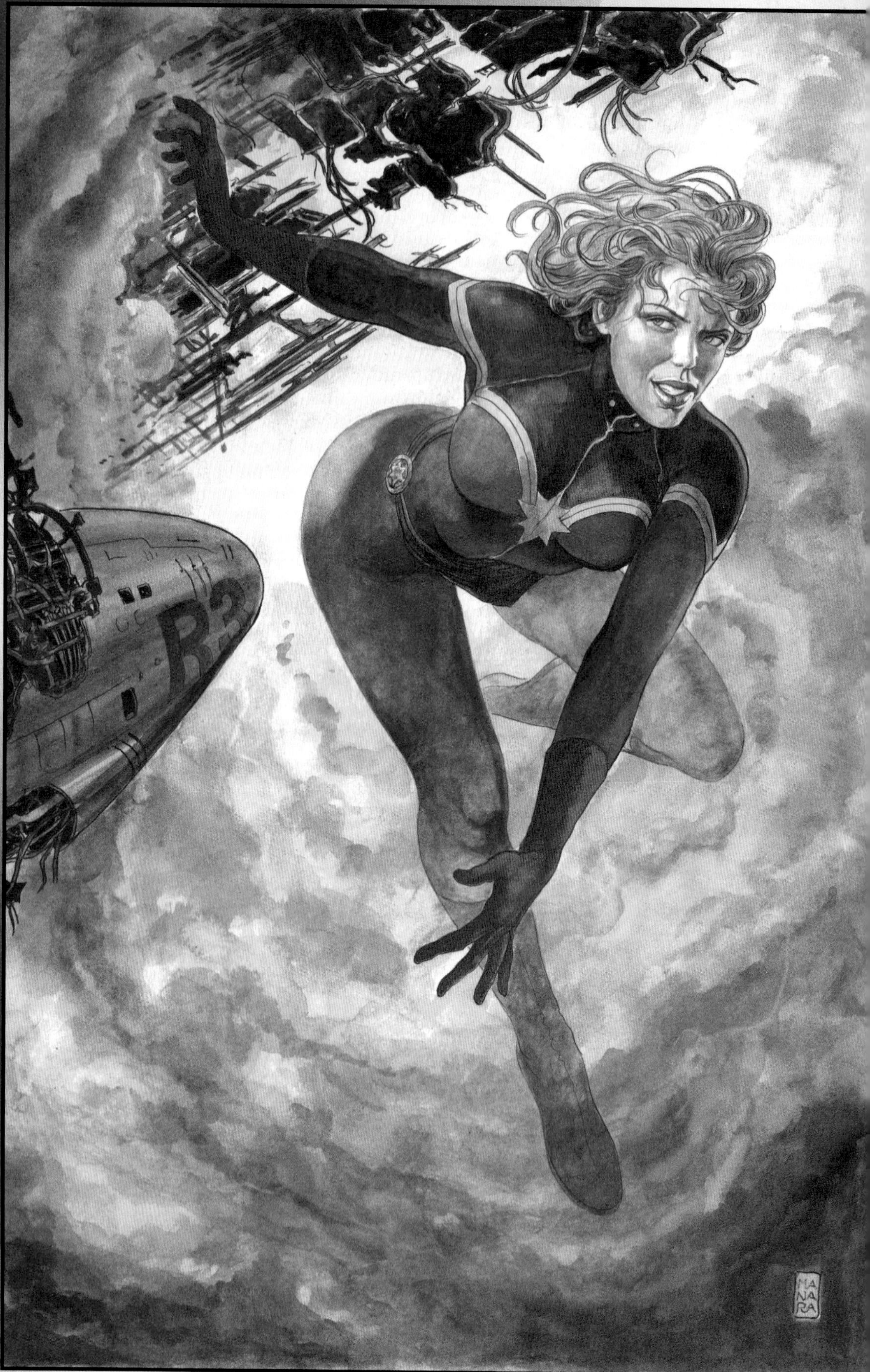

AVENGERS: THE ENEMY WITHIN #1 VARIANT BY MILO MANARA

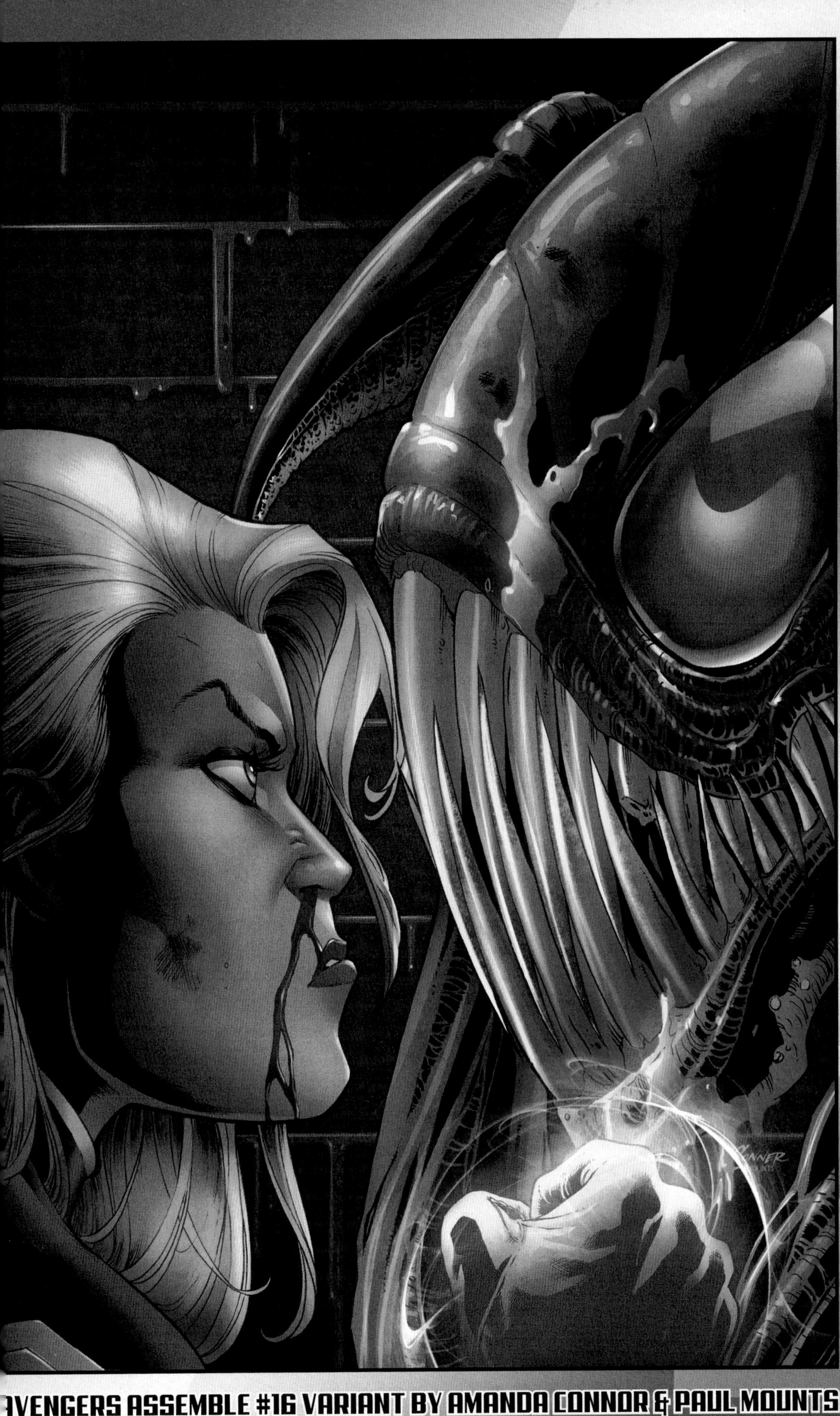

AVENGERS ASSEMBLE #16 VARIANT BY AMANDA CONNOR & PAUL MOUNTS

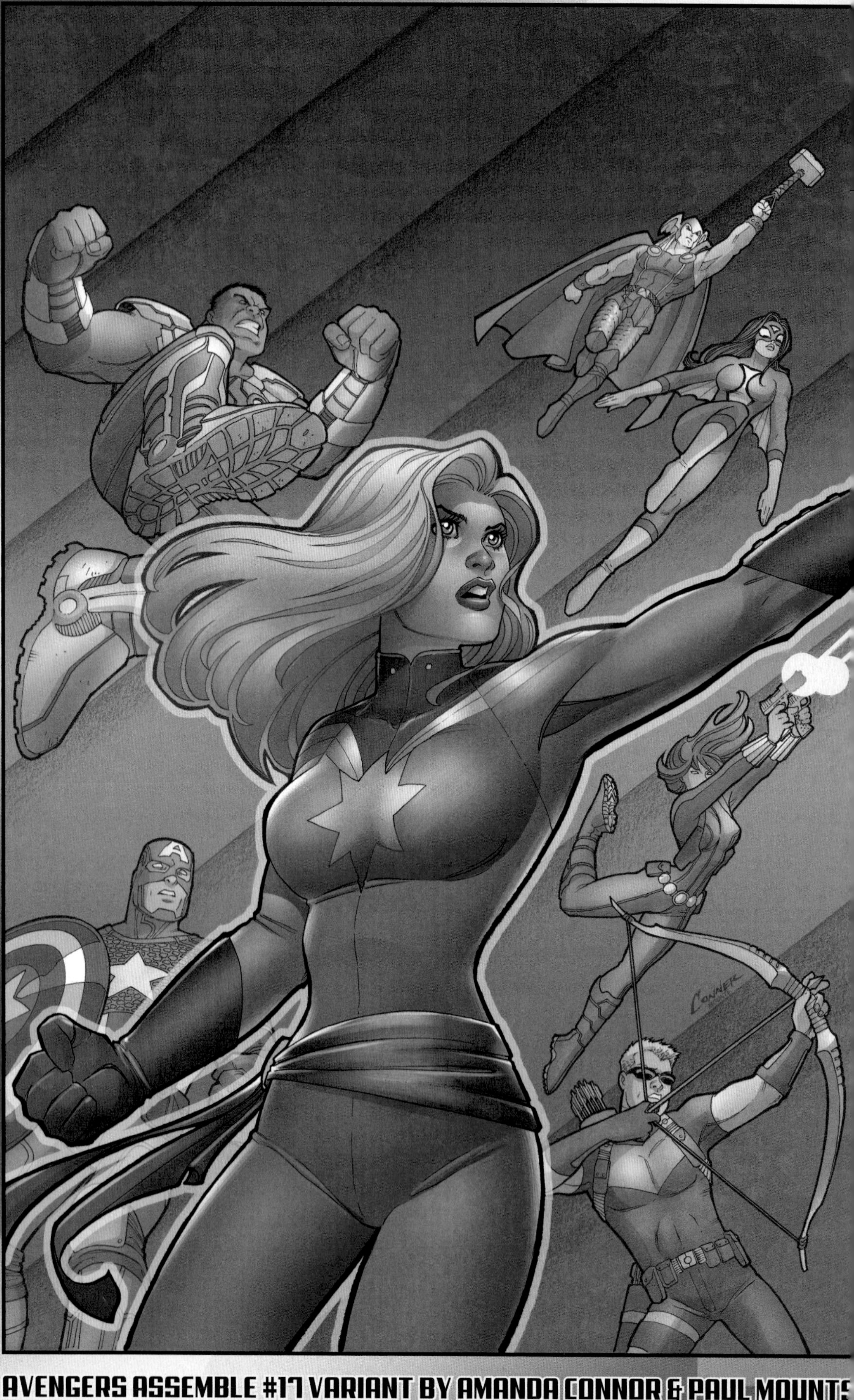
CONNER

AVENGERS ASSEMBLE #17 VARIANT BY AMANDA CONNOR & PAUL MOUNTS

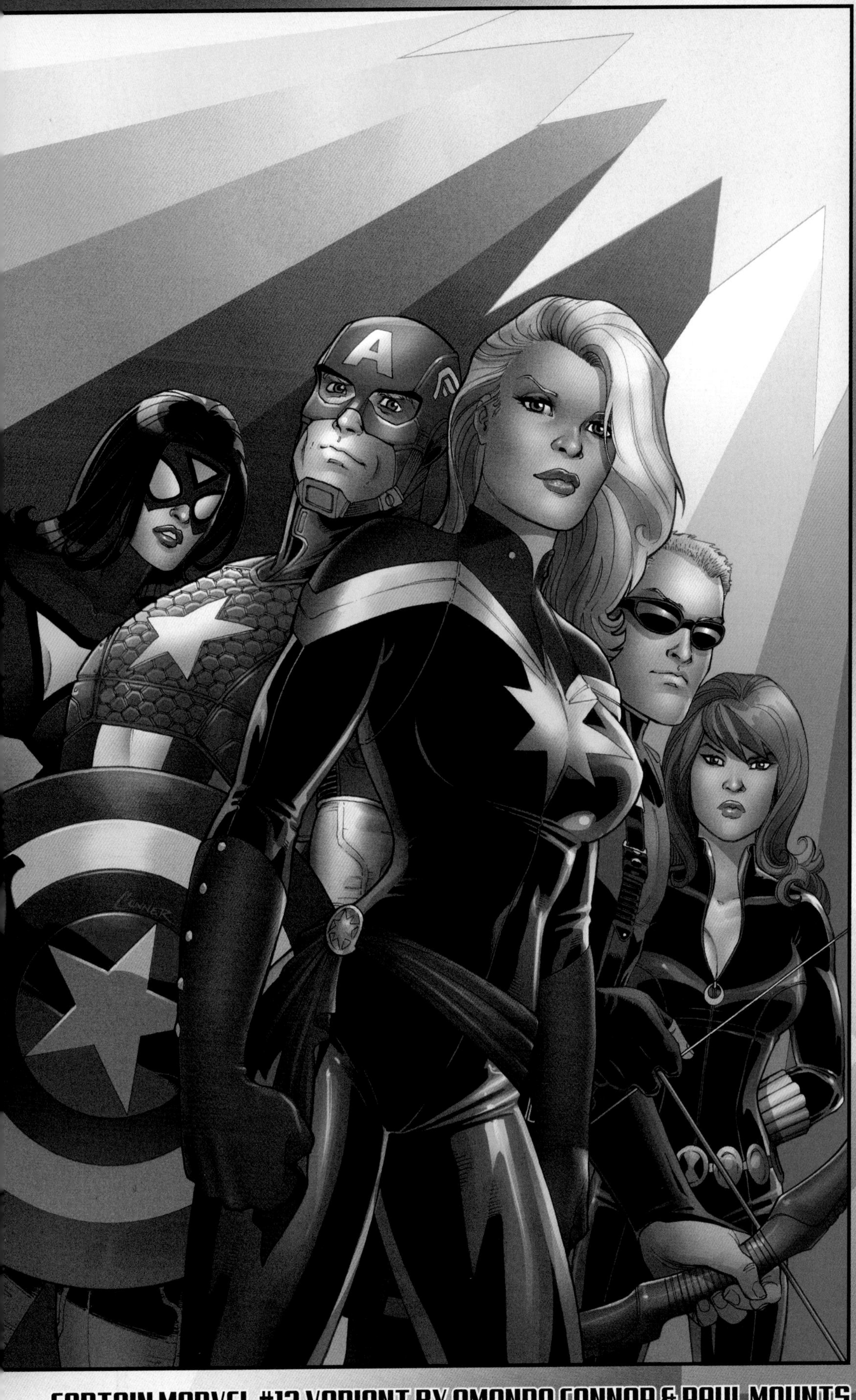

CAPTAIN MARVEL #13 VARIANT BY AMANDA CONNOR & PAUL MOUNTS

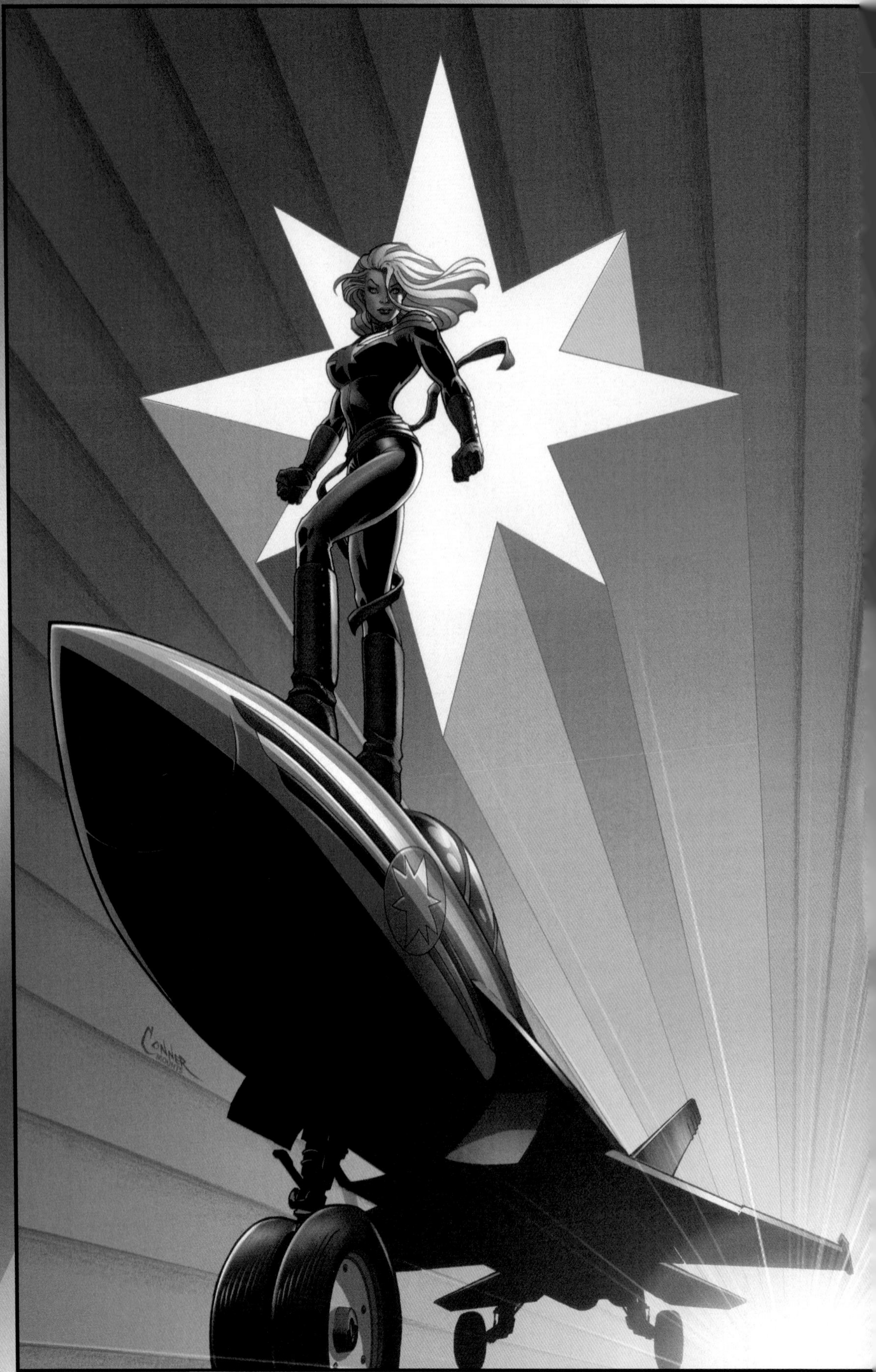

CAPTAIN MARVEL #14 VARIANT BY AMANDA CONNOR & PAUL MOUNTS

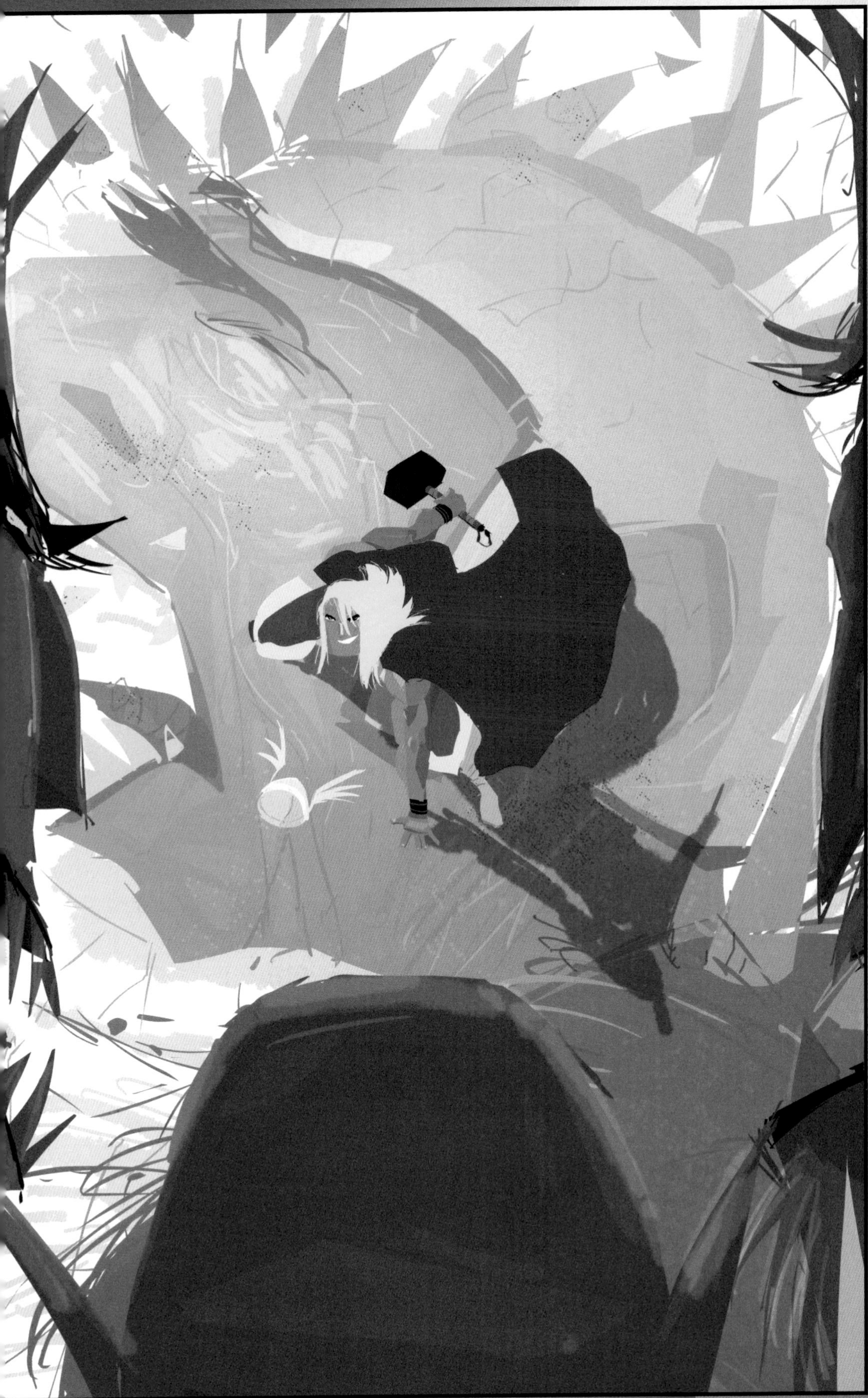

CAPTAIN MARVEL #17 THOR BATTLE VARIANT BY PASCAL CAMPION

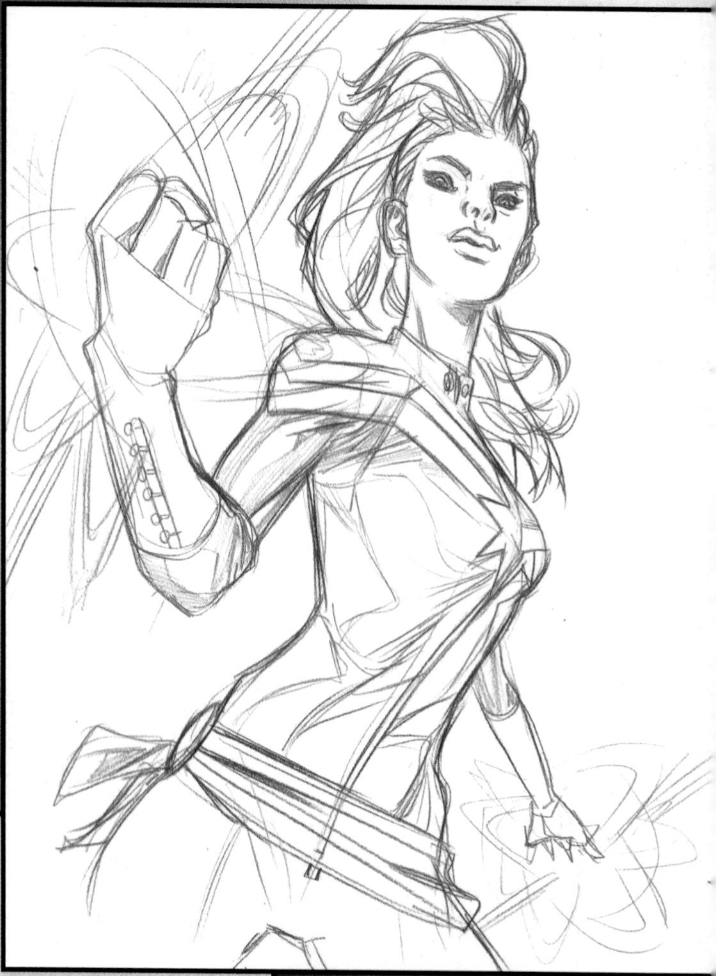

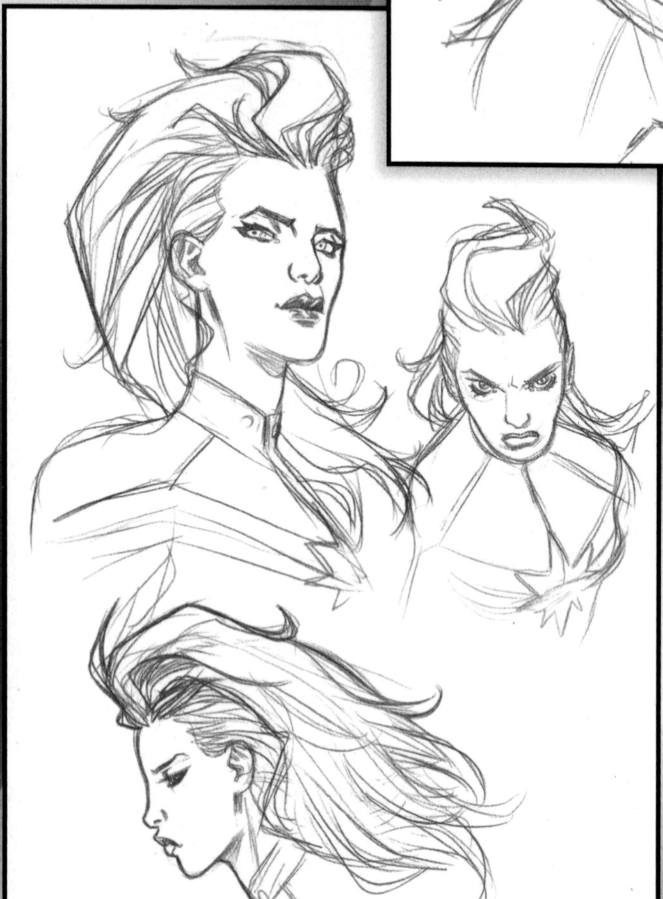

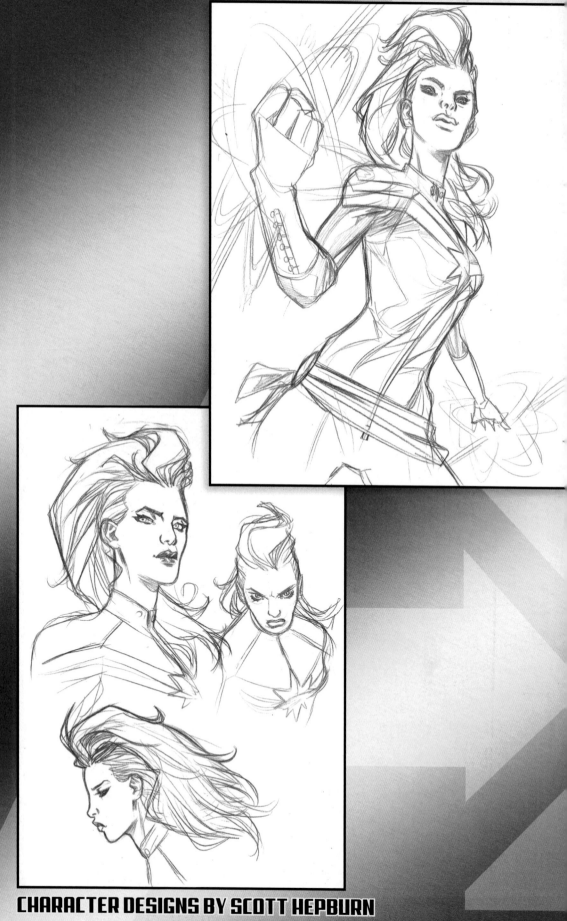

CHARACTER DESIGNS BY SCOTT HEPBURN

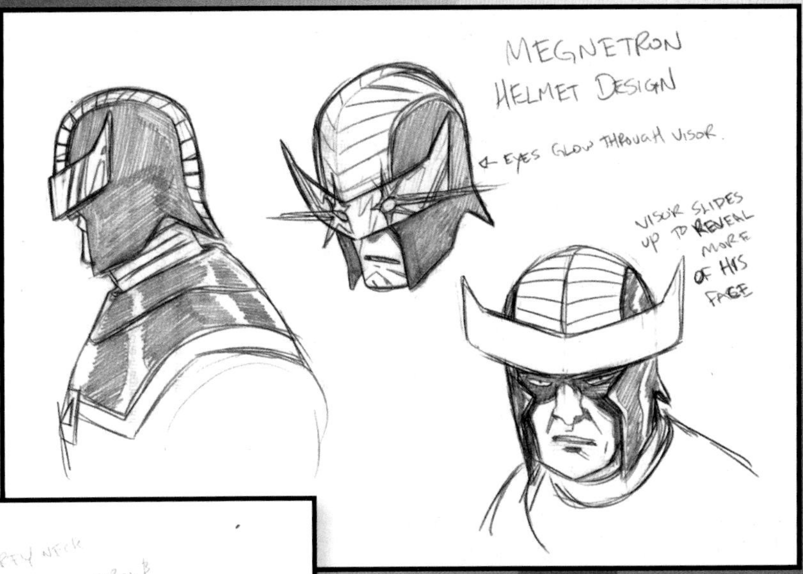
MEGNETRON
HELMET DESIGN
← EYES GLOW THROUGH VISOR.
VISOR SLIDES UP TO REVEAL MORE OF HIS FACE

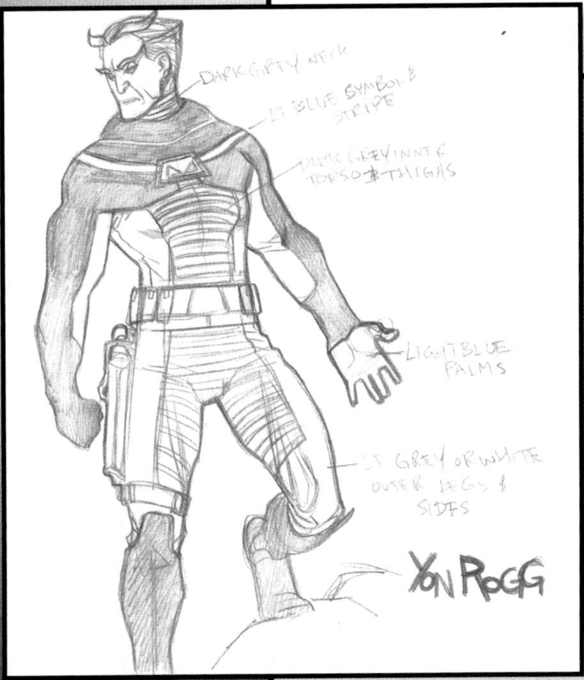
DARK GREY NECK
LT BLUE SYMBOL & STRIPE
DARK GREY INNER TORSO & THIGHS
LIGHT BLUE PALMS
LT GREY OR WHITE OUTER LEGS & SIDES
YON ROGG

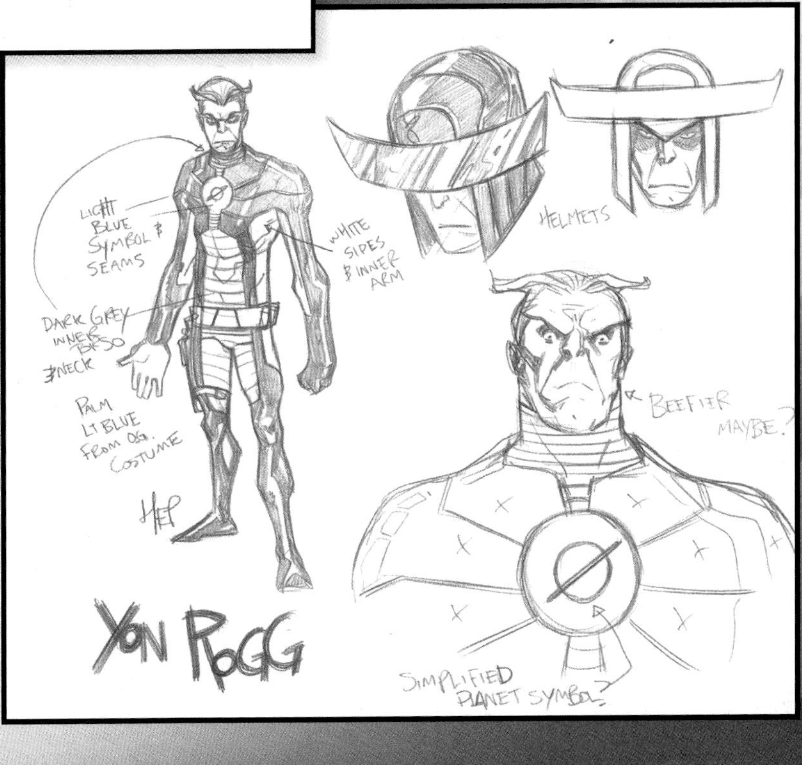
HELMETS
LIGHT BLUE SYMBOL & SEAMS
WHITE SIDES & INNER ARM
DARK GREY INNER TORSO & NECK
PALM LT BLUE FROM OG. COSTUME
BEEFIER MAYBE?
HEP
YON ROGG
SIMPLIFIED PLANET SYMBOL?

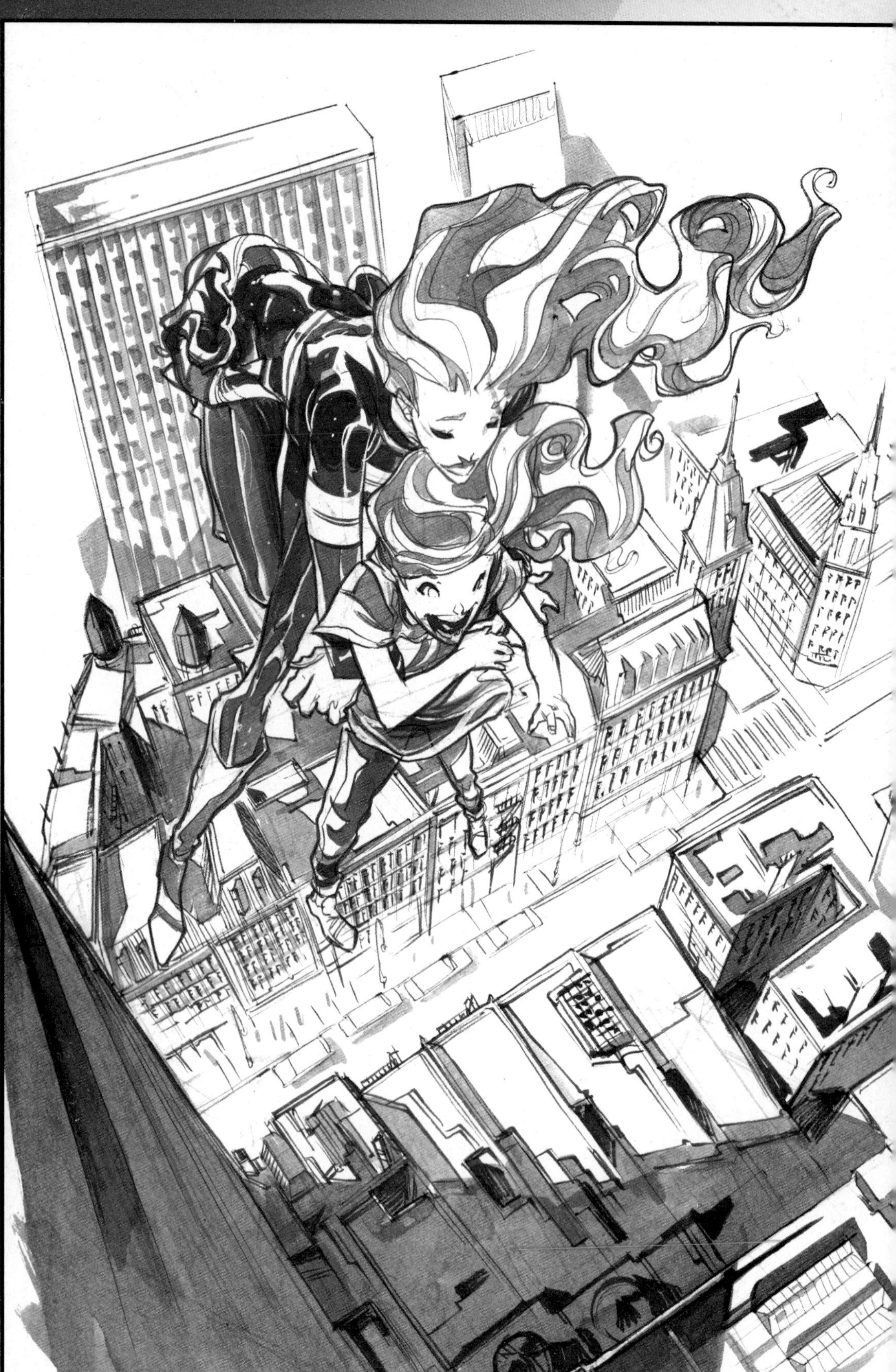

CAPTAIN MARVEL #17, PAGE 8 ARTWORK BY FILIPE ANDRADE